Concepts and Cases of Illicit Finance

Abdul Rafay
University of Management and Technology, Pakistan

IGI Global
PUBLISHER of TIMELY KNOWLEDGE

A volume in the Advances in Finance, Accounting, and Economics (AFAE) Book Series

Published in the United States of America by
IGI Global
Business Science Reference (an imprint of IGI Global)
701 E. Chocolate Avenue
Hershey PA, USA 17033
Tel: 717-533-8845
Fax: 717-533-8661
E-mail: cust@igi-global.com
Web site: http://www.igi-global.com

Library of Congress Cataloging-in-Publication Data

Names: Rafay, Abdul, 1973- editor.
Title: Concepts and cases of illicit finance / edited by Abdul Rafay.
Description: Hershey, PA : Business Science Reference, [2023] | Includes bibliographical references and index. | Summary: "The book shall be an international book whose primary mission is to provide understanding and lessons learned in regard to all aspects of financial & technological crimes, frauds, and corruption in individual, organizational, and societal experiences. The goal of this book is to provide a unique opportunity for researchers to take the shape of experience, implementation, and application. The book shall consist of contents discussing the emergence and practices of financial crimes, frauds, and corruption during the last century and especially in the current technological advancement. It includes various forms of financial/technological crimes including money laundering, corporate frauds, the dark web, and relevant regulatory environment to name a few (See the detailed list of topics)"-- Provided by publisher.
Identifiers: LCCN 2022062309 (print) | LCCN 2022062310 (ebook) | ISBN 9781668485873 (hardcover) | ISBN 9781668485880 (paperback) | ISBN 9781668485897 (ebook)
Subjects: LCSH: Commercial crimes.
Classification: LCC HV6768 .C6545 2023 (print) | LCC HV6768 (ebook) | DDC 364.16/8--dc23/eng/20230201
LC record available at https://lccn.loc.gov/2022062309
LC ebook record available at https://lccn.loc.gov/2022062310

This book is published in the IGI Global book series Advances in Finance, Accounting, and Economics (AFAE) (ISSN: 2327-5677; eISSN: 2327-5685)

British Cataloguing in Publication Data
A Cataloguing in Publication record for this book is available from the British Library.

For electronic access to this publication, please contact: eresources@igi-global.com.

Advances in Finance, Accounting, and Economics (AFAE) Book Series

Ahmed Driouchi
Al Akhawayn University, Morocco

ISSN:2327-5677
EISSN:2327-5685

Mission

In our changing economic and business environment, it is important to consider the financial changes occurring internationally as well as within individual organizations and business environments. Understanding these changes as well as the factors that influence them is crucial in preparing for our financial future and ensuring economic sustainability and growth.

The **Advances in Finance, Accounting, and Economics (AFAE)** book series aims to publish comprehensive and informative titles in all areas of economics and economic theory, finance, and accounting to assist in advancing the available knowledge and providing for further research development in these dynamic fields.

Coverage

- Risk Analysis and Management
- Economics Geography
- Economic Indices and Quantitative Economic Methods
- Applied Finance
- Public Finance
- International Economics
- Health Economics
- Evidence-Based Studies
- Theoretical Issues in Economics, Finance, and Accounting
- Accounting information systems

IGI Global is currently accepting manuscripts for publication within this series. To submit a proposal for a volume in this series, please contact our Acquisition Editors at Acquisitions@igi-global.com or visit: http://www.igi-global.com/publish/.

The Advances in Finance, Accounting, and Economics (AFAE) Book Series (ISSN 2327-5677) is published by IGI Global, 701 E. Chocolate Avenue, Hershey, PA 17033-1240, USA, www.igi-global.com. This series is composed of titles available for purchase individually; each title is edited to be contextually exclusive from any other title within the series. For pricing and ordering information please visit http://www.igi-global.com/book-series/advances-finance-accounting-economics/73685. Postmaster: Send all address changes to above address.

Titles in this Series

For a list of additional titles in this series, please visit: http://www.igi-global.com/book-series/advances-finance-accounting-economics/73685

Perspectives on the Transition Toward Green and Climate Neutral Economies in Asia
Patricia Ordóñez de Pablos (The University of Oviedo, Spain) Mohammad Nabil Almunawar (Universiti Brunei Darussalam, Brunei) and Muhammad Anshari (Universiti Brunei Darussalam, Brunei)
Business Science Reference • © 2023 • 465pp • H/C (ISBN: 9781668486139) • US $325.00

Revolutionizing Financial Services and Markets Through FinTech and Blockchain
Kiran Mehta (Chitkara Business School, Chitkara University, India) Renuka Sharma (Chitkara Business School, Chitkara University, India) and Poshan Yu (Soochow University, China & Australian Studies Centre, Shanghai University, China)
Business Science Reference • © 2023 • 340pp • H/C (ISBN: 9781668486245) • US $265.00

Circular Economy Implementation for Sustainability in the Built Environment
Nicoleta Cobîrzan (Technical University of Cluj-Napoca, Romania) Radu Muntean (Transilvania University of Braşov, Romania) and Raluca - Andreea Felseghi (Technical University of Cluj-Napoca, Romania)
Business Science Reference • © 2023 • 300pp • H/C (ISBN: 9781668482384) • US $250.00

Sustainable Growth and Global Social Development in Competitive Economies
Andrei Jean Vasile (Petroleum-Gas University of Ploiesti, Romania) Mile Vasić (European Marketing and Management Association, Banja Luka, Bosnia And Herzegovina) and Predrag Vukovic (Institute of Agricultural Economics, Belgrade, Serbia)
Business Science Reference • © 2023 • 320pp • H/C (ISBN: 9781668488102) • US $250.00

The Past, Present, and Future of Accountancy Education and Professions
Nina T. Dorata (St. John's University, USA) Richard C. Jones (Hofstra University, USA) Jennifer Mensche (St. Joseph's University, USA) and Mark M. Ulrich (CUNY Queensborough Community College, USA)
Business Science Reference • © 2023 • 240pp • H/C (ISBN: 9781668454831) • US $215.00

Changing World Economic Order in the Post-Pandemic Period
Sushanta Kumar Mahapatra (The ICFAI Foundation for Higher Education (IFHE) (Deemed), Hyderabad, India) and Vishal Sarin (Lovely Professional University, India)
Business Science Reference • © 2023 • 305pp • H/C (ISBN: 9781799868965) • US $260.00

Principles of Financial Control in the Public Sector
Plamena Georgieva Nedyalkova (University of Economics, Bulgaria)
Information Science Reference • © 2023 • 190pp • H/C (ISBN: 9781668488836) • US $185.00

IGI Global
PUBLISHER of TIMELY KNOWLEDGE

701 East Chocolate Avenue, Hershey, PA 17033, USA
Tel: 717-533-8845 x100 • Fax: 717-533-8661
E-Mail: cust@igi-global.com • www.igi-global.com

Dedication

Great things are done when men and mountains meet;
this is not done by jostling in the street –
William Blake in "Great things are done"
(c. 1807-1809)

This book by Professor Abdul Rafay, is dedicated to (the late) **Sheikh Ejaz Ahmad (1940-1998)** and **Dr. Gohar Ejaz.**

Sheikh Ejaz Ahmad (the late) *was a visionary Pakistani businessman of his time. Sheikh Ejaz Ahmad laid the foundation of the Ejaz Group of companies in 1950 for the international trading of commodities. From 1962 to 1985, he was an iconic leader of the business community and gained the monumental title of 'King of Commodities' in Karachi. In fact, he was an institution in himself, and the history of commodity trading is incomplete without him. He became a member of the Senate of Pakistan in 1985.*

May Allah rest his soul in peace.

Currently, **Dr. Gohar Ejaz**, *a visionary businessman and philanthropist in Pakistan, is the torch bearer for this father's mission.*

Being a philanthropist, his services in the field of health and education have uplifted the lives of millions of Pakistanis. He demonstrated exemplary humanitarian service during natural disasters in Pakistan. He is the chairman of Sheikh Ejaz Ahmad Trust and Gohar Ejaz Foundation. Sheikh Ejaz Ahmad Trust provides premium quality medical equipment for the care and comfort of patients. The trust established state of art free of cost dialysis center at Jinnah Hospital, a public sector hospital in Lahore Pakistan. Gohar Ejaz Foundation provides merit-based scholarships to students from across the country.

Being the Patron-in-Chief of the All-Pakistan Textile Mills Association (ATMA), he is a staunch supporter of Export-led economic growth and worked tirelessly for improving the export-oriented textile sector of Pakistan. He was the force behind the 40% increase (FY18: \$13 billion to FY22: \$19.4 billion) in textile exports of Pakistan.

Dr. Gohar was awarded Hilal-i-Imtiaz (2023) & Sitara-i-Imtiaz (2014) by the Government of Pakistan for business leadership and philanthropic services. He is also a regular guest speaker at seminars organized around the globe by academic institutions, multilateral and bilateral economic institutions and NGOs.

Editorial Advisory Board

Table of Contents

Detailed Table of Contents

The purpose of this chapter is to explore the basis and scope of civil and criminal liability for insider trading under the federal securities laws of the United States. Insider trading involves the use of non-public corporate information by those with access to it in order to trade in the corporation's securities. Such conduct involves a breach of the insider's fiduciary duty of confidentiality and is considered to be a form of fraud in the market as well. In addition, others to whom inside information has been disclosed and who trade on it may face liability. In its overall approach, the chapter reviews and illustrates these issues through a discussion of key cases and with reference to regulations issued by the US Securities & Exchange Commission.

Informal remittance channels operate in various jurisdictions to promote illegal activities which are detrimental to the global efforts of combating money laundering. Here, in this chapter, Hawala is considered the main informal remittance channel. The economic and social implications of Hawala are very significant when it comes to a weak regime of AML/CFT. Therefore, the focus of this chapter is on weak AML/CFT regimes even though the discussed practices take place across the globe. A global initiative to limit or control informal remittance channels may support the global initiatives of anti-money laundering. However, it has also to bear in mind that informal remittance services are used globally as a very efficient and low-cost remittance channel despite the allegations of using them by criminals. Therefore, it is very important to implement proper systems and controls to regulate informal remittance channels while making them available for all segments of society.

The collapse of Enron and its auditor Arthur Andersen was one of the biggest events in US corporate history and it had long-lasting repercussions in the corporate world. Following the Enron – Arthur Andersen scandal, the US Congress passed the Sarbanes Oxley Act (SOX). The legislation was designed to strengthen existing securities regulations and enacted harsh penalties on lawbreakers. SOX was one of the first and heavy responses to corporate fraud. Since the passage of SOX, debates revolving around the costs and benefits of it have prevailed and several studies investigated its effectiveness to prevent future financial crimes. This study first reviews the chronology of the events leading to SOX, followed by a brief discussion of the rules and regulations established by SOX. The empirical evidence presented by previous studies on the effectiveness of legislation and the harsh penalty Enron's auditor had received are assessed and evaluated.

Cryptocurrencies have sparked global transformations in digital technology and financial services, leading to deliberations on regulatory frameworks. India is cautiously working towards regulatory clarity and legalizing Cryptocurrency usage, as it becomes the country with the most cryptocurrency users. The Indian regulatory body is vigilant, monitoring progress and warning the public about associated risks. Despite regulatory efforts, India has seen a worrisome rise in cyber-frauds, cryptocurrency crimes, and money laundering involving digital currencies. This chapter focuses on the regulatory ambiguity in India, which inadvertently fosters an environment for crypto criminals. Through case studies, it highlights the gravity of the situation and the urgent need for legislative action to combat scams and money laundering. The author concludes optimistically, expecting India to establish robust crypto regulations to effectively address these challenges.

The implications of money laundering activities in developing economies have yielded mixed findings. However, existing studies have not specifically examined the role of anti-money laundering (AML) regulations in relation to entrepreneurial development. This study aims to fill this gap by analyzing the impact of AML regulations on entrepreneurship in Africa. The analysis utilizes data from 21 African nations for 2012-2018. The empirical analysis employs panel-corrected standard errors (PCSEs) and instrumental variable (IV) regression. The results demonstrate a significant positive impact of AML regulations on entrepreneurship. It is also revealed that AML regulations bolster institutional quality, thereby fostering entrepreneurship. Moreover, the study finds that AML measures facilitate financial development, further promoting entrepreneurial growth in Africa. Importantly, these results remain robust even after conducting a thorough robustness check. Consequently, the study advocates for the implementation of effective AML regulations to enhance the African business environment.

Section 2
Financial Fraud and Corrupt Practices

Organized tax frauds include circular frauds which are very complex in EU member states. Circular fraud is a way of the organized and systematic extraction of money from the state budget by exploiting the shortcomings of the tax system. The destination principle is based on the same tax treatment and the same market position of domestic and imported goods, but it also enables circular fraud. New member countries of the EU are struggling with circular fraud. Losses in the territory of the EU are measured in billions of euros and thus the negative effects on the budgets of those countries are growing. Tax frauds also involve countries outside Europe (UAE, Hong Kong, Russia). On the other hand, in tax havens, illegally acquired money is transferred as a part of the money laundering process. Monitoring and suppression are becoming more and more demanding because the center of gravity has moved to the domain of intangible assets due to the evolution of the internet. The regulatory bodies of the EU are trying hard to combat circular fraud and VAT abuse.

Government effectiveness has emerged as an important factor in the relationship between corruption and the process of financial development. This chapter explores the relationship between corruption control, government effectiveness and financial development in 14 low- and high-income countries over the period 2005–2020 to determine the applicability of the grease the wheels and the sand the wheels hypotheses. Panel data for the two country groups were analysed after overcoming heterogeneity and endogeneity issues. Diagnostic tests were used to increase robustness. The analysis revealed that an increase in corruption control led to a decrease in financial development due to highly effective governments in high-income countries. In contrast, an increase in corruption control led to an increase in financial development due to inefficient governments in low-income countries. The main conclusions of the study are that the grease the wheels hypothesis is applicable to high-income countries and the sand the wheels one is applicable to low-income countries.

Preface

The editing of a book on illicit finance has never been more thrilling and demanding. Over the past few decades, this field of interest has experienced remarkable growth, garnering attention from the G20[1] to the World Economic[2] Forum, and influencing both global and national economic agendas. In today's world, the alarming surge in illicit finance has elevated the importance of addressing these issues in developed and developing countries alike. Consequently, a new regulatory regime, characterized by strict compliance and robust processes, has emerged as a response to combat these challenges.

Throughout history, societies and communities have been greatly affected by the looming specter of illicit finance, with havoc being wreaked across the ages. Even as far back as 1350, the gravity of forgery and counterfeiting was recognized by the statute of Purveyors, which classified them as treasonable offenses. Devastating financial consequences can be unleashed by these illicit activities, affecting both companies and individuals. In the contemporary landscape, illicit finance continues to be a formidable and escalating problem, with businesses and nations being cast in dark shadows, regardless of their size or industry. Addressing these challenges becomes imperative at both macro and micro levels to effectively reduce illicit finance. The task of finding robust and innovative solutions to tackle these pervasive issues is grappled with by countries and organizations.

Discussing illicit finance remains a difficult topic. As society fights with the ever-increasing complexity and frequency of fraudulent practices, understanding and confronting these issues head-on become paramount. Shedding light on these crimes, engaging in discussions about preventive measures, and implementing robust regulatory frameworks are essential steps toward mitigating the profound impact of illicit finance on individuals, organizations, and entire nations. The contemporary world has witnessed the emergence of various insidious sources of illicit finance, ranging from identity fraud, cyber fraud, phishing, hacking, and Ponzi/pyramid schemes to insider trading, embezzlement of funds, window dressing, tax evasion, kickbacks, graft, influence peddling, nepotism, and the misuse of resources, among others. Among the various forms of fraud, cybercrimes loom as the most significant threat, closely followed by customer fraud and asset misappropriation. Interestingly, this era is witnessing a convergence of multiple challenges: the triple threat of fraud, compliance risks, and cyber-attacks, all of which are on the rise. Simultaneously, environmental, geopolitical, financial, and social pressures are further complicating the already challenging task of fraud prevention.

In the current century, technological advancements have revolutionized the landscape of fraud, making it both easier to commit and more sophisticated to detect and prevent. Comprehensive AI-driven platforms have emerged to handle the flow of illicit finance. Leveraging data analytics, artificial intelligence, and machine learning, these platforms play a pivotal role in effectively tracking illicit finance. Governments and organizations are embracing these cutting-edge solutions to proactively monitor the situation. By harnessing the power of these advanced technologies, societies can build robust defenses to protect the interests of individuals and businesses alike. As technology continues to evolve, the fight against fraud and corruption is set to intensify, necessitating a collaborative effort between policymakers, law enforcement, and the private sector to stay ahead of these ever-evolving threats. Through such collective action, a more secure and trustworthy environment may be created for all.

The way is paved for a more transparent and ethical world by breaking the silence and facing the harsh realities of these crimes. A collective commitment from governments, businesses, civil society, and individuals is called for to foster integrity, strengthen accountability, and safeguard the welfare of society as a whole. By upholding the values of honesty, fairness, and justice, a path can be forged toward a more resilient and just future. Efforts to combat fraud and corruption should be multifaceted and proactive. Transparent and accountable governance practices must be upheld, and strict enforcement of anti-corruption laws is essential. Whistleblower protection systems empower individuals to report wrongdoing without fear of retaliation, encouraging them to come forward with valuable information. Internal audit policies and corporate compliance programs can serve as vital checks and balances, ensuring organizations adhere to ethical standards and regulatory requirements.

Public awareness campaigns and educational initiatives are powerful tools to foster a culture of integrity and ethics. By engaging citizens and businesses, we can collectively work towards building a society that values transparency and actively rejects corrupt practices. Collaboration between governmental bodies, law enforcement agencies, private sectors, and international organizations, such as the UNODC, is crucial for a coordinated and effective approach to combating fraud and corruption on a global scale.

The sustainability of a transparent society is currently facing significant risks. To ensure a safer working environment and effectively combat illicit finance within society, it is crucial to implement robust anti-fraud and anti-corruption policies. These policies may encompass a wide range of measures, including anti-corruption strategies, transparent governance procedures, bribery laws, whistleblower systems, internal audit policies, and corporate compliance programs. Promoting a transparent and accountable society requires persistent efforts and a collective commitment to upholding the principles of integrity and justice. By instilling a strong anti-corruption culture and actively implementing anti-fraud policies, we can safeguard the foundations of a sustainable and prosperous future for all.

CONTEXT AND ORGANIZATION OF THIS VOLUME

Regardless of whether you are a beginner or a seasoned researcher, this book will deepen the discourse about illicit finance. I am hopeful that this book is a fascinating and invaluable guide for understanding the theory, practice and cases of finance frauds in today's world.

This book consists of twelve chapters by writers from twelve countries. Twenty One authors contributed from disparate parts of the world;

Americas: USA, Brazil
Europe: Portugal, Croatia, Türkiye
Asia: India, Pakistan, Sri Lanka
Middle East: UAE, Oman
Africa: Ghana, Nigeria

The first chapter "Liability for Insider Trading Under US Federal Securities Law" by Kurt M. Saunders, and Luis Perez, examines civil and criminal liability concerning insider trading under the federal securities laws in the United States. Insider trading occurs when individuals with access to non-public corporate information use it to trade in the company's securities. This behavior violates the insider's fiduciary duty of confidentiality and is considered fraudulent in the market. Furthermore, individuals who receive inside information and trade based on it may also be held accountable. The chapter explores these matters through the analysis of significant cases and relevant regulations issued by the US Securities & Exchange Commission.

The second chapter "AML/CFT Regulations and Informal Remittance Services: The Case of Hawala" by S G Sisira Dharmasri Jayasekara, and Abdul Rafay examines examines informal remittance channels and their connection to illegal activities, which undermines global efforts to combat money laundering. The main focus is on *Hawala*, as a prominent informal remittance channel, and its significant economic and social implications in weak anti-money laundering and counter-financing of terrorism (AML/CFT) regimes. While a global initiative to regulate informal remittance channels could support anti-money laundering initiatives, it is essential to recognize their widespread use as efficient and low-cost remittance channels, despite their association with criminal activities.

The third chapter, "How Harsh the Legislation Should be to Prevent Financial Crimes?: Lessons After Enron Scandal" by Perihan Iren, and Moo Sung Kim, discusses that the Enron and Arthur Andersen scandal, which caused significant repercussions in the corporate world, led to the enactment of the Sarbanes Oxley Act (SOX) by the US Congress. This study reviews the events leading to SOX, discusses its rules and regulations, and evaluates empirical evidence from previous studies regarding the legislation's effectiveness and the harsh penalty imposed on Enron's auditor.

The fourth chapter, "Regulatory Ambiguity in India: A Breeding Ground for Crypto Criminals" by Sachin Shah, and Abdul Rafay, describes that the emergence of cryptocurrencies has brought significant digital technology and financial service changes worldwide, prompting discussions on regulatory frameworks. In India, where cryptocurrency usage is rapidly growing, the government is cautiously working towards legalizing its usage while closely monitoring associated risks and warning the public. Through case studies, the chapter emphasizes the seriousness of the situation and advocates for urgent legislative action to combat scams and money laundering.

The fifth chapter, "Anti-Money Laundering Regulations and Entrepreneurship: The Case of Africa" by Folorunsho Ajide, discusses that money laundering activities in developing economies have produced mixed results in previous studies, but their specific impact on entrepreneurial development has not been thoroughly explored. This chapter addresses this gap by analyzing the influence of anti-money laundering (AML) regulations on entrepreneurship in Africa, utilizing data from 21 African nations between 2012 and 2018. AML regulations are found to improve institutional quality, thereby fostering entrepreneurship, and facilitating financial development, further promoting entrepreneurial growth in Africa. These robust findings emphasize the importance of implementing effective AML regulations to enhance the business environment in the African region.

The sixth chapter, "Circular Frauds and Abuses of VAT: The Case of the European Union" by Valentina Vinšalek Stipic, looks at organized tax fraud, particularly circular fraud, that presents a complex challenge within the EU member states. New EU member countries are facing significant struggles with this type of fraud, leading to substantial financial losses in the billions of euros and negatively impacting national budgets. Tax fraud is not limited to Europe, as countries like UAE, Hong Kong, and Russia are also involved. Additionally, tax havens play a role in facilitating money laundering processes. Monitoring and suppressing these fraud activities are becoming more difficult, particularly with the increasing focus on intangible assets in the digital era.

The seventh chapter, "Corruption, Government Effectiveness and Financial Development: An Empirical Analysis" by Faris Nasif Alshubiri, investigates the relationship between corruption control, government effectiveness, and financial development in 14 low- and high-income countries from 2005 to 2020. It aims to determine the relevance of the "grease the wheels" and "sand the wheels" hypotheses. It is concluded that the "grease the wheels" hypothesis applies to high-income countries, while the "sand the wheels" hypothesis applies to low-income countries.

The eighth chapter, "Examining the Link Between Corruption and Bank Credit: The Case of Sub-Saharan Africa" by Ibrahim Nandom Yakubu, Alhassan Bunyaminu, and Alhassan Musah, investigates the impact of corruption on the expansion of bank credit in Sub-Saharan Africa between 2000 and 2017. The study finds a significant positive relationship between corruption and bank credit. Additionally, the research reveals that banking sector stability leads to a reduction in bank credit, while economic growth and inflation have a notable influence on increasing bank credit. Crucial measures are suggested to promote integrity and responsible lending practices within the banking sector. Recommendations include implementing robust whistleblowing procedures to report corrupt transactions associated with credit advancement, fostering transparency and accountability, and enforcing strict non-price constraints to regulate lending practices effectively.

The ninth chapter, "Inconsistencies in the Disclosures of Discount Rates: The Case of Financial Reporting in Portugal" by Miguel Assunção, and Fábio Albuquerque, explains that the significance of the discount rate in financial reporting has gained prominence over time, warranting attention from international standard-setting bodies. This chapter uses archival research and content analysis to evaluate mandatory and voluntary disclosure levels concerning discount rates. The chapter emphasizes the importance of understanding the appropriate set of items to be disclosed and the factors influencing their disclosure. Aligning these efforts with legal authorities' compliance measures can help reduce information asymmetries and enhance transparency in entities' financial reporting.

The tenth chapter, "Occupational Frauds in Highly Regulated Banking Industry: The Case of India" by Beemamol M., identifies that globally, the banking industry has experienced a significant increase in occupational fraud, with India also witnessing a rise in fraudulent activities by bank officials. This chapter investigates five notable cases of high-value occupational fraud perpetrated by top management personnel in Indian banks. The study identifies multiple contributing factors, including greed, social comparison, corrupt ideology, lack of ethics, a sense of entitlement and ego, hubris, and a hyper-competitive culture. The study's findings lay the groundwork for future empirical research and offer valuable insights to enrich the existing literature on this subject.

The eleventh chapter, "The Effect of Corruption Perception on Foreign Direct Investment: The Case of Latin America" by Thiago Corni Ferreira, Viviani Silva Lírio, Felippe Clemente, and Tayo Oke, explores the relationship between corruption, as measured by Transparency International's Corruption Perception Index (CPI), and Foreign Direct Investment (FDI) inflows in Latin American countries from 2012 to 2019. The study employs a panel data model to determine whether corruption "greases the wheels" or "sands the wheels" of FDI. Surprisingly, the results indicate that the CPI does not have a significant impact on FDI inflows during this time period and sample.

The twelfth chapter, "The Political Economy of Corruption: The Case of Lebanon" by Fatih Kırşanlı, discusses that Lebanon is currently experiencing an unprecedented socioeconomic and political crisis, despite once being a prominent financial center. The civil war in the late 20th century greatly damaged its banking sector, and from 1990 to 2019, the country's economy gradually collapsed, leading to a severe depreciation of the Lebanese lira against foreign currencies. This chapter explains the collapse and a so-called Ponzi scheme orchestrated by Lebanese central and commercial banks. It identifies rampant corruption as the primary cause of these issues, examining factors like financial engineering, the Beirut Explosion, political deadlock, and economic turmoil from a political economy perspective. The chapter also discusses foreign interventions, and terror financing problems, while offering policy recommendations for Lebanon's political economy and highlighting areas for future research.

I express my gratitude to all the contributors and external reviewers who have provided valuable critiques to ensure the chapters that meet the minimum acceptable standard. While the publisher and I, as the Editor, have made our best efforts in preparing this book, we do not make any representations or warranties regarding the accuracy or completeness of its contents. Specifically, we disclaim any implied warranties of merchantability or fitness for a particular purpose. The strategies, suggestions, or any information in this book may not be suitable for every specific situation, and individuals should consult with a professional as needed. Neither the publisher nor the Editor will be liable for any loss of profit or any other commercial damages, including but not limited to special, incidental, consequential, or other damages.

Abdul Rafay
University of Management and Technology, Pakistan.
August 2023

ENDNOTES

1 **Group of Twenty (G20)**: It is an intergovernmental forum comprising of the European Union and nineteen industrialized and developed countries. It is a primary venue for international economic and financial cooperation.

2 **World Economic Forum (WEF)**: It is an international non-governmental forum based in Switzerland, to discuss the state of the world by engaging business, political, academic, and other leaders of society.

Section 1

Legislation for Money Laundering and Financial Fraud

Chapter 1
Liability for Insider Trading Under US Federal Securities Law

Kurt M. Saunders
California State University, Northridge, USA

Luis Perez
California State University, Northridge, USA

ABSTRACT

The purpose of this chapter is to explore the basis and scope of civil and criminal liability for insider trading under the federal securities laws of the United States. Insider trading involves the use of non-public corporate information by those with access to it in order to trade in the corporation's securities. Such conduct involves a breach of the insider's fiduciary duty of confidentiality and is considered to be a form of fraud in the market as well. In addition, others to whom inside information has been disclosed and who trade on it may face liability. In its overall approach, the chapter reviews and illustrates these issues through a discussion of key cases and with reference to regulations issued by the US Securities & Exchange Commission.

INTRODUCTION

Insider trading[1] is the use of non-public corporate information by those with access to it in order to trade in the corporation's securities. Under current law, an insider[2] who fails to disclose material, non-public information before trading on it will be liable for insider trading and may be subject to civil and criminal sanctions. Liability for insider trading has a curious history in the United States. At one time, it was not illegal. Later, it was treated as a form of common law fraud by nondisclosure. In 1934, the US Congress enacted the Securities & Exchange Act, which contained an anti-fraud provision, and prohibited fraud and deception in the sale and purchase of securities. As applied by the courts and through rules issued by the Securities & Exchange Commission (SEC), the practice and prosecution of insider trading became more closely aligned with the duty of confidentiality and its breach by those who owe such duty who trade on inside information[3].

DOI: 10.4018/978-1-6684-8587-3.ch001

Since the enactment of the 1934 statute, the scope of who qualifies as an "insider" has been expanded, and liability has been extended to those who receive and trade on tips from insiders. The main purpose of this chapter is to examine the prohibition of insider trading under US securities law. The chapter begins by considering the meaning of insider trading and tracing the historical development of civil and criminal bases of liability under US securities regulation statutes. Next, the chapter explores the scope of who is considered to be an "insider" and explains the interrelationship of insiders with the traditional fiduciary duties of loyalty and confidentiality (Hensen, 2021). In addition, the chapter considers the liability of "*tippers*[4]" and "*tippees*[5]" and how courts have applied the concept of misappropriation to extend the ambit of liability for insider trading. Finally, the chapter examines emerging issues and trends in insider trading prosecution concerning shadow trading, tipping on the dark web, trading in digital assets such as non-fungible tokens, and the liability of "temporary insiders" working in the gig economy.

HISTORICAL DEVELOPMENT OF THE LAW OF INSIDER TRADING

Investigations of corporate officers, celebrities, and politicians for insider trading are conventional news in the interconnected world of business in the 21st century. In the first three quarters of 2022, the US Securities and Exchange Commission[6] filed 20 new complaints against parties that the agency claims could be found guilty of insider trading. It would then be reasonable to assume that 2022 will be the first year where SEC complaints increased, at least since 2018, prior to the start of the pandemic. Notably, insider trading has not always been unlawful. In fact, insider trading was, during a specific period in time, considered a practice that was common among professionals who traded and dealt with securities. Those who held positions within a corporation and had the ability to acquire material information that might affect the price of its securities were not barred from personally trading on those securities, even if the information remained unknown to the general public. This was also true of those who received tips or advice from insiders. However, with time, the overall perception of the practice started to change.-

The Inception of Securities Markets in the United States

Insider trading within the United States can be traced to very early in the country's development. Even with vast economic differences found in the colonies in the latter half of the 18th century, which were mostly due to the colonies' use of varied currencies, their investor market participants were nonetheless active. The country's first stock exchange platform, the Philadelphia Stock Exchange, came about in 1790 and attested to the country's economic growth as founded on the increasingly popular practice of speculating in government-issued assumption bonds (Markham, 2002; Wright, 2005; Teweles *et al.*, 1982). The bonds were issued by the federal government when it assumed debts incurred by the colonies during the Revolutionary War by issuing debt certificates. In fact, during the time when Congress was debating the debt assumption, some officials with access to negotiations and information about the matter profited by purchasing the depreciated certificates and redeeming them at a higher price when the US government assumed this debt (Markham, 2002). Even though far from perfect, the country began to move in the direction of progress in terms of securities trading activities given its increased activity in the market.

These trading developments occurred only two centuries after the initial stock trading markets in Europe that surfaced during the early 17th century and which allowed economies in that region to develop in a healthy manner (Geisst, 2004). Implementing an organized stock-trading platform was considered necessary if the United States would want to efficiently develop (Geisst, 2004). Of course, such optimism, mixed with unavoidable inexperience, would not yield perfection without some cost. It was during this time when securities traders and investors of this era would witness the rise of insider trading practices due to the market's weak regulation in combination with its inability to anticipate greater economic twists and turns that occur in vulnerable markets.

A Notorious Early Insider Trader

In 1791, William Duer, an English colonial who was able to become an experienced merchant and hold important financial positions in the northern states, devised a plan with the purpose of enriching himself at the expense and ignorance of others within the private sector given his upper hand in having access to key sources of financial information (Geisst, 2004; Cowen, 2000). Duer's plan was to loan immense amounts of money in an attempt to swindle the American securities marketplace of "*US debt securities as well as the stocks of the [Bank of the United States] and the Bank of New York*" (Cowen, 2000). Lamentably for Duer, his plan, in conjunction with the addition of timely market factors at the time, caused the prices of securities to peak in January of 1792, and abruptly decline continuously for the remaining months of that same quarter (Cowen, 2000). The halting of the issuance of credit by the banks would further hinder Duer's remaining possibility of achieving his objective or at least incurring huge financial losses. Interestingly, the sum of these factors, which are also often given as causes for the financial crisis of 1792, is what facilitated the discovery of the Duer scheme by the press.

While insider trading was not itself an unlawful practice during the time, defaulting on debts was sufficient to send someone to prison. Duer's acquisition of the securities using information drawn from his financial capacity as secretary to the Board of the Treasury is what amounted to insider trading. Eventually, due to the market crises of 1792 coupled with his inability to settle his debts, Duer, managed to default on the contracts and financial responsibilities he had entered by employing borrowed money and which would have him sent to debtors' prison where his passing would happen only a few years later in 1799. Duer, while part of an unsuccessful scheme, would nevertheless earn the title of the first imprisoned insider trader in US history given that he was "*the first individual to use the knowledge gained from his official position to [yield a jail sentence from] speculative trading*" (Cowen, 2000; Geisst, 2004). Duer's misconduct and conviction led to the negative perception of insider trading due to the deleterious impact it had on the market of his time.

Further Development of Securities Trading

The Duer scandal and market crisis of 1792 proved to be a learning experience for those involved in securities trading and led many investors and traders to come together and acknowledge the weaknesses of the market and aim to lessen investor vulnerability. A debate between those who supported the idea of regulation of trading practices and those who opposed it would be furthered by the 1792 crisis. This particular self-regulation initiative, which is notable given it was executed by the participants of the market themselves, took place in May 1792 when a small group of stock traders agreed to sign "The Buttonwood Agreement" (MacDonald, 2017).

This agreement ensured that a set of customs be followed by those who wished to engage in securities transactions between those who signed. As speculative trading on the Philadelphia Stock Exchange kept rising in popularity, the founders of the Buttonwood Agreement further formalized their improvements by mimicking the structure of the Philadelphia Exchange (Wright, 2005). This decision led the New York-based market to become an even more regulated entity than it had initially been. In 1817, the group that had created the exclusive platform for trading in 1792, would give birth to a new association named the New York Stock and Exchange (MacDonald, 2017). Only two-and-a-half decades later, the network would receive its present-day denomination, "New York Stock Exchange" ("NYSE") (MacDonald, 2017).

Around the same time, the Supreme Court somewhat undercut the successful self-regulation efforts made by the securities trading participants when it decided on a case that would have consequences for the insider trading topic. The case of *Laidlaw v. Organ* (1817) involved the use of non-public information that was likely to affect the price of a commodity when it became public. Henry Organ arranged to purchase tobacco from Laidlaw several hours before the Treaty of Ghent was announced. The treaty ended the War of 1812 and lifted a trade embargo on US tobacco exports. Organ had learned from his brother that the treaty was about to be announced and that this would result in higher tobacco prices but did not inform Laidlaw before the sale. Laidlaw sued, and on appeal, the Supreme Court ruled in favor of Organ. Chief Justice John Marshall explained that a purchaser of commercial goods is not obliged to (1) disclose material information about a commodity that will inevitably increase its price even when the seller is not aware of it or asks about it, or (2) refrain from transacting given such knowledge (Laidlaw v. Organ, 1817).

The Supreme Court's reasoning was that ruling otherwise would mean that the law would require information equity on all commercial deals, which is practically impossible. Additionally, the Court believed that requiring the disclosure of all known pertinent information would be uncharacteristic of a buyer's natural role and interest in pursuing the best deal. This decision, more importantly, signaled to speculators that they could engage in transactions of valuables with fluctuating prices without being legally obliged to disclose all known material information about the items, even when that same information was not yet known to the other party or to the general public (Markham, 2002). In effect, this meant that insider trading in securities was permissible.

19th Century Insider Trading Events

Even against a backdrop of participant-based regulation efforts, radical and pronounced examples of insider trading took place in the plain daylight of the 1800s. There was no pity for victims of the practice since profits obtained at the least possible cost were all that mattered for insider traders during this time. Even the US Treasury itself had to learn a costly lesson from these financial malefactors. The "Credit Mobilier Scandal" case is a second early and yet significant example where organizational insiders employed privileged information to scheme for financial benefit. It constitutes one of the biggest financial scandals of US history involving the federal government.

In 1864, alongside additional Union Pacific Railroad partners, Union Pacific executive Oakes Ames plotted a scheme to misappropriate governmental funds. During the time, railroad expansion and businesses involved in furthering this objective were crucial to the development of the stock exchange markets given that most of the securities being issued throughout the period were from entities linked with the Railroad Industry (Teweles *et al.*, 1982). The group created and managed a sham subcontracting company named Credit Mobilier of America, and overcharged Union Pacific for the westward railroad expansions being financed and requested by the government by the Union Pacific Company (Geisst, 2004). The group would also issue stocks of Credit Mobilier to further enrich themselves and their partners. Some of these issued stocks would even conclude in the hands of politics in order to obtain their favor in potentially hiding the scheme. Eventually, the scandal was made public by the media (Kens, 2009). Of course, given how insider trading was seen as customary of the market, there were no legal repercussions for the executives involved in the scandal. In truth, all high-profile individuals involved were absolved of any and all criminal charges (Geisst, 2004; Riggs, 2015). Moreover, the subjects involved were in fact able to go on and develop their careers without issue (Riggs, 2015). On the other hand, the scandal created an increased awareness of the existence of corruption within the country as well as additional reform efforts to cushion scandalous events. (Olson & Mendoza, 2015; Geisst, 2004).

The Most Hated Insider Trader in 19th Century America

Perhaps the most notorious and ruthless of the machinators of the late railroad era, however, was an investor and robber baron Jason "Jay" Gould. His market manipulations ranged from inaccurate disclosure of information to employees of private company information in trading to bribes to persuasion of presidential colleagues, and while perhaps not entirely surprising, attempted kidnapping (Geisst, 2004).

Gould's actions would even earn him the title of "the most hated man in America" to the extent that he, on one occasion, barely escaped from an angry mob in New York as a result of one of his dealings in the gold market (Geisst, 2004). Gould, as a fully realized investor and market influencer, would routinely express his financial dealings via articles published by his newspaper company, the *New York World,* in order to manipulate companies, their securities' value, the entire market, and its participants (Geisst, 2004).

Bribes were known to Gould as he once induced legislators to authenticate illegally generated and issued stock (Riggs, 2015). Furthermore, Gould once coerced presidential connections to influence transactions involving gold, a commodity that was imperative to hold control of the market during the late 1860s and which Gould would want to corner in order to further his projects that would yield great profits at the expense of others (Geisst, 2004). Even upon the realization that Gould was merely employing a speculation machination, President Ulysses S. Grant failed in preventing Gould from profiting from his millionaire gold transactions as he was clever enough to manage to avoid losses by getting rid of the gold prior to the decline of the commodity value (Geisst, 2004).

As individuals who develop expertise in their field and execute their work with flair, Jay Gould sometimes took creative approaches to unethical securities trading. To illustrate, Gould, as a financially successful trader, would at times provide seemingly overly-generous trading tips to people (A recipient of pertinent inside information is contemporarily considered a tippee) in order to make them trade or even behave as he wished. Consider how Gould once tipped a "pastor of a wealthy church" who requested trading advice in regard to Pacific Mail securities, but, to the spiritual leader's surprise, Gould offered more than counsel (Boland, 1985). Gould guaranteed the investment's success by financially insuring it. Any losses the pastor incurred would be covered by Gould. Naturally overjoyed with such an offer, the pastor bought onto the idea and even went and tipped additional individuals/traders by sharing how no other than Gould himself had tipped and insured him on the matter. This, of course, had its intended effect of persuading numerous secondary tippees on acting upon what appeared to be an exclusive tip. In due course, the financial advice endorsed to the pastor proved faulty, yet a loyal Gould covered the losses incurred by the pastor. Nevertheless, Gould disclosed how those secondary tippees were "*...the people I was after*" (Boland, 1985). More specifically, Gould explained how merely made use of the pastor in order to draw the attention of additional traders who would act upon the tip but who, unlike the pastor, held no financial cushion/insurance on the matter from Gould (Boland, 1985). In other words, this formula would guarantee Gould a profit by artificially influencing the transactions of secondary tippees, facilitated by his reputation, and which would only cost Gould a small fee to execute.

Insider Trading: 20th Century Events and the Dawn of Regulation

In the Union Pacific Dividend Scandal of 1906, director Edward Harriman capitalized on his knowledge that Union Pacific and its affiliated company, Southern Pacific would increase dividend rates. Not only did he allow himself to make a profit on such information, but by further extending the time between when additional company insiders became aware of the dividend news and the moment when the news was finally made public, he facilitated insiders of both companies and tippees of those insiders to profit from personal transactions on company securities made prior to the final disclosure of the dividend news to the general public. The regularity of insider trading during this period and as it relates to this particular instance can be best described by Harriman himself: "*any employee who was not 'in' on the Pacific deal ought to be discharged for incompetency*" (Perino, 2019). This scandal, however, led to public discussion in the newspapers of the time about the lack of laws prohibiting insider trading. Observers and a majority general public of various political perspectives and social viewpoints decried the overall situation as a betrayal of trust, an abuse of corporate power, the advancement of personal gain from the ignorance of others, as well as the inefficacy of directorial fraud regulations of the time (Perino, 2019).

It was in the 1909 landmark case of *Strong v. Repide* (1909) in which the United States Supreme Court identified the practice of insider trading as an unwelcome practice within the business realm. The Court determined that a "company official is obliged to disclose her identity and non-public information when she trades the company stocks" (Salinger, 2005). The case involved Francisco Repide, the majority shareholder and director of Philippine Sugar Estates Development Company, Limited. The company's ownership of islands in the Philippines, at the time a US territory, prompted an offer to purchase stock from the Philippine government. Given his position within the company, Repide ultimately held full authority on whether to accept or decline the offer. In order to defraud his co-owners, including Eleanor Strong, Repide employed a broker with instructions to hire an additional or secondary broker as a way to remain anonymous to obtain all of the remaining shares held by Strong. With the acquisition of Strong's shares, Repide finalized the sale of the lands which allowed him to realize a profit from their increased value.

The Court expressed its interest in providing a cushion of legal protection to shareholders, like Strong, who are involved in a fiduciary relationship with directors and who may also be shareholders of the same company, like Repide. Special circumstances, like the existing company policy agreement between the owners of the Philippines-based company that prescribed a meeting prior to a sale of significant company real estate, supported the Supreme Court's holding in favor of Strong. Additionally, the Court based its reasoning on multiple state-level precedents and the Philippine Civil Codes that support a fiduciary duty of disclosure as well as prohibit obtaining contractual consent via fraud.

The finding in the *Strong* case of "special circumstances" – such as active concealment of the purchaser's identity or failure to disclose information that could materially affect the price of the stock – served as a standard for insider trading liability. In fact, it was the exception to the general rule of no liability, and the need to prove special circumstances limited its application. In the case of *Goodwin v. Agassiz* (1933), for example, the directors and officers of Cliff Mining Corporation, a company that operated in the extraction of minerals in the northern Michigan region, learned of the discovery of substantial copper deposits on land it had been exploring and purchased shares on the open market. One shareholder,

Homer Goodwin, who had sold his stock before the information became public, sued. The Supreme Court of Massachusetts ruled that there were no special circumstances involved in the case due to the speculative nature of the information, and therefore the board and officers had no duty to disclose the information before trading (ABM, 1934; Wartzman, 2002).

In the period before the beginning of the 1930s, absent special circumstances amounting to fraud, those with access to inside information could engage in insider trading without concern for any legal penalties. Notably, between the middle of the 19th century through the end of the initial decade of the 20th century, eleven out of sixteen court decisions involving insiders and securities fraud[7] were held in favor of the insiders (Boland, 1985). However, as discussed in the next section, securities regulation and the treatment of insider trading in the United States soon took a more serious turn at the federal level.

THE BASIS AND EXTENT OF LIABILITY UNDER RULE 10B-5

During the depth of the Great Depression and in the aftermath of the stock market crash of 1929, the United States Congress launched the current system of federal securities regulation by enacting the Securities Act of 1933. The 1933 Act is concerned with regulating the offering of securities and promoting the disclosure of information needed by investors to make informed decisions about purchasing securities (Palmiter, 2011). A year later, Congress further enacted the Securities and Exchange Act of 1934 to supplement the Securities Act of 1933. As with the 1933 Act, the main purpose of the 1934 Act was to protect investors by promoting public disclosure of material information about issuers of securities. The 1934 statute requires disclosures of information in statements filed at the time of registration of securities to be traded, as well as periodic and ongoing reporting of information thereafter. In order to further ensure investor confidence and the integrity of the securities market, the statute also limits the ability of corporate insiders to profit from trading in the shares of their issuers (Loss, 1988). The 1934 Act also established the Securities and Exchange Commission (SEC) as the federal agency tasked with implementing and enforcing securities laws.

Defined in the 1934 Act as an "insider" are officers and directors of corporations that have registered equity securities as required by the statute, as well as owners of more than 10 percent of such equity securities (15 US Code § 781(b)(1)(d)). In enforcing the 1934 Act over the years, however, the SEC and the courts have broadened the range of persons who are considered insiders. In addition, section 16(a) of the 1934 Act requires insiders to disclose their ownership of their corporation's securities within 10 days of acquiring the securities (15 US Code § 78p(b)). Moreover, insiders must report any subsequent transactions in the securities within two business days after the trade. Section 16(b) prohibits an insider from profiting from short-swing trading in his or her corporation's shares. Any short-swing profits made by an insider may be recovered by the issuer if the profits resulted from the purchase and sale, or the sale and purchase, of any class of the issuer's equity securities within less than a six-month period (Palmiter, 2011).

Also included in the Securities and Exchange Act of 1934 are provisions designed to prevent fraud, deception, or manipulation in securities transactions and to provide remedies to investors who suffer losses due to such misconduct. Foremost among these provisions is section 10(b) of the statute, which declares unlawful any manipulative or deceptive device in connection with the purchase or sale of any registered security[8] (15 US Code § 78j(b)). The Securities and Exchange Commission has implemented section 10(b) by adopting Rule 10b-5, which states:

It shall be unlawful for any person, directly or indirectly, by use of any means or instrumentality of interstate commerce or of the mails, or of any facility of any national securities exchange,

(a) to employ any device, scheme, or artifice to defraud,

(b) to make any untrue statement of a material fact or to omit to state a material fact necessary in order to make the statements made, in the light of the circumstances under which they were made, not misleading, or

(c) to engage in any act, practice, or course of business which operates or would operate as a fraud or deceit upon any person,

in connection with the purchase or sale of any security (17 C.F.R. § 240.10b-5).

In its application, Rule 10b-5 prohibits trading in securities by any person with non-public confidential information who owes a fiduciary duty of loyalty to the corporation and its shareholders. Rule 10b-5 has been used to deter and punish fraudulent misstatements or nondisclosures of material facts in the sale or purchase of securities, and any shareholder can sue for damages for losses suffered. In addition, Rule 10b-5 prohibits insider trading "*in breach of a duty of trust and confidence that is owed directly, indirectly or derivatively, to the issuer of that security or the shareholders of that issuer, or to any other person who is the source of the material non-public information*" (Regulation 10b-5, 17 C.F.R. § 240.10b5-1). This extension of Rule 10b-5 to insider trading is consistent with Congress' purpose of promoting the integrity of the securities market in which all can compete on a fair and even basis (Loss, 1988). In this sense, the proscription against insider trading is grounded in preventing those who possess material non-public information from exploiting an informational asymmetry to the disadvantage of those without access to the same information.

Who Is an Insider?

Liability for insider trading under Rule 10b-5 applies only to insiders – those persons who have a duty to abstain from trading on inside information until it is made public – but who is an insider? Of course, they include officers, directors, and employees of the corporation, who owe a fiduciary duty of loyalty and confidentiality to the corporation by virtue of their position. However, the courts have extended insider status beyond those who hold such positions. For instance, in the case of *Speed v. Transamerica Corp.* (1947), for a majority shareholder was deemed to be an "insider" because it knew that the actual cash value of a corporate asset was greater than its book value as reported in financial statements. As it turned out, this information was neither public nor known by minority shareholders who had sold their stock to the majority shareholder.

In subsequent cases, the courts have broadly held that an insider is any person who is entrusted with confidential information for a corporate purpose. Accordingly, the SEC and various courts have stated that insiders also include outside consultants, attorneys, accountants, independent auditors, engineers, investment bankers, securities analysts, public relations advisers, news reporters, as well as personnel of government agencies such as the SEC who are provided access to confidential corporate information in filings and disclosures (Palmiter, 2011).

The "Disclose or Abstain" Rule

The fiduciary duty of loyalty owed by insiders encompasses a duty not to disclose confidential information. Insiders breach this fiduciary duty by using the information to purchase or sell the corporation's securities, or by receiving a personal benefit by disclosing the information to someone else who uses it to purchase or sell the corporation's securities. In the foundational case of *SEC v. Texas Gulf Sulphur Corp.* (1968), the court held that the disclosure requirements of Rule 10b-5 impose a duty on insiders either to disclose the information or to abstain from trading in the corporation's securities until the information has been disclosed to the public.

In the *Texas Gulf Sulphur* case, the corporation's officers received positive reports about rich ore deposits discovered during exploratory drilling on a site in Canada. After learning this, but before the news was made public, the officers made substantial purchases of the corporate stock. The court of appeals first noted that the information would have affected the price of the stock and then observed that a reasonable investor would have considered the information relevant in deciding whether to purchase, sell, or hold the stock. As such, the court held that insiders like corporate officers are subject to what became known as the "disclose or refrain" rule. An insider who possesses material, non-public information may not use that information when trading with a person who does not also know it. Rather, the insider must either disclose the information before trading the securities or refrain from trading. An insider who fails to disclose the information before trading on it will be liable under Rule 10b-5.

In 2000, the SEC promulgated Regulation FD, which prohibits corporations from selectively disclosing material non-public information to investment analysts, institutional investors, and other market professionals without making widespread public disclosure at the same time (Regulation FD, 17 C.F.R. § 243.100). The rationale behind Regulation FD is the belief that all investors should have equal access to a securities issuer's disclosures of material information at the same time in order to promote full and fair disclosure (Loss, 1988). Therefore, if an issuer discloses material non-public information to securities market professionals, the issuer must also make public disclosure of the same information.

The Misappropriation Theory of Liability

The traditional approach to insider trading liability considers trading on inside information to be deceptive under Rule 10b-5 because of the fiduciary relationship between insiders and shareholders of the corporation, which results in the duty to disclose or abstain. Over time, another approach to determining liability emerged known as misappropriation theory[9], which applies when an insider uses confidential information from his or her corporation to trade in securities of another corporation. This theory posits that a person violates Rule 10b-5 when he or she uses confidential information in breach of a duty of loyalty and confidentiality owed to the source of the information in order to trade in securities of another corporation (Palmiter, 2011).

In effect, the insider's use of the information in breach of his or her fiduciary duty defrauds the corporation of the exclusive use of that information. The difference between the traditional and misappropriation approaches is based on their focus. Whereas the traditional theory is grounded in the duty owed to shareholders of the corporation, the misappropriation theory is based on the duty owed to the corporation as the source of the information and, more broadly, is concerned with protecting the integrity of the securities market. Thus, once a person who acquires the information uses it to trade, there is fraud in connection with the purchase or sale of securities because the fraud occurs not when he or she obtains the information but when, without first disclosing it, he or she uses the information in the purchase or sale of the securities (Palmiter, 2011).

The Supreme Court endorsed the application of the misappropriation theory in the case of *United States v. O'Hagan* (1997). In this case, O'Hagan was an attorney whose firm was hired by one corporation to make a tender offer for the stock of another corporation. He purchased the stock of the target corporation before the tender offer was announced, and when the tender offer was announced to the public, he made a large profit on the sale of the stock. The SEC indicted O'Hagan for insider trading and he argued that he could not have violated Rule 10b-5 because he owed no duty of confidentiality to the target corporation. On appeal, the US Supreme Court embraced the misappropriation rule. The Court held that O'Hagan's use of non-public material information about the tender offer he had acquired from the corporation his firm had represented in order to trade in securities of the other corporation was illegal.

Following the *O'Hagan* decision, the SEC issued Rule 10b5-2 to broadly define the duty of confidentiality in misappropriation cases. Rule 10b5-2 provides that a duty of trust and confidence exists "whenever a person agrees to maintain information in confidence; and whenever the person communicating the material non-public information and the person to whom it is communicated have a history, pattern, or practice of sharing confidences, such that the recipient of the information knows or reasonably should know that the person communicating the material non-public information expects that the recipient will maintain its confidentiality" (Regulation 10b5-2, 17 C.F.R. § 240.10b5-2). Accordingly, misappropriation extends to situations beyond those involving a fiduciary relationship between the insider and the recipient of inside information.

Tipper/Tippee Liability

Tippees are persons outside of the corporation who are recipients of inside information provided to them by an insider or tipper. A tippee is liable under Rule 10b-5 if it is proved that the (1) tippee knew that the insider/tipper breached a fiduciary duty by disclosing the non-public information, and (2) the tippee used the information to trade in the corporation's securities. On the other hand, a tipper is liable only if he or she also receives a personal benefit, either for pecuniary gain or to make a gift to a friend or relative who trades in the securities, by disclosing the information to a tippee. As to the element of benefit, the different standards of culpability for tippers and tippees can be understood through the lens of fiduciary duty. The tipper's disclosure is a breach of his or her duties of confidentiality and to disclose or abstain, while the tippee's basis of liability results from his or her misappropriation of the information and unjust enrichment from the tipper's breach of duty (Loss, 1988).

The requirement of a benefit to the tipper is demonstrated in the case of *SEC v. Dirks,* (1983). The case involved a securities analyst named Dirks, who received non-public information from Secrist, a former officer of EFA, that EFA assets were overvalued due to corporate fraud. Dirks also informed his clients of this information. The SEC sued. The Supreme Court held that Secrist received no personal benefit from the disclosure. Rather, he did so to reveal the fraud to the public. As such, because Dirks had no fiduciary duty to conceal the information, he did not violate Rule 10b-5 by passing the information on to Secrist.

To be liable, the tippee must know or should have known, that the tipper breached a fiduciary duty by disclosing the information. Moreover, in order to find that the tipper engaged in insider trading, he or she must have received a benefit in exchange for disclosing the information to the tippee. The benefit received by the tipper need not always be pecuniary. For instance, a tipper's benefit may be to impress others with his or her knowledge of inside information. In *Salman v. United States* (2016), the tipper was an investment banker who disclosed inside information regarding pending mergers and acquisitions to his brother to assist him financially. The US Supreme Court held that a tipper obtains a personal benefit when the tipper makes a gift of confidential information to a tippee who is a relative or friend with the intent to benefit that person. This holding has been interpreted by some courts to mean that insider/tippers are liable when they disclose material, non-public information to any tippee with an intent to benefit the tippee, even without any other personal or financial benefit to the insider/tipper.

Table 1. The scope of tipper/tippee liability

Transaction	Result
Insider sells or purchases securities using inside information	Insider is liable for insider trading and breach of fiduciary duty
Insider/Tipper sells or gives inside information to a Tippee, who sells or purchases securities	Tippee is liable for insider trading; Insider/Tipper is liable for breach of fiduciary duty
Insider/Tipper sells or gives inside information to a Tippee in exchange for a benefit, and Tippee sells or purchases securities	Tippee is liable for insider trading; Insider/Tipper is liable for insider trading and breach of fiduciary duty

Sanctions for Insider Trading

Those found to have engaged in insider trading may be subject to civil liability for damages and penalties as well as criminal sanctions. As to civil penalties, any person who sold or purchased securities of the same class as those traded by the insider in violation of Rule 10b-5 may bring a private action against the insider. Pursuant to section 20A of the 1934 Act, a person found liable for insider trading is liable for the total amount of the profits gained or loss avoided due to the violation of Rule 10b-5. The action must be filed within five years after the date of the last transaction involving insider trading.

In addition, the SEC may bring an action in a US district court to impose a civil monetary penalty against any person who trades on inside information. The amount of the penalty may not exceed three times the profit gained, or loss avoided due to the purchase or sale. In calculating the amount of damages or penalties, the profit gained or loss avoided is the difference between the purchase or sale price of the security and the value of that security during a reasonable period of time after public dissemination of the information. This remedy is known as the disgorgement of profits (Palmiter, 2011). The SEC may also seek an order enjoining the insider or tippee from further trading.

The 1934 Act also provides for liability for criminal violations. Section 32 provides that individuals may be fined up to $5 million and imprisoned for up to 20 years for willful violations of the 1934 Act or SEC rules. Corporations may be fined up to $25 million. Individuals who did not knowingly and willfully violate the law can avoid imprisonment. In addition, the courts can impose a forfeiture of assets, representing profits unlawfully obtained from insider trading. (15 USC. § 78ff(a))

Table 2. Penalties for insider trading

Civil Penalties	Criminal Penalties
● A fine of up to $500,000 along with a cease-and-desist order. ● A potential injunction from a federal district court based on a request by the SEC. ● Disgorgement of profits gained, or losses avoided by the execution of insider trading. ● In an action brought by the SEC, an insider or tippee may be required to relinquish three times the number of profits gained or losses avoided by trading on inside information.	● A fine of up to $5 million for individuals. ● A corporation involved, if any, can be fined up to $25 million. ● Imprisonment of up to 20 years in federal prison for willful violations by an individual

EMERGING ISSUES AND TRENDS

Even though the incidence of insider trading is relatively low when contrasted against other financial crimes, recent annual reports released by the SEC reveal that insider trading cases remain a significant share of the overall total investigated and prosecuted by the agency. Insider trading complaints by the SEC against individuals exceed 20 filings as of September 2022 (Litigation Releases, 2022). Twelve of these complaints concern trading based on undisclosed acquisition news, whereas nine complaints are concerned with trades based on unpublished earnings reports or instances where imminent undisclosed announcements (not related to an acquisition) had a significant impact on the value of the traded shares (Litigation Releases, 2022).

According to a 2019 data-driven study, defendants who are caught trading on material non-public information often profit from the practice, even after being subjected to penalties (Spaic *et al.*, 2019). Another study considered insider trading cases between 1996 and 2016. The findings suggested that the likelihood of insider trading is higher for stocks with greater liquidity because greater trading activity allows insiders to conceal their trades and earn higher profits, and when the amount of material information in a transaction is substantial because the chances of information "leakage" by those involved is more likely. (Patel & Putnins, 2020) The same study discerned that cases involving inside information about mergers and acquisitions and about announcements of quarterly earnings tend to be the most frequent target of prosecution. (Patel & Putnins, 2020)

As the reach of liability for insider trading has expanded, it has come under greater scrutiny by regulators and the investing public. The SEC has increasingly relied on data analytics and circumstantial evidence, which creates an inference of liability, as proof of insider trading. However, a court in a recent case, *SEC v. Clark,* (2021), cautioned the SEC on overreliance on such evidence and dismissed an insider trading case against an alleged mortgage banker tippee whose bold option purchases prior to a corporate acquisition had been red-flagged by the SEC's surveillance databases. The SEC based its case on "suspicious" trading activity after the alleged tipper and tippee, who were brothers, had been in communication with one another. Nevertheless, absent direct evidence of a tip, or testimony supporting the SEC's claim that inside information had been shared, the court dismissed the case because the case was too speculative and did not support an inference of insider trading. (Michaels, 2021).

Even so, the continuous, accelerated technological advances of recent decades have created opportunities for the unscrupulous to exploit their access to inside information to profit personally in new markets. Indeed, the current environment bears many similarities to the period of exploitation by securities traders during the dawn of the railroad era in the 1800s (Geisst, 2004; Teweles *et al.*, 1982). This section considers several such instances of insider trading and the emerging issues or trends they present, including the regulation of shadow trading, misuse of the "dark web" for illicit reconnaissance of material inside information, the issues arising from the trading of non-fungible tokens, and the exposure of independent contractors as "temporary insiders" in the current and growing "gig" economy.

Regulation of Shadow Trading

The recent case of *SEC v. Panuwat* (2022) represents a potentially far-reaching expansion of liability for insider trading in recent years. Matthew Panuwat was senior director of business development at Medivation, a medium-sized biopharmaceutical firm when he learned that the company was about to be acquired by Pfizer, a much larger competitor. This information was both non-public and material as to Medivation's future stock value. Rather than purchasing Medivation stock, which would have led to liability under the traditional theory of insider trading, or stock in Pfizer, which would have led to liability under the misappropriation approach, Panuwat purchased stock options in Incyte, a competing pharmaceutical firm of comparable size to Medivation. Panuwat reasoned that Pfizer's acquisition of Medivation was likely to lead to an increase in the price of Incyte's stock as well, which is exactly what occurred when the acquisition was announced. After Panuwat earned $107,066 from his trade, the SEC charged Panuwat with insider trading.

Panuwat moved to dismiss the charges on the grounds that the non-public information was not material because it did not involve Incyte or breach of his duty of confidentiality to Medivation, and because Incyte was not involved in the acquisition. Thus, he argued that his trading in the stock of an unrelated issuer of securities did not violate Rule 10b-5 under either the traditional or misappropriation bases of liability. The federal district court disagreed, accepting the SEC's new "shadow trading" theory of liability. This practice involves using inside information of one issuer to trade in the stock of another issuer of comparable size and which offers competing or complementary products or services within the same or a related industry (Mehta *et al.*, 2021). A key factor in the court's decision was Medivation's insider trading policy prohibiting employees from using non-public information to profit financially by buying or selling "*the securities of another publicly traded company, including … competitors*" of Medivation (*SEC v. Panuwat,* (2022). As such, Panuwat's violation of this policy was the basis of his knowing breach of duty.

Whether Panuwat's exposure to liability would have been different if Medivation's policy was less restrictive is unclear. If not, then the expansion of insider trading liability to encompass shadow trading is a significant development in light of its focus on prohibiting more remote forms of trading that might compromise the integrity of the market. The theory extends beyond the concerns of the traditional and misappropriation theories – discouraging a breach of a duty of confidentiality and protecting other investors in the securities market – to prohibiting any form of derivative or tertiary trading based on knowledge of non-public information. Do this benefits shareholders and further preserve the integrity of the securities market? Absent an express duty not to engage in shadow trading as in the *Panuwat* case, can such a duty be implied? Such a system of regulation is likely to have a major impact on corporate compliance policies, not only as to their content and employee training but also as to limitations on the ability of employees to trade in those industries related to the business of their employer.

Tipping on the Dark Web

In its early years, the internet offered the promise of "worldwide economic growth and cultural transformation" through the engine of e-commerce (Saunders, 2001). Decades later, a hidden online marketplace has emerged known as the "dark web," a part of the internet accessible through specialized software and designed to facilitate anonymity by obscuring users' identities, including their internet protocol addresses. The anonymity afforded by the dark web allows users to sell and purchase illegal products and services, including illicit drugs, stolen identities, hacking services, and insider trading tips. Such insider tipping gained the attention of the SEC and the US Department of Justice in the case of *SEC v. Trovias* Complaint, 2021).

Using a pseudonym, an individual by the name of Apostolos Trovias sold tips that he claimed consisted of order-book data from a securities trading firm – purportedly material, non-public information – that had been provided to him by an employee of the trading firm (*SEC v. Trovias* Complaint, 2021). Trovias sold those tips through weekly and monthly subscriptions, as well as through one-off sales. Over the course of this scheme, Trovias sold over 100 subscriptions to investors via the dark web, and purchasers traded securities on the basis of tips that Trovias provided to them (*SEC v. Trovias* Complaint, 2021). The SEC discovered the scheme through undercover agents and indicted Trovias, asserting that Trovias employed the dark web as a platform where he repeatedly and covertly sold material non-public information for his own benefit. Alternatively, the SEC alleged that many of Trovias' disclosures were fraudulent misrepresentations of accurate securities data (*SEC v. Trovias* Complaint, 2021).

Considering the current widespread use of social media, messaging apps, and email to exchange information electronically, the Trovias prosecution reveals that the SEC is making increasing use of advanced technology and complex techniques to uncover instances of insider trading (McGinley, 2022). Such tools will be essential in policing the dark web, social media, and areas of the internet where users can exchange information anonymously.

Trading in Digital Assets

A non-fungible token is a "*digital asset that represents real-world objects like art, music, in-game items, and videos. They are bought and sold online, frequently with cryptocurrency, and they are generally encoded with the same underlying software*." (Conti & Broverman, 2022). In recent years, the SEC and Department of Justice have signaled that they will give closer scrutiny to trading in digital assets such as non-fungible tokens ("NFTs"). In 2022, the Department of Justice brought its first prosecution for insider trading involving NFTs. Nathaniel Chastain was a product manager at OpenSea Inc., currently the largest online marketplace for NFTs, and was responsible for choosing which NFTs would be featured for sale on the OpenSea site. The indictment asserted that Chastain used his position as controller of the OpenSea website, which showcased trending NFTs on its homepage which, in turn, would cause their respective prices to increase. More specifically, given his knowledge of upcoming NFTs and their availability on the market, Chastain was able to pre-purchase the forthcoming NFTs and secure profits, sometimes up to a fivefold value from their initial price. In order to conceal his identity in making the purchases, he used anonymous OpenSea accounts and transferred funds through various anonymous digital currency accounts.

Chastain, like Trovias' insider tipping scheme on the dark web, attempted to use advanced technology to conceal his identity for purposes of self-enrichment at the expense of others who lacked access to the non-public information about the future availability of the NFTs. This case is significant because it reflects how an individual can be subjected to legal liability under mail and wire fraud statutes for the execution of insider trading. In addition, the case confirms that regulatory agencies like the SEC are increasing their scrutiny of online platforms and the use of digital technologies and assets to engage in insider trading and whether cryptocurrencies and NFTs are investment contracts that should be considered securities. After charges were brought against Chastain, OpenSea implemented an employee insider trading policy regarding NFTs. The policy prohibits employees from buying and selling from collections or creators while they are featured on the site's homepage and prohibits employees from using confidential information to purchase or sell NFTs, regardless of whether they are available on OpenSea's platform. (Finzer, 2021). It is likely that such self-regulating compliance policies will soon become the norm in the industry.

Inside Information in the "Gig Economy"

The 21st century has witnessed the emergence of a contingent workforce sector of self-employed independent contractors and temporary, freelance jobs known as the "gig economy." These contingent workers serve as business consultants but also in such jobs as drivers for Uber and Lyft, and delivery persons for DoorDash, GrubHub, and Amazon. (Timko, 2019) The recent pandemic significantly expanded the demand for these services and the popularity of remote and contract work. In light of this, suppose a consultant temporarily hired by an issuer of securities encounters inside information, or an Uber driver overhears a conversation between two corporate insider passengers who reveal material, non-public information about the corporation. Can the consultant or driver trade on the basis of these revelations?

An outsider with no relationship to the issuer may also have a duty to disclose or refrain when he or she becomes aware of material non-public information through a relationship of trust or confidence. As the *O'Hagan* case revealed, an attorney employed by a firm representing an issuer incurred a duty of confidentiality as to any insider information he or she learns while working for the issuer. Such individuals are considered to be "temporary insiders" who have "entered into a special confidential relationship in the conduct of the business of the enterprise and are given access to information solely for corporate purposes." (*Dirks v. SEC,* 1983). Temporary insiders may include lawyers, accountants, underwriters, and consultants, and they, like corporate managers and employees, are also prohibited from trading on inside information as reinforced by Rule 10b5-2.

The case of *Kosinski v. United States* (2021) reinforces the continuing application of this rule. Kosinski was retained by Regado, a pharmaceutical company, as the principal investigator for a clinical trial of a drug designed to prevent blood clots in heart patients. Kosinski later began acquiring Regado stock. When subjects in the study began suffering severe allergic reactions to the drug, Kosinski sold all of his Regado stock just before this information was made public. In response to his indictment for insider trading, Kosinski argued that he had no fiduciary relationship with Regado that imposed a duty of confidentiality. However, the court disagreed, finding that Kosinski qualified as a temporary insider because he had been entrusted with Regado's information because of his duty to ensure the integrity and accuracy of the clinical trial.

As a result, an independent contractor like the business consultant who is retained by the issuer has such a duty when he or she becomes aware of inside information obtained during the relationship. What about the Uber driver who overhears what might be considered a tip? A stranger who overhears inside information but has no relationship to the source of the inside information, has no duty to disclose or abstain from trading (Palmiter, 2011). For instance, in *SEC v. Switzer* (1984), Switzer, a university football coach, overheard a conversation in public at a track meet in which Platt, the chief executive officer of a corporation, stated that several companies had made bids to acquire the corporation. He was charged with insider trading as a tippee after he used the information, he overheard to purchase shares in the corporation. However, the court held that Switzer had acquired no fiduciary duty to the shareholders and therefore was not liable for insider trading. Further, there was no proof that Platt had intentionally or recklessly tipped Switzer. This conclusion is further supported when a stranger is not aware that the information overheard is confidential (Loss, 1988).

CONCLUSION

As this chapter has revealed, the act of insider trading, a once-ignored practice, is now a central focus of enforcement actions by securities regulators. Lack of awareness is not a defense for avoiding liability for insider trading, even when a person cannot be labeled an insider as the misappropriation theory supports. Because of these possibilities in a hyper-connected world, business practitioners and academicians should strive to secure a thorough understanding of the legal liabilities, proper disclosure requirements, and the repercussions of insider trading. Finally, the emerging issues and current trends discussed above, when considered alongside the historical development of securities regulation, underscore the evolving reach of insider trading liability in response to changing economic and technological realities.

DECLARATION

The authors declare that the manuscript follows ethical standards and there are no potential conflicts of interest with respect to the research, authorship and/or publication of this chapter.

DISCLAIMER

The contents and views of this chapter are expressed by the authors in their personal capacities. It is not necessary for the Editor and the Publisher to agree with these viewpoints, and they are not responsible for any duty of care in this regard.

ACKNOWLEDGMENT

The authors extend sincere gratitude to

- The Editor and the International Editorial Advisory Board (IEAB) of this book who initially desk reviewed, arranged a rigorous double/triple blind review process, and conducted a thorough, minute, and critical final review before accepting the chapter for publication.
- All anonymous reviewers who provided very constructive feedbacks for thorough revision, improvement, extension, and fine tuning of the chapter.
- All colleagues, assistants and well-wishers who assisted to complete this task.

REFERENCES

ABM. (1934). Corporations: Duty of director to stockholder on stock exchange sales. *Michigan Law Review*, *32*(5), 678–685. doi:10.2307/1280999

Boland, J. C. (1985). *Wall Street's Insiders: How You Can Profit with the Smart Money* (1st ed.). Morrow.

Conti, R., & Broverman, A. (2022, June 13). What is an NFT? Non-fungible tokens explained. *Forbes Advisor*. Retrieved from https://www.forbes.com/advisor/ca/investing/cryptocurrency/nft-non-fungible-token/

Cowen, D. J. (2000). The first bank of the United States and the securities market crash of 1792. *The Journal of Economic History*, *60*(4), 1041–1060. doi:10.1017/S002205070002636X

Dirks v. SEC, 463 US 646 (1983).

Finzer, D. (2021, September 15). Announcement: our commitment to the OpenSea community. *OpenSea Blog*. Retrieved from https://opensea.io/blog/announcements/employee-information-use-at-opensea/

Geisst, C. R. (2004). *Wall Street: a history: from its beginnings to the fall of Enron*. Oxford University Press.

Goodwin v. Agassiz 186 N.E. 659 (Mass. 1933).

Hansen, L. (2021). Regulatory Ambiguity: The Underbelly of Insider Trading. In A. Rafay (Ed.), *Handbook of Research on Theory and Practice of Financial Crimes* (pp. 132–148). IGI Global., doi:10.4018/978-1-7998-5567-5.ch008

Kens, P. (2009). The Crédit Mobilier Scandal and the Supreme Court: Corporate power, corporate person, and government control in the mid-nineteenth century. *Journal of Supreme Court History*, *34*(2), 170–182.

Kosinski v. United States, 976 F.3d 135 (2d Cir. 2021).

Laidlaw v. Organ, 15 US 178 (1817).

Litigation Releases. (2021, September 9). Retrieved from https://www.sec.gov/litigation/litreleases.htm

Loss, L. (1988). *Fundamentals of securities regulation* (2nd ed.). Aspen Publishers.

MacDonald, S. B. (2017). *Separating fools from their money: A history of American financial scandals*. Routledge.

Markham, J. W. (2002). *A Financial History of the United States: From Christopher Columbus to the Robber Barons (1492-1900)* (Vol. 1). ME Sharpe.

McGinley, I. (2022). 'US v. Trovias': Lessons from the first dark web insider trading case. *New York Law Journal*, *267*(48).

Mehta, M. N., Reeb, D. M., & Zhao, W. (2021). Shadow trading. *The Accounting Review*, *96*(4), 367–404. doi:10.2308/TAR-2017-0068

Michaels, D. (2021, December 14). SEC takes rare court loss in insider-trading case. *Wall Street Journal.* Retrieved from https://www.wsj.com/articles/sec-takes-rare-court-loss-in-insider-trading-case-11639515867

Olson, J. S., & Mendoza, A. O. (2015). *American Economic History: A dictionary and chronology.* ABC-CLIO.

Palmiter, A. (2011). *Securities regulation* (5th ed.). Wolters Kluwer.

Patel, V., & Putnins, T. J. How much insider trading happens in stock markets? (January 11, 2020). *American Finance Association (AFA) Annual Meeting.* Retrieved from http://dx.doi.org/10.2139srn.3764192

Perino, M. A. (2019). The lost history of insider trading. *University of Illinois Law Review, 2019*(3), 951–1004.

Regulation FD, 17 C.F.R. § 243.100.

Riggs, T. (Ed.), *Gale encyclopedia of US economic history* (2nd ed., Vol. 1, pp. 312–314). Gale Group.

Rule 10b5-2, 17 C.F.R. § 240.10b5-2.

Rule 10b-5, 17 C.F.R. § 240.10b5-1.

Salinger, L. M. (Ed.) (2005). Insider trading. In Encyclopedia of White-Collar and Corporate Crime (Vol. 2, pp. 428-432). SAGE.

Salman v. United States, 580 US _, 137 S. Ct. 420 (2016).

Saunders, K. M. (2001). *Practical internet law for business.* Artech House.

SEC v. Clark, 2021 WL 6932689 (E.D. Va. 2021).

SEC v. Panuwat, 2022 WL 633306 (N.D. Cal. 2022).

SEC v. Switzer, 590 F. Supp. 756 (W.D. Okla. 1984).

SEC v. Texas Gulf Sulphur Corp., (401 F.2d 833 (2d Cir. 1968).

SEC v. Trovias, Complaint, No. 1:21-cv-05925 (S.D.N.Y. Jul. 9, 2021), ECF No. Retrieved from https://www.sec.gov/litigation/complaints/2021/comp-pr2021-122.pdf

Spaic, A., Nolasco, C. A., Tsai, L. C. F., & Vaughn, M. S. (2019). Does insider trading pay? An analysis of trading and tipping activities in insider trading litigation. *Journal of Financial Crime, 26*(2), 647–664. doi:10.1108/JFC-07-2018-0068

Speed v. Transamerica Corp., 71 F. Supp. 457 (D. Del. 1947).

Strong v. Repide, 213 US 419 (1909).

Teweles, R. J., Bradley, E. S., Farwell, L. C., & Leffler, G. L. (1982). *The stock market* (4th ed.). Wiley.

Timko, M. (2019). The gig economy: An annotated bibliography. *Northern Illinois University Law Review, 39,* 361–378.

United States v. O'Hagan, 521 US 642 (1997).

Wartzman, R. (2002, July 3). A 1920s insider trade was ruled by court to be merely a perk. *Wall Street Journal*. Retrieved from https://www.wsj.com/articles/SB1025637858937126040

Wright, R. E. (2005). *The first Wall Street: Chestnut Street, Philadelphia, and the birth of American finance*. University of Chicago Press. doi:10.7208/chicago/9780226910291.001.0001

ADDITIONAL READING

Securities Act of 1933, 15 USC. § 77a *et seq.*

Securities and Exchange Act of 1934, 15 USC. §78a *et seq.*

ENDNOTES

1. *Insider Trading* is the purchase, sale, or holding of securities by employing material, non-public information.
2. *Insiders* are those in a corporation or affiliated with an issuer of securities who have knowledge of, or who have been entrusted with, material non-public information, including officers, directors, employees, attorneys, accountants, consultants, and underwriters, among others.
3. *Inside information* is confidential data, information, or knowledge that has not yet been made accessible to the general public. Inside information can be either material or immaterial for the purposes of insider trading. Also known as non-public or privileged information.
4. A *tipper* is an insider who provides inside information to the tippee, and who may be liable for insider trading if he or she receives a benefit in return.
5. A *tippee* is a recipient of material, non-public information from an insider/tipper who uses the information to purchase, sell, or hold securities.
6. *The Securities and Exchange Commission* (SEC) is an independent US federal government agency institutionalized in 1933 to regulate securities trading and issuances, with additional responsibility for the oversight of securities markets and agents operating within the securities industry.
7. Securities fraud is a misstatement or omission of a material fact made with a scienter, which is relied upon by others in connection with the purchase or sale of securities, and which causes the purchasers or sellers to suffer economic loss as a result.
8. Security is an instrument commonly traded in speculation markets and recognized as a medium of investment and evidence of an obligation of the issuer, or as a share, participation, or other interest in an enterprise. Examples include stocks, bonds, debentures, and options.
9. Misappropriation theory is a theory of liability applied to find that a person violates Rule 10b-5 when he or she uses confidential information in breach of a duty of loyalty and confidentiality owed to the source of the information in order to trade in securities of another corporation.

Chapter 2
AML/CFT Regulations and Informal Remittance Services:
The Case of Hawala

S. G. Sisira Dharmasri Jayasekara
https://orcid.org/0000-0001-8006-3252
Central Bank of Sri Lanka, Sri Lanka

Abdul Rafay
https://orcid.org/0000-0002-0285-5980
University of Management and Technology, Pakistan

ABSTRACT

Informal remittance channels operate in various jurisdictions to promote illegal activities which are detrimental to the global efforts of combating money laundering. Here, in this chapter, Hawala is considered the main informal remittance channel. The economic and social implications of Hawala are very significant when it comes to a weak regime of AML/CFT. Therefore, the focus of this chapter is on weak AML/CFT regimes even though the discussed practices take place across the globe. A global initiative to limit or control informal remittance channels may support the global initiatives of anti-money laundering. However, it has also to bear in mind that informal remittance services are used globally as a very efficient and low-cost remittance channel despite the allegations of using them by criminals. Therefore, it is very important to implement proper systems and controls to regulate informal remittance channels while making them available for all segments of society.

INTRODUCTION

Often crimes are driven by the motive of money where the criminals perceive that money can buy anything to satisfy them. This desire force criminals to earn more money to earn further in the laundering process. The process of money laundering functions as a vehicle for criminals to achieve their malicious objectives. Money laundering is a threat to countries in which the main objective is the well-being of

DOI: 10.4018/978-1-6684-8587-3.ch002

the citizens. The global initiatives to prevent money laundering and terrorist financing (ML/TF) evolved with the establishment of the Financial Action Task Force (FATF) in 1989. Since then, the FATF has engaged in activities that are aimed at the efforts of countries to strengthen the framework of anti-money laundering and combating the financing of terrorism (AML/CFT). In that context, it sets international standards that aim to prevent illegal activities and the harm they cause to society. On the other hand, the FATF works closely with the countries to generate the necessary political will to bring about national legislative and regulatory reforms in these areas. However, the effectiveness of global initiatives in combating ML is questionable since it has failed to reduce global financial crimes over the period. For example, UNCTAD (2020) reports that capital flight, which captures trade mis-invoicing and other balance-of-payment transactions, was estimated at $88.6 billion, on average, during 2013–2015 or around 3.7 percent of African GDP. The capital flight between 2000–2015 was $836 billion or 2.6 percent of GDP. UNODC (2020) reports that the estimated amount of money laundered globally in one year is about 2% to 5% of global GDP or $800bn–$2tn in current US dollars. These estimates may include formal as well as informal channels. However, when it comes to informal channels these figures may even bigger. In an Indian case, an alleged hawala dealer and his accomplices have "generated" black money worth ₹ 565 crores from their global networks and it is also reported that he has facilitated parking of funds abroad by Indian nationals through his international hawala transaction structure created in India and various other jurisdictions (India News, 2020). Ouédraogo (2017) finds that the quality of governance, the quality of institutional settings, and the unemployment rates are major determinants of the size of the informal economy and a high level of corruption and poor institutional settings favour an increase of the informal economy. Weak AML/CFT regimes also characterise these fundamental issues and hence informal economy plays a vital role in economic activities. The weak regimes are often subject to the close monitoring of FATF. However, these countries fall into deficient regimes once they were evaluated again for compliance as well as the effectiveness of the AML/CFT regime.

Therefore, it is questionable whether the FATF is on the correct track to achieving its objectives.

The FATF works to prevent related threats to the integrity of the international financial system which come from criminals. The criminals can use formal as well as informal channels to move criminal proceeds from one place to another sometimes it may be from one country to another. Formal channels are operated through financial institutions (FIs) where FIs are subjected to the regulatory framework of the country in terms of the AML/CFT regime. The FIs develop proper AML/CFT programs within the institutions in order to comply with AML/CFT regime. The non-compliance with the regulatory requirements will be dealt with following proportionate and dissuasive sanctions. Therefore, criminals are a little bit reluctant or think twice before using formal channels to remit criminal proceeds through the formal financial system.

Financial institutions are subject to stringent regulations in most jurisdictions. This mechanism becomes stronger when they operate across countries. and the strong and effective implementation of sound AML/CFT systems and controls in the FIs is a barrier to criminals accessing the formal system. This forces criminals to use informal remittance services to move criminal proceeds for the intended purposes across borders as well as within a country. The regulatory mechanism of the informal sector is not strong as the formal sector. The informal sector is not subject to professional management and strict AML/CFT regulations which limits the quality of conducting customer due diligence, and limited monitoring of informal service providers and agents which forces them to gather minimum sender/receiver information or no information. The informal remittance services include Hawala, Uncial, and any other forms of unlicensed money transfer services. This chapter uses the term Hawala to represent all these unlicensed money value transfer services despite the slight differences among them for the chapter. Hawala operates in an informal environment often without regulations. Having quoted an indictment, DOJ (2018) defines hawala as an alternative form of money remittance which operates outside of traditional banking or financial systems. Hawala transactions occur through brokers who are typically located in different locations which may be different countries or different cities. These transactions are performed solely on the trust that exists between the brokers. Hawala transactions are not backed by any financial instruments but rely on trust. Therefore, DOJ (2018) states that the hawala system, which originated on the Indian subcontinent, does not rely on promissory instruments; rather, it relies on trust and long-established connections between brokers that are typically based on familial, ethnic, religious, and regional and/or cultural grounds. Hence, it is observable that the Hawala transactions transfer only the value of the money, but it does not involve transferring the money itself which makes regulation of Hawala business difficult because Hawala transactions restrict the movement of foreign currencies across borders. Kelejian & Mukerji (2022) state that Hawala is a vast informal funds transfer system providing speedy, untraceable funding and money laundering for global terrorism.

This background analysis shows that there is an opportunity for criminals to use formal as well as informal systems to launder money. However, this chapter will focus on informal remittance services. Accordingly, this chapter will discuss the evolution of the Hawala system, requirements for regulation of informal remittance services, the impact of informal remittance services on weak economies, and finally concludes with a discussion.

EVOLUTION OF THE HAWALA SYSTEM

Hawala is a well-evolved informal remittance channel through a specific segment of the community which is characterized by common features like religion and community. This has basically emerged and developed in the Asian context. The meaning of the term Hawala can take different views, but it performs the same function. For example, Schramm & Taube (2003) state that. the Arabic term hawala can be translated as payment or debt transfer whereas in Hindi, it can also mean trust or to be precise some valuable artefact that is passed on to a trusted third party for delivery. The Hawala system emerged as a trustable remittance service for traders when a formal system was not available. Schramm & Taube (2003) show that the roots of the hawala financial system can be found in the very early medieval commerce in premodern societies of the Near and Middle East, which contained a multitude of institutional incalculability. They further state that a formal legal system and regulatory framework were not available at that time to support the requirements of merchants who were engaged in informal remittance services.

Therefore, the Hawala system was concentrated on geographically small areas where the area was controlled by tribal laws. Often, the ethnic groups practiced the Hawala system which was a restrictive practice to the growth of Hawala business outside the community. The transactions moved away from the community creating uncertainty over the trust of transactions. However, this problem has been addressed by the common recognition of the values of the Koran and sharia at least from a moral perspective legally binding (Gärber, 1992). The evolution of an institutional solution to the problem of coordinating economic interaction was decisively influenced and strongly guided by the Koran's moral directives as to how business was to be conducted (Amereller, 1995). During this course of time, an extensive group of institutions came into existence, which is collectively referred to today as Islamic banking and eventually, the hawala system established itself as an efficient institutional arrangement (Schramm & Taube, 2003).

REGULATIONS OF INFORMAL REMITTANCE SERVICES

The objectives of the Financial Action Task Force (FATF) are to set standards and promote effective implementation of legal, regulatory, and operational measures for combating money laundering, terrorist financing and other related threats to the integrity of the international financial system. The hawala system is recognized as an informal financial system that may affect the formal financial system as well as the strength of an AML/CFT regime of a country. Therefore, Recommendation 14 requires countries to take measures to ensure that natural or legal persons that provide money or value transfer services (MVTS) are licensed or registered, and subject to effective systems for monitoring and ensuring compliance with the relevant measures. This category included formal as well as informal remittance service providers such as Hawala[1]. However, this area has not been addressed by many countries in order to achieve the common goal of preventing criminals from using formal as well as informal channels for laundering criminal proceeds. The following tables show the compliance level of Recommendation 14, Money or value transfer services, by the strategically deficient AML/CFT regimes which are under the scrutiny of FATF.

Table 1. Compliance level of Recommendation 14 by deficient AML/CFT regimes[2] -June 2022

No.	Country	Compliance Level	Factor(s) underlying the rating as reported in mutual evaluation report
01	Albania	Compliant	• No significant issues
02	Barbados	Largely Compliant	• Needs to make necessary amendments to the law and MVTS should be licensed or registered
03	Burkina Faso	Partially Compliant	• Absence of dissuasive sanctions for unauthorized or unregistered MVTS. • There is no requirement for the agents of MVTS providers to be licensed or registered. • MVTS providers are not required to include agents in the AML/CFT programs or monitor them for compliance.
04	Cambodia	Largely Compliant	• The penalty is not proportionate and dissuasive for illegal MVTS providers. • MVTS providers are not required to include agents in the AML/CFT programs or monitor them for compliance.
05	Cayman Islands	Largely Compliant	• MVTS providers are not required to include agents in the AML/CFT programs or monitor them for compliance. • MVTS monitoring does not fully extend to the requirements of the terrorism law.
06	Gibraltar	Largely Compliant	• There is no explicit requirement for MVTS to include agents in their AML/CFT programs or monitor them.
07	Haiti	Partially Compliant	• The definition of MVTS is limited and not in keeping with the FATF Standards. • No measure(s) for ensuring that MVTS that use agents include them in their AML/CFT programs and monitor their activities.
08	Jamaica	Largely Compliant	• Legislation does not provide remit or powers to sanction unlicensed MVTS. • No active identification of unregistered MVTS providers
09	Jordan	Largely Compliant	• There is no legal provision to supervise postal services for their compliance with the AML/CFT requirements
10	Mali	Partially Compliant	• Absence of dissuasive sanctions against unlicensed or unregistered MVTS providers. • There is no requirement to for agents of MVTS providers to be licensed or registered with any competent authority.
11	Morocco	Largely Compliant	• There is no requirement for MVTS providers to maintain a list of their agents. • Absence of a requirement for the MVTS providers to include agents in AML/CFT programs.
12	Myanmar	Non- Compliant	• There is no mechanism to identify unauthorized MVTS providers. • There is no information about scope and scale of hundi, so unable to determine whether proportionate and dissuasive sanctions have been applied. • There is no mandate for the regulator to undertake supervision of MVTS.
12	Nicaragua	Partially Compliant	• There is no mechanism to identify unauthorized MVTS providers. • There is no power for the regulator to carry out supervision and to issue respective sanctions for non-compliance. • There is no training and monitoring mechanism for agents of MVTSs providers.

Continued on following page

Table 1. Continued

No.	Country	Compliance Level	Factor(s) underlying the rating as reported in mutual evaluation report
13	Pakistan	Partially Compliant	• There is no proportionate and dissuasive sanctioning regime for illegal MVTS providers. • There is no mechanism to be licensed and registered for Pakistan Post and payment booths. • Lack of requirement to monitor agents for compliance with AML / CFT programs. • Pakistan Post is not subjected to AML/CFT supervision
14	Panama	Partially Compliant	• MVTS providers are not required to include agents in the AML/CFT programs or monitor them for compliance. • Remittance and Currency Exchange houses are not subject to the licensing regime.
15	Philippines	Largely Compliant	• There are limitations to the identification and sanctioning process for unregistered MVTS providers.
16	Senegal	Largely Compliant	• There is no legislation regulating MVTS providers using agents
17	Türkiye	Largely Compliant	• There are limitations to identifying unregistered MVTS providers
18	Uganda	Partially Compliant	• Inadequate monitoring of Mobile Money Service Providers. • Limitations of monitoring agents of MVTS providers.
19	United Arab Emirates	Largely Compliant	• There is no evidence as to how to identify the natural or legal persons that carry out MVTS without a license.

Source: FATF (2022)

Most of the deficient jurisdictions had placed satisfactory compliance regimes for formal money value transfer service providers. However, the problem was with the regulation of informal MVTS providers such as *Undial* and *Hawala.* Often, these informal service providers operate in an informal economy where the jurisdictions do not have a clear understanding of the size of the informal economy and its functions. For example, Lara-Rodríguez (2021) finds evidence of a rule of informality in the province of Choco, where armed illegal groups settle down underground states toward illegal economic activities, and where centralized and decentralized state organizations get rid of their responsibilities. Therefore, the availability of information is limited and hence it is very difficult to estimate the volume of Hawala transactions. Scholars often assume that actual figures are much higher than official reports, and in light of the informality of the hawala system and the unreliability of official figures, it is fair to assume the real level of remittance receipts is indeed higher (Hoye, 2022). The availability of limited information is a barrier to coming up with a sound mechanism to mitigate exposed ML/TF risk from informal sectors. This position becomes worse regarding emerging economies and deficient AML/CFT regimes. For example, having recognized the unreliability of data, Hoye (2022) estimates that Somalia had received US$ 2 billion as of 2020 and also states this amount may count to 24–45% of Somali GDP. Therefore, the impact of informal remittance channels is significant in deficient regimes over strong regimes.

IMPACT OF INFORMAL REMITTANCE SERVICES

The impact of informal remittance services on emerging countries is very significant from many perspectives over developed countries. Kelejian & Mukerji (2022) state that Hawala, a vast informal funds transfer system providing speedy, untraceable funding and money laundering for global terrorism where the issue is quite relevant given the rise of terrorist organizations such as the Islamic State, with vast and difficult to track cash earnings. Often, these terrorist organisations emerge in weak AML/CFT regimes. Literature provides that Hawala thrives in countries with under-developed financial markets (Looney, 2003; Kelejian & Mukerji, 2022). Often, developed countries can retain their powerful currencies within the country since Hawala moves only the value of transactions across borders. Informal money remittance services affect the position of the balance of payments as well as the net foreign reserves of weak economies (Jayasekara, 2022). However, it is required to bear in mind that the position of foreign reserve position is determined by various factors. The informal remittance services will also be an influential factor depending on the size of the market. On the other hand, the international trade position of a country is determined by the competitive advantage of the country over its competitors. The trade competitiveness of a country will be determined by various factors and the trade competitiveness will determine the position of international trade as well as the balance of payment of a country. The main motive of this chapter is to discuss the implications of informal remittance services on weak economies. Hence, this chapter will not discuss the issues related to the competitiveness of international trade which will impact the position of balance of payment and depletion of foreign reserves of a country.

Criminals always target readily available options to create opportunities to move money for the intended purposes. The easy access to informal channels paves the way for the criminals who are waiting to grab every possible chance to generate more money from criminal activities. For example, in the Sri Lankan context, the investigators reveal that an individual has obtained money from an associate of the drug dealer who resides abroad, and that money has been sent using the Hawala system to him, from a foreign country (Daily News, 2022). The use of Hawala for drug trafficking is a proposition that drug trafficking seems to be extensively used in the informal economy. The attractiveness of informal channels is also enhanced by the strength of the regime of anti-money laundering and countering the financing of terrorism (AML/CFT) of a country. The strong regimes discourage criminals from using the formal financial system hence they tend to use informal channels. On the other hand, cash-intensive businesses such as vehicle dealers, textile businesses, pawning centers, Gem and Jewelry dealers, and real estate dealers among others are usually engaged in the Hawala business which is a convenient and effective channel for criminals to launder money which is generated from criminal activities. For example, a vehicle dealer who operates an informal remittance service can bank proceeds that are derived from drug trafficking or money of drug traffickers to appear them derived from his business. He will justify these deposits to the financial institutions as the proceeds of selling vehicles. And such businesses can use part of illegal proceeds to meet the expenditure of the business reducing the amount of banking. For example, a textile business can use criminal proceeds to expand the textile business using criminal proceeds This background analysis shows that there is an opportunity for criminals to use informal channels extensively for money laundering.

Nature of Hawala System

A sizable informal economy is a common feature of most weak economies. For example, World Bank (2020) reveals that around 70 percent of the workforce of Sri Lanka is informally employed and there are generally three reasons to be concerned about high informality namely poverty, productivity, and public finance. ILO (2022) also states that almost two-thirds of total employment in Sri Lanka is in the informal sector. Department of Census and Statistics (2020) also reveals that the total employment contribution to the informal sector in Sri Lanka in 2020 is 58.1%. Some examples of the weak and strong AML/CFT regimes and the respective significance of the informal economy are shown below.

Table 2. Size of informal economy of weak and strong AML/CFT regimes

No.	Weak Country	Informal Economy (%)	No.	Strong Country	Informal Economy (%)
01	Albania	30.4	01	Austria	9.2
02	Barbados	23.7	02	China	8.6
03	Burkina Faso	31.2	03	Germany	15.0
04	Cambodia	36.6	04	Ireland	13.8
05	Jamaica	31.7	05	Japan	10.2
06	Mali	33.8	06	New Zealand	11.3
07	Morocco	29.6	07	Singapore	11.3
08	Myanmar	24.7	08	Switzerland	8.0
09	Pakistan	32.4	09	UK	11.6
10	Philippines	34.2	10	US	8.1

Source: World Bank (2021)

The above information shows that the size of the informal economy in AML/CFT weak regimes is substantial over the AML/CFT strong regimes. This composition and macroeconomic implications due to Covid 19 pandemic have provided opportunities to criminals to exploit the opportunities from the informal economy. Some of the common instances of using Hawala and the structures of such transactions or mechanisms are discussed below.

Investments in virtual assets using Hawala

Investment in virtual assets is an emerging trend that uses Hawala in many countries where the stance of the government on virtual assets is not clear. Such neutral countries neither regulate nor monitor the transactions related to virtual assets. For example, Sri Lanka has recognized the growing interest in virtual currencies both domestically and internationally and announced to the public that the Central Bank of Sri Lanka has not given a license or authorization to any entity or company to operate schemes involving virtual currencies, including cryptocurrencies, and has not authorized any Initial Coin Offerings (CBSL,2018). This neutral stance affects not only the interest of the public but also could amount to breaches of AML/CFT laws. Tsang (2019) reveals that most African countries stay crypto neutral where the governments tend to warn their citizens about the risks of trading crypto and possible financial losses and urge them to be particularly cautious when dealing with virtual currencies.

The limitation of foreign currencies for investments in virtual assets and other restrictions of the countries has forced the interested parties to use Hawala for investments. The increased awareness of the formal sector on risk exposure is a barrier to potential investors and hence they try to use the available other alternatives. Hawaladars coordinate local investors and abroad migrant communities on the other end to structure the transactions of virtual assets. An investment agent in the local context collects funds from the interested parties. This may happen through his bank account. The other agent in the international context collects worker remittances from the migrant workers which have to be remitted to the family members of the migrant workers. The collected foreign remittance proceeds are invested in virtual assets and the relevant amount of worker remittances are credited to the accounts of beneficiaries using the locally collected investment proceeds. Ultimately, without having movement of foreign currencies across borders local people can invest in global cryptocurrencies. This process is shown below.

Figure 1. Use of the banking system and hawala to invest in Cryptocurrencies
Source: Jayasekara (2022)

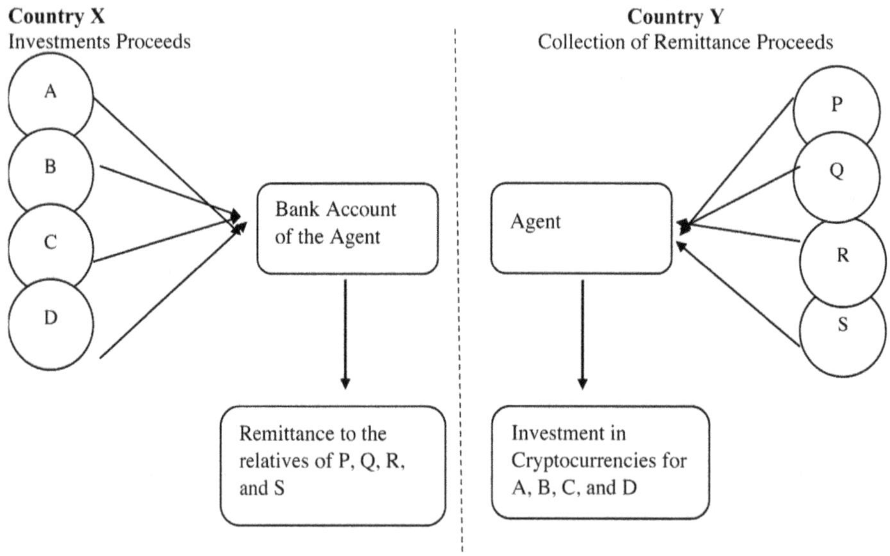

Financing foreign educational expenses

The second type of Hawala transaction is related to remitting foreign educational expenses. A lesser number of students get the opportunity of higher university education in most emerging countries forcing a sizable number of students to go abroad for higher studies. When a country is in the default category in terms of the sovereign rating, it is very difficult to remit educational expenses through a formal financial system. Hence, parents often rely on informal channels.

Table 3. Outflow of tertiary-level students from financially stressed countries

No.	Country	Sovereign Rating			Total number of students abroad
		Moody[3]	S&P[4]	Fitch[5]	
01	Venezuela	C	B-	-	31,707
02	Zambia	-	SD	RD	4,900
03	Sri Lanka	Ca	SD	RD	29,002
04	Lebanon	C	SD	RD	20,264
05	Belarus	Ca	SD	RD	24,545

Source: UNESCO (2022); Countryeconomy.com (2022)

For example, the number seems to be very significant given the current unfavorable position of balance of payments in these countries which has arisen as pressure from the external sector. The limited opportunities within the countries for higher education and the interest of parents in foreign education as a result of limited trust and confidence in the local policies have forced the students to overseas education. However, the prevailing economic crises have forced parents to remit educational expenses through informal channels due to the shortage of foreign currencies in the banking system. The hawala system is used in this context as a convenient tool. Hawaladars collect the amounts to be remitted from the parents or guardians and make the collected funds available to the students in order to bear the relevant expenses. In addition to the trust, quality of service and timeliness, Hawaladars provide the best exchange rate over formal financial institutions. The Hawaladars also used the mechanism which was elaborated in figure 1 to process the transactions. Therefore, the deficient countries need to reassess their policy stance considering the growing number of cryptocurrency transactions and the shift of Hawaladars to crypto-related transactions. This shift may become a huge challenge in combating financial crimes and money laundering. On the other hand, these transactions are not recorded in national accounts since they happen in the informal economy and hence, the national accounts will not provide accurate information for policymaking. The growth of an informal economy is also an impediment to the national combating ability of money laundering.

Remitting the disposal proceeds of assets of migrants

The movement of people across countries has become a trend in the current global labour market which included migration as well as other forms of movement for foreign employment. When people migrate from one country to another, they have to transfer the accumulated wealth to the new place of residence. This process is easy and convenient if the home country does not have controls or limitations of foreign reserves to process the transactions. On the other hand, weak regimes of taxation also force migrants to use informal channels to transfer their asses. The restrictions and weak tax regimes force migrants to use hawala to transfer money to the countries where they are going to reside. The migrants use the formal banking system as well as informal channels to transfer funds through the Hawala system.

Figure 2. Use of Hawala to remit funds of migrants
Source: Jayasekara (2022)

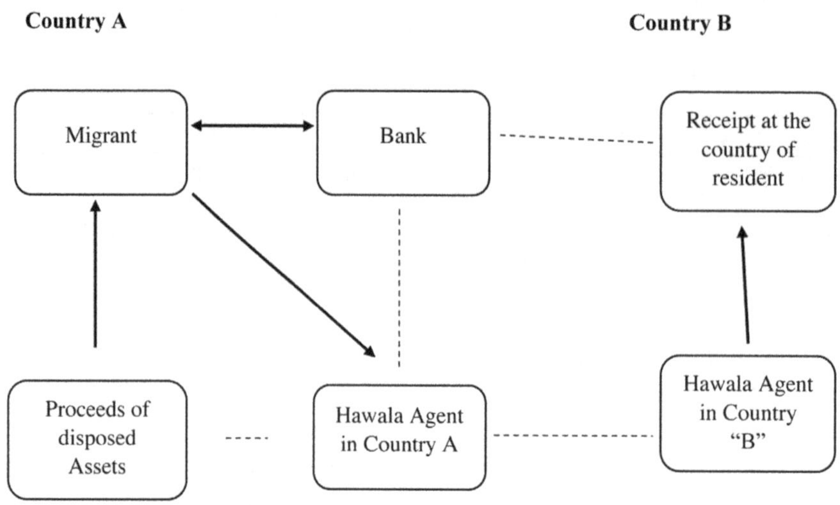

The growth of Hawala business is a challenge for AML/CFT weak regimes because it further expands the contribution of the informal economy of the country. On the other hand, the increased trust and confidence in the Hawala system will reduce the trust in the formal financial system. This position will further deteriorate when the transaction costs of the formal system are high over the informal system. The outcome of this puzzle affects the effectiveness of the AML/CFT regime of the country because crimes grow in informal sectors. Drug trafficking grows in informal segments because drug traffickers prefer to use physical cash and use cash-intensive businesses to cover illegal activities. Having conducted field interviews UNODC (2018) reports that three main methods are used in Afghanistan to move funds in the context of opiate trafficking. The first involves traditional bank or money exchange transfers, the second is based on the basic barter of opiates for goods (mainly cars) and the third involves informal money transfer systems such as hawala. UNODC (2018) further states that within Afghanistan, the use of hawala as a means of payment for drug shipments is common, partly because of the limited use of the formal banking system for all financial transactions. The use of Hawala for drug trafficking is not only related to weak AML/CFT regimes but there is evidence of using Hawala in strong AML/CFT regimes. For example, DOJ (2018) shows that the convicted person has participated in a Hawala conspiracy that was moving money generated from drug sales in Canada to the United States to pay for multi-kilogram drug shipments that were purchased in Los Angeles and then routed back to Canada for distribution. These examples provide evidence that drug traffickers use Hawala to move criminal proceeds across the countries despite the strength of the AML/CFT regime. Therefore, policymakers should assess the real requirement of having an informal remittance service in a country in view of strengthening the AML/CFT regime. The following figure shows the process of using Hawala for drug trafficking.

Figure 3. Use of informal remittance services for drug trafficking
Source: Jayasekara (2022)

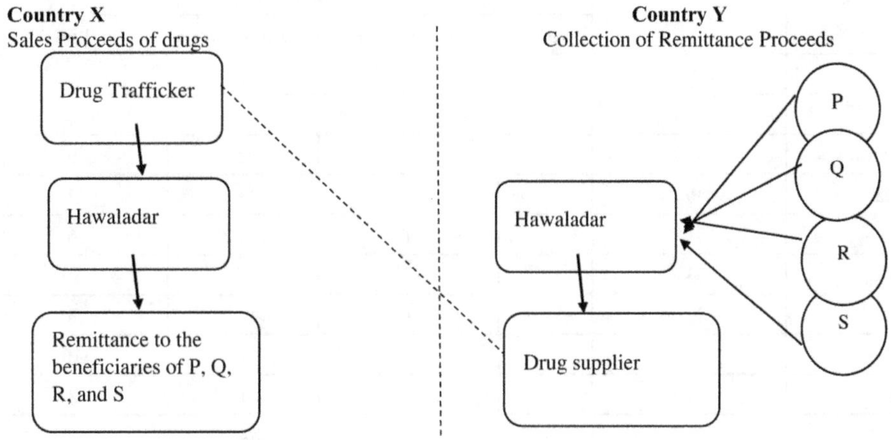

DISCUSSION AND CONCLUSION

The strength of an AML/CFT regime is a very important factor in controlling financial crimes. However, it can be observed that the existence of a mere strong AML/CFT regime does not prevent all financial crimes. Often, larger crimes happen in stronger AML/CFT regimes. The composition of the informal economy and its growth is a significant deterrent factor in combating many crimes. Therefore, the growth of the Hawala system in a weak AML/CFT regime limits the effectiveness of the implementation of a sound AML/CFT regime. It is a common observation that most of the deficient AML/CFT regimes are ineffective or effective in a few areas in terms of the mutual evaluations conducted using the FATF methodology. On the other hand, the size of the informal economy of these countries in terms of gross domestic product is significant. The dominance of the informal economy is a hindrance to strengthening the AML/CFT regime where most of the criminal activities take place in the informal sector. Therefore, policy measures are required to reduce the size of the informal economy where the formalization process will introduce proper systems and controls by which the use of formal systems for criminal activities will be reduced. This process will improve the quality of the AML/CFT regime and will reflect in future mutual evaluation reports.

Table 4. Level of the effectiveness of weak AML/CFT regimes

No.	Weak Country	Informal economy %	Level of effectiveness in terms of immediate outcomes of FATF methodology				Total
			High	Substantial	Moderate	Low	
1	Albania	30.4	-	2	7	2	11
2	Barbados	23.7	-	-	4	7	11
3	Burkina Faso	31.2	-	-	2	9	11
4	Cambodia	36.6	-	1	3	7	11
5	Jamaica	31.7	-	1	4	6	11
6	Mali	33.8	-	-	1	10	11
7	Morocco	29.6	-	1	7	3	11
8	Myanmar	24.7	-	-	1	10	11
9	Pakistan	32.4	-	-	1	10	11
10	Philippines	34.2	-	1	4	6	11

Source: World Bank (2021); FATF (2022)

The limitations of strategic policies in weak AML/CFT regimes are a common problem and hence such countries have failed in all aspects. The temporary measures which are focused on solving evolving phenomena may result in further weakening of the AML/CFT regime of a country. Having studied weak AML/CFT regimes, Jayasekara (2022) states that mere reactive regulations will not help to solve the long prevailed structural problems of an economy and suggests an entrepreneurial regulatory framework to solve the structural issues. On the other hand, the shift to a regime of entrepreneurial regulation from a traditional postmortem type of regulatory regime is challenging because the policymakers are reluctant to move for the change since they were developed in the traditional regime.

DECLARATION

The authors declare that the manuscript follows ethical standards and there are no potential conflicts of interest with respect to the research, authorship and/or publication of this chapter.

DISCLAIMER

The contents and views of this chapter are expressed by the authors in their personal capacities. It is not necessary for the Editor and the Publisher to agree with these viewpoints, and they are not responsible for any duty of care in this regard.

ACKNOWLEDGMENT

The authors extend sincere gratitude to

• The Editor and the International Editorial Advisory Board (IEAB) of this book who initially desk reviewed, arranged a rigorous double/triple blind review process, and conducted a thorough, minute, and critical final review before accepting the chapter for publication.

• All anonymous reviewers who provided very constructive feedbacks for thorough revision, improvement, extension, and fine tuning of the chapter.

• All colleagues, assistants and well-wishers who assisted to complete this task.

REFERENCES

Amereller, F. (1995). Hintergru¨nde des ‘‘Islamic banking. *Schriften zum Internationalen Recht, 71.*

CBSL. (2018). *Public awareness on virtual currencies in Sri Lanka.* Colombo: Central Bank of Sri Lanka. Retrieved from doi:https://www.cbsl.gov.lk/en/news/public-awareness-on-virtual-currencies-in-sri-lanka

Countryeconomy.com. (2022). *Sovereigns ratings list.* Retrieved from https://countryeconomy.com/ratings

Daily News. (2022). *Illegal assets investigation division nabs suspect linked to drug dealer.* The Associated Newspapers of Ceylon Ltd.

Department of Census and Statistics. (2020). *Sri Lanka labour force survey.* Department of Census and Statistics.

DOJ. (2018). *Monrovia man found guilty in 'Hawala' scheme to move money for international drug trafficking organizations, included drug cartels.* California: US Department of Justice. Retrieved from https://www.justice.gov/usao-cdca/pr/monrovia-man-found-guilty-hawala-scheme-move-money-international-drug-trafficking

FATF. (2022). *Mutual Evaluations.* Financial Action Task Force. Retrieved from https://www.fatf-gafi.org/publications/mutualevaluations/?hf=10&b=0&s=desc(fatf_releasedate)

Gärber, A. (1992). *slam, finanzielle Infrastruktur und wirtschaftliche Entwicklung.* Frankfurt: Peter lANG.

Hoye, J. M. (2022). Famine, remittances, and global justice. *World Development Perspectives, 27*, 100446. doi:10.1016/j.wdp.2022.100446

ILO. (2022). *Informal economy in Sri Lanka and the Maldives.* Geneva: International Labour Organisation. Retrieved from https://www.ilo.org/colombo/areasofwork/informal-economy/lang--en/index.htm

India News. (2020). *Hawala dealer Naresh Jain generated black money worth ₹ 565 crore: Probe agency.* Press Trust Of India. Retrieved from https://www.ndtv.com/india-news/hawala-dealer-naresh-jain-generated-black-money-worth-rs-565-crore-enforcement-directorate-2320129

Jayasekara, S. D. (2022). Trade-based money laundering and informal remittance services: implications on the sustainability of the balance of payments of a small open economy. *Journal of Money Laundering Control, ahead-of-print.* doi:10.1108/JMLC-03-2022-0042

Kelejian, H. H., & Mukerji, P. (2022). Causal factors of terrorist attacks on countries, and corresponding spill-overs between them. *European Journal of Political Economy*, *72*, 102092. doi:10.1016/j.ejpoleco.2021.102092

Lara-Rodríguez, J. S. (2021). How institutions foster the informal side of the economy: Gold and platinum mining in Choco, Colombia. *Resources Policy*, *74*, 101582. doi:10.1016/j.resourpol.2020.101582

Looney, R. (2003). Hawala: The terrorist's informal financial mechanism. *Middle East Policy*, *10*(1), 164–167. doi:10.1111/1475-4967.00099

Ouédraogo, I. M. (2017). Governance, Corruption, and the Informal Economy. *Modern Economy*, *8*(2), 256–271. doi:10.4236/me.2017.82018

Schramm, M., & Taube, M. (2003). Evolution and institutional foundation of the hawala financial system. *International Review of Financial Analysis*, *12*(4), 405–420. doi:10.1016/S1057-5219(03)00032-2

Tsang, D. (2019). *Crypto-Friendly countries: Crypto regulation around the world.* Retrieved from https://blog.lumiwallet.com/crypto-regulation-around-the-world/

UNCTAD. (2020). Tackling illicit financial flows for sustainable development in Africa. Geneva: *United Nations Conference on Trade and Development.*

UNESCO. (2022). *Global flow of tertiary-level students.* Quebec: UNESCO Institute of Statistics. Retrieved from http://uis.unesco.org/en/uis-student-flow

UNODC. (2018). *Afghan opiate trafficking along the northern route.* Vienna: United Nations Office on Drugs and Crime. Retrieved from https://www.unodc.org/rpanc/en/Sub-programme-4/afghan-opiate-trafficking-along-the-northern-route.html

UNODC. (2020). *Money-Laundering and globalization.* Vienna: United Nations Office on Drugs and Crime. Retrieved from https://www.undp.org/unodc/in/money-laundering/globalization.html

World Bank. (2020). *Informality, job quality, and welfare in Sri Lanka.* Washington: The World Bank. Retrieved from https://documents.worldbank.org/en/publication/documents-reports/documentdetail/341681597688560604/informality-job-quality-and-welfare-in-sri-lanka

World Bank. (2021). *Informal economy database.* Washington: The World Bank. Retrieved from https://www.worldbank.org/en/research/brief/informal-economy-database

ADDITIONAL READING

APG. (2015). *Mutual Evaluation Report -Sri lanka.* Sydney: APG Secretariat.

CBSL. (2021). *New Order issued under Foreign Exchange Act to Preserve the Foreign Exchange Position of Sri Lanka.* Colombo: Central Bank of Sri Lanka. Retrieved from https://www.cbsl.gov.lk/sites/default/files/cbslweb_documents/press/pr/press_20210702_new_order_issued_under_foreign_exchange_act_e.pdf

CBSL. (1987-2020). *Annual Report.* Colombo: Central Bank of Sri Lanka. Retrieved from https://www.cbsl.gov.lk/sites/default/files/cbslweb_documents/publications/annual_report

DMT. (2022). *Total Vehicle Population.* Department of Motor Traffic. Colombo: Department of Motor Traffic. Retrieved from https://dmt.gov.lk/images/PDF/statistics/pop2015.pdf

FATF-Egmont Group. (2020). *Trade-Based Money Laundering: Trends and Developments.* Paris: Financial Action Task Force. Retrieved from www.fatf-gafi.org/publications/methodandtrends/documents/trade-based-money-laundering-trends-anddevelopments

Fernando, S. (2022). *Central Bank remittance incentive fails spectacularly.* The Morning - Sri Lanka New.

Gerboth, D. L. (1973). Research, intuition, and politics in accounting inquiry. *The Accounting Review, 48*(3), 475–482.

IMF. (2022). *IMF Executive Board Concludes 2021 Article IV Consultation with Sri Lanka.* Washington: International Monetary Fund. Retrieved from https://www.imf.org/en/News/Articles/2022/03/02/pr2254-sri-lanka-imf-executive-board-concludes-2021-article-iv-consultation-with-sri-lanka

Inalcik, H. (1969). Capital formation in the ottoman empire. *The Journal of Economic History, 29*(1), 97–140. doi:10.1017/S0022050700097849

Jayasekara, S. D. (2021). Deficient regimes of anti-money laundering and countering the financing of terrorism: Agenda of digital banking and financial inclusion. *Journal of Money Laundering Control, 24*(1), 150–162. doi:10.1108/JMLC-04-2020-0035

Labib, S. Y. (1969). Capitalism in Medieval Islam. *The Journal of Economic History, 29*(1), 79–96. doi:10.1017/S0022050700097837

Narcotic Bureau. (2019). *Sri Lanka Police.* Retrieved from https://www.police.lk: https://www.police.lk/images/narcotic_bureau/2019/march/3_significant_drugs_seized_in_sri_lanka_2018.pdf

SLBFE. (2020). *Outward Labour Migration in Sri Lanka.* Colombo: Sri Lanka Bureau of Foreign Employment. Retrieved from http://slbfe.lk/file.php?FID=588

UNODC. (2022). *Annual Drug Seizures.* United Nations Office on Drugs and Crime. Retrieved from https://dataunodc.un.org/data/drugs/Annual%20Drug%20Seizures

Worstall, T. (2022). *Op-Ed: How Sri Lanka became the island of a thousand errors.* Dhaka: Dhaka Tribune. Retrieved from https://www.dhakatribune.com/business/2022/01/22/op-ed-how-sri-lanka-became-the-island-of-a-thousand-errors

ENDNOTES

1 MVTS refers to financial services that involve the acceptance of cash, cheques, other monetary instruments or other stores of value and the payment of a corresponding sum in cash or other forms to a beneficiary by means of communication, message, transfer, or through a clearing network to which the MVTS provider belongs. Transactions performed by such services can involve one or

more intermediaries and final payments to a third party and may include any new payment methods. Sometimes these services have ties to particular geographic regions and are described using a variety of specific terms, including hawala, hundi, and fei-chen.

2 These countries are subject to increased monitoring of the FATF due to strategic deficiencies which were identified in respect of anti-money laundering, countering terrorist financing, and proliferation financing. This list is often externally referred to as the "grey list". The selected list comprises the countries which were identified as deficient countries as of 20.09.2022.

3 C, in default; Ca, extremely speculative

4 B-, Highly speculative; SD, In default with little prospect for recovery

5 RD, In default with little prospect for recovery

Chapter 3
How Harsh Should the Legislation Be to Prevent Financial Crimes?
Lessons After the Enron Scandal

Perihan Iren
Zayed University, UAE

Moo Sung Kim
Zayed University, UAE

ABSTRACT

The collapse of Enron and its auditor Arthur Andersen was one of the biggest events in US corporate history and it had long-lasting repercussions in the corporate world. Following the Enron – Arthur Andersen scandal, the US Congress passed the Sarbanes Oxley Act (SOX). The legislation was designed to strengthen existing securities regulations and enacted harsh penalties on lawbreakers. SOX was one of the first and heavy responses to corporate fraud. Since the passage of SOX, debates revolving around the costs and benefits of it have prevailed and several studies investigated its effectiveness to prevent future financial crimes. This study first reviews the chronology of the events leading to SOX, followed by a brief discussion of the rules and regulations established by SOX. The empirical evidence presented by previous studies on the effectiveness of legislation and the harsh penalty Enron's auditor had received are assessed and evaluated.

INTRODUCTION

Once a financial crime is discovered, it results in penalties for the culprits and their collaborators, as well as new rules, and legislation in order to prevent similar cases from happening in the future. Past corporate fraud events have severely hurt the public. At the very least, small investors lost their investments, tens of thousands of people became unemployed as the firms committing the crime started to

DOI: 10.4018/978-1-6684-8587-3.ch003

disappear slowly and the public lost its confidence in the corporate and accounting world. While only a few white-collared criminals made millions of dollars, the public at large suffered. Therefore, preventing future financial crimes is critical to protect investors and reinstate confidence in the system (Rafay, 2023). Also, the severity of the punishment of the culprits sets the tone for the ones who would contemplate committing similar crimes in the future.

The collapse of Enron and its auditor Arthur Andersen had long-lasting repercussions in the corporate world. Following the Enron – Arthur Andersen scandal, the US Congress passed the Sarbanes Oxley Act (SOX), which was one of the most notable responses to corporate fraud. When the SOX passed, many criticized it as an unnecessary interference of the government in the financial markets. Since the passage of SOX, several studies investigated its effectiveness of it to prevent future crimes. This chapter elaborates on the penalties and legislative response following the Enron - Arthur Andersen scandal.

The Enron-Arthur Andersen scandal had been the most important corporate and accounting fraud in history and it still hides lessons to draw for corporations, auditors, and regulators. The scandal and the legislative response to it (SOX) find themselves a place in textbooks so that younger generations who didn't witness the events are educated about the consequences of unethical practices through the Enron example. Even after twenty years, the effects of SOX appear to be an important topic to explore for researchers in a way that they continue publishing research papers revolving around the impact of SOX. Most recently, James and Lirey (2022) investigated the effect of SOX on firms' propensity to save; Kim and Luo (2022) examined if the level of customer concentration moderates the impact of SOX on firms' earning management; Hillier *et al.* (2022) studied the impact of SOX on executive risk-taking incentives; Shi *et al.* (2022) examined the effect of SOX on firms' earning management practices; Pozner *et al.* (2022) reviewed the change in the firms' response to earnings restatements; Gayle *et al.* (2022) investigated the effects of SOX on CEO compensation plans and incentives, just to cite a few of the most recent research papers. There is still a flux of ongoing research studying the effects of SOX. For example, Pincus (2020) replicates the highly cited work of Cohen *et al.* (2008) and calls for future research on the longer-term impact of the SOX. This chapter provides a review of empirical studies investigating the effectiveness of SOX and the penalty imposed on Arthur Andersen.

The collapse of Enron and its auditor Arthur Andersen was one of the biggest in US history. Enron's shareholders lost $74 billion when the company's share price quickly saw a downfall. Enron's 20,600 employees lost their jobs and pensions. Within the same year, telecommunications giant WorldCom had also committed fraud by concealing its falling profitability. The cases about Tyco and Adelphia followed the others. Immediately after these massive scandals, new rules and regulations were introduced in order to promote the accuracy of the financial reporting of public companies. In July 2002, Sarbanes Oxley Act (SOX) was passed by the US Congress. The new legislation was designed to strengthen existing securities regulations and enacted harsh penalties on lawbreakers. SOX was one of the first and heavy responses to corporate fraud. Since the passage of SOX, debates revolving around the costs and benefits of it have prevailed and several studies investigated the effectiveness of it to prevent future crimes. The corporate world has seen other frauds after Enron and some were quite massive, such as Lehman Brothers in 2008 and Madoff in 2008. Nonetheless, none of the frauds after were as impactful as Enron was. Although Enron is history now, its long-lasting impact on corporate policies and legislation is still relevant and is worth examining.

This chapter first reviews the chronology of the events leading to SOX, followed by a brief discussion of the new rules and regulations established by SOX. Then the empirical evidence presented by previous studies on the effectiveness of legislation is assessed and the harsh penalty Enron's auditor Arthur Andersen received is evaluated.

Enron-Andersen Scandal

Enron was founded in 1985 and it soon became one of the fastest-growing companies in the United States. It was named by Fortune as the "America's Most Innovative Company" between 1996 to 2001 for these six consecutive years. However, behind its shiny cover, it had massive accounting and corporate fraud. By the spring of 2001, concerns about Enron's true financial health started to be voiced in the financial world. In December 2001, Enron could no longer conceal and sustain the losses and declared bankruptcy. The collapse of Enron had long-lasting repercussions in the financial world. The public was mischievously deceived as the financial troubles of Enron were obscured with the help of its auditor, Arthur Andersen. The bankruptcy of Enron was the largest in the US As the evidence of the fraud lasting several years started to emerge, the scale of the scandal grew in size.

Before the Enron scandal, Arthur Andersen was one of the five biggest accounting firms at that time with offices in 84 countries. Auditors' reputation is one of the most important criteria in assessing the reliability of their audited financial statements (Firth, 1990). DeAngelo (1981) claims that large auditors deliver higher quality audits since they have more to lose if they don't maintain their audit quality. As one of the biggest audit firms at that time, Arthur Andersen's audits were deemed to be credible. However, by the end of 2001s and early 2002s, as the evidence on the financial fraud Arthur Andersen collaboration surfaced, the credibility of the auditing firm quickly nosedived. Following the failure of Enron, Arthur Andersen was deeply disgraced and shortly disappeared from the financial world.

Timeline of Events

In July 1985, Houston Natural Gas merged with InterNorth and formed Enron. Enron was an energy company trading natural gas. In the 1990s the firm positioned itself as a trader of energy derivative contracts. Enron acted as an intermediary and assisted natural gas producers to hedge the risk of energy price changes. In exchange for a fee, the firm was negotiating derivative contracts on behalf of its customers. The firm quickly grew and started to trade derivate contracts for a broad range of commodities such as coal, paper, steel, and energy. Enron launched the first global commodity trading website, EnronOnline in 1999. In August 2000, Enron shares hit an all-time high. Although the firm continuously reported profits, its troubles dated back 1990s. On January 30, 1992, the Securities and Exchange Commission (SEC) allowed Enron to use mark-to market accounting instead of traditional, accrual accounting. Using mark-to-market accounting, the firm was able to write unrealized future gains from some trading contracts into current income statements and delude the market with an impression of higher current profits. Besides, Enron used special purpose entities (SPEs) and transferred its troubled operations to these limited partnerships. By transferring the troubled assets to SPEs, those assets were kept off Enron's books and changed the profitability of the company significantly. November 1997 marks the start of Enron's complex series of transactions using SPEs that enable it to hide debts. Some of those SPEs were actually run by Enron's Chief Financial Official (CFO) Andrew Fastow. Enron kept on its risky business and continued to conceal its losses for many years. Only by April 2001, several financial analysts became skeptical and started to question Enron's earnings. On October 16, 2001, the firm filed its first quarterly loss of $638 million and disclosed a $1.2 billion reduction in shareholder equity. The same day, Moody's investors' service stated that it is considering lowering its credit rating on Enron debt securities. Soon enough, on October 19, 2001, Enron came into the spotlight of SEC investigations. In November, the firm admitted accounting errors and filed documents with SEC revising its financial statements for the previous five years to account for $586 million in losses. In the meanwhile, Enron agreed to be acquired by Dynegy for around $9 billion. However, a few days after, Enron announced the restatement of third quarter earnings and disclosed that a $690 million debt is due. About one week after this announcement, Dynegy backed out of the deal. On December 2, 2001, Enron filed for bankruptcy, which is the biggest in US history. 4,000 employees of Enron lost their jobs. The firm's stock price fell from its highest value of $90.75 in August 2000 to $0.26 by December 2002, hurting many small investors and wiping out the pension plans of Enron's employees, which were mainly tied to the company stock. In the following years, several Enron executives and some of their immediate families (wife of Enron's CFO Andrew Fastow) were indicted on charges of fraud and served prison time.

Throughout all the years when Enron utilized dubious accounting practices, Arthur Andersen was both the auditor and a consultant for the company. On November 29, 2001, SEC expanded its investigation on Enron to include its auditor, Arthur Andersen. On January 10, 2002, Arthur Andersen informed the SEC, the Department of Justice and Congress that it had destructed evidence by shredding Enron's audit documents. Reputation-related concerns after this news caused some Arthur Andersen clients to change their auditing firms. In February 2002, the board of Enron released the Powers report which cleared the board and highly criticized Arthur Andersen's role as the auditor. The Powers Report clearly described how Enron used a web of partnerships to conceal Enron's true financial situation and accused Arthur Andersen of failing to perform its professional duties. On March 14, 2002, Arthur Andersen was indicted. From that day on, the ability of the firm to survive was uncertain. Two days after the indictment, SEC announced that companies are required to obtain extra assurances from Arthur Andersen audit reports signed after March 14, 2002. In May 2002, former Arthur Andersen Partner David Duncan testified at the court and admitted that he obstructed justice by ordering his team to destruct the documents related to Enron. On June 15, 2002, Arthur Andersen was convicted of obstruction of justice and lost its license to engage in public accounting. Until the date it was found guilty, Arthur Andersen continued its audits of its remaining clients. Following the conviction, all the remaining clients of Arthur Andersen were forced to change their auditors. On August 31, 2002, Arthur Andersen surrendered its license and laid off around 80,000 employees. Three years later, US Supreme Court overturned the obstruction of justice verdict for Arthur Andersen but by that time there was not much left from the firm except a couple of hundred employees managing its lawsuits and the glorious days of the accounting giant were long gone. In 2008, SEC filed a settled action against former Arthur Andersen Partner David Duncan. In the litigation report, it is noted that in the years 1998 to 2000, Duncan signed on behalf of Arthur Andersen materially false and misleading audit reports although he allegedly was aware of the significant risks Enron had been carrying over the years. A summary of the timeline of events can be found in Appendix A.

Sarbanes Oxley Act (SOX)

As a response to financial fraud that happened in the early 2000s, on July 30, 2002, US Congress passed the Sarbanes Oxley Act (SOX). The new legislation was designed to strengthen existing securities regulations and enacted harsh penalties on lawbreakers. The act got its name from its two sponsors: Senator Paul S. Sarbanes and Representative Michael G. Oxley. SOX was constructed as reforms and additions to the Securities Exchange Act of 1934 and the Investment Advisers Act of 1940. The act is a very detailed and extensive piece of legislation. It consists of eleven titles, or sections, describing enhanced rules on transparency and responsibilities of corporate boards. The core areas of the change introduced by SOX are imposing legal responsibility on corporate executives, introducing enhanced accounting regulations, and establishing new protections. The act requires SEC to implement rules and monitor compliance with the law.

One of the novelties brought by the legislation was introducing corporate responsibility. The act imposes liability on senior corporate officers. Senior management is held responsible to establish an adequate internal control structure and ensure that financial reports are accurate (Nakitende *et al.*, 2021). The law also imposes criminal penalties for any officers who submit non-complying financial statements to the Securities and Exchange Commission (SEC). The act requires the management to submit a year-end disclosure report which includes reporting of material changes in financial condition. It also mandates enhanced reporting requirements for financial transactions, including off-balance sheet items. Besides, the law has introduced protection for whistleblowers. Public companies are prohibited from retaliating against employees who report fraud and/or testify about fraud. In addition, SOX requires the change of audit partner every five years and prohibits audit firms from providing many non-audit services. As a response to this regulation, big auditing firms formed their consulting services into separate entities.

Moreover, the act has created the Public Company Accounting and Oversight Board (PCAOB) to watch over public audit companies, enhance the quality of auditing and ensure independent auditing. Before SOX, auditing firms were required to obtain state licenses only and were expected to mostly self-regulate themselves. After SOX, all accounting firms that audit public firms were required to register with PCAOB. PCAOB is a non-profit private corporation monitoring the auditors of publicly traded firms. It is PCAOB's responsibility to inspect and ensure compliance at the registered accounting firms. PCAOB's core mission is to protect investors and the public interest by investigating and disciplining audit firms. Particularly after the misconduct of Arthur Andersen, the legislation aimed to prevent corporate managers from meddling with an independent financial audit. The act made it illicit for any corporate officer attempting to interfere with audits through manipulation, fraud, and coercion.

The implementation of SOX has brought many criticisms along with it. Some argued that these stringent rules and regulations pose a great burden, particularly on smaller firms seeking public funds; takes too much management time and is very expensive to keep up with the compliance costs. However, Congress has granted several delays to these costly disclosures for smaller firms with market capitalizations of less than $75 million. Later, these delays were made permanent by Dodd-Frank Act in 2010. Others claimed that the growing marginal cost of being a public company would outweigh the benefits and cause existing public firms to go private, prevent new ones to go public and reduce the cross-listings in the US Supporting this stance, Piotroski and Srinivasan (2008) found that after SOX, smaller international firms were more likely to list in the UK stock exchange instead of the US stock exchanges. However, firms that chose to list in the UK are smaller, less profitable, less likely to hire a big accounting firm as its auditor and more likely from developed countries. The characteristics of firms choosing the UK to list their shares are as expected since the compliance cost for SOX is a concern for smaller firms. On the other hand, the firms that prefer listing in the US exchanges after SOX are larger and more profitable companies from less developed countries. Although the fact of reduction in the cross-listed firms in the US may seem like a disadvantage of SOX, this may result in a net gain in market capitalization as the market capitalization of these larger cross-listing firms in total is expected to be more than the market capitalization of many smaller firms. In sum, many studies have examined the effectiveness of SOX in preventing future financial crimes to see if the marginal benefits of strict regulations would compensate for its projected costs. In the next section, some of these studies will be reviewed.

Effectiveness of SOX

A number of previous studies have presented empirical evidence of the positive impact of SOX on firm practices (Kedia *et al.*, 2010; Qian *et al.*, 2009). Some showed that post-SOX the audit quality has increased (Cohen *et al.*, 2008; Daniel *et al.*, 2008; Dyck *et al.*, 2010; Lobo & Zhou, 2006), while some others have documented the benefits of SOX in improving the accounting quality of US companies. For example, Koh *et al.* (2008) and Bartov and Cohen (2009) observed less accrual-based earnings management to meet analyst forecasting, following the implementation of SOX. In a similar fashion, Lobo and Zhou (2006) showed improved conservatism after SOX, in terms of the timely recognition of bad news. This shows that firms learned an important lesson, particularly after the concealment of Enron's losses by Arthur Andersen. Besides, Dyck *et al.* (2010) documented an increased role of auditors in detecting financial fraud following the implementation of SOX. Daniel *et al.* (2008) showed that firms engage less in earnings management for dividend payouts post-SOX implementation. Kedia *et al.* (2010) found that before SOX, firms were more likely to copy their peers' poor accounting practices. Brochet (2010) documented that the transparency of insider trading has enhanced and became more informative after SOX. Arping and Sautner (2013) analyzed the impact of SOX on corporate transparency and showed that cross-listed firms in the US became significantly less opaque post-SOX.

After the implementation of SOX, accounting and audit quality may have also improved. DeFond and Lennox (2011) report that after SOX and the enactment of PCAOB, the number of audit firms has reduced particularly due to the exit of several small audit firms. The authors argue that compared to remaining auditors, exiting auditors were of lower quality. Hence, SOX improved audit quality by encouraging low-quality auditors to exit the market.

However, the majority of the studies examined the impact of SOX immediately after its implementation. During this period, the benefits gained in terms of improvements in audit quality may not entirely be the result of SOX itself. Instead, it could be market discipline and/or a combination of complementary provisions contemporaneously provided, such as changes in the stock exchange guidelines (Coates & Srinivasan, 2014). Also, a longer period of time may be needed to pass new legislation to discover and take advantage of any ambiguities and circumvent new rules. Prior literature shows that real earnings management (abnormal operating cash flow, product costs and discretionary expenses) has increased to substitute accrual-based earnings management, which decreased after SOX implementation (Chaochharia & Grinstein, 2007; Cohen *et al.*, 2008; Lobo & Zhou, 2006). These studies show that the passage of SOX didn't alter the fundamental behavior of managers, as they carried on their quest in looking for ways to elude regulations for their own benefit. Besides, as time passes, the concern about stricter rules may wear off, causing both internal and external monitoring to loosen. Hence, the audit quality may return to its level prior to SOX after a certain period of time. Therefore, it is also important to conduct the long-term effects of SOX on audit quality. Using conservatism (Basu, 1997) as a measure of audit quality, Kim *et al.* (2019) found a significant positive change in conservatism over the long run. These results confirm that the concerns about the timing effect or the tendency of the opportunistic escape of managers do not reduce the effectiveness of SOX.

Another strand of literature has investigated if the claims that the cost of SOX would encourage firms to delist and prevent them to go public or discourage cross-listing in the US exchanges are valid or not.

Engel *et al.* (2007) found that smaller, less liquid firms with low growth prospects went private after the implementation of SOX. Talley (2009) also found similar results and reported that smaller firms went private post-SOX. Bova *et al.* (2013) found that smaller private companies in the US are less likely to raise financing through an IPO when compared to a control sample of firms in the UK Leuz *et al.* (2008) showed that the number of companies that deregister their common stock and suspend their SOX compliance and SEC reporting requirements have increased after SOX. The authors argue that deregistering firms are smaller, have weaker accounting quality and corporate governance, poorer performance and fewer growth opportunities. Piotroski and Srinivasan (2008) found that fewer foreign firms listed in US exchanges after SOX when compared to before the SOX era. Although the results of all these studies may be seen as a support for the criticisms of SOX, Leuz (2007) documented that going private trends in the UK were quite similar to those in the US post-SOX. Bartlett (2009) argues that going private doesn't necessarily exempt companies from the compliance with SOX, since going private usually entails the issuance of high-yield debt which require SEC reporting and SOX compliance. Also, Gao *et al.* (2013) showed that the decreasing trend in the IPOs is dated before SOX. Furthermore, in spite of the decrease in the number of IPOs, the pricing of the IPOs was improved after SOX. Johnson and Madura (2009) showed that US IPOs were not as underpriced when compared to a matched sample of Canadian IPOs which are not subject to SOX.

Dyck *et al.* (2010) documented that after the implementation of SOX, SEC's total fraud detection rate increased from 5% to 10%, making the SEC become more likely to detect corporate fraud. Anginer *et al.* (2012) examined options backdating cases and found that smaller firms were more engaged in that practice, while larger firms were more likely to be detected and brought to court by the SEC. In sum, although at the beginning the rules and regulations set by SOX seemed to be strict and costly, studies show the effectiveness of it in detecting and preventing future financial crimes (Rafay, 2021).

The Demise of Arthur Andersen

The auditor of Enron, Arthur Andersen, was one of the most important actors in the Enron scandal. The auditing firm was found guilty of obstruction of justice in matters related to the audit of Enron. When the scandal broke out, Arthur Andersen was one of the biggest five auditing firms with offices in 84 countries. It had global revenues of $9.3 billion and US revenues of $4.3 billion (Hawkins & Cohen, 2003). On March 15, 2002, the Department of Justice indicted Arthur Andersen on the felony charge of obstructing justice as a result of its involvement in the Enron case. On May 31, 2005, the United States Supreme Court has reversed Arthur Andersen's criminal conviction but by that time Arthur Andersen was already a history in the auditing industry. Following the events in 2002, the firm had to close its operations, which resulted in job losses for over 80,000 professionals worldwide. Some argued that this was a very harsh punishment (Ainslie, 2006), while some argued that certain individuals who committed the act should have been prosecuted instead of the entire firm (Krishnan, 2007). Although there is some evidence that suggests that the quality of the audits performed by the Houston office (which audited Enron) was inadequate, there is no systematic evidence on whether this lack of audit quality was pervasive throughout all of Andersen's operations (Kim *et al.*, 2019). Comparing the clients of Arthur Andersen's Houston office and Houston clients of other auditing firms, as well as Arthur Andersen's Atlanta office, Krishnan (2005) found that Arthur Andersen's Houston clients reported bad news on a less timely basis, indicating more aggressive accounting practices. Furthermore, Kim *et al.* (2019) examined if there were other Arthur Andersen offices that helped the clients to delay the recognition of publicly available bad news and found that only six of the twenty city-level offices of Arthur Andersen were less conservative than their main competitors (PricewaterhouseCoopers-PwC, Ernst & Young -EY, KPMG, Deloitte). The majority of city-level offices of Arthur Andersen utilized a more conservative approach than the Houston office and other Big Four offices in the same city. These results support the claim of critiques of the punishment of Arthur Andersen that it was quite harsh to close all the offices while only a few were engaged in financial fraud. However, along with the passage of SOX, the punishment of Arthur Andersen could establish a model not to follow for other accounting firms.

Besides, it should be noted that this scandal had rippling effects on the whole market and auditing industry. The unearthing of the massive scandal casted doubts on the audits of other firms done by Arthur Andersen. For example, following the Enron case, Chaney and Philipich (2002) found negative abnormal returns for Arthur Andersen's clients. Krishnamurthy *et al.* (2006) reported a significant negative market reaction to Arthur Andersen's clients when the news about Arthur Andersen's indictment was announced. Similarly, Cahan and Zhang (2006) examined the level of changes in the abnormal accruals of ex-Andersen clients and found that being audited by Arthur Andersen was seen as a significant source of litigation risk by successor auditors. Krishnan (2007) showed that earnings conservatism has increased for ex-Arthur Andersen clients that switched to other big auditing firms. Furthermore, he showed that before the scandal, the earnings of Arthur Andersen clients were less sensitive to bad news relative to the earnings of non-Arthur Andersen clients. However, after the demise of Arthur Andersen, ex-clients of Arthur Andersen's sensitivity to bad news have significantly increased. Krishnan *et al.* (2007) showed that for large ex-Arthur Andersen clients, new auditors were more conservative. Doogar *et al.* (2003) found that around the dates of exposure of the Enron-Arthur Andersen scandal, investor uncertainty increased and raised general concerns regarding financial statement quality. Furthermore, the risk of litigation has increased in the auditing industry. Chi (2004) found that post Enron scandal, on average, audit fees have increased. Feldman (2006) showed a positive and significant relationship between audit fees and changes in market concentration, suggesting that the departure of Arthur Andersen from the Big Five auditing firms has enabled the remaining Big Four firms to take the grip and exercise market power.

Some studies reviewed auditors' performance during the 2008 global financial crisis to see if rules and regulations brought by SOX were effective in improving auditing quality and if Arthur Andersen's sad end has set the right tone for lawbreakers. Sikka (2009) reviewed audit reports for failing firms during the 2008 global crisis and showed that Bear Stearns received an unqualified audit report on January 28, 2008, meaning that the auditors were satisfied with the company's financial reporting. However, interestingly, a few months after the clean audit report, Bear Stearns failed on March 14, 2008. Similarly, Thornburg Mortgage, the second largest independent mortgage provider in the US, received an unqualified audit opinion on February 27, 2008, from KPMG. Later, on March 4, 2008, KPMG withdrew its clean audit report shortly before Thornburg's bankruptcy. Northern Rock received an unqualified audit report on July 25, 2007. Yet shortly after in August and September, it suffered a bank run. After receiving clean audit reports from their auditors, many banks asked for financial support from the state. For example, US Bancorp received its clean report from E&Y on February 20 and a few months later, on November 14, it received $6 billion in bail-out funds from the government. Consistent with these, Desai *et al.* (2016) showed that during the time before the 2008 global crisis, auditors were not able to assess bank risk correctly while short sellers were able to see and take advantage of these weaknesses. When the Global Financial Crisis broke out in 2008, it was only six years after the Enron-Arthur Andersen scandal and the memory of the consequences of the massive fraud should still be fresh. Hence, any purposeful wrongdoings committed by auditors would be very surprising. Thus, some studies argued that contrary to the reports on the inability of auditors to spot problems in the firms they perform the audits, SOX significantly helped to improve the financial and auditing systems. For example, Jin *et al.* (2011) found that when a small and mid-sized US bank hired auditors specialized in banking, their chances of failing in the crisis were lower. Yeh *et al.* (2011) showed that banks with fully independent audit committees prior to the crisis performed better during the global financial crisis of 2008.

CONCLUSION

When the SOX passed, many criticized it as an unnecessary interference of the government in the financial markets. Many have claimed that such centralization of corporate governance and extra stringent rules and regulations to abide by would place severe financial burdens on particularly smaller firms seeking public funds; takes too much management time and is very expensive to keep up with the compliance costs. However, as time passed these claims were shown to be wrong and indeed the legislation was a successful one. Implementation of SOX has altered the relationship between the companies and the auditing firms and enhanced the transparency and reliability of financial reporting. Previous studies have shown that SOX has changed the firms' unethical behaviors, increased corporate transparency, increased audit quality and contributed to limiting future financial frauds. Both short-run (immediately after the SOX implementation) and long-run (many years after the SOX implementation) analyses show the positive impact of SOX on a firm's accounting practices. Besides, although the studies document that the punishment for Arthur Andersen was harsh, it represented a good lesson for firms and auditing companies as an example not to follow in the future and encourage firms to improve audit quality and employ ethical approaches. Following the success of SOX and the general perception that stricter rules and regulations would assist in preventing further crimes, several other countries passed SOX-type regulations (i.e., Canada (2002), Germany (2002), South Africa (2002), France (2003), Australia (2004), India (2005), Japan (2006), etc.)

The Enron-Arthur Andersen scandal did not only affect the clients and investors of these two firms but had effects on the whole market, the auditing industry and the public at large. The size of the scandal was so big that it put the auditing profession in the spotlight. Although the new rules and regulations commanded by SOX seemed to be very ambitious at the beginning, as time passes, it is seen that these rules have enhanced transparency and prevented other potential scandals at a big scale so far. Similarly, even though the punishment of Arthur Andersen may seem to be quite harsh, it set a great example for the results of financial fraud. Hence, sometimes it may be necessary to throw the baby out with the bath water.

DECLARATION

The authors declare that the manuscript follows ethical standards and there are no potential conflicts of interest with respect to the research, authorship and/or publication of this chapter.

DISCLAIMER

The contents and views of this chapter are expressed by the authors in personal capacities. It is not necessary for the Editor and the Publisher to agree with these viewpoints, and they are not responsible for any duty of care in this regard.

ACKNOWLEDGMENT

The authors extend sincere gratitude to

- The Editor and the International Editorial Advisory Board (IEAB) of this book who initially desk reviewed, arranged a rigorous double/triple blind review process, and conducted a thorough, minute, and critical final review before accepting the chapter for publication.
- All anonymous reviewers who provided very constructive feedbacks for thorough revision, improvement, extension, and fine tuning of the chapter.
- All colleagues, assistants and well-wishers who assisted to complete this task.

REFERENCES

Ainslie, E. K. (2006). Indicting corporations revisited: Lessons of the Arthur Andersen prosecution. *The American Criminal Law Review*, *43*, 107–125.

Anginer, D., Narayanan, M. P., Schipani, C. A., & Seyhun, H. N. (2012). Should size matter when regulating firms? implications from backdating of executive options. *New York University Journal of Legislation and Public Policy*, *15*, 1–44.

Arping, S., & Sautner, Z. (2013). Did SOX section 404 make firms less opaque? Evidence from cross-listed firms. *Contemporary Accounting Research*, *30*(3), 1133–1165. doi:10.1111/j.1911-3846.2012.01188.x

Bartlett, R. P. (2009). Going private but staying public: Reexamining the effect of Sarbanes-Oxley on Firms' Going Private Decisions. *The University of Chicago Law Review. University of Chicago. Law School*, *76*, 7–44.

Bartov, E., & Cohen, D. A. (2009). The "Numbers Game" in the pre- and post-Sarbanes Oxley Eras. *Journal of Accounting, Auditing & Finance*, *24*(4), 505–534. doi:10.1177/0148558X0902400401

Basu, S. (1997). The conservatism principle and the asymmetric timeliness of earnings. *Journal of Accounting and Economics*, *24*(1), 3–37. doi:10.1016/S0165-4101(97)00014-1

Bova, F., Minutti-Meza, M., Richardson, G., & Vyas, D. (2014). The Sarbanes-Oxley Act and exit strategies of private firms. *Contemporary Accounting Research*, *31*(3), 818–850. doi:10.1111/1911-3846.12049

Brochet, F. (2010). Information content of insider trades before and after the Sarbanes Oxley Act. *The Accounting Review*, *85*(2), 419–446. doi:10.2308/accr.2010.85.2.419

Cahan, S. F., & Zhang, W. (2006). After Enron: Auditor conservatism and ex-Andersen clients. *The Accounting Review*, *81*(1), 49–82. doi:10.2308/accr.2006.81.1.49

Chaney, P. K., & Philipich, K. L. (2002). Shredded reputation: The cost of audit failure. *Journal of Accounting Research, 40*(4), 1221–1245. doi:10.1111/1475-679X.00087

Chaochharia, V., & Grinstein, Y. (2007). Corporate governance and firm value: The impact of the 2002 governance rules. *The Journal of Finance, 62*(4), 1789–1825. doi:10.1111/j.1540-6261.2007.01257.x

Chi, W. (2004). The effect of the Enron-Andersen affair on audit pricing. SSRN *Electronic Journal. 886. https://doi.org/* doi:10.2139/ssrn.614884

Coates, J. C., & Srinivasan, S. (2014). SOX after ten years: A multidisciplinary review. *Accounting Horizons, 28*(3), 627–671. doi:10.2308/acch-50759

Cohen, D. A., Dey, A., & Lys, T. Z. (2008). Real and accrual-based earnings management in the pre- and post-Sarbanes Oxley periods. *The Accounting Review, 83*(3), 757–787. doi:10.2308/accr.2008.83.3.757

Daniel, N. D., Denis, D. J., & Naveen, L. (2008). Do firms manage earnings to meet dividend thresholds? *Journal of Accounting and Economics, 45*(1), 2–26. doi:10.1016/j.jacceco.2007.11.002

DeAngelo, L. E. (1981). Auditor size and audit quality. *Journal of Accounting and Economics, 3*(3), 183–199. doi:10.1016/0165-4101(81)90002-1

DeFond, M. L., & Lennox, C. S. (2011). The effect of SOX on small auditor exits and audit quality. *Journal of Accounting and Economics, 52*(1), 21–40. doi:10.1016/j.jacceco.2011.03.002

Desai, H., Rajgopal, S., & Yu, J. J. (2016). Were information intermediaries sensitive to the financial statement-based leading indicators of bank distress prior to the financial crisis? *Contemporary Accounting Research, 33*(2), 576–606. doi:10.1111/1911-3846.12161

Doogar, R., Sougiannis, T., & Xie, H. (2003). *The impairment of auditor credibility: Stock market evidence from the Enron-Andersen saga* (Working paper). University of Illinois at Urbana-Champaign.

Dyck, A., Morse, A., & Zingales, L. (2010). Who blows the whistle on corporate fraud? *The Journal of Finance, 65*(6), 2213–2253. doi:10.1111/j.1540-6261.2010.01614.x

Engel, E., Hayes, R. M., & Wang, X. (2007). The Sarbanes Oxley Act and firms' going private decisions. *Journal of Accounting and Economics, 44*(1-2), 116–145. doi:10.1016/j.jacceco.2006.07.002

Feldman, E. R. (2006). A basic quantification of the competitive implications of the demise of Arthur Andersen. *Review of Industrial Organization, 29*(3), 193–212. doi:10.100711151-006-9117-5

Firth, M. (1990). Auditor reputation: The impact of critical reports issued by government inspectors. *The RAND Journal of Economics, 21*(3), 374–387. doi:10.2307/2555615

Gao, X., Ritter, J. R., & Zhu, Z. (2013). Where have all the IPOs gone? *Journal of Financial and Quantitative Analysis, 48*(6), 1663–1692. doi:10.1017/S0022109014000015

Gayle, G. L., Li, C., & Miller, R. A. (2022). Was Sarbanes Oxley costly? Evidence from optimal contracting on CEO compensation. *Journal of Accounting Research, 60*(4), 1189–1234. doi:10.1111/1475-679X.12436

Hawkins, D. F., & Cohen, J. (2003). *Arthur Andersen LLP. Case 9-102-061*. Harvard Business School.

Hillier, D., McColgan, P., & Tsekeris, A. (2022). How did the Sarbanes Oxley Act affect managerial incentives? Evidence from corporate acquisitions. *Review of Quantitative Finance and Accounting*, *58*(4), 1395–1450. doi:10.100711156-021-01028-6

James, H. L., & Lirely, R. (2022). The propensity to save: The effect of Sarbanes Oxley Act. *Review of Financial Economics*, *40*(1), 77–96. doi:10.1002/rfe.1140

Jin, J. Y., Kanagaretnam, K., & Lobo, G. J. (2011). Ability of accounting and audit quality variables to predict bank failure during the financial crisis. *Journal of Banking & Finance*, *35*(11), 2811–2819. doi:10.1016/j.jbankfin.2011.03.005

Johnson, J., & Madura, J. (2009). The pricing of IPOs post-Sarbanes-Oxley. *Financial Review*, *44*(2), 291–310. doi:10.1111/j.1540-6288.2009.00219.x

Kedia, S., Koh, K., & Rajgopal, S. (2010). *Evidence on contagion in corporate misconduct* (AFA 2011 Denver Meetings Paper). SSRN Electronic Journal. Retrieved from https://papers.ssrn.com/sol3/papers.cfm?abstract_id=1571538

Kim, M. S., Dandu, J., & Iren, P. (2019). The effect of SOX on audit quality. *Journal of Financial Crime*, *26*(3), 897–909. doi:10.1108/JFC-08-2018-0088

Kim, R., & Luo, W. (2022). Customer concentration and earnings management: Evidence from the Sarbanes Oxley Act. *European Accounting Review*, *31*(4), 905–936. doi:10.1080/09638180.2020.1858915

Koh, K., Matsumoto, D. A., & Rajgopal, S. (2008). Meeting or beating analyst expectations in the post-scandals world: Changes in stock market rewards and managerial actions. *Contemporary Accounting Research*, *25*(4), 1067–1098. doi:10.1506/car.25.4.5

Krishnamurthy, S., Zhou, J., & Zhou, N. (2006). Auditor reputation, auditor independence, and the stock-market impact of Andersen's indictment on its client firms. *Contemporary Accounting Research*, *23*(2), 465–490. doi:10.1506/14P1-5QRR-1NAF-3CE1

Krishnan, G. V. (2005). Did Houston clients of Arthur Andersen recognize publicly available bad news in a timely fashion? *Contemporary Accounting Research*, *22*(1), 165–193. doi:10.1506/EGQD-BTG1-4RHD-7MU6

Krishnan, G. V. (2007). Did earnings conservatism increase for former Andersen clients? *Journal of Accounting, Auditing & Finance*, *22*(2), 141–163. doi:10.1177/0148558X0702200205

Krishnan, J., Raghunandan, K., & Yang, J. S. (2007). Were former Andersen clients treated more leniently than other clients? Evidence from going-concern modified audit opinions. *Accounting Horizons*, *21*(4), 423–435. doi:10.2308/acch.2007.21.4.423

Leuz, C. (2007). Was the Sarbanes Oxley Act of 2002 really this costly? A discussion of evidence from event returns and going-private decisions. *Journal of Accounting and Economics*, *44*(1-2), 146–165. doi:10.1016/j.jacceco.2007.06.001

Leuz, C., Triantis, A., & Wang, T. (2008). Why do firms go dark? Causes and economic consequences of voluntary SEC deregistrations. *Journal of Accounting and Economics*, *45*(2-3), 181–208. doi:10.1016/j.jacceco.2008.01.001

Lobo, G. J., & Zhou, J. (2006). Did conservatism in financial reporting increase after the Sarbanes Oxley Act? Initial evidence. *Accounting Horizons*, *20*(1), 57–73. doi:10.2308/acch.2006.20.1.57

Nakitende, M. G., Rafay, A., & Waseem, M. (2021). Frauds in Business Organizations: A Comprehensive Overview. In A. Rafay (Ed.), *Handbook of Research on Theory and Practice of Financial Crimes* (pp. 21–38). IGI Global., doi:10.4018/978-1-7998-5567-5.ch002

Pincus, M. (2020). Did accrual earnings management decline and real earnings management increase Post-SOX? A re-examination and replication. *Journal of Financial Reporting*, *7*(2), 179–205. doi:10.2308/JFR-2019-0009

Piotroski, J. D., & Srinivasan, S. (2008). Regulation and bonding: The Sarbanes-Oxley Act and the flow of international listings. *Journal of Accounting Research*, *46*(2), 383–425. doi:10.1111/j.1475-679X.2008.00279.x

Pozner, J. E., Mohliver, A., & Moore, C. (2022). Shine a light: How firm responses to announcing earnings restatements changed after Sarbanes Oxley. In K. Martin, K. Shilton, & J. Smith (Eds.), *Business and the Ethical Implications of Technology* (pp. 121–137). Springer. doi:10.1007/978-3-031-18794-0_8

Qian, J., Strahan, P. E., & Zhu, J. L. (2009). *The economic benefits of the Sarbanes Oxley Act?: Evidence from a natural experiment*. Financial Institutions Center, Wharton School, University of Pennsylvania.

Rafay, A. (Ed.). (2021). *HandBook of Research on Theory and Practice of Financial Crimes. Pennsylvania*. IGI Global., doi:10.4018/978-1-7998-5567-5

Rafay, A. (Ed.). (2023). *Concepts, Cases, and Regulations in Financial Fraud and Corruption. Pennsylvania*. IGI Global., doi:10.4018/978-1-6684-5007-9

Shi, Y., Nie, D., & Chen, L. (2022). Management earnings forecasts, earnings management, and the Sarbanes Oxley Act. *Journal of Forensic & Investigative Accounting*, *14*(1), 106–132.

Sikka, P. (2009). Financial crisis and the silence of the auditors. *Accounting, Organizations and Society*, *34*(6-7), 868–873. doi:10.1016/j.aos.2009.01.004

Talley, E. (2009). Going-Private decisions and the Sarbanes Oxley Act of 2002: A cross-country analysis. *Journal of Law Economics and Organization*, *25*(1), 107–133.

Yeh, Y. H., Chung, H., & Liu, C. L. (2011). Committee independence and financial institution performance during the 2007-08 credit crunch: Evidence from a multi-country study. *Corporate Governance*, *19*(5), 437–458. doi:10.1111/j.1467-8683.2011.00884.x

APPENDIX

Table 1. Timeline of Events in the Enron-Arthur Andersen Scandal

Date	Event
July 1985	The merger of Houston Natural Gas and InterNorth to form Enron
30 January 1992	Permission granted by the SEC to Enron to use mark-to-market accounting instead of traditional, accrual-based accounting
November 1997	Start of a series of transactions using SPEs to hide losses
29 November 1999	Launch of the first global commodity trading website, EnronOnline
August 2000	All-time highest share price: $90.75
April 2001	Skepticism of financial analysts about Enron's profitability Rising concerns regarding Enron's true financial situation
16 October 2001	Filing of first quarterly loss of $638 million. Announcement of a $1.2 billion reduction in shareholder equity. An announcement by Moody's Investor Service that it is re-evaluating Enron's credit rating on its debt securities.
19 October 2001	Initiation of SEC investigations on Enron
8 November 2001	Filing of documents with the SEC and revising the financial statements for the past five years totaling $586 million in losses
9 November 2001	The deal made to be acquired by Dynegy
19 November 2001	Announcement of restatement of third quarter earnings and disclosure that $690 million debt is due
28 November 2001	Announcement of Dynegy backing off from the deal to purchase Enron as Enron's credit ratings sink
29 November 2001	Inclusion of Arthur Andersen in the SEC's investigation of the Enron case
2 December 2001	The bankruptcy of Enron Stock price falls to $0.26 Thousands of people lost their jobs
10 January 2002	Arthur Andersen admits shredding thousands of pages of Enron's audits documents
February 2002	Powers report by Enron's board accusations by the board to Arthur Andersen of not fulfilling its professional duties
14 March 2002	The indictment of Arthur Andersen
May 2002	Arthur Andersen's partner Duncan admits to destructing documents and obstructing justice
15 June 2002	Conviction of Arthur Andersen
30 July 2002	Passage of the Sarbanes Oxley Act (SOX) from the US Congress
31 August 2002	Arthur Andersen surrenders its accounting license and lays off 80,000 employees
31 May 2005	Overturn of the obstruction of justice verdict for Arthur Andersen
January 2008	Filing of settled action against Arthur Andersen partner Duncan

Chapter 4
Regulatory Ambiguity in India: A Breeding Ground for Crypto Criminals

Sachin Shah
Tata Consultancy Services, India

Abdul Rafay
https://orcid.org/0000-0002-0285-5980
University of Management and Technology, Pakistan

ABSTRACT

Cryptocurrencies have sparked global transformations in digital technology and financial services, leading to deliberations on regulatory frameworks. India is cautiously working towards regulatory clarity and legalizing Cryptocurrency usage, as it becomes the country with the most cryptocurrency users. The Indian regulatory body is vigilant, monitoring progress and warning the public about associated risks. Despite regulatory efforts, India has seen a worrisome rise in cyber-frauds, cryptocurrency crimes, and money laundering involving digital currencies. This chapter focuses on the regulatory ambiguity in India, which inadvertently fosters an environment for crypto criminals. Through case studies, it highlights the gravity of the situation and the urgent need for legislative action to combat scams and money laundering. The author concludes optimistically, expecting India to establish robust crypto regulations to effectively address these challenges.

INTRODUCTION

When Satoshi Nakamoto penned down its original whitepaper and introduced to the world "*Bitcoin*" and *blockchain technology*, no one had ever imagined that virtual currencies a.k.a. *cryptocurrencies* will bring a tsunami of changes in the world of digital technology and financial services. There are approximately 300 million crypto users across the world as of 2021 (Tuwiner, 2023). The number of users joining this bandwagon over the past decade is astonishing and the incredible growth of 190% from the year 2018 to 2020 evidences the same fact. India is not behind in joining this bandwagon and is estimated to have more than 100 million users (Tuwiner, 2023) which distinguishes it as the country

DOI: 10.4018/978-1-6684-8587-3.ch004

with more cryptocurrency users than any other country. This definitely puts India in the league among countries in imbibing new technology and adopting new innovation and is very well acknowledged by its key regulator – The Reserve Bank of India (RBI) too. That is why the regulator is taking a very cautious approach in formulating the regulatory framework around cryptocurrencies in India.

Though this approach is in line with the approach adopted by various regulators across the globe, however, India is still lagging behind in terms of providing regulatory clarity and necessary directives for recognizing the cryptocurrency despite being tagged as the country with the largest pool of users. The April 2018 notification by RBI on prohibition on dealing in *virtual currencies* a.k.a. cryptocurrencies demonstrate this regulatory limbo and the subsequent verdict by the Hon. Supreme Court of India overruling the same notification indicates the state of regulatory ambiguity. This verdict turned out to be a key game changer as it not only exacerbated the confusion around using the cryptocurrency but also triggered a spate of headaches for the RBI in terms of not providing necessary guidelines to the regulated entities but also containing the instances where cryptocurrency is been used as a conduit for carrying frauds and money laundering activities.

It may be noted that despite the lack of regulatory framework for the regulated entities coupled with the volatility in the cryptocurrency market, Indians are still attracted to the use of cryptocurrencies completely unaware of the related risks. With the growing trend of cryptocurrency users, India also witnessed worrying growth in the number of instances of cyber-frauds, crypto crimes and money laundering activities involving cryptocurrency.

In this chapter, the author aims to highlight the absence of a regulatory framework related to cryptocurrencies in India and how criminals are exploiting this loophole to carry out criminal activities including money laundering and fraud. The concerns are supplemented by reference to the major cryptocurrency-related incidents carried out to perpetrate fraud and money laundering activity.

GLOBAL CRYPTOCURRENCY REGULATIONS – A SILOED APPROACH

The last two decades are known for the birth and evolution of cryptocurrency and its impact on the banking and financial services sector. The way *cryptocurrency* has emerged and started disrupting the financial services ecosystem has been a focal point for a lot of governments and regulators across the globe. As per the information available in the public domain, there are more than 300 million people around the world who use or own cryptocurrencies in 2022. There are approximately 6000 different types of cryptocurrencies available with a market capitalization of USD 1.06 trillion (Tuwiner, 2023). The fact that there are close to 18000 business globally that accepts cryptocurrency payments evidences the wider acceptance of cryptocurrencies. India as a country is not immune to this development and has emerged as the country with the largest holder of cryptocurrencies in the world.

Despite this unprecedented growth in the evolution of cryptocurrencies, the regulations around them are yet to evolve and strengthen. Considering the existing crypto regulations globally one can see that there is an uncoordinated and siloed approach to tackle the risks related to the usage of cryptocurrencies and leveraging the benefits it offers to the wider banking and financial services system. World Bank along with several regulators has raised concerns about the risks posed by cryptocurrency to global financial stability and has called for a coordinated approach to harness the benefits and contain various risks it injects into the ecosystem, like money laundering risk, regulatory risk, liquidity risk, etc. Adding to the concerns is the quicker pace of new applications and models like *tokenization*, *decentralized finance*

(DeFi), Non-fungible Tokens (NFTs) and *Decentralized Autonomous Organizations* (DAOs) which has challenged the existing models and regulations. In other words, it forced the regulators and the governments to revisit their existing pool of regulations related to cross-border data flows, intellectual property rights and capital controls and make necessary amendments.

Considering the volatility, technological challenges and the increased threat to global financial stability there is a clear need for global coordination and the necessary regulations around cryptocurrencies. Currently, the existing regulations are at various maturity levels in terms of receptivity and building the regulatory framework to regulate the usage of cryptocurrencies. Countries like the United States, Singapore, El Salvador already are at an advanced maturity level in terms of having necessary regulations, however, countries like India are still taking a cautious approach in adapting cryptocurrencies and building regulations around them following the age-old belief that "prevention is better than cure". Though the overall aim and approach are aimed towards financial stability, preventing misusage and criminalization and promoting innovation but the lack of coordination among all the countries is still one of the biggest challenges to have robust and strong regulation.

INDIAN CRYPTOCURRENCY REGULATIONS AND ITS EVOLUTION

India in recent times is emerging as a major economic power and recently surpassed the United Kingdom to become the fifth-largest economy in the world. The last decade has been a witness to major economic developments and that also includes continuing its evolutionary journey in the field of financial services. With the entry of multiple FinTech firms, it also has the unique distinction of being the country with the largest holder of cryptocurrencies. As per the estimates available in the public domain, India has more than 100 million cryptocurrency holders and it is estimated that the cryptocurrency-tech market will add an economic value of USD 184 billion by 2030 (Analytics Insight, 2022).

These interesting statistics are very much on the radar of the Government of India (GoI) and RBI which is the apex regulator in India. Considering the risk involved, the potential of the misuse of cryptocurrencies, absence of any regulatory or legal framework, RBI cautioned the general public way back in 2013 and advised them not to deal with cryptocurrencies. However, as cryptocurrencies gained popularity at a global level, their (mis) usage also got prominent and widespread in India. In the subsequent section of this chapter, it will be explained further as to how the cryptocurrencies were widespread in their misuse which resulted in a loss to the public. One of the key reasons for such misuse of cryptocurrencies in India was the absence of crypto regulation. Though RBI reiterated its stance and cautioned the public multiple times and also released follow-up notifications in the years 2017 and 2018 advising not to deal in cryptocurrencies, there was no concrete development on the formulation of the crypto regulations.

In the year 2018 when RBI again issued the notification and advised the Regulated Entities (REs) not to deal in cryptocurrencies or provide services for facilitating any person or entity in dealing with or settling cryptocurrencies, there was a big hue and cry among the cryptocurrency service provider which majority were the crypto exchanges operating in the currency. The RBI notification was challenged in the court of law and Honorable Supreme Court reversed the said directive by RBI and removed the bank on cryptocurrencies by opining that in the absence of any legislation, RBI cannot impose any restrictions in the dealing of cryptocurrencies. This was a big win for the crypto-lobbyist in India and since then there is a state of limbo as far as the formulation of crypto regulation in India is concerned. The unofficial grapevine, however, is that the REs are still following abundant caution while dealing in cryptocurrencies and this has proved to be a major barrier to the growth of the cryptocurrency market in India.

This was not the end of the regulatory limbo. Though it was a big blow to RBI and the GoI, however, it also gave a big push to the efforts in formulating a country-wide legislative framework. By this time, GoI and the law enforcement agencies also noticed the tax evasion via cryptocurrency trading and hence it became all the more important to expedite the process of formulating the crypto regulations in India. This tax evasion was happening via the crypto exchange platform and as per the information available in the public domain it is alleged that these exchanges facilitated a tax evasion of an estimated USD 12.6 million (Shumba, 2022). Subsequently, GoI imposed a tax on the income generated from "*virtual digital assets*" (a.k.a. cryptocurrencies, virtual currencies). This action by GoI was construed as a step to legitimize dealing in cryptocurrencies. However, the finance minister Ms. Nirmala Sitharaman clarified that imposing tax should not be interpreted as a step in the direction of legitimizing cryptocurrencies. She said that *"taxing income from cryptos and other virtual digital assets should be seen as a step to legitimize them. Rather, it is a means to check the source and trail but not to legitimize them (FE Online, 2022)"*. She further added that *"We haven't said that this is currency. We haven't said that this has intrinsic value, but certain operations are taxable for the sovereign and that is why we have taxed (FE Online, 2022)"*.

This decision by the GoI proved to be a masterstroke in curbing cryptocurrency dealings or cryptocurrency trading. Though the trading volumes plunged by 90-95% (Newar, 2022), the risk still remains in the overall ecosystem and the public at large is still vulnerable to increased frauds and scams involving cryptocurrency. If one analyzes these scams, it will be easy to infer that the only solution to curb these scams, frauds and misuse of cryptocurrency is to have legislation in place.

CRYPTOCURRENCY SCAMS AND SELECT CASE STUDIES

To understand the impact of the absence of appropriate crypto regulations and the legislative framework, one must go through the various scams which have occurred in India over the past two decades. The trend in India is no different from the global trend where the money laundering instances involving crypto spiked by nearly 30% between 2020 and 2021 (Dey & Kumar, 2022). As per the same report, cybercriminals laundered USD 8.6 billion worth of cryptocurrencies in 2021 as appeared in Outlook India 2022. It is estimated that, as of June 2022, Indian crypto investors have lost about INR 1 trillion (USD 0.0133 trillion) to multiple fake crypto exchange scams as appeared in Tomorrow Makers, 2022. These scams and money laundering instances will also act as a case study for the academic circle and will clearly demonstrate how the absence of a legislative framework coupled with the low level of education and greed can result in major scams and penetrate the social structure where employment and poverty is a major issue even in the 21st century. It may be noted that the moot point conveyed here is not to blame the socio-economic issues like poverty or unemployment but to reinforce the point that how these socio-economic challenges supplement the criminal activities and play havoc on the masse in terms of financial losses.

If one ponders the biggest twelve scams in India involving cryptocurrency which amounted to approximately USD 9 billion and analyzes the modus-operandi and the legal fate of such investigations, one can clearly identify the focus areas which are imminent from RBIs perspective. The high-level snapshot of the biggest crypto scams reported in India is diagrammatically depicted below:

Figure 1. Biggest crypto scams in India
(Source: Inc42.com)

Ponzi Schemes	Key Accused	Scam Size	Number Of People Duped
bitconnect	Divyesh Darji, Satish Kumbhani	INR 41,000 Cr+	NA
GAINBITCOIN	Amit Bhardwaj, Ajay Bhardwaj, Vivek Bhardwaj	INR 20,000 Cr+	8,000+
MORRIS COIN	Nishad K	INR 1200 Cr	11 Lakh
Regalcoin (REC)	Divyesh Darji	INR 7,000 Cr	NA
DEKADO	Divyesh Darji, Ranjeet Saxena	INR 1,000 Cr	NA
	Amit Lakhanpal	INR 500 Cr	15,810
Karnataka Crypto Scam	Sri Krishna Sriki	INR 400 Cr	NA
Plutoexchange	Umesh Verma	INR 2 Cr	43
	Ranganath DS	NA	2,000
OneCoin	Rjua Ignatova	$10 Mn ($265 Mn globally)	NA
Ether Trade Asia	Nishid Wasnik	INR 500 Cr	5,000
ATC Coin	Subhashchand Jewria	INR 100 Cr	NA

The most prominent of these instances is – The GainBitcoin Scam. This was one of the early scams involving cryptocurrency in India and occurred from 2014 to 2018 affecting 8000 victims with an estimated scam size of USD 3 billion. The accused brothers leveraged the *Multi-Level-Marketing* (MLM) business model to trap the innocent public by setting up the crypto exchange BitEx and offering Bitcoin mining contracts. Under this scheme, the investors were promised 10% monthly returns for an investment for 18 months and a payout in bitcoin. As the MLM pyramid grew and more and more people were involved in the chain, the whole scheme started to have problems and started faltering on the payout commitments. Besides this, the alleged culprit brothers gave MCAP which was one of the types of pre-mined tokens having negligible value. The investigation is still undergoing; however, the main accused has already died due to kidney failure in 2022.

The next crypto scam is the – The Bitconnect Scam which was operated from 2016 to 2018 and was having a scam size of approximately USD 5.5 billion. It is also considered one of the biggest Ponzi schemes globally. This Ponzi scheme was operated by an entity headquartered in the United Kingdom and the Indian franchisee was operating from the Diamond Capital of India – Surat. This scam draws similarity to GainBitcoin Scam where the masterminds introduced BitConnect Coins (BCC) and marketed them as an investment option with a daily interest return of 1% which will get doubled in 100 days. The most interesting thing about this scam is that it involved high-profile investors which includes senior police and government officers, state ministers and members of the legislative assembly. The accused of this scam are absconding and hence there is no progress at all in this scam.

The next scams to be analyzed are – The Regal Coin and The Dekado Coin Scam. The mastermind of both these scams was the same accused who was heading the India franchise in the Bitconnect Scam. The modus-operandi in both these scams were that of MLM schemes which were heavily leveraged in the lack of knowledge and people's greed. In the Regal Coin case, The Regal coins were marketed as tokens promising lucrative returns from 1% to 7% depending on the MLM layer on which the investor is sitting. Apart from the promised returns, the scheme was made more attractive by promising bonus returns to the tune of 2% to 5% depending on investment levels. The mastermind also leveraged technology to trap innocent investors where access was provided to applications and the daily dashboards were published showing returns. The Regal Coin was also listed on a few international exchanges however its value became zero from more than USD 70 quoted in 2017.

The Dekado Coin Scam also followed the same *modus-operandi* which promised monthly returns of 40-70% by investing in Dekado Coins. This scam involved people from various countries, i.e., India, Indonesia, Netherlands and the African continent and hence had global footprints. In this scam also, investors were given access to websites that later were shut down resulting in huge losses to the investors. The investigations are still going on however at a slow pace.

The next scam is as recent as that of 2020 where the gullible public was defrauded by luring to invest in Morris Coin by the mastermind and promising them a daily return and other attractive bonus for each referral to the Ponzi scheme MLM chain. The mastermind duped close to 1 million people under the guise of an *Initial Coin Offering* (ICO) through his companies like Long Rich Global, Long Rich Technologies and Morris Trading Solutions. The case is under investigation; however, the mastermind is absconding.

During the investigation, it was found that the cryptocurrencies were bought from the proceeds of crime and the money obtained through investors was used for the purchase of immovable properties, various cryptocurrencies, luxury cars and for spending in luxury hotels and resorts.

One more such instance of a crypto scam is – The Ether Trade Asia Scam which operated from 2020-2021 and posed as one of the trading platforms promising daily returns to the tune of 3%.

Apart from these scams or Ponzi Schemes, recently law enforcement authorities also identified the involvement of cryptocurrency in undertaking money laundering. One such instance is the investigation against one of the largest crypto exchanges which was accused of involvement in money laundering to the tune of USD 0.5 billion (Thakur, 2022). As per the information available in the public domain, investigating agencies found the remittance of illegal cash with anonymity and no details of the beneficiaries.

In this instance, 'proceeds of crime' were converted by criminals into cryptocurrency and transferred the same to various crypto wallet service providers based out of tax heaven countries like Cayman Island. These remittances are then brought back to the country via shell companies. It was also noted that these transactions were not having any audit trail in the blockchain which made it easy for criminals to transfer the proceeds of crime irrespective of location and nationality of beneficiary.

In such similar instance involving money laundering, investigating agencies arrested a person who was involved in following a similar *modus operandi* for money laundering. This person was found to be involved in transferring a large amount of 'proceeds of crime' derived from illegal betting and transferring the same by converting it into cryptocurrency. It is believed that these cryptocurrencies were purchased on behalf of non-Indian nationals and were then transferred to different wallets outside India. This case is very well linked back to the investigation of an online betting case where a few Chinese nationals were involved in setting up entities in India to carry the online betting scam and international *hawala* transfers.

In a similar instance, fraud worth USD 0.15 billion was identified where the fraudsters duped the public by posing as fake exchanges. These criminals were very tech-savvy and they used fake domains and social media accounts to reach out and convince the users to invest in fake exchanges. Once the investors are trapped and invest their own money, the criminals then will approach them as investigative agents or pose as other investors and get important details like card details or bank details. These details were then used to carry out other criminal activities. This scan is known as "CoinEgg Scam" (BI Bureau, 2022).

CRYPTOCURRENCY ECOSYSTEM – KEY CHALLENGES

The multiple scams and the involvement of cryptocurrency in undertaking money laundering activity in India raise some serious questions for the regulators and the government. Though all the efforts are been made to formulate a legislative and regulatory framework, however, there are some key challenges that needs to be tackled immediately. A few of these challenges are mentioned as below.

Absence of Watchdog

One of the major reasons for the slow investigations into cryptocurrency scams is the absence of a watchdog at a national level. Though the investigations are pursued by other investigative agencies, however, the need is to have a specialized watchdog or a national agency that specializes in the investigation of cryptocurrency-related matters. It may be noted that as technology is advancing and criminals are becoming more tech-savvy the need for such specialized national agency is the need of the hour. Since such investigations required specialized investigation and technical skills, it will be prudent that such a national agency or watchdog office is established to focus only on cryptocurrency-related scams and related instances.

Revamped Judicial System

The second challenge is related to the first one and that is the new-age judiciary system. The existing system is too old and not tech-savvy. Adding to that the absence of a legislative framework makes it easy for criminals to beat the system and avoid any legal actions against them. The scams mentioned above are classic examples where the mastermind or the prime accused could obtain bail and abscond even before the legal proceedings are initiated against them. This clearly demonstrates that the current judiciary system needs to come up the curve and requires it to be more tech-savvy and digital in its approach. This will ensure that the legal framework is not skewed towards the criminals and the public at large also has faith that they will get quicker justice.

Upskilling the Investigative Agencies

The crypto ecosystem is a very complicated system and it is very difficult to understand the nuances. The way criminals are beaten in terms of their knowledge and the innovative techniques to defraud the public, the investigative agencies are behind the curve. They are not appropriately equipped either in terms of knowledge level or providing the right kind of tools to carry out such investigations. Hence the cases fall under the crack and the investigations run into years and years without any concrete results. It is this very important that the investigative agencies are appropriately skilled and the right kind of investigative tools are provided to them so as to conclude the investigations and restore the public trust.

Enhanced Public Awareness

Going by the case studies mentioned in the above section, one common theme which is identified is the lack of knowledge. The innocent public doesn't have the knowledge and hence falls under the trap of criminals or such scams. It is thus important that various agencies within the government take initiatives to increase public awareness. This will surely bring results in the long run and will be the best counter mechanism to beat criminal activities.

CONCLUSION

The regulatory ambiguity is slowly turning out to be a breeding ground for crypto criminals in India. Hence a swift and quick action to put a regulatory framework around the cryptocurrencies in India is the need of the hour. The case studies discussed in the chapter clearly demonstrate the urgency of putting a legislative and regulatory framework if India wants to contain cryptocurrency-related scams and money laundering instances. There are various challenges, as mentioned in the above section that needs to address on high priority by the GoI and RBI. The regulator and the government are aware of these challenges and have taken several measures including regulatory notifications and several other communications made in the public domain to increase awareness of cryptocurrency and its pitfalls and also advise the public to be cautious while dealing with cryptocurrencies. The work is also under progress to formulate the appropriate legislative framework and finalize the regulator to handle all cryptocurrency-related matters. As the famous poet George Herbert right said, 'Where There is a Will There is a Way'. It is just a matter of time before India will come strong on the crypto regulations and execute this phrase, both in letter and spirit by having an appropriate legislative and regulatory framework around cryptocurrency soon.

DECLARATION

The authors declare that the manuscript follows ethical standards and there are no potential conflicts of interest with respect to the research, authorship and/or publication of this chapter.

DISCLAIMER

The contents and views of this chapter are expressed by the authors in their personal capacities. It is not necessary for the Editor and the Publisher to agree with these viewpoints, and they are not responsible for any duty of care in this regard.

ACKNOWLEDGMENT

The authors extend sincere gratitude to

- The Editor and the International Editorial Advisory Board (IEAB) of this book, who initially desk reviewed, arranged a rigorous double/triple-blind review process, and conducted a thorough, minute, and critical final review before accepting the chapter for publication.
- All anonymous reviewers who provided very constructive feedback for thorough revision, improvement, extension, and fine-tuning of the chapter.
- All colleagues, assistants and well-wishers who assisted to complete this task.

REFERENCES

Analytics Insight. (2022, January 23). *Cryptocurrency in India: Demographic survey of the domestic cryptocurrency market*. Retrieved from https://www.analyticsinsight.net/cryptocurrency-in-india-demographic-survey-of-the-domestic-cryptocurrency-market/

Bureau, B. I. (2022, June 21). Crypto scammers have reportedly stolen Rs. 1000 crore off Indian users by posing as fake exchanges. *Business Insider India*. Retrieved from https://www.businessinsider.in/cryptocurrency/news/indian-investors-may-have-lost-almost-1000-crore-in-crypto-scam-according-to-a-new-report/articleshow/92358876.cms

Dey, P., & Kumar, H. (2022, January 28). 30% rise in money laundering activity in crypto in 2021. *Outlook*. Retrieved from https://www.outlookindia.com/business/30-rise-in-money-laundering-activity-in-crypto-in-2021-finds-study-news-48007

Newar, B. (2022, July 05). Indian crypto trading volumes slump following hefty taxes. *Cointelgraph*. Retrived from https://cointelegraph.com/news/indian-crypto-trading-volumes-slump-following-hefty-taxes

Online, F. E. (2022, April 19). Nirmala Sitharaman's latest statement on cryptocurrency tax: Here's why Govt imposed 30% crypto tax, 1% TDS. *Financial Express*. Retrieved from https://www.financialexpress.com/business/blockchain-nirmala-sitharamans-latest-statement-on-cryptocurrency-tax-heres-why-govt-imposed-30-crypto-tax-1-tds-2496309/

Shumba, C. (2022, March 28). India identifies 11 crypto exchanges accused of tax evasion. *CoinDesk*. Retrieved from https://www.coindesk.com/policy/2022/03/28/india-identifies-11-crypto-exchanges-accused-of-tax-evasion/

Thakur, P. (2022). Over Rs. 4000 Cr laundered via cryptos unearthed By ED in 1 year. *Times of India*. Retrieved from https://timesofindia.indiatimes.com/india/over-rs-4000cr-laundered-via-cryptos-unearthed-in-1-year/articleshow/87939180.cms

Tuwiner, J. (2023, January 1). *63+ Cryptocurrency statistics, facts & trend*. Retrieved from https://buybitcoinworldwide.com/cryptocurrency-statistics/#:~:text=Key%20Cryptocurrency%20Statistics%3A&text=300%2B%20million%20people%20around%20the,cryptocurrency%20users%20are%20bitcoin%20owners

ADDITONAL READING

Statista. (2023). *Number of identity-verified cryptoasset users from 2016 to December 2022 (in millions)*. Retrieved from https://www.statista.com/statistics/1202503/global-cryptocurrency-user-base/

KEY TERMS AND DEFINITIONS

Cryptocurrency: A cryptocurrency is a digital currency, which is an alternative form of payment created using encryption algorithms.

Virtual Currency: Virtual currency is a type of unregulated digital currency. It is not issued or controlled by a central bank. Examples of virtual currencies include Bitcoin, Litecoin, and XRP.

Bitcoin: Bitcoin is a decentralized digital currency that can be transferred on the peer-to-peer bitcoin network.

Cyber-fraud: Cyber fraud is the crime committed via a computer with the intent to corrupt another individual's personal and financial information stored online.

Crypto-crime: It is a crime that is an example of cybercrime related to theft (or the otherwise illegal acquisition) of cryptocurrencies and some of the methods or security vulnerabilities commonly exploited.

Money Laundering: It a predicate offense and a crime that includes concealment of the origins of illegally obtained money, typically by means of transfers involving foreign banks or legitimate businesses.

Tokenization: Tokenization is the process of replacing sensitive data with unique identification symbols that retain all the essential information about the data without compromising its security.

Decentralized finance (DeFi): Decentralized finance (DeFi) is an emerging financial technology based on secure distributed ledgers similar to those used by cryptocurrencies.

Non-fungible Tokens (NFTs): Non-fungible tokens are unique cryptographic tokens. They are digital watermarks that can be used to establish provenance and ownership of many types of assets, from tweets to artwork and real estate.

Decentralized Autonomous Organizations (DAOs): A decentralized autonomous organization (DAO) is an emerging form of legal structure that has no central governing body and whose members share a common goal to act in the best interest of the entity.

Chapter 5
Anti-Money Laundering Regulations and Entrepreneurship:
The Case of Africa

Folorunsho Ajide
https://orcid.org/0000-0003-3231-2423
University of Ilorin, Nigeria

ABSTRACT

The implications of money laundering activities in developing economies have yielded mixed findings. However, existing studies have not specifically examined the role of anti-money laundering (AML) regulations in relation to entrepreneurial development. This study aims to fill this gap by analyzing the impact of AML regulations on entrepreneurship in Africa. The analysis utilizes data from 21 African nations for 2012-2018. The empirical analysis employs panel-corrected standard errors (PCSEs) and instrumental variable (IV) regression. The results demonstrate a significant positive impact of AML regulations on entrepreneurship. It is also revealed that AML regulations bolster institutional quality, thereby fostering entrepreneurship. Moreover, the study finds that AML measures facilitate financial development, further promoting entrepreneurial growth in Africa. Importantly, these results remain robust even after conducting a thorough robustness check. Consequently, the study advocates for the implementation of effective AML regulations to enhance the African business environment.

INTRODUCTION

Goal 16 of the United Nations (UN) sustainable development agenda is specifically concerned with peace, a just and inclusive society which can be achieved by reducing insecurity and, the fight against crime (UN, 2019). Money laundering is a global concern and has been recognized to have a direct link to crime funding. It involves a situation where the perpetrators conceal proceeds of crime-related activities through the mainstream of the financial system, cross-border trading, or other efforts to make

DOI: 10.4018/978-1-6684-8587-3.ch005

it legitimate within an economy (Hendriyetty & Grewal, 2017). Money laundering constitutes a crime, and its reduction has been acknowledged to promote financial integrity, effective governance, well-being, and sustainable development in general (Canhoto, 2021). Various efforts are now put in place to formulate laws, regulations, and policies to combat money laundering issues in the economy (Ball *et al.*, 2015). Consequently, anti-money laundering (AML) refers to the initiatives such as financial action task force, sharing of intelligence and setting measures to combat issues related to money laundering. AML strengthens trust, confidence and transparency in the financial system and economy as a whole (Yildirim & Rafay, 2021). Given these critical roles, AML regulations have important impacts on business and entrepreneurial development in developing nations.

Interestingly, there are many channels by which money laundering may affect entrepreneurial ventures. Schumpeter (1934) explains the role of finance as a business fundamental for stimulating entrepreneurial effectiveness for growth and development in the economy. This theoretical proposition has gained empirical attention. A high level of financial development ensures efficient allocations of finances and induces growth through entrepreneurial productivity (Ajide, 2020; Ibrahim & Alagidede, 2020). However, in a situation of an underdeveloped financial system, scholars suggest that financial markets may hunt entrepreneurship and economic growth (Williams, 2019; Ajide & Ojeyinka, 2022). One of the factors that may reduce the effectiveness of financial development is money laundering activities. Raweh *et al.* (2017) hint that the financial system serves as the main channel for money laundering in which the proceeds from illegal transactions are launched into the economy. It destabilizes financial firms by eroding the integrity of the financial market and trust (Mekpor *et al.*, 2018). This necessitates the introduction of anti-money laundering regulation to enhance the efficiency of financial development in promoting entrepreneurship. Money laundering may also affect entrepreneurship through the weak institutional framework. A country with poor-quality institutions would have a high size shadow economy and money laundering transactions. As such, formal channel of shifting money becomes riskier due to poor institutions. Money laundering hampers legitimate business initiatives and promotes corrupt practices in government institutions. It increases inefficiencies and costs of conducting business venturing, making outputs less competitive. (Loayza *et al.*, 2019).

Sharman (2012) opines that the quality of AML regulations can be enhanced only if domestic regulatory arms of the economy are effective and strong enough for the application of international AML compliance. It also depends on the extent of the leadership authority in formulating laws and good policies for effective implementation. The economic rationale of money laundering control suggests that the significant financial burdens of AML regulations may reduce the revenue of the government for infrastructural development (Rafay, 2021a). This limits the ability to provide a conducive entrepreneurial environment (Reuter & Truman, 2004; Geiger & Wuensch, 2007). Niyetullayev and Almond (2014) suggest that laundered funds may be used for productive ventures and promote economic activities, entrepreneurship, and national development. Few studies investigating the role of AML regulations in the economic system suggest that AML promotes foreign direct investment, bank stability, financial development, and economic growth (Ofoeda *et al.* 2022a; Ofoeda *et al.* 2022b; Issah *et al.* 2022; Ofoeda *et al.* 2020). Ofoeda *et al.* (2022b) reveal that AML regulations rebrand the country's image and assist in attracting foreign investors. However, little or nothing is known about how AML regulations may influence entrepreneurial activities in developing nations. Djankov *et al.* (2006) opine better regulatory quality assists nations to grow faster, by supporting the entrepreneurial ecosystem. To this end, the present study proposes that an effective AML regulatory framework would be expected to promote better entrepreneurial outcomes, eliminate inefficient firms, and woo investors' confidence by upholding the integrity of the financial system.

The objective of this chapter is to examine the impact of anti-money laundering (AML) regulations on entrepreneurship in Africa. The contributions of this study are hereby summarized. The study focuses on African nations due to the prevalence of money laundering cases in the region. Some countries in Africa have been enlisted to have potential threats to the international financial system. Although countries like Ethiopia and Tunisia are said to operate an effective AML framework, Botswana, Ghana, Mauritius, and Zimbabwe are classified as high-risk nations (Issah *et al.* 2022). This study also analyzes the transmission channels of AML systems in Africa including financial development and quality of institutions. There is a lack of empirical evidence to showcase the implications of AML regulations on entrepreneurial development. The results show that AML regulations promote entrepreneurial development in Africa. In addition, the study shows that AML regulations boost the quality of institutions to promote entrepreneurial development. With AML regulations, the study finds that financial development is strengthening to protect entrepreneurs. These results identify the consequences of AML regulations and their vulnerability in the African region.

This chapter is organized into 5 subsections. The next section presents the literature review and hypotheses of the paper. Section 3 presents the methodology while section 4 presents the results and discussion of findings. In section 5, the conclusion and policy recommendations are presented.

LITERATURE REVIEW AND HYPOTHESES

AML Regulations and Entrepreneurship in Africa: An Overview

Money laundering activities flourish where structures can be set up to hide the ownership and nature of funds in the economy (Campbell, 2018). A successful money laundering operation can only take place where the perpetrators enjoy some degree of confidentiality (Warf, 2002). Weak regulation policy, tax havens, banking secrecy and confidentiality principles, and non-disclosure of firms' ownership serve as a foundation for successful money laundering activity in Africa (Christensen, 2012; Gilmour, 2020). Because this activity devastates the country's financial system and overall well-being, the role of anti-money laundering (AML) regulation is very important in restoring the entrepreneurial environment and building trust in the financial system and the economy as a whole. La Porta *et al.* (1998) state that an effective legal system enables information sharing, and transparency and fosters customer trust and confidence. The AML regulation ensures information symmetry and promotes efficiency and competition in the business environment. Table 1 reveals the Basel AML regulation index in selected African nations for 2014 and 2016. The index is computed from five important components of economic and financial crime data, namely: quality of countering activities on the financing of terrorism framework, financial transparency and standards, Bribery and corruption, public transparency and accountability, and legal and political risks (Agoba *et al.* 2019; Ofoeda *et al.* 2020; Rafay, 2023). The score ranged from 0 (lower risk) to 10 (high risk).

The table shows that all the countries have a higher risk of money laundering activities except Egypt, South Africa and Tunisia which have moderate risk profiles of economic and financial crimes related activities. Among the measures put in place by the government are the 1999 Algiers convention, the

2002 AU's intergovernmental meeting on the prevention of terrorism in Africa and the establishment of Financial Intelligent Units and personnel training to combat financial crimes in the regions.

Table 1. Anti-money laundering regulations index for selected countries in Africa (0=Low Risk 10=High Risk)

Country	2014	2016
Algeria	6.61	6.50
Botswana	5.84	5.95
Egypt	5.18	4.74
Lesotho	7.14	7.24
Liberia	7.52	7.41
Mali	8.06	7.86
Mauritius	5.74	5.82
Morocco	5.61	5.59
Namibia	6.69	6.64
Nigeria	7.14	6.97
Rwanda	n/a	6.70
Senegal	5.43	5.37
Sierra Leone	7.09	7.12
South Africa	4.95	4.86
Sudan	7.74	7.85
Togo	7.05	n/a
Tunisia	5.06	4.62
Uganda	7.84	8.01
Zambia	7.40	7.32
Zimbabwe	7.02	6.98
Tanzania	7.03	7.08

Source: Compiled by author from Basel Institute on Governance. N/A denotes not available.

Other measures include the adoption of the OAU convention on terrorism and collaboration with multinational organizations to formulate laws to criminalize the perpetrators of money laundering activities in Africa. These have helped in reducing entrepreneurial tension and further provide competitive opportunities for young entrepreneurs[1]. For instance, Togo is ranked top 10 economies in doing business regulatory reforms. Nigeria and Kenya have also improved in six areas of business environment reforms, while Somalia and South Sudan do not implement any reforms as shown in the Doing Business report (2020)[2].

Table 2. Average New business density

Sub-regions	2014	2016
Africa Eastern and Southern	n/a	2.01
Africa Western and Central	0.56	0.59
Sub-Saharan Africa	n/a	1.42
Arab World	0.59	0.69
Central Europe and the Baltics	0.29	3.53
East Asia & Pacific	4.91	6.29
Europe & Central Asia	3.50	3.87
Latin America & Caribbean	1.83	1.73
South Asia	0.09	0.12

Source: Extracted from World Bank – Doing business database

Table 2 shows the trend of entrepreneurial development proxied by the new business density for 2014 and 2016 by regions. It shows that South Asia has the lowest new business commencement followed by African regions while East Asia & Pacific has the highest rate of business registration per 1000 adults followed by Europe & Central Asia. This means that entrepreneurship in most African countries is still in the developing stage.

Table 3. Ease of doing business scores.

Sub-regions	2015	2016	2017	2018
Africa Eastern and Southern	49.76	50.57	51.72	52.92
Africa Western and Central	45.24	46.04	47.23	48.43
Middle East & North Africa	56.38	56.83	57.76	59.14
Sub-Saharan Africa	47.69	48.49	49.67	50.86
Least developed countries	45.49	46.13	47.05	48.22

Source: Extracted from World Bank – Doing business database

Furthermore, Table 3 presents the ease of doing business scores by sub-regions in Africa. It shows that Middle East & North African regions have consistently improved in the ease of doing business, followed by Eastern and Southern Africa. Overall, compared with least developed countries, African sub-regions are doing better. Several studies have shown that entrepreneurship has contributed immensely to economic growth and job creation in Africa (Abor & Quartey, 2010). However, most African nations still lag in regulations and inadequate infrastructures (Legas, 2015).

THEORIES, EMPIRICS AND HYPOTHESIS

AML Regulations and Entrepreneurship

Schumpeter (1934) regards entrepreneurship as the key ingredient for the development process. Entrepreneurs combine economic resources and coordinate such resources for economic changes via innovation and technology (Mishra & Zachary, 2014; Ajide, & Dada, 2023). Entrepreneurship involves new business creation and re-organising economic activities leading to disequilibrium that emerges through modern innovations and technology. Many factors have been discussed in the literature to affect entrepreneurship including macroeconomic factors, regulations, and social factors (Munemo, 2021; Ajide & Ojeyinka, 2022). However, little attention is given to the analysis of how crime, illicit finance and money laundering activities influence entrepreneurship.

Matti and Ross (2016) opine that crime increases uncertainties in the business environment with harmful effects on the entrepreneurial decision of business location. The economic theory of crime suggests that crime operations are being guided by the cost-benefit-analysis. The decision to engage in crime is a rational one emerging from the benefits of such operations (Becker, 1968). Becker's theory assists in modelling the nexus between entrepreneurship and money laundering activities (Matti & Ross, 2016). Money laundering activities grow with organized crime with devastating impacts on entrepreneurial development and economic growth (Raweh *et al*., 2017). Crime distorts the existence of business opportunities and entrepreneurial decisions. It increases the costs of doing business (Kuratko *et al*., 2000).

Higher costs of production discourage entrepreneurial activities and raise opportunity costs due to uncertainties in predicting the next course of action. Money laundering encourages crimes including bribery, human trafficking, gambling, embezzlement, prostitution rings and smuggling, with harmful effects on a country's reputation and its ability to attract entrepreneurs and foreign investors (Baldwin, 2004; Rafay, 2021b). Money laundering activities affect the locations of businesses (Rosenthal & Ross, 2010). Higher levels of money laundering activities increase the risk profile of a country and make it unattractive to local and foreign entrepreneurs. In the presence of money laundering, entrepreneurs spend more to provide security for business assets. Therefore, anti-money laundering regulations may do better for the business environment and economy in general (Wei, 2000). Concerning this, many nations have embraced anti-money laundering regulation policies. It is also essential to note that economic regulations can be discussed within two main frameworks: public choice and public interest theory (Pigou, 1932; Munemo, 2021).

The public interest theory suggests that government regulation is necessary to safeguard the public from the failure of market forces (Pigou, 1932). This kind of regulation is introduced to protect the consumers from harmful impacts of externalities and poor quality of goods and services from the providers. However, the public choice theorists view that the introduction of regulation is not necessarily benevolent; therefore, it may lead to inefficiencies due to the selfish interest of the politicians and government bureaucrats (Stigler 1971; Shleifer & Vishny, 1993). This implies that regulations can be a tool for controlling new firm creation. It may reduce competition and raise the existing firms' profiles. Porter's hypothesis also reveals that a fairly regulation policy can promote innovation, efficiency and reduce transaction costs (Chambers & O'Reilly, 2021). Therefore, anti-money laundering regulations may positively or negatively impact entrepreneurial activities. Munemo (2021) also suggests that trade regulations serve as a barrier to export entrepreneurship. Klapper *et al*. (2004), and Dreher and Gassebner (2013) document that excess regulations may serve as a disincentive for business creation. Omri

(2020) shows that institutional regulation increases the level of entrepreneurship. This study proposes, therefore, that:

H1: AML regulations significantly stimulate entrepreneurial development.

Institutions, AML Regulations and Entrepreneurship

In the literature, studies suggest that institutions are fundamental for entrepreneurial development (Ajide, 2022; Babajide *et al.*, 2021). Institution/governance is a set of norms and traditions being practiced by regulatory authorities (Amjad, Arshed & Anwar, 2021). The new institutional theory emphasizes that institutional arrangement shapes the actions of economic agents (North, 1990). This theory provides the basis for understanding how institutions may influence entrepreneurial ventures in the economy (Sobel, 2008; Baumol, 1996). There are two important distinctions that should be made in analyzing the economics of institutions: inclusive institutions and extractive institutions (Munemo, 2021). Inclusive institution or governance guarantees business and economic freedom with strong protection of property rights. This type of institution is the most appropriate for national development and efficient entrepreneurial resource allocation (North, 2000; Williamson, 2000; Acemoglu & Robinson 2012). It encourages entrepreneurship with adequate protection of individual freedom and property rights while extractive economic institutions represent the exact opposite of inclusive economic institutions in which government regulations are not business-friendly (Williamson, 2000). Therefore, good economic institutions should foster anti-money laundering activities and prevent criminal activities that may emerge from money laundering. A good institutional arrangement would make anti-money laundering regulations effective and denies corrupt officials any opportunity to conceal the origin of any illegal funds. An inclusive economic institutional arrangement ensures transparency and fosters entrepreneurial development.

The interactions of Anti-money laundering regulations with a business-friendly institutional framework are expected to control corruption and entice entrepreneurial activities. Although money laundering erodes the confidence and integrity of the financial system, it is expected that a good institutional system should flitter some ill-gotten money and uphold the integrity of the system by providing effective anti-money laundering tactics (Amjad, Arshed & Anwar, 2021). It is expected that an effective anti-money laundering regulation within a framework of good institutions would promote financial development and attract entrepreneurs. Entrepreneurial firms would benefit from an anti-money laundering system built on inclusive economic institutions because it creates healthy competition and the same level playing field for all firms in the economy. Money laundering may also allow firms to benefit from illicit proceeds and subsidize the cost of borrowing which is reflected in prices of products and services below market rates (McDowell & Novis, 2001). The study of Vaithilingam and Nair (2007) reveals that governance with an efficient legal system lowers money laundering. Alemika (2013) documents that political instability strengthens crime and money laundering activities. Okunlola (2014) shows that money laundering distorts the weak quality of institutions. The institutional and business environment promotes the effectiveness of regulations and thrives very well on transparency (Ajide & Ojeyinka, 2022). Therefore, country regulations should promote transparency in anti-money laundering (Campbell, 2018). This study proposes that:

H2: Good institutional framework strengthens the effectiveness of AML regulations in promoting entrepreneurship.

AML Regulations, Financial Development and Entrepreneurship

Schumpeter (1934) emphasizes that a good financial system should mobilize financial resources for growth and entrepreneurial development while Patrick (1966) opines that the financial sector is very important in the promotion of entrepreneurial venturing (Ajide & Ojeyinka, 2022). However, money laundering activities may erode the efficient functions of the financial system and further reduce the strength of the system due to the loss of confidence and integrity that emerged from money laundering issues. Therefore, the introduction of anti-money laundering schemes may have noticeable impacts on entrepreneurship through the channel of the financial system. Conventionally, it is believed that AML regulations would strengthen the financial development to deliver its mandate of encouraging entrepreneurship and further influences economic growth. Financial development stimulates entrepreneurial development and economic prospects by ensuring the efficient allocation of financial resources (Levine, 1998; Omri, 2020; Dutta & Meierrieks, 2021). Law *et al.* (2013) disclose that the financial system may not promote economic development if the system is corrupt and legally inefficient leading to mobilizing funds to unproductive enterprises. AML regulations reduce corruption and further enhance investors' protection and direct funds to productive activities in the economy. It ensures the stability of the financial sector and guarantees the survival of financial institutions. Ofoeda *et al.* (2022a) investigate the modulating roles of AML regulations in foreign direct investment (FDI)-growth nexus and report that the positive impact of FDI on growth is more effective in the presence of AML regulations. In Ofoeda *et al.* (2022b), the authors establish AML regulation stimulates FDI in a global sample. Based on this, this study proposes the third hypothesis (H3):

H3: the interactive effects of AML regulations and financial development significantly stimulate entrepreneurship.

METHODOLOGY

Empirical Model

The empirical strategies are in two stages. The study estimates the impact of AML regulations on entrepreneurship (Hypothesis 1) while controlling for the impact of other variables. For the second stage, the study uses mediation analysis to test the significance of the transmission mechanisms (i.e., Hypotheses 2 & 3). To do this, the author specifies equations (1-3). Equation (1) is used to examine the impact of AML regulations on entrepreneurship (Hypothesis 1(*H1*)) as stated below:

$$EN_{it} = \beta_0 + \beta_1 AML_{it} + \delta' X_{it} + \varepsilon_{it} \tag{1}$$

i and *t* are country and year identity respectively; *EN* is the dependent variable representing entrepreneurship. AML (anti-money laundering) regulations are an independent variable and *X* stands for the vector of other variables that influence entrepreneurship. Equation (2) is specified to test *Hypothesis (H2):*

$$EN_{it} = \beta_0 + \beta_1 AML_{it} + \beta_2 IQ_{it} + \beta_3 \left(AML \times IQ \right)_{it} + \delta' X_{it} + \varepsilon_{it} \quad (2)$$

IQ is the institutional quality and *AML×IQ* is the interactive term of AML and IQ. This is used to test the strength of institutional quality in enhancing the effectiveness of AML regulations on entrepreneurship. If $\beta 3$ is positive and significant, it implies that institutional quality assists in reducing the risk of money laundering activities towards entrepreneurial development, otherwise, it increases the risks. Finally, equation (3) is specified to test H*ypothesis 3 (H3):*

$$EN_{it} = \beta_0 + \beta_1 AML_{it} + \beta_2 FD_{it} + \beta_3 \left(AML \times FD \right)_{it} + \delta' X_{it} + \varepsilon_{it} \quad (3)$$

FD is the financial development and *AML×FD* is the interactive term to assess the effectiveness of the strength of AML regulations and FD on entrepreneurship. If $\beta 3$ is positive and significant, it implies that AML assists in reducing the risk of money laundering activities in the financial system towards entrepreneurial development, otherwise, it increases the risks. As stated earlier, X stands for the vector of control variables that influence entrepreneurship in Africa.

In the 3 equations, the control variables are inflation (Inf) to proxy macroeconomic instability, foreign direct investment inflow (FDI) is used to capture the influence of multinational firms in the domestic economy, infrastructural development (LAIDI), economic growth (GR), and business regulation (STUP) measured as the number of requirements to register a business. This study also controls the presence of economic globalization (LEGLO). The choice of control variables is informed by the extant literature. Literature suggests that entrepreneurship and economic growth have interconnections (Rodrigues Brás & Soukiazis, 2018; Adusei, 2016; Wennekers *et al.*, 2005). Munemo (2018) explains that growth may be negative or not significantly influence entrepreneurship in Africa due to its non-inclusiveness. Inflation (Inf) is one of the macroeconomic environments that may negatively influence entrepreneurial development if it is too harsh for entrepreneurs. It creates uncertainties for business (Parker, 2009). FDI should influence entrepreneurial development due to the spillover effects of foreign innovation and its learning impacts on domestic firms (Munemo, 2018). Infrastructural development also creates a conducive environment for entrepreneurial activities to survive (Audretsch *et al.* 2015; Ajide, 2020). It is also expected that globalization would positively influence entrepreneurship because it opens many potential opportunities for African businesses (Ajide, *et al.* 2021; Coulibaly *et al.* 2017).

Estimation Techniques

The empirical strategies of the study take two stages. First, the models (1)-(3) are estimated via the panel-corrected standard errors (PCSEs) estimation technique. This technique is efficient in the presence of any potential autocorrelation and heteroscedasticity in the datasets. It also corrects for interconnection between cross-sectional units that may lead to contemporaneous errors. Unlike feasible generalized least squares, it is more appropriate for the case of short-period dimension panel datasets (Beck & Katz, 1995). For the second stage, this study further employs the instrumental variable (IV)-regression technique as a robustness test. The technique is useful in the correction of any endogeneity or reversed causality that may occur among the variable of interest. This technique is an extension of pooled ordinary least squares. In its implementation, the study uses the lagged value of the variable as an instrument to follow the extant literature (Ajide & Soyemi, 2022; Ferede, 2019).

Data and Measurement of Variables

The study covers 21 African countries selected based on data availability. These countries are Algeria, Botswana, Egypt, Lesotho, Liberia, Mali, Mauritius, Morocco, Namibia, Nigeria, Rwanda, Senegal, Sierra Leone, South Africa, Sudan, Tanzania, Togo, Tunisia, Uganda, Zambia, and Zimbabwe. The period of study is from 2012 to 2018. This period is chosen because AML data started in 2012 while entrepreneurship data started in 2006. To have a balanced panel, the period of study starts in 2012 and ends in 2018. Data for this study are obtained from various sources which include World development indicators, the KOF Globalization database, the World Bank Doing Business database, the African Infrastructure index database, and Basel Institute on Governance. In specific, the study proxied entrepreneurship as a new business density obtained from the World Bank entrepreneurship snapshot database while the Basel AML regulation index is obtained from Basel Institute on Governance. Data on infrastructure are obtained from the African infrastructure development database. Economic globalization data are obtained from the KOF Globalization database which covers de jure and de facto measures of economic globalization. The number of requirements to register a business is sourced from the Doing Business database. Institutional index data are obtained from World Governance indicators. IMF Data on broad-based financial development is used to proxy financial development in Africa. Other data are sourced from World Development indicators. Table 4 summarizes the measurement and sources of the data.

Table 4. Source of Data and Measurement of Variables.

Variable	Measurements	Sources of data
Entrepreneurship (EN)	New businesses registered per 1000 population of age between 15 and 64	Entrepreneurship database of World Bank
Business regulation (Startup)	Number of procedures to register new ventures	Entrepreneurship database of World Bank
AML Regulation Index (AML)	Originally, the AML index ranged from 0=Low Risk and 10=High Risk. However, the author rescales the index using. AML (re-scaled) = −1*(AMLR-10) for better interpretation, implying a higher score for AML regulation effectiveness.	Basel Institute on Governance
Financial Development (FD)	Index of broad-based financial system development	IMF database
Foreign direct investment (FDI)	FDI inflow (% of GDP)	World Development Indicators
Economic growth (GR)	GDP per capita (annual growth)	=do=
Inflation (Inf)	Inflation, CPI (annual %)	=do=
Economic globalization (LEGIO)	Natural log of economic globalization	KOF Globalization Index database
Infrastructure (LAIDI)	Aggregate African Infrastructure Development index, a natural log is taking.	African Development Bank Group
Institutional Index (IQ)	It is measured as the average index of the six institutional indicators provided by the World Governance database that ranged from -2.5 to +2.5. The followings are the indicators: control of corruption (COR), government effectiveness (GOE), political stability and absence of violence/terrorism (POS), regulatory quality (REQ), rule of law (ROL) and voice and accountability (VOA)	World Governance database

Source: compiled by the author

The Basel AML regulation index is an index for assessing the money laundering risk and terrorist financing activities. The assessment focuses on the effectiveness of anti-money laundering regulations to reduce or eradicate money laundering/terrorist financing in the economy (Memdani *et al.* 2021). The index ranges from 0 (lowest risk) to 10 (highest risk). However, we re-scale the AML index using the formula below:

AML (re-scaled) = −1*(AMLR-10) (4)

This helps for a better interpretation of the direct coefficient of AML regulation and the indirect coefficients that emerged when interacting AML with FD and IQ. The use of this formula follows the extant literature (Ofoeda *et al.* 2022a; Ofoeda *et al.* 2022b). Therefore, a high figure means lower risk, implying a more effective AML regulation. In other words, a higher score corresponds to the effectiveness of AML regulation in reducing money laundering activities. Tables 5 and 6 show the descriptive analysis and pairwise correlation between the variables. The mean value of new business density (a proxy for entrepreneurship) is 2.241 with a maximum value of 20.090. AML regulation index is on average 3.484 on a scale of 10 points, implying that African countries still need to do more to have a more effective regulatory framework. However, some countries in the continent still have their AML index up to 5.878 (maximum).

Table 5. Descriptive statistics

Variable	Obs.	Mean	Std.Dev.	Min	Max
EN	147	2.241	3.904	0.008	20.090
Inf.	147	6.361	7.389	-2.409	36.906
FDI	147	3.994	8.822	-1.032	84.894
LEGLO	147	49.504	10.532	32.443	85.185
LAIDI	147	31.411	23.961	6.608	85.846
STUP	147	7.857	2.729	4	14
AML(Re-scaled)	147	3.484	0.903	1.990	5.878
IQ	147	-0.418	0.591	-1.660	0.853
FD	147	0.216	0.134	0.056	0.626

Source: Author's Calculation

Table 6. Pairwise correlation

Variable	EN	AML (Re-scale)	Inf.	FDI	GR	LEGLO	LAIDI	STUP	IQ	FD
EN	1.000									
AML(Re-scaled)	0.326*	1.000								
Inf.	-0.141	-0.057	1.000							
FDI	-0.118	-0.190*	-0.045	1.000						
GR	-0.086	-0.100	-0.076	0.174*	1.000					
LEGLO	0.544*	0.259*	-0.316*	0.039	-0.001	1.000				
LAIDI	0.411*	0.644*	-0.090	-0.228*	-0.155	0.400*	1.000			
STUP	-0.063	-0.167*	0.314*	-0.170*	-0.043	-0.346*	0.050	1.000		
IQ	0.664*	0.321	-0.424*	-0.062	-0.003	0.694*	0.331*	-0.299*	1.000	
FD	0.529*	0.562*	-0.132	-0.112	-0.196*	0.601*	0.694*	-0.173*	0.582*	1.000

Source: Author's Calculation - *Denotes 5% level of significance

Pairwise correlation coefficients among the variables are significant at a 5 percent level. In specific, there is a significant positive relationship between AML regulations and new business creation as shown in Table 6. In addition, the coefficients of the variables are below the threshold value of 0.8. Therefore, there is no evidence of multicollinearity. Also, the relationship between AML and entrepreneurship is presented in Figure 1, showing that there is a positive relationship between AML (Re-scaled) and entrepreneurship. In other words, an effective AML promotes entrepreneurial development in Africa. This relationship is further elAborated in the regression results presented in the next section.

Figure 1. The relationship Between Re-scaled AML and entrepreneurship
Source: own chart

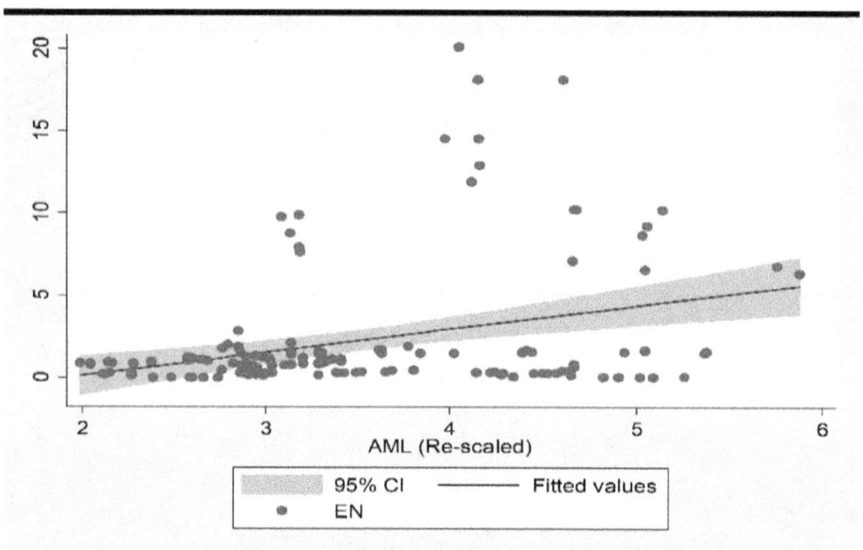

EMPIRICAL ANALYSIS AND FINDINGS

Baseline Results

The results of the models estimated are reported in Table 7. It shows that the coefficients of AML are positive and significant; implying that AML regulations impact entrepreneurial development positively. This indicates that entrepreneurs are interested in locations that can give the best entrepreneurial conditions. The prevalence of money laundering activities has several implications for a nation. One relates to reputational risks and blacklisting in the international scene. Reputational damage may increase transaction costs and increase entrepreneurial risks. In this case, a good AML framework would reduce the level of risk and uncertainty associated with entrepreneurial investment. It further enhances transparency in the entrepreneurial environment.

Table 7. Results from panel-corrected standard errors (PCSEs)

Variable	(1)	(2)	(3)
AML (Re-scaled)	0.612* (0.080)	1.068** (0.011)	0.138** (0.004)
Inf.	-0.003 (0.830)	0.073** (0.001)	-0.010 (0.505)
FDI	-0.028*** (0.000)	-0.003 (0.501)	-0.032*** (0.000)
GR	-0.044 (0.568)	-0.033 (0.527)	-0.013 (0.860)
LEGLO	23.309*** (0.000)	1.258 (0.538)	20.296*** (0.000)
LAIDI	1.041 (0.221)	1.990*** (0.001)	-0.077 (0.892)
STUP	0.1789** (0.019)	0.139*** (0.002)	0.190*** (0.003)
IQ		-4.129* (0.098)	
IQ× AML(Re-scaled)		2.399*** (0.001)	
FD			-4.141 (0.411)
FD× AML(Re-scaled)			2.565*** (0.017)
Constant	-41.715*** (0.000)	-6.403* (0.092)	-33.842*** (0.000)
Wald test-chi	666.28***	274.63***	590.27***
R-sq.	0.366	0.582	0.393
No. of group	21	21	21

On the transmission channels, it is widely agreed that the institutional quality of Africa is weak (Olaniyi & Oladeji, 2021). The estimated results also confirm this stance because the direct coefficient of institutional quality is negative and significant. This implies that weak institutions distort the economic fortunes of entrepreneurs in Africa. However, the interactive impact of institutions and AML regulations are positive and significant, implying that AML regulation assists in improving institutional quality and further encourages entrepreneurial development. The entrepreneurial intention is attracted to the economies with sound AML regulations and strong quality institutions because of the potential economic prosperity (Ajide & Osinubi, 2022; Ofoeda *et al.* 2022a). Nations with recurrence incidence of money laundering are featured with high levels of policy issues, exchange rate volatility and instability in other macroeconomic parameters. This may discourage entrepreneurial mindsets. However, an effective system of AML should be expected to enhance a stable business environment and attract new firm creations.

Furthermore, the results in column (3) show the coefficient of financial development is negative and significant; implying that financial development does not spur entrepreneurship in Africa. This result further emphasizes the results of Ajide and Ojeyinka (2022). The authors explain that financial development is very weak and that there is a threshold for the financial system that must be reached before improving entrepreneurship. Accordingly, the coefficient of the interactive variable of financial development and AML regulation is positive and significant; implying that AML regulations help in improving and wooing confidence in African financial development. Overall, the results suggest that if African nations implement sound AML regulations, they are better positioned to attract domestic and foreign entrepreneurs. Countries with sound institutional quality would have good protection for property rights and there would be stable political and business environments which are very important for entrepreneurial development.

On the control variables, the coefficients of inflation, business regulations and infrastructures are positive and significant while the coefficient of FDI is negative. These results support the submission of Audretsch *et al.* (2015) that infrastructural development promotes entrepreneurship and that of Ajide and Ojeyinka (2022) who document that good business regulation and macroeconomic instability promote entrepreneurship in Africa. Inflation promotes entrepreneurial ventures mainly to compensate for a drop in real income from employment or job loss during economic crises or natural disasters (Klapper & Love, 2011; Munemo, 2018). Our results also suggest that the impact of FDI is negative and significant illustrating the results of Munemo (2018) and Zheng and Musteen (2018). These authors suggest that FDI may crowd out entrepreneurial activities because they compete with local producers who are lagging in technology and advanced innovations. In addition, local entrepreneurs may be hired by multinational corporations for wage employment with attractive wages and salaries. Consequently, the level of entrepreneurial activities may shrink in the African economy. Furthermore, the coefficient of economic globalization is positive and significant; implying that globalization improves entrepreneurship. This result is consistent with the submission of Coulibaly *et al.* (2017).

Testing for Robustness

The usual empirical challenge in examining the nexus between entrepreneurship and its determinant is the issue of endogeneity due to variable omission biasedness and simultaneity (Wooldridge, 2012). The omitted variables may occur due to the inability to include all determinants of entrepreneurship as control variables in the model while the simultaneity issue may be due to reversed causality between dependent variables and its determinants. Based on this, this study further utilizes instrumental variable estimation techniques to address the endogeneity issue of the model. To do this, the study follows the extant literature to regress the entrepreneurship variable on its first lag in the first stage regression while the fitted value is used to instrument the main regression (Asongu & Tchamyou, 2015; Ferede, 2019).

Table 8. Results from IV- regression

Variable	(1)	(2)	(3)
AML(Re-scaled)	1.889** (0.021)	0.644* (0.071)	0.360** (0.018)
Inf.	0.041 (0.510)	0.067** (0.018)	0.035 (0.293)
FDI	-2.057** (0.042)	-0.008 (0.511)	-0.045** (0.017)
GR	0.591 (0.121)	-0.017 (0.921)	-0.061 (0.369)
LEGLO	40.682*** (0.000)	3.780 (0.181)	46.389*** (0.000)
LAIDI	-7.370 (0.112)	2.699*** (0.002)	-0.943 (0.412)
STUP	-0.833* (0.059)	-0.006 (0.914)	0.362** (0.011)
IQ		-3.450** (0.017)	
IQ× AML(Re-scaled)		1.813*** (0.000)	
FD			-25.995*** (0.003)
FD× AML(Re-scaled)			5.535*** (0.001)
Constant	-37.464*** (0.001)	-9.866** (0.031)	-74.974*** (0.000)
Wald test-chi	33.80***	124.11***	100.41***
Hansen's J /P-vale	0.490	0.385	0.975
No. of group	21	21	21

The results of IV-regression are reported in Table 8; showing that AML regulations improve entrepreneurship. In addition, there is not much difference when comparing these results with that of PSCEs in terms of sign and significance. However, the parameters estimated are robust and more efficient. Hansen's J–statistic shows that the instruments used are valid. The Wald test is significant and robust, showing the overall significance of the model.

CONCLUSION AND POLICY RECOMMENDATIONS

The existing bodies of literature suggest the implications of money laundering on economic growth and development. However, none of this study specifically devotes attention to the role of anti-money laundering regulations on entrepreneurial development. This study, therefore, examines the role of AML regulations in African entrepreneurship. This is done in two ways; it assesses the direct impact of AML regulations on entrepreneurship. Second, the study also examines the indirect impacts of AML regulations on entrepreneurship through two transmission channels: quality of institutions and financial development. The study relies on data from 21 African nations from 2012 through 2018. Using panel-corrected standard errors (PCSEs) estimation technique and instrumental variables' regression, the study shows that AML regulations improve entrepreneurship in the selected African economies.

On the results of transmission channels, the AML regulations strengthen the institutions for the promotion of new business creation. Further analysis shows that AML regulations enhance the integrity of financial development in encouraging entrepreneurial intentions in Africa. These findings support the three hypotheses developed for the study. It shows that AML regulations are important in fast-tracking entrepreneurial development; thereby supporting public interest theory. In addition, the indirect effect shows that AML regulations strengthen institutional quality in boosting African entrepreneurship. This reiterates the preposition of new institutional theorists that institutional framework may complement governments' regulations to enhance the efficiency of institutional authorities in the economy to bring out positive outcomes.

Based on these outcomes, the following recommendations emerged. First, an effective AML regulatory framework should be implemented to promote entrepreneurial intentions in African nations. Second, countries should formulate policies to protect the integrity and transparency of the financial sector. Third, AML laws and compliances should be incorporated into the institutional structure to strengthen entrepreneurial development. This will help to combat corruption and enhance the reputation of African regions in the international environment. Adequate supervisory schemes on AML compliances would help in making the financial system effective in the promotion of African entrepreneurship.

One of the main limitations of this study relates to the regional analysis. It does not look at the policy specificities of each country within Africa. This limitation is related to the short period of the data (2012-2018). Future studies should overcome this shortcoming whenever the data are available for the country's level analysis. Future studies can also look at other transmission channels in which AML regulations may impact entrepreneurship.

DECLARATION

The author declares that the manuscript follows ethical standards and there are no potential conflicts of interest with respect to the research, authorship and/or publication of this chapter.

DISCLAIMER

The contents and views of this chapter are expressed by the author in his personal capacity. It is not necessary for the Editor and the Publisher to agree with these viewpoints, and they are not responsible for any duty of care in this regard.

ACKNOWLEDGMENT

The author extends sincere gratitude to

- The Editor and the International Editorial Advisory Board (IEAB) of this book, who initially desk reviewed, arranged a rigorous double/triple-blind review process, and conducted a thorough, minute, and critical final review before accepting the chapter for publication.
- All anonymous reviewers who provided very constructive feedback for thorough revision, improvement, extension, and fine-tuning of the chapter.
- All colleagues, assistants and well-wishers who assisted to complete this task.

REFERENCES

Abor, J., & Quartey, P. (2010). Issues in SME development in Ghana and South Africa. *International Research Journal of Finance and Economics*, *39*(6), 218–228.

Acemoglu, D., & Robinson, J. A. (2012). *Why Nations Fail.* Crown Business.

Adusei, M. (2016). Does entrepreneurship promote economic growth in Africa? *African Development Review*, *28*(2), 201–214. doi:10.1111/1467-8268.12190

Agoba, A. M., Abor, J. Y., Osei, K., Sa-Aadu, J., Amoah, B., & Dzeha, G. C. O. (2019). Central Bank independence, elections and fiscal policy in Africa: Examining the moderating role of political institutions. *International Journal of Emerging Markets*, *14*(5), 809–830. doi:10.1108/IJOEM-08-2018-0423

Ajide, F. M. (2020). Infrastructure and Entrepreneurship: Evidence from Africa. *Journal of Developmental Entrepreneurship*, *2*(1), 1–20.

Ajide, F. M., & Dada, J. T. (2023). Poverty, entrepreneurship, and economic growth in Africa. *Poverty & Public Policy*, *15*(2), 1–28. doi:10.1002/pop4.368

Ajide, F. M., & Ojeyinka, T. A. (2022). Financial development and entrepreneurship: Insights from Africa. *Journal of Financial Regulation and Compliance*, *30*(5), 596–617. doi:10.1108/JFRC-09-2021-0079

Ajide, F. M., & Osinubi, T. T. (2020). Foreign aid and entrepreneurship in Africa: The role of remittances and institutional quality. *Economic Change and Restructuring*, *55*(1), 193–224. doi:10.100710644-020-09305-5

Ajide, F. M., Osinubi, T. T., & Dada, J. T. (2021). Economic Globalization, Entrepreneurship, and Inclusive Growth in Africa. *Journal of Economic Integration*, *36*(4), 689–717. doi:10.11130/jei.2021.36.4.689

Ajide, F. M., & Soyemi, K. A. (2022). Oil Rent, entrepreneurial start-ups, and institutional quality: Insights from African oil-rich countries. *Entrepreneurial Business and Economics Review*, *10*(1), 35–49. doi:10.15678/EBER.2022.100103

Alemika, E. E. (2013). *The impact of organized crime on governance in West Africa*. Friedrich Ebert-Stiftung.

Amjad, M. M., Arshed, N., & Anwar, M. A. (2021). Money Laundering and Institutional Quality: The Case of Developing Countries. In A. Rafay (Ed.), *Money Laundering and Terrorism Financing in Global Financial Systems* (pp. 91–107). IGI Global., doi:10.4018/978-1-7998-8758-4.ch004

Asongu, S. A., & Tchamyou, V. S. (2015). The impact of entrepreneurship on knowledge economy in Africa. *Journal of Entrepreneurship in Emerging Economies*, *8*(1), 101–131. doi:10.1108/JEEE-08-2015-0045

Audretsch, D. B., Heger, D., & Veith, T. (2015). Infrastructure and entrepreneurship. *Small Business Economics*, *44*(2), 219–230. doi:10.100711187-014-9600-6

Babajide, A., Lawal, A., Asaleye, A., Okafor, T., & Osuma, G. (2020). Financial stability and entrepreneurship development in sub-Sahara Africa: Implications for sustainable development goals. *Cogent Social Sciences*, *6*(1), 1798330. doi:10.1080/23311886.2020.1798330

Baldwin, F. N. Jr. (2004). The financing of terror in the age of the internet: Willful blindness, greed or a political statement? *Journal of Money Laundering and Control*, *8*(2), 127–158. doi:10.1108/13685200510621154

Ball, K., Canhoto, A. I., Daniel, E., Dibb, S., Meadows, M., & Spiller, K. (2015). *The private security state? Surveillance, consumer data and the war on terror*. Copenhagen Business School Press.

Baumol, W. J. (1996). Entrepreneurship: Productive, unproductive, and destructive. *Journal of Business Venturing*, *11*(1), 3–22. doi:10.1016/0883-9026(94)00014-X

Beck, N., & Katz, J. N. (1995). What to do (and not to do) with time-series cross-section data. *The American Political Science Review*, *89*(3), 634–647. doi:10.2307/2082979

Becker, G. (1968). Crime and punishment: An economic approach. *Journal of Political Economy*, *76*(2), 169–217. doi:10.1086/259394

Campbell, L. (2018). Dirty cash (money talks): 4AMLD and the money laundering regulations. *Criminal Law Review (London, England)*, *2*, 102–122.

Canhoto, I. A. (2021). Leveraging machine learning in the global fight against money laundering and terrorism financing: An affordances perspective. *Journal of Business Research*, *131*, 441–452. doi:10.1016/j.jbusres.2020.10.012 PMID:33100427

Chambers, D., & O'Reilly, C. (2021). The economic theory of regulation and inequality. *Public Choice*, *193*(1-2), 63–78. doi:10.100711127-021-00922-w

Christensen, J. (2012). The hidden trillions: Secrecy, corruption, and the offshore interface. *Crime, Law, and Social Change*, *57*(3), 325–343. doi:10.100710611-011-9347-9

Coulibaly, S. K., Erbao, C., & Mekongcho, M. T. (2017). Economic globalization, entrepreneurship, and development. *Technological Forecasting and Social Change*, *127*(C), 271–280.

Djankov, S., McLiesh, C., & Ramalho, R. M. (2006). Regulation and growth. *Economics Letters*, *92*(3), 395–401. doi:10.1016/j.econlet.2006.03.021

Dreher, A., & Gassebner, M. (2013). Greasing the Wheels? The Impact of Regulations and Corruption on Firm Entry. *Public Choice*, *155*(3-4), 413–432. doi:10.100711127-011-9871-2

Dutta, N., & Meierrieks, D. (2021). Financial development and entrepreneurship. *International Review of Economics & Finance*, *73*, 114–126. doi:10.1016/j.iref.2021.01.002

Ferede, E. (2021). Entrepreneurship and personal income tax: Evidence from Canadian provinces. *Small Business Economics*, *56*(4), 1765–1781. doi:10.100711187-019-00226-w

Geiger, H., & Wuensch, O. (2007). The fight against money laundering: An economic analysis of a cost-benefit paradox on. *Journal of Money Laundering Control*, *10*(1), 91–105. doi:10.1108/13685200710721881

Gilmour, P. M. (2020). Lifting the veil on beneficial ownership: Challenges of implementing the UK's registers of beneficial owners. *Journal of Money Laundering Control*, *23*(4), 717–734. doi:10.1108/JMLC-02-2020-0014

Hendriyetty, N., & Grewal, S. B. (2017). Macroeconomics of money laundering: Effects and measurements. *Journal of Financial Crime*, *24*(1), 65–81. doi:10.1108/JFC-01-2016-0004

Ibrahim, M., & Alagidede, I. P. (2020). Asymmetric effects of financial development on economic growth in Ghana. *Journal of Sustainable Finance & Investment*, *10*(4), 371–387. doi:10.1080/20430795.2019.1706142

Issah, M., Antwi, S., Antwi, S. K., & Amarh, P. (2022). Anti-Money Laundering Regulations and Banking Sector Stability in Africa. *Cogent Economics & Finance*, *10*(1), 2069207. doi:10.1080/23322039.2022.2069207

Klapper, L., Laeven, L., & Rajan, R. (2004). *Barriers to entrepreneurship* (NBER Working Paper, Paper No: 10380), National Bureau of Economic Resaerch.

Klapper, L., & Love, I. (2011). The impact of the financial crisis on new firm registration. *Economics Letters*, *113*(1), 1–4. doi:10.1016/j.econlet.2011.05.048

Kuratko, D. F., Hornsby, J. S., Naffziger, D. W., & Hodgetts, R. M. (2000). Crime and small business: An exploratory study of cost and prevention issues in US firms. *Journal of Small Business Management*, *38*(3), 1–13.

La Porta, R., Lopez-de-Silanes, F., Shleifer, A., & Vishny, R. W. (1998). Law and finance. *Journal of Political Economy*, *106*(6), 1113–1155. doi:10.1086/250042

Law, S. H., Azman-saini, W. N. W., & Ibrahim, M. H. (2013). Institutional quality thresholds and the finance – growth nexus. *Journal of Banking & Finance*, *37*(12), 5373–5381. doi:10.1016/j.jbankfin.2013.03.011

Legas, H. (2015). Challenges to entrepreneurial success in Sub-Saharan Africa: A comparative perspective. *European Journal of Business and Management*, *7*(11), 23–35.

Levine, R. (1998). The legal environment, banks, and long-run economic growth. *Journal of Money, Credit and Banking*, *30*(3), 596–613. doi:10.2307/2601259

Loayza, N., Villa, E., & Misas, M. (2019). Illicit activity and money laundering from an economic growth perspective: A model and an application to Colombia. *Journal of Economic Behavior & Organization*, *159*, 442–487. doi:10.1016/j.jebo.2017.10.002

Matti, J., & Ross, M. (2016). Does crime affect entrepreneurship? A discussion of the current literature. *Journal of Entrepreneurship and Public Policy*, *5*(3), 254–272. doi:10.1108/JEPP-05-2016-0018

McDowell, J., & Novis, G. (2001). The consequences of money laundering. *Economic Focus*, *6*(2), 6–8.

Mekpor, E. S., Aboagye, A., & Welbeck, J. (2018). The determinants of anti-money laundering compliance among the Financial Action Task Force (FATF) member states. *Journal of Financial Regulation and Compliance*, *26*(3), 442–459. doi:10.1108/JFRC-11-2017-0103

Memdani, L., Kademi, T. T., & Rafay, A. (2021). Effect of Terrorism Financing on selected Global Indices: The Case of 2015 Paris Attacks. In A. Rafay (Ed.), *Money Laundering and Terrorism Financing in Global Financial Systems* (pp. 183–205). IGI Global., doi:10.4018/978-1-7998-8758-4.ch008

Mishra, C. S., & Zachary, R. K. (2014). *The Theory of Entrepreneurship*. Palgrave Macmillan. doi:10.1057/9781137371461

Munemo, J. (2018). Entrepreneurial success in Africa: How relevant are foreign direct investment and financial development? *African Development Review*, *30*(4), 372–385. doi:10.1111/1467-8268.12345

Munemo, J. (2021). The effect of regulation-driven trade barriers and governance quality on export entrepreneurship. *Regulation & Governance*, *16*(4), 1119–1140. doi:10.1111/rego.12384

Niyetullayev, N. N., & Almond, P. (2014). Money laundering and the shadow economy in Kazakhstan. *Journal of Money Laundering Control*, *17*(2), 128–140. doi:10.1108/JMLC-05-2013-0015

North, D. (1990). *Institutions, Institutional Change and Economic Performance*. Cambridge University Press. doi:10.1017/CBO9780511808678

Ofoeda, I., Agbloyor, E. K., & Abor, J. Y. (2022b). How do anti-money laundering systems affect FDI flows across the globe? *Cogent Economics & Finance*, *10*(1), 2058735. doi:10.1080/23322039.2022.2058735

Ofoeda, I., Agbloyor, E. K., Abor, J. Y., & Osei, K. A. (2020). Anti-money laundering regulations and financial sector development. *International Journal of Finance & Economics*, *24*(2), 1–20.

Ofoeda, I., Agbloyor, E. K., Abor, J. Y., & Osei, K. A. (2022a). Foreign direct investment, anti- money laundering regulations and economic growth. *Journal of International Development*, *34*(3), 670–692. doi:10.1002/jid.3582

Okunlola, O. C. (2014). Money Laundering: A Threat to Sustainable Democracy in Nigeria. *Journal of Economics and Sustainable Development*, *5*(2), 85–98.

Olaniyi, C. O., & Oladeji, S. I. (2021). Moderating the effect of institutional quality on the finance–growth nexus: Insights from West African countries. *Economic Change and Restructuring*, *54*(1), 43–74. doi:10.100710644-020-09275-8

Omri, A. (2020). Formal versus informal entrepreneurship in emerging economies: The roles of governance and the financial sector. *Journal of Business Research*, *108*, 277–290. doi:10.1016/j.jbusres.2019.11.027

Parker, S. C. (2009). *The Economics of Entrepreneurship*. Cambridge University Press. doi:10.1017/CBO9780511817441

Patrick, H. T. (1966). Financial development and economic growth in underdeveloped countries. *Economic Development and Cultural Change*, *14*(2), 174–189. doi:10.1086/450153

Pigou, A. (1932). *The Economics of Welfare* (4th ed.). Macmillan.

Rafay, A. (Ed.). (2021a). *Money Laundering and Terrorism Financing in Global Financial Systems*. IGI Global., doi:10.4018/978-1-7998-8758-4

Rafay, A. (Ed.). (2021b). *HandBook of Research on Theory and Practice of Financial Crimes*. IGI Global., doi:10.4018/978-1-7998-5567-5

Rafay, A. (Ed.). (2023). *Concepts, Cases, and Regulations in Financial Fraud and Corruption*. IGI Global., doi:10.4018/978-1-6684-5007-9

Raweh, B. A., Erbao, C., & Shihadeh, F. (2017). Review the literature and theories on anti-money. *Asian Development Policy Review*, *5*(3), 140–147. doi:10.18488/journal.107.2017.53.140.147

Reuter, P., & Truman, E. M. (2004). *Chasing Dirty Money: The Fight against Money Laundering*. Institute for International Economics.

Rodrigues Brás, G., & Soukiazis, E. (2018). The determinants of entrepreneurship at the country level: A panel data approach. *Entrepreneurship Research Journal*, *9*(4), 20160060. doi:10.1515/erj-2016-0060

Rosenthal, S., & Ross, A. (2010). Violent crime, entrepreneurship and cities. *Journal of Urban Economics*, *67*(1), 135–149. doi:10.1016/j.jue.2009.09.001

Schumpeter, J. A. (1934). *Theorie Der Wirtschaftlichen Enwicklung* [the Theory of Economic Development]. (R. Opie, Trans.). Duncker and Humblot.

Sharman, J. (2012). Chasing kleptocrats' loot: Narrowing the effectiveness gap. *U4 Issue*. Retrieved from https://www.cmi.no/publications/4514-chasing-kleptocrats-loot

Shleifer, A., & Vishny, W. (1993). Corruption. *The Quarterly Journal of Economics*, *108*(3), 599–617. doi:10.2307/2118402

Sobel, R. S. (2008). Testing Baumol: Institutional quality and the productivity of entrepreneurship. *Journal of Business Venturing*, *23*(6), 641–655. doi:10.1016/j.jbusvent.2008.01.004

Stigler, G. (1971). The theory of economic regulation. *The Bell Journal of Economics and Management Science*, *2*(1), 3–21. doi:10.2307/3003160

U.N. (2019). About the Sustainable Development Goals. United Nations. https://www. un.org/sustainabledevelopment/sustainable-development-goals/. Accessed 26 April 2022.

Vaithilingam, S., & Nair, M. (2007). Factors affecting money laundering: Lesson for developing countries. *Journal of Money Laundering Control, 10*(3), 352–363. doi:10.1108/13685200710763506

Warf, B. (2002). Tailored for Panama: Offshore banking at the crossroads of the Americas. *Geografiska Annaler. Series B, Human Geography*, *84*(1), 33–47. doi:10.1111/j.0435-3684.2002.00112.x

Wei, S. J. (2000). How taxing is corruption on international investors? *The Review of Economics and Statistics*, *82*(1), 1–11. doi:10.1162/003465300558533

Wennekers, S., Van Stel, A., Carree, M., & Thurik, R. (2010). The relationship between entrepreneurship and economic development: Is it U-shaped? *Foundations and Trends in Entrepreneurship*, *6*(3), 167–237. doi:10.1561/0300000023

Williams, K. (2019). Do political institutions improve the diminishing effect of financial deepening on growth? Evidence from developing countries. *Journal of Economics and Business*, *103*, 13–24. doi:10.1016/j.jeconbus.2018.11.003

Williamson, O. (2000). New Institutional Economics. *Journal of Economic Literature*, *38*(3), 595–613. doi:10.1257/jel.38.3.595

Wooldridge, J. (2012). In Introductory econometrics: A modern approach (5th ed.). South-Western: Cengage Learning.

Yildirim, Y., & Rafay, A. (2021). Anti-Money Laundering in Insurance Sector: The Turkish Case. In A. Rafay (Ed.), *Money Laundering and Terrorism Financing in Global Financial Systems* (pp. 108–127). IGI Global., doi:10.4018/978-1-7998-8758-4.ch005

Zheng, C., & Musteen, M. (2018). The impact of remittances on opportunity-based and necessity-based entrepreneurial activities. *Academy of Entrepreneurship Journal*, *24*(3), 1–13.

ENDNOTES

1 Doing Business Report 2019. World Bank Group.

2 Doing Business Report 2020. World Bank Group.

Section 2
Financial Fraud and Corrupt Practices

Chapter 6
Circular Frauds and Abuses of VAT:
The Case of the European Union

Valentina Vinsalek Stipic
Veleučilište "Nikola Tesla" u Gospiću, Croatia

ABSTRACT

Organized tax frauds include circular frauds which are very complex in EU member states. Circular fraud is a way of the organized and systematic extraction of money from the state budget by exploiting the shortcomings of the tax system. The destination principle is based on the same tax treatment and the same market position of domestic and imported goods, but it also enables circular fraud. New member countries of the EU are struggling with circular fraud. Losses in the territory of the EU are measured in billions of euros and thus the negative effects on the budgets of those countries are growing. Tax frauds also involve countries outside Europe (UAE, Hong Kong, Russia). On the other hand, in tax havens, illegally acquired money is transferred as a part of the money laundering process. Monitoring and suppression are becoming more and more demanding because the center of gravity has moved to the domain of intangible assets due to the evolution of the internet. The regulatory bodies of the EU are trying hard to combat circular fraud and VAT abuse.

INTRODUCTION

With the entry into the European Union, i.e. the adoption of European directives (including the VAT Directive), the new member states become more exposed to the risks of financial fraud of all kinds. Organized tax frauds, including circular frauds, are taking on increasingly complex forms in the countries of the European Union, and thus the negative effects on the budgets of those countries are growing. Furthermore, tax frauds increasingly involve countries outside of Europe (e.g. UAE, Hong Kong, Russia........) and tax havens where illegally acquired money is transferred (part of the money laundering process). Like any tax, VAT is susceptible to evasion and fraud. But its credit and refund mechanism offer unique opportunities for abuse, and this has recently become an urgent problem in the European

DOI: 10.4018/978-1-6684-8587-3.ch006

Union (Keen & Smith, 2006). After the accession of the Republic of Croatia to the European Union, the establishment of companies without employees, without assets and with minimal share capital, which is usually not located at the address of the company's headquarters, was noticed. The initial information on the basis of which the Tax Administration detected such companies was obtained based on requests for international legal assistance in the field of VAT, and on the basis of observed suspicious requests for VAT refunds. The goods that are the subject of circular fraud are, for the most part, suitable for transport, that is, they take up little space, and at the same time, are of high value. The goal of tax evaders is to transfer goods in the chain as quickly as possible while making as much profit as possible (Beebeejaun *et al.*, 2023). According to all its characteristics, gold belongs to these goods, so for example in 2013, after the Republic of Croatia joined the European Union, the gold trade grew exponentially. According to data from the National Bureau of Statistics, 2.8 tons of gold were exported in 2014, most of which was exported to Italy, and slightly less to Slovenia. Therefore, the tax authorities were forced to participate in new trends and protect the state budget as soon as possible. In circular frauds, several companies in at least two EU member states participate in transactions. Companies trade in various goods, usually of high value, but circular frauds are increasingly common in services (trade in CO_2 emissions, electricity). It is difficult to detect data on losses for the budget in the area of VAT in the matter of circular fraud. The losses of the European Union for the year 2014 related to VAT are estimated at around €135.5 billion (CIS, 2014). In the 2013 tax gap analysis study, the estimated losses of VAT revenue involving VAT fraud amounted to €193 billion (CIS, 2013).

However, the Center for Social and Economic Research (CASE) produced a Study and report on the VAT gap in the EU-28 member states of the European Union in 2016, which states a VAT gap of €522 billion. The most common frauds are related to gold, trade in secondary raw materials, mobile phones, tablet devices, gaming consoles, coffee, cereals, chocolate bars, etc. There are also so-called conduit companies that are under increased monitoring and on the Eurofisc list. In the case of circular frauds, the most significant thing is the development of risk analysis in order to prevent fraud (preventive action), given that when fraud occurs, money for the state budget is irretrievably lost, the company disappears (MTIC - Missing Trader Intra Community) and regardless of the implemented tax supervision and established tax liabilities, the amount remains unpaid and losses accumulate. Globalization has led to new paradigms and concepts of public finance management. The goal of realizing the concept is to build a free, moral and cohesive society based on universal social inclusion and a market economy (Vinšalek Stipić, 2020).

In this chapter, a systematic investigation of the issue of circular fraud and abuse of VAT in the European Union was undertaken using the desktop research method. The problem of circular VAT fraud was analyzed in detail using the method of critical thinking. Using the empirical method, the occurrence of circular VAT frauds was demonstrated experientially, and the problem of circular VAT frauds in the EU was recognized using the rationalization method based on rational consideration. The methods of abstraction and generalization led to certain knowledge about the researched problem, on the basis of which research conclusions were reached, while the inductive and deductive methods enabled the overview of general knowledge based on individual facts related to the subject of research. Considering the nature of the research to which it belongs, the economic analysis method was applied to the field of economic sciences. The method of macroeconomic analysis was applied in this research to analyze phenomena, relationships, processes and problems caused by circular frauds and abuses of VAT in the EU.

THE CONCEPT OF CIRCULAR FRAUD

The world itself has a current account surplus (Gros, 2017) a logical impossibility that must result from measurement error or misreporting-possible fraud. This fact - called the world's own surplus - prompted Krugman (2010) to develop a humorous theory about "interstellar trade" that could be at the root of the global surplus. For very good reasons, economists usually consider bilateral current account balances to be irrelevant from a macroeconomic perspective (Feenstra *et al.*, 1999). However, they are of great importance for bilateral economic relations, especially in the context of trade conflicts, currency unions and external imbalances. Helbling and Terrones (2009) suggest that time lags in international transport may lead to delays in recording imports relative to exports. According to this explanation, lengthy shipping processes and high growth rates distort trade figures, which lends itself to tax fraud. Academic literature emphasizes the link between insufficient trade and export restrictions, Fisman and Wei (2009) measure art smuggling as a bilateral difference in trade figures, and Vézina (2015) shows that export disappearance is often the result of resource export restrictions. Braml & Felbermayr (2022) argue that companies over-declare the true value of their exports in order to obtain VAT refunds for goods sold on the domestic market. The resulting export statistics are inflated and do not match the corresponding import figures. Similar to the differences in trade in services between the EU and the US (Braml & Felbermayr, 2019), the UK contributes quite significantly to the differences in trade in services within the EU: the total own surplus in services in the EU is €141 billion. Within the euro area, this figure is only 39 billion euros (Chesson *et al.*, 2018). The unification of Europe opened the door to a large market that was supposed to facilitate and simplify the flow of goods, services and capital. Of course, the enlargement of the European Union has increased the possibility of abuse of the benefits offered by the duty-free union. Namely, even though the European Union abolished borders and facilitated cross-border crossings between Union members, the members themselves remained independent both within their geographical borders and in the adoption and enforcement of certain laws that are sluggish in relation to the speed of financial fraud.

Carousel fraud is one of the most significant forms of VAT fraud in the EU, and it is estimated that member states lose about 100 billion euros a year because of it. The appearance of circular frauds appeared due to the shortcomings of the system itself with the taxation of Value Added Tax (VAT) between the member states of the Union. Commercial companies that participate in fraud use the shortcomings of the VAT system, which has been in use in the Union since January 1993, when the common market was established and all obstacles to duty-free business between member states were abolished. The VAT system that came into force at that time was designed so that the tax is calculated in the destination member state at the rate and conditions applicable to it. The method of taxation of such transactions is basically taxation as in the case of exporting from one state and importing into another state of the Union. Zero-rate taxation applies to such sales of goods between members of the union. The justification for this type of taxation is justified by the fact that it equalizes imported and domestic products in terms of taxation because VAT was used as input tax for the production of domestic products. When this kind of system was adopted and implemented, it was considered a temporary system until a new solution was adopted, but it is still in use today and greatly facilitates circular fraud.

The appearance of such types of transactions and fraud within the tax system of the entire European Union, and not only within individual members, resulted in the reaction of the Union's bodies so that for coordination between members and greater flexibility in the detection of financial fraud, the Office europèen de lutte anti-fraude (OLAF) was established.

Office de Lutte Anti-Fraude – OLAF

Social audit and social responsibility have become the focus of sustainable community development in order to respond to risks and challenges to the sustainability of public finances (Vinšalek Stipić, 2022). Office europèen de lutte anti-fraude (OLAF) is an independent investigative office for the fight against fraud within the EU and was founded in 1999. OLAF conducts investigations in all members of the European Union and other countries that have agreed to do so, and all of this is aimed at preventing fraud and all those illegal activities that have a harmful effect on the Union, such as corruption. OLAF does not act independently but cooperates with the investigative bodies of the member states in whose territory it operates. Although the office is relatively small (500 employees with a budget of 50 million euros), its benefits are manifold when detecting fraud. In order for fraud investigations to be effective, OLAF has the authority to conduct external administrative investigations between member states and certain non-member states, but with which the Union has cooperation agreements, all with the aim of fighting against fraud, corruption and any other illegal activities they have for the consequences of adverse effects for the financial interests of the European Union. The powers give OLAF the possibility of investigations by accountants in delegations as well as conducting administrative investigations within the institutions of the Union. OLAF, as an umbrella anti-fraud organization, by coordinating between member countries and direct contacts between the police and judicial authorities, develops strategies and assists in the adoption of legal acts to combat fraud. Given that OLAF represents a commission in the scope of fraud prevention, it undertakes to protect all "whistleblowers", witnesses and other persons who entrust the Office with information about corruption or fraud, and to guarantee the confidentiality of data from all its operations.

Anti-fraud Coordinating Structures – AFCOS

Anti-fraud coordinating structures (AFCOS) is a system through which the coordination of legislative, administrative and operational activities is carried out with the aim of protecting the financial interests of the European Union and direct cooperation with the European Commission's Anti-Fraud Office (OLAF). All members of the Union are included in the AFCOS network. It includes the bodies that manage and use the aid funds of the European Union and the bodies that deal with combating fraud, corruption or any other form of irregularity in the system, which includes all the most important ministries and bodies of the executive power, such as the Ministry of Justice, the Ministry of the Interior, The Ministry of the Economy, the Administration for the Public Procurement System, the Central State Office for Administration, the State Audit Office, the Ministry of Finance, the supervisory bodies of the Ministry of Finance, the bodies of the Tax Administration, the Customs Administration, the Financial Police, etc. The department within the system performs a coordinating role and is the contact point for OLAF - and, if necessary, includes other representatives of state bodies in the work of the AFCOS network. All bodies in the AFCOS system are obliged to cooperate with the Ministry of Finance - Department for Suppression of Irregularities and Frauds and to mutually exchange information and provide assistance related to issues of protection of the financial interests of the EU.

CIRCULAR FRAUDS WITHIN THE EUROPEAN UNION

In all member states of the European Union, some form of attempted fraud of the VAT system has been detected, whether it is micro, small, medium or large. Circular fraud within the European Union takes place in the following way:

For example, company Alpha from a member state of the Union sells goods to company Beta on the Croatian market (or some other member state of the Union) and is exempt from paying taxes, that is, company Beta calculates VAT and input tax on the input invoice of company Alpha. The next step is the sale of goods by the company Beta (according to) the company Gamma with the calculation of VAT. The amount of calculated VAT should be paid by the company Beta within the legally specified period, but it is not paid, while the company Gamma reports this VAT as input tax. Then the Beta company ceases to operate, that is, it disappears and becomes a disappearing company "missing trader". During this time, the entrepreneur Gamma continues to sell goods to the entrepreneur Delta, and Delta sells those goods to the company Omega, etc. In order to conceal the real reason for the sale, each of the companies calculates a symbolic price difference so that it realizes the minimum profit value and thus creates the appearance of an orderly business. In the end, the company Omega exports goods to third countries without VAT, while using input tax and claiming a refund from the state budget. During the inspection, it is determined that the company Delta has properly declared VAT as a liability and the tax administration has no reason but to refund the VAT to the company Omega. Companies between the acquirer in Croatia and the supplier to the member country are in fact used to cover up the traces of the completed transactions. Such companies are called "buffers". These are companies that normally work on the territory of Croatia and unconscionably participate in circular fraud. After a period of time, the Tax Administration will block and foreclose the account of the company Beta. But the Beta company works in a rented space and has no assets, VAT cannot be collected. The biggest curiosity of this business is that this action cannot be interpreted as tax evasion because the company Beta duly declared its obligation, so it is difficult to prove the intention of tax evasion.

Types and Functioning of Missing Trader Intra-community Fraud (MTIC Fraud)

Every tax system has in common that the simpler the system and with fewer tax rates, the harder it is to cheat, in fact, the easier it is to control. Complicated tax systems, which are also changing, are suitable for all kinds of tax fraud, especially VAT due to the high tax rate. From missing trader intra-community (MTIC) fraud, fraud within the Union through a company that disappears, there are two types of fraud: circular fraud - carousel fraud and acquisition fraud - acquisition fraud and a hybrid version of contra trading (Ainsworth, 2009).

Carousel fraud is a financial fraud that results in damage to the state budget through abuse of the VAT system (Ainsworth, 2006). Goods or services are purchased without VAT from EU member states. The acquirer sells the goods with VAT included and disappears before paying the VAT to the state, and the final buyer claims input tax from the state. Acquired goods are resold to a large number of trading companies. They never end up in retail on the domestic market, i.e. they do not become available for consumption, but are returned fictitiously or actually to the country of origin or are used to start a new chain of fraud, which is where the name circular fraud comes from.

Acquisition fraud implies the sale of imported goods at a zero VAT rate on the domestic black market (Van Erven *et al.*, 2017). After the sale, the importer does not charge VAT on taxable supplies, which allows him to sell the goods cheaper than other market participants. Since it does not collect VAT, it directly damages the state budget. In this case, the criminal offense is easily proven because it is about legally imported goods that are recorded in the warehouse. The goods are sold for cash without tax, so they are more competitive on the market, but they remain recorded in the bookkeeping, so they are discovered very simply and very quickly, therefore the processing is easier. The biggest problem here is the rare and slow control by the tax authorities, so an entrepreneur can sell "black" for years.

Contra trading is used by fraudsters to prevent MTIC from detecting fraud. Contra trading perpetrators often try to hide complicating trading methods (Sokanović, 2020). The term counter trader refers to a taxpayer who participates in two separate types of chain of transactions, one of which is legal and is carried out with the aim of concealing a circular fraud. This is in fact a circular fraud involving entrepreneurs who operate legally and serve to divert attention from dubious businesses. For each delivery in the chain, they calculate a certain profit and thus show a real business event. This is intended to avoid the appearance of legal work. As these are old entrepreneurs with already well-established businesses, it is difficult to prove that this is an apparent legal business.

New Models of Circular Fraud

The damage suffered by the member states of the Union due to circular frauds is a big problem and loss, therefore a great effort is being made to suppress such frauds. In the illegal operations of the described circular frauds, goods of high value, which are small in volume and highly sought after on the market for the sake of quick and simple placement, take part. These are usually mobile phones, game consoles, gold, watches, designer clothes and shoes. As it is a commodity, the problem for perpetrators is that the commodity can be traced, so detecting fraud is easier. With the development of the digital form of trading, supervision is becoming more and more complicated and requires more knowledge and time spent, as well as means to find fraud. Recently, there has been a form of trade in various certificates and trade rights that are subject to VAT. This form of trade is interesting because there are no additional costs, and monitoring is much more difficult. After the entry into force of the Kyoto Protocol in 2005, the trade in certificates or rights for CO_2 emissions, so-called Carbon credits with certificates of European Union Allowances (AUAs), Certified Emission Reductions (CERs) and Emission Reduction Units (ERUs). Trade was not only carried out between entrepreneurs who have a surplus or deficit of certificates, but other investment funds, banks, insurance companies and others who saw profit in it also joined the trade. Already in 2009, the turnover of certificates grew to more than 100 billion euros, and according to published data, the turnover in 2011 was more than 129 billion euros (World Bank, 2011). CO_2 emission certificates are intangible assets that disappear from circulation after use and are very difficult to trace once they cross the border. Soon, the perpetrators of circular fraud joined the trade in CO_2 certificates by importing them without VAT from member countries and then selling them on the domestic market. From August 2008, the real expansion of trade began, but behind it, there were circular frauds. In France, Denmark, the Netherlands, Spain and Great Britain, the turnover of CO_2 certificates reached previously unimaginable amounts. In March 2009, the Dutch tax authority FIOD first linked an unusual increase in the turnover of CO_2 certificates to possible circular fraud. It is estimated that in the period from August 2008 to March 2009, the CO_2 certificates alone caused damage to the mentioned countries in the amount of more than 5 billion euros (Europol, 2009). The Netherlands immediately changed the tax law for these transactions so that instead of the seller, the person liable to pay VAT became the acquirer, which made trade-in certificates in that country no longer suitable for circular fraud, as a reverse charge mechanism VAT. Immediately after that, trade-in said certificates almost stopped, which meant that the measure was justified. This decision was in contradiction with the VAT Directive of the Union, but in this case, the Netherlands was guided by the protection of its fiscal interests. Soon, many other countries followed the Dutch example, and the trading of CO_2 certificates in these countries fell by up to 90%. One year later, in March 2010, Directive 2010/23/EU was adopted, which allows the mechanism of reverse VAT collection for certain services that may be subject to VAT fraud (Council Directive 2010/23/EU). The perpetrators of circular frauds then moved the trading of CO_2 certificates to countries that had not introduced the reverse charge mechanism, such as Poland, Italy and the Czech Republic. In 2010, the Italian Guardia di Finanza carried out a large-scale operation and closed about 150 companies in eight Italian regions. It is estimated that so far, they have damaged Italy by around 500 million euros in VAT on CO_2 certificates (Europol, 2009). In the same year, a chain of circular frauds with CO_2 certificates was also discovered in the Czech Republic. Apart from the domain of CO_2 certificates, it is expected that the increased activity of perpetrators of circular fraud could be directed at special segments in gas and electricity trading (Europol, 2010). At the end of 2012, circular frauds involving copper cathodes used in the metal industry were observed in the UK, Germany and the Netherlands. All this proves that the perpetrators of circular fraud are increasingly shifting from classic types of goods to areas of the high technology sector and that there is probably a whole range of goods in material and immaterial form that they trade, which the supervisory authorities have not yet been able to spot. In Italy, in 2010, it was discovered that the subject of circular fraud was an intangible asset for which it was unthinkable to put it in such a context: VOIP - voice over internet protocol. Two of Italy's largest telecommunications companies participated in that fraud: Telecom Italia and FastWeb. It is estimated that the total damage is around EUR 400 million VAT. It is interesting that two things are traded in VOIP transactions: 1) equipment, which can be tracked, and 2) minutes, which requires expert knowledge to track (Ainsworth, 2010).

CHARACTERISTICS OF VAT CIRCULAR FRAUD

Value Added Tax (VAT) is an indirect consumption tax levied on most sales of goods and services. The basis of VAT is the added value of the economic entity. VAT is calculated for registered tradesmen and end customers who are not business entities. The Goods and Services Tax (GST) is the equivalent of VAT applied in countries such as India, Canada, Australia and New Zealand. It is interesting that VAT has not found acceptance in the United States, despite numerous attempts by various politicians to create momentum for the introduction of VAT as a federal tax. VAT evasion covers all countries that have indirect taxation systems, including VAT and GST (Frunza, 2018). The Netherlands showed the most significant progress in the fight against circular VAT fraud. Over the years, in the Dutch FIOD unit in the Central Department for VAT Fraud, which is part of the specially organized FIOD unit in Amsterdam for VAT fraud, the characteristics of participants in chain frauds have been determined. There are different forms of circular fraud that are modified over time. The most common circular frauds are those in which a non-existent entrepreneur appears in chain transactions and the so-called counter-circular frauds in which a chain with a non-existent entrepreneur is disguised by another chain of companies. In the chain, each company has its own role, and accordingly, the following companies are distinguished:

Missing traders do not fulfill their tax obligations, do not pay VAT, and in most cases do not submit tax reports (Podlipnik, 2012). Such companies do not perform real business activities. Most often, these companies are mailboxes or companies registered at the address of a fake office, and when Tax

Administration officials visit such a taxpayer, they do not find anyone at the address. Directors of such companies are usually foreign nationals known as strawmen (Talisse & Aikin, 2006). The characteristic of such companies is that when the money comes into the account, it leaves immediately, so in these cases there are no quick action mechanisms to confiscate the funds.

Buffer firms are those that sit between a disappearing trader or other buffer firm and a broker. As a regular taxpayer, the Buffer company submits VAT reports and settles value-added tax obligations (Sokanović, 2020). Its role is to facilitate an investigation that would quickly reveal the connection between the disappearing trader and the broker (end customer in the chain) who is requesting a VAT refund. The more buffer companies are there in the chain, the more difficult is the job of tax inspectors in detecting circular fraud. Most often, there is one buffer company in the chain, although there can be more. A buffer company can also be a well-known trader that is not necessarily established for the purpose of tax fraud and tries to give the impression of a serious company that does not only participate in tax fraud but can also happen to carry out real trading activities in part. Most often, such enterprises have a small margin and small amounts of VAT to pay.

The broker (end customer), located at the end of the chain, buys goods from a buffer company or from a Missing trader (Frunza, 2013) and delivers to another EU member state. In this way, he has an exempt delivery and realizes the right to input tax, considering that he procures the goods in the country. Given that the disappearing trader will not pay the VAT obligation in the event of a VAT refund, there will be direct damage to the budget.

A *Conduit Company* is a company established with the aim of engaging in fraud in order to enable tax evasion (Podlipnik, 2012). There is no tax administration that has not encountered this type of company. The most common characteristics of a Conduit Company are the following: high income, few employees and no obligation to pay taxes to the state budget. A company buys goods in one member state and immediately sells them to another member state, so there is no legal obligation to pay tax. These types of companies are usually cooperative in their relations with the tax administration and try to leave the impression of a serious company, some of them pay tax on profit since they have a small margin. However, it may happen that such companies remain liable for other taxes (profit tax, income tax) and ultimately there is a loss for the budget. The problem with Conduit Company is that such companies are part of a fraudulent chain between several member states and the loss of VAT occurs in another state as well.

Examples of VAT circular fraud

Detecting tax fraud is a very complex process, and tax inspectors should focus on the following facts: company history (owners, directors, income, tax reports); relations between companies (orders, contacts, etc.); transport documentation (forwarders and transport documentation); payments; the way of storing goods; prices and margin; documents and contracts; business logic transactions, etc.

It is evident from the mentioned fraud model that the loss of VAT will occur in Member State 2 where the disappearing trader is registered. Various companies take part in circular frauds, which play different roles in VAT fraud and have certain characteristics, such as high-risk goods, loss of VAT at a disappearing trader who collects it but does not pay it into the state budget, price reduction, cross-border trade, high amounts accounts, wholesale trade, a sudden increase in turnover by several tens of times, no warehouse and stock of goods, a small number of employees, goods are not insured, third countries are included (for example Dubai) and similar.

Figure 1. The simplest model of circular fraud

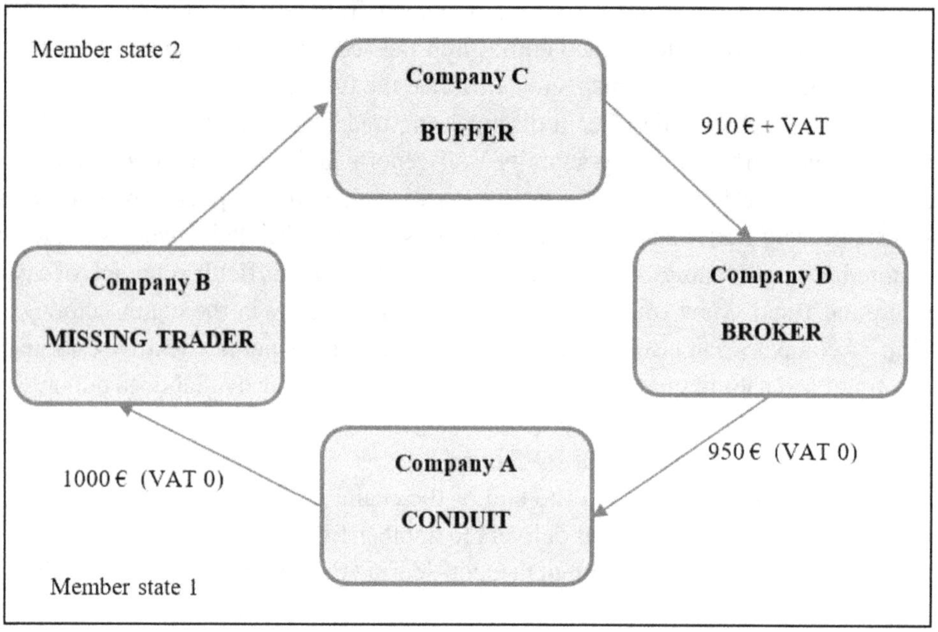

Example 1. Example of a new Conduit Company. The presented situation is a real example of a newly established Croatian company for the implementation of VAT abuse in the Republic of Croatia – company characteristics: Newly founded company; Director and founder foreign citizen; Small share capital (usually the lowest according to legal possibilities); The company has no assets and has one employed person (company director); High amounts of initial transactions for a newly founded company (around €100,000.00); Small margin; The company operates in a rented apartment, and after a few months it is transferred to a virtual office (mail address and accounting services of the company); There is no warehouse (he keeps the goods with the forwarder if necessary); The supplier is paid only after the customer's payment; There is a change of the founder and the headquarters of the company; Trilateral affairs. The newly established taxpayer Alpha applied for a VAT identification number in the Republic of Croatia and started doing business in the EU market. The goods are bought in Poland and sold to a Cypriot company (coffee, chocolate bars, hygiene items). The delivery goes to the warehouse in Slovakia. In other transactions, goods are imported from Serbia and sold to Poland. The taxpayer pays VAT on imports and uses it as input tax in the declaration, and considering that he has tax-free deliveries to another member state of the Union, he has the right to deduct input tax.

Figure 2. Presentation of the circular fraud of the newly established Conduit Company

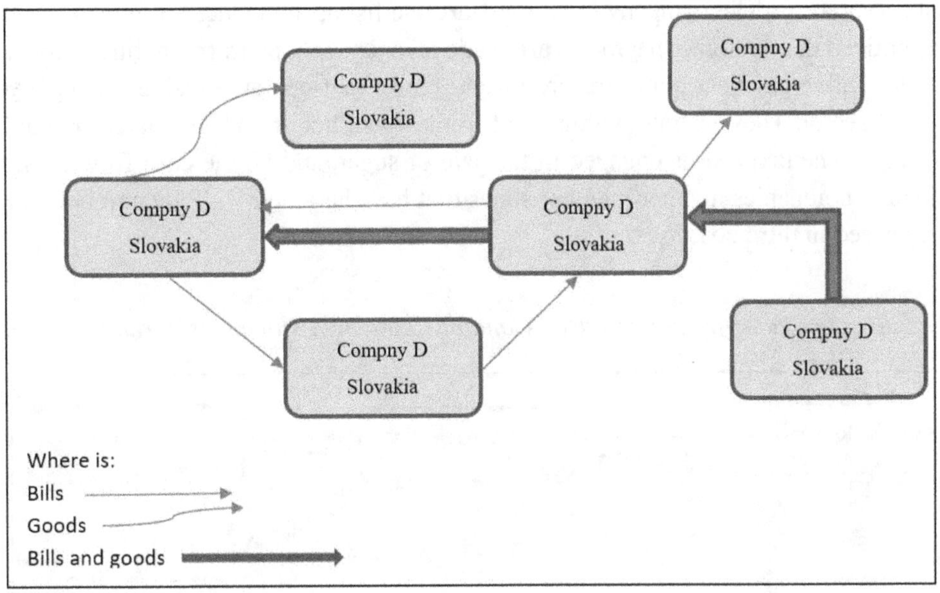

In order not to damage the taxpayer's budget when importing goods from the Customs Administration, increased monitoring (red route) is required, which includes a detailed inspection of the goods and documentation, as well as constant cooperation between the Customs and Tax Administration. Also for deliveries to another member state, when all domestic checks have been exhausted, it is necessary to send a request for the exchange of information in order to determine whether the VAT was paid at the destination and to whom the goods were further sold. The company is on the Eurofisc list as a conduit company and is under increased monitoring at the competent Tax Administration Branch. From the aforementioned characteristics, it is evident that the company has all the characteristics of a potential participant in circular fraud. Considering that many members of the Union (and especially those that have just joined) have a large number of such companies, it is necessary to continuously monitor them in order not to damage the state budget, since the company can show debts on the basis of other taxes (e.g. profit tax, income) if it disappears the liabilities will not be able to be collected because such a company has no assets.

Example 2. Example of the purchase of a Conduit Company (which was dormant). The presented situation is a real example of a conductor company, a purchased company that was dormant, registered in the Republic of Croatia – characteristics of the company: Purchased dormant company by foreign nationals; The company has no assets; The company has no employees; Directors and owners are foreigners; Trilateral affairs; Small share capital (usually the lowest according to legal possibilities); There is no office space; No warehouse; Payments to suppliers are made after receipt of money from customers; Big margin. The company buys goods in one member state and sells them to another member state. The goods do not enter the territory of the country where the company is registered. Based on received requests for international exchange of information, it was established that the taxpayer does business with disappearing merchants in other member states. Considering this fact, the taxpayer's VAT ID number was suspended and the case in question is suitable for Multilateral control (MLC). MLC - multilateral control implies a coordinated control of the tax liability of one or more taxpayers organized by two or more participating countries, but at least one must be a member of the EU and must have common or complementary interests. The company is on the Eurofisc list as a conductor company. With the taxpayer, it was noticed that customer payments are made on a payment platform in third countries. Paying platforms - alternative payment platforms are virtual banks that operate outside the legally regulated global financial sector. They operate within legal frameworks but are not regulated by national regulatory authorities. The taxpayer is engaged in the sale of sugar, and all the cash flow from the sale is given as a loan to companies in other member states that have had their VAT ID number abolished and to companies based in third countries.

Figure 3. Display of circular fraud purchased Conduit Company (which was dormant)

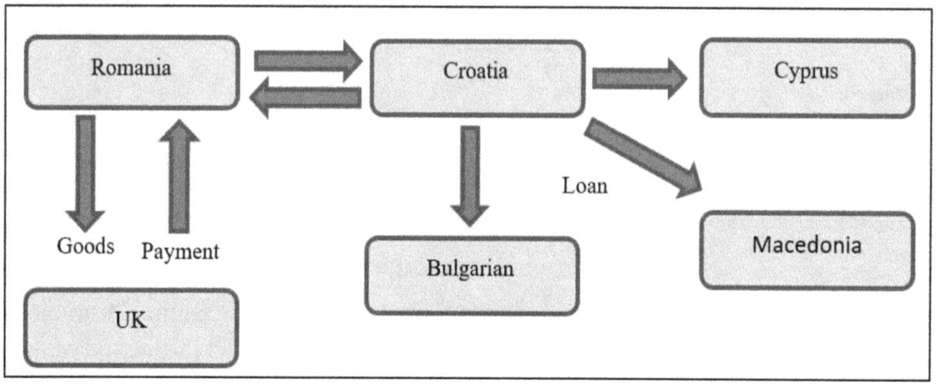

The taxpayer reported a profit tax liability that he did not pay, and the income for the state budget was lost. In the case in question, the potential criminal liability of the responsible persons (foreign nationals) could be considered for extracting money from the company that will not be returned and thus the company was rendered unable to fulfill its tax obligations.

Example 3. Fraud with high-risk goods (computer games and mobile phones). The presented situation is a real example of a circular fraud involving actors from Croatia, the Netherlands and the United Kingdom – characteristics of the company: Medium taxpayer in terms of size; Existence of significant assets (real estate, warehouses, movable property, land, etc.); It has been operating on the Croatian market for many years; Founders and directors are Croatian citizens; Regularly settles tax obligations. For the taxpayer in question, an inquiry was submitted from another member state as to whether the taxpayer is a regular taxpayer, given that he is engaged in trade in risky goods in the EU. After receiving the notification, it was established that the taxpayer purchased the goods from a UK taxpayer with a Dutch VAT identification number. The goods are shipped from the Netherlands to the Republic of Croatia. After four days, the same goods are reshipped to the Netherlands to another taxpayer based in the United Kingdom with a valid NL VAT identification number. The Croatian taxpayer declares the acquisition in the Republic of Croatia, declares the VAT liability and the right to input tax (accounting category) and submits a declaration for the same goods as exempt from VAT with regard to delivery to another member state. There are certain illogicalities in the said transaction as follows. It is illogical that a Croatian taxpayer would transport goods purchased from the Netherlands back to the Netherlands (within four days). In the process of tax supervision, the following must be established: Is the transport documentation correct? Was the transport from the Netherlands to Croatia and back from Croatia to the Netherlands actually carried out, because only if the conditions according to the VAT Act are met, then the taxpayer has the right to exemption. There are justified doubts that the goods did not leave the Netherlands or, if they entered the Republic of Croatia, they were not sold in the Netherlands and that they remained in Croatia, in which case there would be a loss of VAT because the 25% VAT was not calculated on the goods in question.

Figure 4. Presentation of circular fraud with high-risk goods

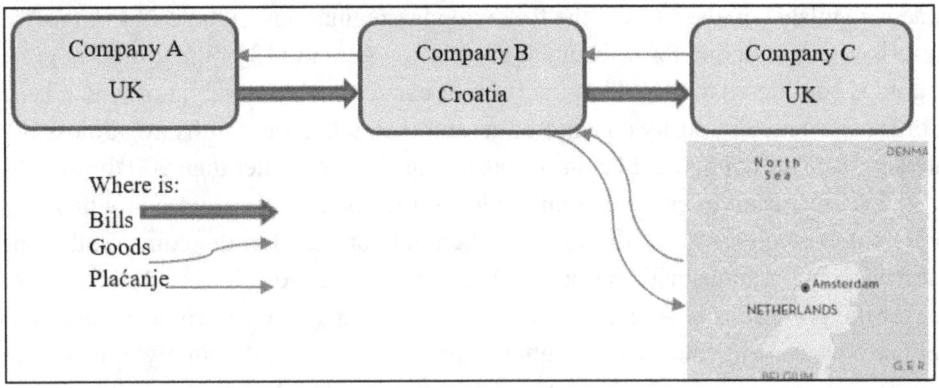

Considering transactions within the European Union and doing business with taxpayers registered in other member states of the Union (a British company with a Dutch VAT number), in order to determine the actual transactions, it is necessary to send a request for international data exchange for suppliers and carriers in order to determine the actual transactions. The case is also suitable for multilateral control since it would be possible to determine the transactions and where the goods in question were sold, and whether they were actually delivered to another member state. If the goods came to Croatia and were not actually sold, that is, delivered back to the Netherlands, there would be a loss of VAT for the Croatian budget, as VAT at the rate of 25% should be calculated on the delivery in question.

Example 4. Fraud with high-value goods (gold). Gold scams were spotted in the Czech Republic and Finland, as well as in non-EU countries. The member states suffered losses in the gold trade, and the budget of the Republic of Croatia was significantly damaged. Croatian companies that played different roles in that chain participated in the chain transactions: disappearing traders, shield companies and brokers who ultimately made a profit since they reported deliveries to other member states that are tax-free) and submitted requests for VAT refund - considering that they procured gold domestically from shield companies (buffers). At some brokers, the turnover has increased by 100 times in the current year compared to previous years. The characteristics of the companies appearing in the chain are:

a) Disappearing merchants: they don't exist at their address, they don't submit tax reports, they don't have property, they don't have business premises, they don't have employees, they withdraw money from the giro account immediately after the customer's payment and there is no trace of them.

b) Buffers - shield companies, newly established companies, change founders, directors, directors and founders are foreigners, move from one regional office of the tax administration to another, regularly submit reports, and settle small VAT tax obligations in order to act as regular taxpayers.
c) Brokers - the last in the chain who carry out deliveries to another EU member state, and buy gold from a taxpayer in the Republic of Croatia and based on that, submit a request for a VAT refund.

It was noticed by the taxpayers that there was no delivery of gold, that is, that the taxpayers in the chain do not have credible documentation of the purchase and sale of gold and that if there was the delivery of gold, it was in very small quantities in the part of purchases from citizens. In the Republic of Croatia, the gold trade is regulated on the basis of the following tax regulations: Article 114 of the Value Added Tax Act prescribes an exemption for investment gold, while Article 113 of the same Act prescribes that investment gold is considered to be gold in the form of bars or bars, the weight of which is accepted on the market of precious metals, purity equal to or greater than 995 thousandths, regardless of whether it is represented by securities or not, gold coins of purity equal to or greater than 900 thousandths, minted after 1800, which are currently or were legal tender in the country of origin and which are normally sold at a price not exceeding 80% of the value of the gold contained in the coins on the open market, and which are not sold for numismatic purposes. According to the provisions of Article 115 of the same Law, except for the provisions of Article 114 of the Law, a taxpayer who produces investment gold or converts gold into investment gold, has the right to choose for taxation the supply of investment gold he makes to other taxpayers. As the trade in gold in 2014 amounted to 2.8 tons of gold according to official data, it is illogical that a large number of companies, which participated in fraudulent activities, traded in gold, and have no resources or credible documentation on the purchase of gold. In order to determine the actual business events of companies participating in VAT fraud, it is necessary to send requests for international exchange of data in the field of VAT (SCAC inquiries) in order to determine whether the delivery and purchase of gold has actually been carried out. In such cases, it is also necessary to establish the credibility of the purchase blocks (for foreign citizens and Croatian citizens), since it often happens that they are fictitious with the aim of extracting money from the company. It is important to check all the companies in the chain in order to determine their possible connection either through the founder or the director, which can be one of the important facts in the evidentiary procedure. What are the losses based on the fictitious gold trade, there is no available data, the problem is that the losses are present with VAT and income (stated VAT refunds as well as cash withdrawals from ATMs with the initial participant of the fraud, according to which the income calculation was made will not be able to charge, since it is a disappearing merchant)? In the Republic of Croatia, there have also been certain cases related to fictitious gold trade in which money laundering took place. Most of the cases have not yet been legally concluded, and the data on fraud cannot be considered final. In order to reduce the possibility of fraud in future periods, a good pre-registration control is needed. The gold scam is given in the following schematic representation.

Figure 5. Presentation of circular fraud with high-value goods (gold)

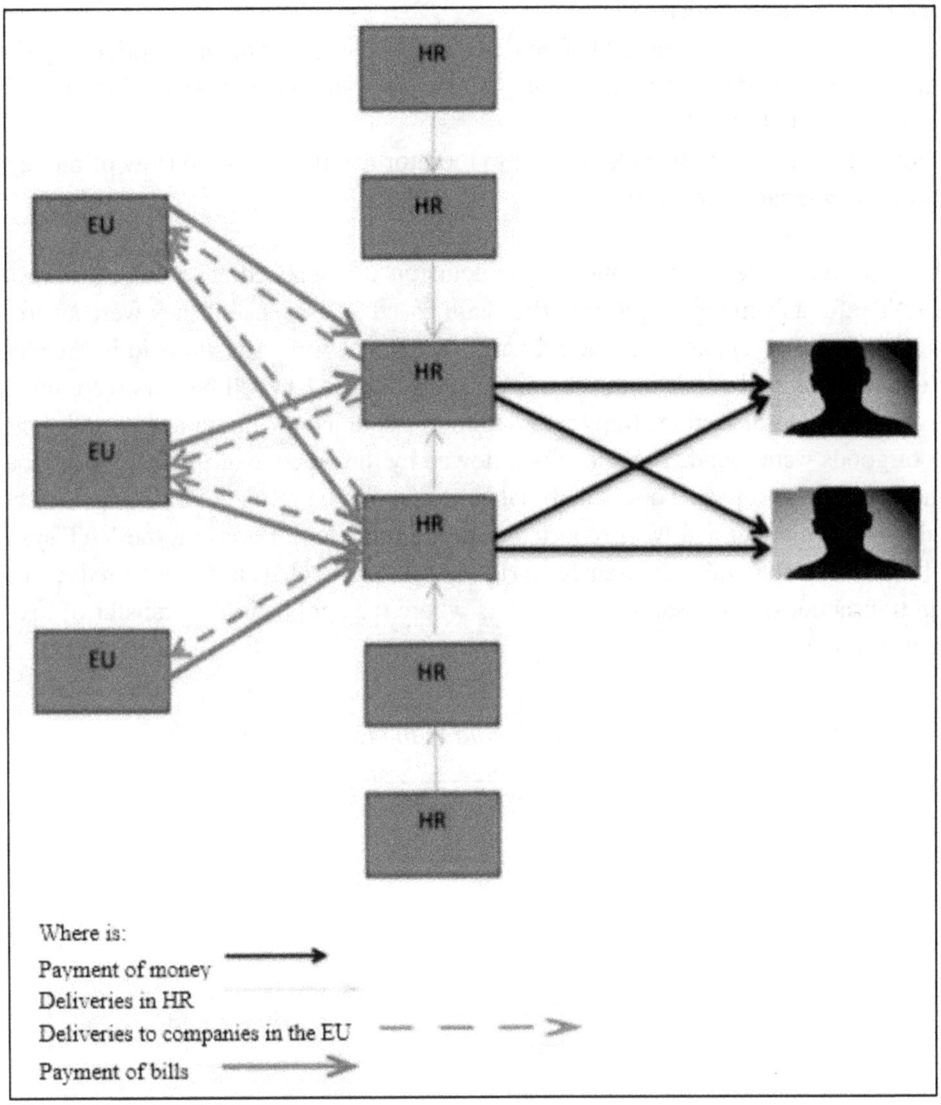

Example 5. Abuse of the gold fraud of the Czech Republic. In the Czech Republic, the taxpayer unfoundedly asserted the right to deduct input tax with the intent to defraud regarding the purity of the gold and by applying the transfer of tax liability. In the case of taxpayers, there was only a circulation of documentation, and there was no actual circulation of goods. Responsible persons of the companies involved have already been accused of participating in financial fraud in the past. The right to deduct input tax has been denied. In case of justified suspicion that certain companies are involved in tax fraud with gold, it is important to determine the following:

a) collect as much evidence as possible that points to intentional malfeasance by the participants involved.

b) the final goal is to prove suspicions about the entire economic activity and the origin of the goods that did not prove to be satisfactory.
c) cooperation with experts in the field of gold business, the average purchase price of gold, purity of gold, the origin of gold of lower purity, and security of gold transport, given that these are transactions above €200,000.00.
d) close contact with the Czech bank in order to monitor the history of the flow of money in the accounts of the companies involved.

After the collected evidence, the following conclusion was reached: The Tax Administration can withhold a VAT refund from any taxpayer in the chain based on evidence if they were aware of participating in the fraud. Taxpayers knew or should have known that VAT was not paid in the chain, mostly for transactions without real goods in the chain. Disappearing traders and brokers were involved in the chain, where fraudulent transactions (only circulation of documents without actual deliveries) and unclear origin of goods were found. The above is followed by the practice of the European Court Halifax C255/02, in which the European Court ruled that VAT will not be refunded based on transactions that have no real economic effect and were reported with the intention of abusing the VAT system. In the VAT Act of the Czech Republic, the transfer of tax liability is applied in order to reduce tax evasion, especially in transactions with disappearing traders where the application of transfer of tax liability is the only legal solution.

Figure 6. Presentation of the circular fraud with gold in the Czech Republic

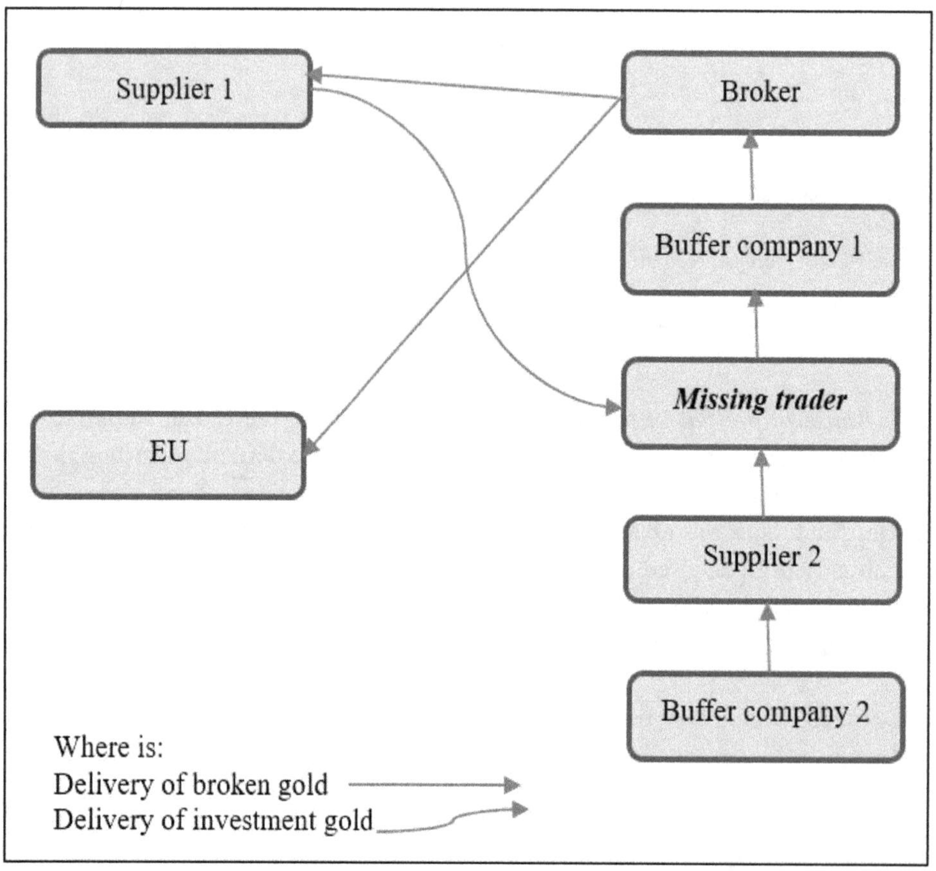

Legal and natural persons (registered for VAT purposes) operating in the field of gold, jewelry trade, dental medicine, pharmacy, scientific research, etc., are subject to the application of this regime. The application of the domestic transfer of tax liability (according to the Czech VAT Law) stipulates that it is applied only to domestic transactions: gold, permits for greenhouse gas emissions (carbon credits), construction works, scrap iron and waste. The VAT Directive-(112/2006/EC) regulates what is considered investment gold and transactions are exempt from VAT.

Example 6. Abuse of the gold fraud of the Republic of Finland. The gold fraud case was initiated by the Finnish Financial Intelligence Unit of the National Bureau of Investigation where the gold was transported by plane to Helsinki by the company O. The responsible person of the company is known to the police from previous years in which he participated in VAT fraud. In order to establish additional facts, the officers of the Office organized the monitoring of the movement of gold toward Sweden. They found that the handover of gold for Norway was carried out in the parking lot, which was transported in the trunk of an old car and was not reported to Customs (green route – the absence of customs control). The Office for the Prevention of Money Laundering contacted the Tax Administration and the following was determined:

a) company A reported deliveries in VIES.
b) the acquisition was reported, but not the sale.
c) the cash flow was determined from the bank statements: the receipt of money from the Norwegian company H, which forwarded the money to the Belgian company T.
d) the payment from the Norwegian company was made on behalf of company S.

Transaction participants had the following roles:

a) Spanish company (bogus company), only invoices without actual deliveries, reported acquisition in the VAT system.
b) Belgian company T as a producer of investment gold
c) Norwegian company H (there is a loss of VAT when the company asserts the right to deduct input tax)
d) Norwegian company S, which does not report transactions in Norway, has an account with a Norwegian company.
e) the Finnish company O is an unknown company in Finland (it does not have an account with the Norwegian company (S) but has an account with a Norwegian company.
f) payment of investment gold from company H to company O, in favor of company S (value €11,185,000)
g) loss of VAT in Norway in the amount of €2.2 million.

After the detection of possible circular VAT frauds and their further repetitions, the Amadeus database and Europol were of great importance. The Amadeus database is a European database that contains 11 million companies from 41 European countries that are combined from 30 national registers. The database contains data on income, expenses, total turnover, type of activity, ownership data and other relevant data for checking the company. Europol is the European Police Office, the criminal intelligence agency of the European Union that started its work in 1999. A schematic view of gold fraud abuse transactions in the Republic of Finland is shown as follows:

Figure 7. Presentation of the circular fraud with gold in the Republic of Finland

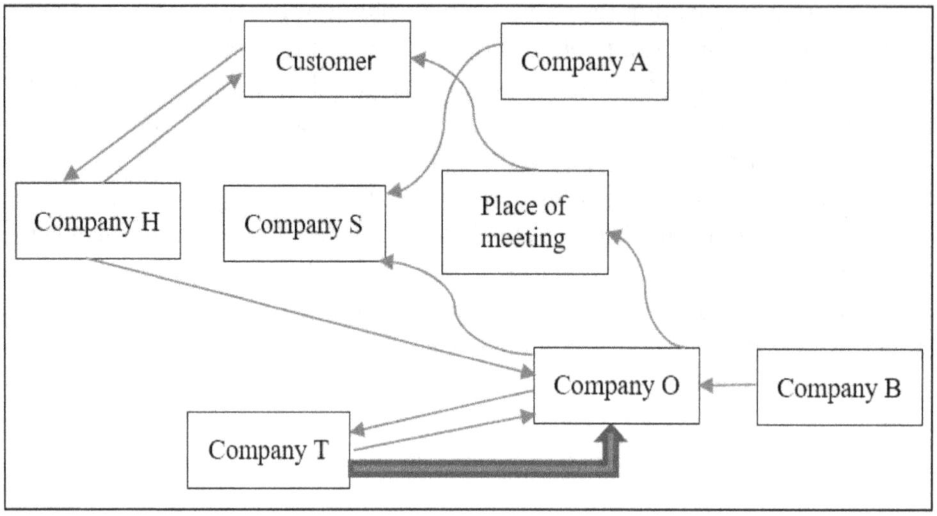

In this case, the following important facts were established: by looking at the Amadeus database, it was established that company S is registered in Norway under the trade name of a Swedish entrepreneur (Mr. "R") who lives in Sweden. Mr. "R" is a member of the board of company H. The police were notified in order to hold a meeting at Europol and to warn the Norwegian Tax Administration about possible VAT fraud. During the next delivery of gold, the cooperation of the Finnish, Swedish and Norwegian police was agreed upon, which resulted in the arrest of two people who smuggled the gold to the end customer in Norway. Gold in the value of €900,000.00 was taken and no one reported it missing. As can be seen from the mentioned case of VAT fraud where several member states are involved, the cooperation of all member states as well as those that are not (Norway) at the operational level (police, anti-money laundering office, tax administration as well as Europol) is necessary because only joint cooperation can achieve results. Although certain losses on the basis of VAT have already occurred, further losses were prevented and part of the gold was confiscated.

PRE-REGISTRATION CONTROL FOR THE PURPOSE OF REDUCING CIRCULAR FRAUD

The reduction of tax fraud in future periods will depend on a well-organized pre-registration control. The damage suffered by the EU member states due to circular frauds is a big problem and a loss of budget money, so greater efforts should be made to suppress such frauds. Tax inspectors perform analysis, assessment and processing of data on risks and risky taxpayers, VAT supervision, especially VAT refund supervision, and determining the economic strength of VAT, which is of essential importance for the early detection of risky taxpayers. The data form contains a series of questions for newly established legal entities (general information about the taxpayer, keeping business books, activities of the taxpayer, warehouses, number of employees, long-term assets) and the following should be attached: decision on registration in the court register, lease agreements, special licenses for carrying out activities, insurance policies, information on membership in trade associations, international or professional associations, list of current and potential customers as well as foreign customers.

Business analysis based on risk assessment is a management measure or tool that includes the determination, analysis and management of risks relevant to the truthfulness and credibility of financial statements in accordance with generally accepted accounting methods, taking into account events inside and outside the company. Risk analysis and assessment do not represent a simple approach to the problem of money laundering (Rafay, 2021), but rather a more difficult path, in which proper judgment is extremely important for the entire system. In order for the risk assessment to be as real as possible, it is necessary to concentrate on the actual risk and try to maximize the benefits for the social community as the basic benefit of introducing this approach and as a measure for risk identification, prevention or reduction (Vinšalek Stipić & Blažević, 2011). The Tax Administration has recognized the role of risk analysis and good pre-registration control with the aim of detecting "fictitious" taxpayers. When registering, taxpayers in most cases submit data on their own initiative to the competent office of the Tax Administration, and in the event that they do not do so, the authorized officers according to the provisions of the Act require the following data: a copy of the decision of the Commercial Court on the establishment, a copy of the notification on the classification of the business entity according to the corresponding activity to which the company belongs, a copy of the contract on opening a transaction account in the bank, copies of signature cards, a copy of the contract with the bookkeeping service, a copy of the lease contract. After the accession of new member states to the European Union, taxpayers who carry out transactions with foreign countries are initially assigned VAT identification numbers, while other taxpayers must request a VAT identification number. The tax administration can refuse to assign or revoke the assigned VAT identification number if it determines that there are no longer reasons for registration for VAT purposes or if the taxpayer misuses the VAT identification number. In case of suspicion of fraud, the Tax Administration will cancel the VAT identification number by decision. The Value Added Tax Act introduced the suspension of the VAT identification number for taxpayers in case of suspicion of misuse of the VAT identification number, which enabled faster action in combating VAT fraud. The experiences of member states (Sweden) apply different mechanisms to prevent tax fraud. Sweden applies a questionnaire in the pre-registration control procedure for risky taxpayers - potential disappearing traders. A small number of entrepreneurs meet the criteria for a potential "disappearing merchant." This type of questionnaire is sensitive and is used in exceptional cases in cooperation with employees who are specialized in the field of fraud. The characteristics of the recommended questions for risky taxpayers (potential disappearing traders) is a larger number of questions and they must be relevant in each individual case. The experiences of member states (Sweden) have shown that many "disappearing traders" who intend to disappear after a short period do not answer questions and often give up the request for registration, i.e the assignment of a VAT identification number. By comparing the data required during registration in relation to Sweden, it is evident that the Tax Administration of the Republic of Croatia required detailed data from taxpayers starting businesses (questionnaire for assessing economic strength) even a few years before joining the European Union. One of the basic prerequisites for the fight against VAT fraud is a quality analysis of taxpayers who start a business (registration in the VAT system, allocation of a VAT ID number) as well as a visit to them because the faster the detection of risky taxpayers results in less damage to the state budget. Some member states (Lithuania) refuse to register taxpayers in the VAT system and to assign a VAT identification number to taxpayers who have participated in tax fraud and if it is determined that they do not have the conditions to perform a real economic activity. In such cases, it is not enough to fulfill one condition, but several of them (cumulative fulfillment). Lithuania is one of the member states that, by applying the risk analysis when entering the VAT system, 40% of requests were rejected.

Every year EU member states lose billions of euros in VAT revenue due to fraud. Since the EU VAT system is undergoing a deep modernization, the European Commission invests a considerable amount of work in modernizing the EU VAT system and the remaining risks of fraud cannot be ignored. A different approach and the use of new technologies allow member states to remove significant obstacles that currently prevent an effective fight against VAT fraud (Lamensch, 2018). Only a greater number of facts established by assessment results in the prevention of the activities of fictitious and non-disappearing companies, which results in a reduction of opportunities for circular VAT fraud.

CONCLUSION

After the accession of new member states to the European Union, greater opportunities for VAT fraud appear. In the EU area, various fraudulent activities of newly established companies, companies that were dormant and subsequently activated, as well as companies that had debts and were sold to new owners who insisted on the assignment of a VAT ID number before the actual purchase of such a company, appear. The largest part of circular fraud is related to trade in gold, secondary raw materials, gas and electronic equipment (mobile phones, consoles, computer games, etc.). However, other goods have also appeared in fraudulent activities, so any goods can be the subject of circular as well as chain fraud. As far as services are concerned, so far no fraudulent activities have been noticed in the area of carbon credits (CO_2 certificates) and electricity, but all member states of the European Union should be vigilant and monitor the electricity market in order to detect possible fraudulent activities in time, and therefore prevent potential fraud. In the member states, the electricity market is closely monitored, taxpayers who are registered for this activity are visited, and experts from the relevant field are invited when training officials. Taking into account the experiences of the member states, it is necessary to follow the trends of the European Union countries that are successfully combating VAT fraud. One of the best examples is Belgium, which in just two years managed to reduce fraud-related losses by 85%, with the fact that it brought a common approach for better cooperation of all competent authorities and focused its activities on detecting fraud organizers, i.e. preventing their activities, and not to disappearing merchants. In the most serious cases of fraud, it is necessary to establish expert teams and the cooperation of all relevant authorities (Tax Administration, Police, State Attorney's Office, Customs Administration and Office for the Prevention of Money Laundering) in order to react in a timely manner. From the experience of the member states, especially the Netherlands and Belgium, all member states should learn in order to react efficiently when new frauds appear and be ready to protect their budget.

DECLARATION

- The author declares that the manuscript follows ethical standards and there are no potential conflicts of interest with respect to the research, authorship and/or publication of this chapter.

DISCLAIMER

- The contents and views of this chapter are expressed by the author in her personal capacity. It is not necessary for the Editor and the Publisher to agree with these viewpoints, and they are not responsible for any duty of care in this regard.

ACKNOWLEDGMENT

The author extends sincere gratitude to

- The Editor and the International Editorial Advisory Board (IEAB) of this book who initially desk reviewed, arranged a rigorous double/triple blind review process, and conducted a thorough, minute, and critical final review before accepting the chapter for publication.
- All anonymous reviewers who provided very constructive feedbacks for thorough revision, improvement, extension, and fine tuning of the chapter.
- All colleagues, assistants and well-wishers who assisted to complete this task.

REFERENCES

Ainsworth, R. T. (2006). *Carousel fraud in the EU: A digital VAT solution* (Working Paper No. 06-23). Boston University School of Law. Retrieved from https://papers.ssrn.com/sol3/papers.cfm?abstract_id=924189

Ainsworth, R. T. (2009). *The morphing of MTIC fraud: VAT fraud infects tradable CO_2 permits* (Working Paper No. 09-35). Boston University School of Law. Retrieved from https://papers.ssrn.com/sol3/papers.cfm?abstract_id=1443279

Ainsworth, R. T. (2010). *VoIP MTIC - The Italian job (Operazione 'Phuncards-Broker')*. (Working Paper No. 10-09). Boston University School of Law. Retrieved from https://papers.ssrn.com/sol3/papers.cfm?abstract_id=1596608

Beebeejaun, A., Gunputh, R., & Rafay, A. (2023). Base Erosion and Profit Shifting (BEPS) in International Taxation System: The Case of Mauritius in the light of OECD/G20 initiatives. In A. Rafay (Ed.), *Concepts, Cases, and Regulations in Financial Fraud and Corruption* (pp. 259–277). IGI Global., doi:10.4018/978-1-6684-5007-9.ch011

Braml, M. T., & Felbermayr, G. J. (2019). What do we really know about the transatlantic current account? *CESifo Economic Studies*, *65*(3), 255–274. doi:10.1093/cesifo/ifz012

Braml, M. T., & Felbermayr, G. J. (2022). The EU self-surplus puzzle: An indication of VAT fraud? *International Tax and Public Finance*, *29*(5), 1075–1097. doi:10.100710797-021-09713-x

Chesson, A., Marilyn, T., & Haynes, J. (2018). *Asymmetries in trade data: Diving deeper into UK bilateral trade data*. Office for National Statistics. Retrieved from https://backup.ons.gov.uk/wp-content/uploads/sites/3/2018/01/Asymmetries-in-trade-data-diving-deeper-into-UK-bilateral-trade-data.pdf

CIS. (2013). *Croatia in figures 2013.* Croatian Institute of Statistics Retrieved from https://podaci.dzs.hr/media/w4jo4fmk/croinfig_2013.pdf

CIS. (2014). *Croatia in figures 2014.* Croatian Institute of Statistics Retrieved from https://podaci.dzs.hr/media/h40htohq/croinfig_2014.pdf

Europol. (2009). Review of Europol 2009. Retrieved from https://data.europa.eu/data/datasets?catalog=europol&showcatalogdetails=true&locale=hr

Feenstra, R. C., Hai, W., Woo, W. T., & Yao, S. (1999). Discrepancies in international data: An application to China-Hong Kong Entrepôt trade. *The American Economic Review*, *89*(2), 338–343. doi:10.1257/aer.89.2.338

Fisman, R., & Wei, S. J. (2009). The smuggling of art, and the art of smuggling: Uncovering the illicit trade in cultural property and antiques. *American Economic Journal. Applied Economics*, *1*(3), 82–96. doi:10.1257/app.1.3.82

Frunza, M. (2013). Aftermath of the VAT fraud on carbon emissions markets. *Journal of Financial Crime*, *20*(2), 222–236. doi:10.1108/13590791311322382

Frunza, M. C. (2018). *Value Added Tax Fraud.* Routledge., doi:10.4324/9781315098722

Gros, D. (2017, July 27). Is Germany's current account surplus bad for the world economy? *CEPS Commentary*. Retrieved from http://gesd.free.fr/gros2012.pdf

Helbling, T., & Terrones, M. E. (2009). From deficit to surplus: Recent shifts in global current accounts. *World Economic Outlook*, 35–39.

Keen, M., & Smith, S. (2006). VAT fraud and evasion: What do we know and what can be done? *National Tax Journal*, *59*(4), 861–887. doi:10.17310/ntj.2006.4.07

Krugman, P. (2010). The theory of interstellar trade. *Economic Inquiry*, *48*(4), 1119–1123. doi:10.1111/j.1465-7295.2009.00225.x

Lamensch, E. M. (2018). *VAT fraud: Economic impact, challenges and policy issues*. EPRS: European Parliamentary Research Service. Retrieved from https://policycommons.net/artifacts/1335646/vat-fraud/1942306/

Podlipnik, J. (2012). Missing trader intra-community and carousel VAT frauds-ECJ and ECtHR case law. *Croatian Yearbook of European Law & Policy*, *8*(1), 457–472. doi:10.3935/cyelp.08.2012.135

Rafay, A. (Ed.). (2021). *Money Laundering and Terrorism Financing in Global Financial Systems.* IGI Global., doi:10.4018/978-1-7998-8758-4

Sokanović, L. (2020). *Fraud in criminal law: A normative and criminological analysis of fraudulent crime in croatia and the regional context.* Duncker & Humblot.

Talisse, R., & Aikin, S. F. (2006). Two forms of the straw m an. *Argumentation*, *20*(3), 345–352. doi:10.100710503-006-9017-8

Van Erven, G. C., Carvalho, R. N., de Holanda, M. T., & Ralha, C. (2017, June). Graph database: A case study for detecting fraud in acquisition of brazilian government. In *2017 12th Iberian Conference on Information Systems and Technologies (CISTI)* (pp. 1-6). IEEE. 10.23919/CISTI.2017.7975974

Vézina, P. L. (2015). Illegal trade in natural resources: Evidence from missing exports. *Inter Economics, 142*, 152–160. doi:10.1016/j.inteco.2014.09.001

Vinšalek Stipić, V. (2020). Korporativno upravljanje i ekonomija trećeg puta. *Obrazovanje za poduzetništvo – E4E: Znanstveno stručni časopis o obrazovanju za poduzetništvo, 10*(1), 132–146.

Vinšalek Stipić, V. (2022). The concept and importance of social audit for sustainable community development. *BH Ekonomski forum, 16(1)*, 151–165. Retrieved from https://ef.unze.ba/OJS/index.php/BHF/article/view/255

Vinšalek Stipić, V., & Blažević, L. (2011). Upravljanje primjenom pristupa temeljenog na procjeni rizika poslovanja i rizika od pranja novca. *Praktični Menadžment - stručni časopis za teoriju i praksu menadžmenta, II*(3), 73–79. Retrieved from https://www.bib.irb.hr/996346

World Bank. (2011). World trade report 2011. Retrieved from https://www.wto.org/english/res_e/booksp_e/anrep_e/world_trade_report11_e.pdf

ADDITIONAL READING

AFCOS. (1996). Council Regulation (Euratom, EC) No 2185/96 of 11 November 1996 concerning on-the-spot checks and inspections carried out by the Commission in order to protect the European Communities' financial interests against fraud and other irregularities. Retrieved from https://eur-lex.europa.eu/legal-content/EN/TXT/?uri=CELEX:31996R2185

Council Directive. 2010/23/EU. Retrieved from https://eur-lex.europa.eu/LexUriServ/LexUriServ.do?uri=OJ:L:2010:072:0001:0002:EN:PDF

OLAF. (2021). The OLAF report 2021. Retrieved from https://anti-fraud.ec.europa.eu/system/files/2022-07/olaf-report-2021_en.pdf

UNFCCC. (2008). Kyoto protocol reference manual on accounting of emissions and assigned amount. Retrieved from https://unfccc.int/sites/default/files/08_unfccc_kp_ref_manual.pdf

Chapter 7
Corruption, Government Effectiveness, and Financial Development:
An Empirical Analysis

Faris Nasif Alshubiri
Dhofar University, Oman

ABSTRACT

Government effectiveness has emerged as an important factor in the relationship between corruption and the process of financial development. This chapter explores the relationship between corruption control, government effectiveness and financial development in 14 low- and high-income countries over the period 2005–2020 to determine the applicability of the grease the wheels and the sand the wheels hypotheses. Panel data for the two country groups were analysed after overcoming heterogeneity and endogeneity issues. Diagnostic tests were used to increase robustness. The analysis revealed that an increase in corruption control led to a decrease in financial development due to highly effective governments in high-income countries. In contrast, an increase in corruption control led to an increase in financial development due to inefficient governments in low-income countries. The main conclusions of the study are that the grease the wheels hypothesis is applicable to high-income countries and the sand the wheels one is applicable to low-income countries.

1. INTRODUCTION

Corruption has become a pivotal factor in the development of economies. As such, Dincer (2019), Ades and di Tella (1999) and others have focused on the following question in various ways: Does corruption help or hinder the process of financial development? In addition, government effectiveness has emerged as an important factor in this relationship. For example, Ehrlich and Lui (1999), Adsera *et al.* (2003) asserted that government effectiveness plays a prominent role in the project start-up process by

DOI: 10.4018/978-1-6684-8587-3.ch007

facilitating or hampering the provision of governmental advantages and any needed facilities. Government effectiveness also affects taxation, which is an integral part of the project development process.

During the last three decades, international organisations, national governments and non-governmental organisations have prioritised the issue of corruption and confronted the risks it brings to economic and social sectors. The increasing interest in this topic stems from the costs of economic and social corruption, which affect various sectors of society. Among the most important are the effects on investments and economic growth. Park and Khanoi (2017) defined corruption as the abuse of power to achieve private interests. Meanwhile, Shumetie and Watabaji (2019) and Rose-Ackerman (2009) defined corruption as a dishonest and illegal shock. Özbaran (2003) indicated that corruption is the use of the authority of officials to achieve special interests.

The risks surrounding corruption span all economic sectors. However, corruption has the greatest impact on financial institutions, since the financial system is an important part of a state's economy that attracts local and foreign investments and works to provide funds to all economic sectors for the development of society (Shahbaz & Rehman, 2012; Anwar & Nguyen, 2010). Financial sector development enhances economic growth through the advanced technologies used in all financial transactions as well as the accumulation of capital (Dincer, 2019). Financial sector development refers to the financial sector, which seeks to enhance investment by exploiting opportunities to build a strong business sector that engages in business through contracts to hedge any risks and has a diversified investment portfolio as it keeps future savings; this is called the reallocation of resources (Ades & di Tella, 1999).

In addition to the link between corruption and the financial system, this also depends on government effectiveness (Ahmad & Saleem, 2014; Rafay, 2023), which is an indicator used to ensure the integrity of transactions and the efficiency of the bureaucracy and enable infrastructure maintenance in order to support the exchange of goods and the provision of services (Levi, 2006). The World Bank (2018) defined government effectiveness as the degree of awareness of the quality of services and their independence from political pressures.

The academic debate about corruption can be cast from different points of view. For example, Dreher and Gassebner (2013) depicted corruption as an obstacle to the achievement of economic growth and social development by private companies. Others have stated that bribery hinders competition, increases potential public health risks, distorts the incentives granted to companies and lowers ethical standards (Budsaratragoona & Jitmaneerojb, 2020; Beekman *et al.*, 2013). Aidt (2009) and Fisman and Svensson (2007) described corruption as reducing growth by imposing a tax It is a great deal of innovative activity. He also noted that bribery increases production costs for companies and reduces investment due to low returns. Mauro (1995), Brunetti and Weder (1998) and Mo (2001) identified a significant negative relationship between corruption and investment and showed that it hindered economic growth. As a result, international organizations (e.g., the IMF, the World Bank, the UN, and the OECD) have made the fight against corruption a high priority.

Other research has indicated that corruption is beneficial and may sharpen the wheels of commerce, reduce government barriers and business risks, hedge against bureaucrats and promote innovation. Adsera *et al.* (2003) and Bardhan (2002) highlighted situations in which corruption may have favoured development by allowing entrepreneurs to grow out of bribers. Beck and Maher (1986) and Lien (1986) argued that corruption leads to increased efficiency. Lambsdorff (2003) indicated that corruption may be beneficial in countries with ineffective governance but harmful in other places. In this sense, governance quality affects participation in corruption (Scully, 2002). At the company level, Drury *et al.* (2006) found that corruption reduces the time of process work and increases harmony with other countries. They also found that multinational companies that pay more bribes spend more time negotiating with officials from foreign countries, which contradicts the hypothesis of greasing wheels. According to Bologna and Ross (2015), bribery helps buyers obtain licenses at the beginning of projects, allowing them to begin working sooner than if they had followed the usual channels and possibly reducing their start-up costs.

The main justification for the beneficial effects of corruption rests on the so-called hypothesis of grease the wheels (Mendoza *et al.*, 2015). According to this argument, inefficient bureaucracy constitutes an impediment to investment that can be circumvented by offering money to speed up or grease the wheels of the process (Ünlü & Ulusoy, 2021). In a nutshell, the grease the wheels hypothesis states that graft may help save the time of the process, thereby increasing efficiency, investment, and, eventually, growth (Pellegrini & Gerlagh, 2006).

Despite a large number of studies on the aforementioned topic, one of the main reasons is data unreliability. Corruption is difficult to measure. Some have argued that corruption should be measured through the opinions of experts or ordinary citizens, or the number of bribes recorded each year (Iwasaki & Suzuki, 2012; Ko & Samajdar, 2010). Despite the measurement challenges, the literature indicates that corruption may become harmful in the presence of government inefficiency, as the failure of a government to manage the governance of its country increases the distortion of the system, which reflect damage to the level of welfare. This chapter helps bridge the research gap in the literature by comparing how the grease the wheels and the sand the wheels' hypotheses contribute to financial growth and development in low- and high-income countries. These countries have two different levels of income. We tried to diagnose the impact of corruption on financial development, especially when countries have been affected by financial and banking crises. Furthermore, there are limited studies on the analysis of the financial sector and corruption and their relationship to government effectiveness.

The significance of the present study relates to the importance of the financial and banking markets. Their stability is a valuable indicator of economic growth because it provides the majority of financial resources to economies (Chen *et al.*, 2023), especially middle-income economies. An analysis of corruption in financial institutions is important for diagnosing the factors that affect the growth of the banking sector and helping government authorities take appropriate measures to reduce the level of corruption. However, the present study examined banking financial development because local and foreign investors need a sound financial market in order to choose an economy that can help them partially finance their projects by providing credit facilities. The need for sound financial institutions, especially in foreign investment, increases when choosing a host country; it seeks to have regular financial transactions, while financial institutions reduce the cost of finance in the host country by collecting, monitoring and processing investment information (Shafiu *et al.*, 2023). Government efficiency is also a decisive factor in attracting investment, which later reflects on financial development; therefore, the existence of effective government oversight paves the way for sound financial transactions.

In this chapter, we measured the corruption control index and financial development, in which financial development is considered part of the growth of societies and the building of social and economic structures (Coleman, 1990). A combination of technological developments, transparency and corruption control helps build a healthy society based on solid principles and leads to more financial development. Therefore, it is difficult for a closed economy and a weak financial sector to play a prominent role in the financial markets in light of the adoption of corrupt practices.

The main implication of the study is that corruption has a significant impact on social activities. A better and more effective financial sector enhances the spirit of entrepreneurship in a specific industry and among competitors, which enhances social ties. Meanwhile, according to Ades and Di Tella (1999) and Sharma and Mitra (2015), there is less corruption in countries with high levels of market competition; consequently, enhancing financial competition between bank controls reduces corruption and the cost of credit. If the levels of corruption in societies increase, the poor become poorer while the rich become richer, leading to persistent poverty and inequality. Corruption is a negative social phenomenon characterised by deviation from the right path, which is the one that promotes the interests and standards of society. Thus, corruption is not a general phenomenon; rather, it is specific to the lives of individuals in various social activities.

The main objective of this chapter was to examine the impact of corruption control, government effectiveness and financial development in low- and high-income countries. This relationship has been explained by two basic theories: grease the wheels and sand the wheels. The novelty of this chapter lies in its exploration of the interaction between corruption and government effectiveness in the model, which has been missing in the literature.

The rest of this chapter is organized as follows. Section 2 presents the theoretical framework of the grease the wheels and the sand the wheels hypotheses. Section 3 describes the econometric methodology approach. Section 4 discusses the results. Section 5 presents conclusions and policy implications.

2. LITERATURE REVIEW

The debate on the impact of corruption and financial development goes beyond a moralistic view. In many debates, the arguments fall into the greasing the wheels' view or the sanding the wheels' view (Mendoza *et al.*, 2015). According to the former argument, corruption may occur in parallel with a weak quality of governance and reduce the inconveniences caused by that low quality (Méon & Sekkat, 2005). According to the latter argument, although bribery may lead to benefits, it can also impose costs if the quality of governance is low (Méon & Weill, 2010). These two views support the relationship of corruption and low-quality governance. The main issue of governance depends on the goals and policies of the government.

2.1 Hypothesis: Grease the wheels

Poor bureaucratic performance is the most prominent catalyst of government inefficiency, which is a key element of the grease the wheels hypothesis (Campante *et al.*, 2009). Society is characterized by rigidity and bureaucracy more than centralisation in the sense of the existence of a rigid and excessively centralised authority (Kaufmann & Wei, 1999). Lui (1985) indicated that corruption may increase efficiency by reducing time spent in queues. In addition, bribes can speed up work by decreasing the length of the bureaucratic process (Drury *et al.*, 2006).

Huntington (1968) argued that corruption supports tedious bureaucratic regulations and fosters growth, whereas corruption by railroad, utility and industrial corporations promotes growth. Furthermore, corruption improves an ill-functioning bureaucracy by enhancing the quality of its civil servants (Leys, 1965; Bailey, 1966).

Beck and Maher (1986) and Lien (1986) argued that corruption can affect the outcome of a competitive auction if bureaucrats do not have enough information and may affect the decisions made by officials. Regarding what are considered official issues, governments are exposed to bribery from various angles. For example, corruption may play an active role in project selection when government licenses are required (Dreher & Gassebner, 2013). In this scenario, a government license is very similar to a competitive auction, as the licenses tend to go to more generous bribers who can be more efficient (Ellis *et al.*, 2020). Hence, the capacity to offer a bribe is correlated with talent.

Corruption also plays a prominent role in shaping government policies. Bologna and Ross (2015) indicated that bribes could enhance private agents and public policies designed to solve problems related to governance. Bologna (2018) argued that grafts may be used to hedge against bad public policies. This is a true picture once institutions are biased against entrepreneurship (Ghoneim & Ezzat, 2016). By simply impeding inefficient government regulations, corruption may limit its adverse effects. According to other scenarios, grafts may improve the quality of investments (Swaleheen, 2011). Swaleheen and Stansel (2007) found that, in the presence of inefficient government spending, corruption in the form of tax evasion led to a decrease in public taxes, and bribery improved the overall efficiency of investments. According to Adsera *et al.* (2003), corruption may act as a hedge against the political systems of countries, such as expropriation or violence. When corruption is used to avoid those risks, investment risks decrease, and the number of investments increases (Haydaroğlu, 2016).

These studies have suggested that corruption can positively contribute to growth and development because of defective bureaucracy and bad policies. Bribery may lead to benefits; however, under a low-quality institutional environment, it also increases costs, providing a rationale for the sand the wheels hypothesis in some circumstances.

2.2. Hypothesis: Sand the wheels

The positive impact of corruption on the growth of societies with poor bureaucratic performance is a key feature of the sand the wheels hypothesis (Giordano & Lopez-Garcia, 2018). Corruption in civil society institutions may cause a delay in growth if the bribery is made public. Moreover, the ability of civil society to speed up processes is limited when decisions are centralised (Goedhuys *et al.*, 2016). Therefore, every stage of civil society development may be subject to bribery or slow-down projects. Using industrial models of organization, Shleifer and Vishny (1993) indicated that the cost of corruption can be increased once authorization for a project has been granted. Hanousek and Kochanova (2016) stated that an increase in transactions might lead to graft; however, that graft would increase the efficiency of transactions carried out under these circumstances. These circumstances are in line with the sand the wheels hypothesis.

At the macro level, corruption is in the quality of civil society. Corrupt officials have an incentive to maintain illegal actions as well as security and allocate these services in exchange for bribes to preserve corruption in exchange for rent (Kunieda *et al.*, 2014). Bribery improves the social status of individuals through the advantages of corruption. This stems from the argument that corruption makes the more correct decisions; however, agents may take large bribes that may hinder growth (Lee *et al.* 2020). Martins *et al.* (2020) found that market entry may be beneficial to a company but detrimental to its welfare. Furthermore, Pluskota (2020) noted that a company may consider paying a bribe to obtain a license to be its best option unless the profitability of that license is uncertain.

In an environment with inadequate government and public policy institutions, corruption has multiple effects (Rodríguez-Pose & Di Cataldo, 2015). Corruption may increase the number and quality of investments, which is proof that it may not be true for government investment. Tanzi and Davoodi (1997) found that an increase in corruption increases government investment, while Mauro (1998) found that this results in a diversion of public spending towards less efficient allocations. In other words, corruption may lead to unproductive investment sectors, which are unlikely to improve efficiency or result in faster development (Sharma and Mitra, 2015).

Corruption can serve as a way to hedge against political risks and the uncertainty of commercial legislation, and this may be true in the event that corruption does not cause additional risks (Saha & Sen, 2021). In any case, corruption is not an easy process, as it is considered illegal. Compliance with the terms of a bribery agreement may be very weak and lead to opportunism, especially on the bribe's part. As Bardhan (2002) indicated, the inherent uncertainty of corruption leads to ineffective efficiency-enhancing mechanisms. This presumption was supported by Campos *et al.* (1999) and Lambsdorff (2003), who indicated that predictions of corruption have direct effects on capital and investments independent of the level of corruption; therefore, corruption may increase the risks associated with the weakness of governance instead of compensating for it.

Therefore, the present study sought to examine the applicability of the grease the wheels and the sand the wheels perspectives while addressing the following main research question:

- H-1: Is there a significant relationship between corruption control, government effectiveness and financial development in low- and high-income countries?

3. METHODOLOGY AND MAIN EMPIRICAL MODEL

This study examined the grease the wheels and the sand the wheels perspectives on corruption as well as the relationship between corruption control, government effectiveness and financial development in 14 low- and high-income countries. The panel data technique was used to examine data collected from the World Development Indicators (World Bank, 2022) and Worldwide Governance Indicator (WGI, 2022) reports for the period of 2005–2020. Appendix A lists the countries included in the study. The reason behind the selection of the sample for both groups of low and high-income countries is due to the rapid economic development of high-income countries in recent years, while the other low-income countries remain less developed.

The basic functional forms of the corruption, government effectiveness and financial development nexus of the main panel model were described as follows:

$$BAS_{i,t} = \beta_0 + \beta_0 IV_{i,t} + \beta_0 control\ variables_{i,t} + \varepsilon_{i,t} \tag{1}$$

where BAS_{it}, banking stability, is measured by the risk premium on the lending (lending rate minus treasury bill rate, %) proxy of the country *I* at time *t* as the dependent variable. $IV_{i,t}$ are the corruption control (CORR) index and the government effectiveness (GEF) index proxies. The *control variables*$_{i,t}$ are GDP per capita growth (annual %) (GDP); inflation, consumer prices (annual %) (INF); and bank capital to assets ratio (%) (BCA).

The banking system is the main driver of savings and productive capital for any country (Rafay & Gilani, 2016). Therefore, the allocation of resources between productive activities works on a platform of economic prosperity and development (Levine, 1997, 2005). In any case, corruption in credit lending operations reduces the efficiency of capital allocation and works to distribute capital from productive activities to non-productive activities. Hence, the main research question of this chapter was as follows:

Does corruption grease or sand the wheels? and their relationship between corruption with government effectiveness and financial development.

The studied period covered 18 years and included the financial crises in 2007–2008, which is significant because, in most economic sectors, banks avoided pursuing risky activities in their quest to support financial services. The descriptive statistics for all variables of the main econometric model as well as the correlation matrix were analysed. The stationarity of the variables at each level was determined using augmented IPS and Levin-Lin-Chu (LLC) unit root tests (Im, Pesaran & Shin, 2003). The panel data analysis started with basic regression for the panel least squares (PLS), followed by the use of fixed effect (FE), random effect (RE) and feasible general least squares (FGLS). Diagnostic tests were used to increase robustness, and the Wooldridge test for autocorrelation and the modified Wald test for groupwise heteroskedasticity were also used.

The Hausman test was employed to determine whether to use FE or RE. Time series and cross-sectional panel data were used to minimize the multicollinearity problem (De Hoyos and Sarafidis, 2006). The endogeneity problem in the panel data was solved using dynamic intertemporality (Hsiao, 2007). Additionally, the heterogeneity of the panel data was solved based on time and country observations (Baltagi, 2012). The PLS estimator was used as the first test of the hypothesis because it ignores the possibility of group structure and supposes that different periods are in the same trend, so we considered the bias for this estimator. Then, FE and RE were used, and the Hausman test was run because it is the main diagnostic test for selecting the best estimator and avoiding heterogeneity and endogeneity (Wooldridge, 2010). FE regression confirmed that coefficients of variables as a one-time intercept for each subject and individual-specific effects were correlated with independent variables under non-random conditions for each group of a specific fixed quantity.

Meanwhile, RE illustrated the different levels of the values by variance to explain the predictor variables and overcome unobserved heterogeneity during the time period and lack of correlation with the independent variables. To overcome serial correlation and heteroskedasticity issues, the FGLS estimator was used to estimate the coefficients under a multiple linear regression model. Furthermore, the covariance matrix under this estimator evaluated the presence of non-spherical innovations with an unknown covariance matrix.

4. RESULTS

This section explains the results of the study and interprets the grease/sand hypotheses that were tested.

4.1 Descriptive Statistics

Table 1 shows the descriptive statistics for six variables for 14 low- and high-income countries over the period of 2005–2020. The data included 112 observations in each country. Specifically, the lower values refer to GEF for the low- and high-income countries, while the median values for CORR were lower in both country groups. In contrast, the median values for BCA were higher in both country groups. The standard deviations for most variables were higher in the low-income countries than in the high-income ones.

Skewness is a measure of a lack of symmetry. Most variables in each country group had positive skewness except CORR and GEF in the high-income countries and GDP in the low-income countries.

Kurtosis is a measure of heavy-tailed (high kurtosis) or light-tailed (low kurtosis) data relative to a normal distribution. The probability for all variables revealed by the Jarque-Bera test results indicated that the model was significant for the low- and high-income countries, which means that the data did not follow the normal distribution.

Table 1. Descriptive statistics

	CORR	GEF	BAS	GDP	INF	BCA
High- income Countries						
Mean	1.093	1.047	3.520	2.226	3.456	9.922
Median	1.270	1.280	3.186	1.859	2.699	8.656
Maximum	2.340	1.970	12.11	11.14	12.69	21.05
Minimum	-0.260	-0.360	1.007	-7.094	-1.544	5.043
Std. Dev.	0.732	0.652	1.726	2.807	2.791	4.420
Skewness	-0.330	-0.860	2.747	0.001	0.979	1.214
Kurtosis	2.026	2.554	13.31	4.643	3.596	3.527
Jarque-Bera	6.467	14.75	637.4	12.60	19.55	28.82
Probability	0.039	0.000	0.000	0.001	0.000	0.000
Sum	122.4	117.2	394.2	249.3	387.1	1111.2
Sum Sq. Dev.	59.53	47.32	330.8	874.7	865.1	2168.5
Observations	112	112	112	112	112	112
Low-income Countries						
Mean	-0.649	-0.735	16.03	2.648	7.587	12.74
Median	-0.775	-0.715	12.13	3.064	6.484	11.60
Maximum	0.760	0.270	52.30	18.05	20.47	32.57
Minimum	-1.420	-1.340	-3.445	-22.31	-0.309	3.345
Std. Dev.	0.510	0.392	12.31	4.103	4.127	6.129
Skewness	1.202	0.671	1.584	-1.926	0.860	1.064
Kurtosis	3.915	2.903	4.908	16.31	3.447	3.889
Jarque-Bera	30.88	8.458	63.86	896.8	14.74	24.83
Probability	0.000	0.014	0.000	0.000	0.000	0.000
Sum	-72.71	-82.35	1795.9	296.6	849.8	1427.4
Sum Sq. Dev.	28.93	17.13	16826.7	1868.	1890.6	4170.5
Observations	112	112	112	112	112	112

4.2 Correlation matrix

All regressors of the coefficients of correlation are presented in Table 2. Most variables were significant. Furthermore, there was compression between low- and high-income countries. Regarding the high-income countries, there were negative relationships between CORR and BAS (-.404), CORR and GDP

(-.284), BAS and BCA (-.065) and GDP and BCA (-.066) as well as between GEF and BAS, GDP and INF (-.339, -.388, and -.308). Meanwhile, there were positive relationships between the other variables. Regarding the low-income countries, there were negative relationships between CORR and BAS and INF (-.181, -.048), between GEF and BAS and INF (-.334, -.200), between BAS and GDP, INF and BCA (-.210, -.121, -.086) and between INF and BCA (-.204). Meanwhile, there were positive relationships between the other variables. Most variables had low values and strength coefficients, indicating that there was no multicollinearity between predictor and response as two independent and/or control variables (Evans, 1996).

Table 2. Correlation Matrix

VARIABLES	CORR	GEF	BAS	GDP	INF	BCA
	High- income Countries					
CORR	1.000					

GEF	0.799	1.000				
	0.000	-----				
BAS	-0.404	-0.339	1.000			
	0.000	0.000	-----			
GDP	-0.284	-0.388	0.098	1.000		
	0.002	0.000	0.302	-----		
INF	0.099	-0.308	0.112	0.060	1.000	
	0.298	0.000	0.235	0.528	-----	
BCA	0.454	0.221	-0.065	-0.066	0.280	1.000
	0.000	0.019	0.490	0.484	0.002	-----
	Low-income Countries					
CORR	1.000					

GEF	0.776	1.000				
	0.000	-----				
BAS	-0.181	-0.334	1.000			
	0.054	0.000	-----			
GDP	0.080	0.155	-0.210	1000		
	0.401	0.100	0.026	-----		
INF	-0.048	-0.200	-0.121	0.081	1000	
	0.611	0.034	0.202	0.391	-----	
BCA	0.217	0.355	-0.086	0.129	-0.204	1.000
	0.021	0.000	0.364	0.172	0.030	-----

4.3 Unit root tests

Table 3 presents the IPS and LLC unit root test findings for the low- and high-income countries. The findings showed that all variables were stationarity at the level and the first difference, indicating that all variables were integrated in the order I(0).

Table 3. Panel unit root IPS test and LLC test

	CORR	GEF	BAS	GDP	INF	BCA
	High – income countries					
IPS (Level)	-1.56**	-3.63***	-4.63***	- -2.63***	-2.13**	-1.89**
IPS (1St Difference)	-6.80***	-10.7***	-9.94***	-8.39***	-8.07***	-5.60***
LLC test t (Level)	-2.42***	-3.28***	-5.29***	-3.76***	-3.58***	-2.91***
LLC test (1St Difference)	-8.59***	-11.2***	-12.36***	-10.2***	-9.09***	-6.88***
	Low-income Countries					
IPS (Level)	-0.340	-4.28***	-3.206***	-3.47***	-3.01***	-1.23
IPS (1St Difference)	-5.23***	-11.67***	-6.96***	-8.74***	-10.84***	-4.98***
LLC test t (Level)	-2.89***	-4.60***	-3.73***	-4.76***	-5.00***	- -1.66**
LLC test (1st Difference)	-5.95***	-14.1***	-7.74***	-11.12***	-13.22***	-3.95***
Note: The significance levels refer to $p < 0.01$ (***), $p < 0.05$ (**) and $p < 0.1$ (*).						

4.4 PLS

The PLS estimator results for both models for the low- and high-income countries are presented in Table 4. Models 1 and 2 revealed a significant negative relationship between CORR and BAS in low-income countries. A 1% increase in CORR led to a -.733 decrease in BAS. Meanwhile, there was a significant positive relationship between CORR and BAS in high-income countries. A 1% increase in CORR led to a 3.95 increase in BAS. In addition, there was a significant negative relationship between GEF and BAS in low-income countries. A 1% increase in GEF led to a -12.77 decrease in BAS. The control variables were significant in all models except Model 2 for BCA. Specifically, there was a significant negative relationship between GDP and BAS in the low- and high-income countries and a significant negative relationship between INF and BAS in the low-income countries. Furthermore, there was a significant positive relationship between BAS and INF and BCA in high-income countries.

Table 4. Panel Least Squares

VARIABLES	Model (1) High–income countries BAS	Model (2) Low–income countries BAS
CORR	-.733***	3.95***
	(.232)	(1.03)
GEF	-.288	-12.77***
	(.370)	(1.99)
GDP	-.047*	-.238**
	(.026)	(.096)
INF	.061**	-.409***
	(.026)	(.075)
BCA	.035*	.082
	(.018)	(.053)
Constant	4.20***	11.16***
	(.320)	(1.35)
R-squared	.261	.439
F-statistic	7.520	16.60
Prob(F-statistic)	.000	.000
Cross-sections	7	7

Note: The significance levels refer to $p < 0.01$ (***), $p < 0.05$ (**) and $p < 0.1$ (*).

4.5 FE and RE regressions

FE and RE were run to overcome the heterogeneity problem, and the Hausman test was used to select which one was the best estimator for the present study. The findings were consistent with those of the PLS estimator. As shown in Table 5, there was a significant positive relationship between GEF and BAS in high-income countries and an insignificant relationship between CORR and BAS in low-income countries. The results for INF and BAS for low- and high-income countries were consistent with the PLS estimator results. Furthermore, the results for BCA and BAS in high-income countries were consistent with the PLS estimator results. Meanwhile, the probability of the Wald chi2(5) value and the F-value were significant in both models, implying that the models were appropriate and fit.

Table 5. FE and RE regressions

	Model (1)	Model (2)
	High–income countries	Low–income countries
VARIABLES	BAS	BAS
	FE	RE
CORR	-4.38***	1.34
	(1.60	(3.69)
GEF	2.92*	-16.94***
	(1.73)	(4.82)
GDP	.012	-.123
	(.056)	(.141)
INF	.225***	-.461***
	(.075)	(.140)
BCA	.248*	.119
	(.148)	(.147)
Constant	1.98	6.76
	(2.08)	(9.56)
F (5, 100)	3.47	-
Prob > F	.006	-
Wald chi2(5)	-	44.76
Prob > chi2	-	.000
Cross-sections	7	7
Modified Wald test for groupwise heteroskedasticity -chi2 (6)	1190.7	191.85
Prob.	.000	.000
Wooldridge test for autocorrelation - Prob	.0255	.0037
Hausman test	.001	1.00

Note: The significance levels refer to $p < 0.01$ (***), $p < 0.05$ (**) and $p < 0.1$ (*).

4.6 FGLS estimator

To overcome problems of heteroskedasticity and serial correlation, the FGLS estimator was used. As shown in Table 5, this estimator confirmed the PLS results in both models and the FE and RE results in some models. The probability of the Wald chi2(5) value was significant in both models, implying that all models were appropriate and fit.

Table 6. Feasible Generalized Least Squares Regression

VARIABLES	Model (1)	Model (3)
	BAS	BAS
	High–income countries	Low–income countries
CORR	-1.58***	5.85*
	(.441)	(3.32)
GEF	.622	-17.41***
	(.511)	(4.59)
GDP	-.003	-.392
	(.056)	(.262)
INF	.134*	-.605**
	(.069)	(.267)
BCA	.049	.068
	(.038)	(.158)
Constant	3.65***	11.80***
	(.542)	(4.34)
Wald chi2(5)	29.45	26.45
Prob > chi2	.000	.000
Cross-sections	7	7
Panels:	All models showed no autocorrelation	
Correlation	All models showed homoscedastic	
Note: The significance levels refer to p < 0.01 (***), p < 0.05 (**) and p < 0.1 (*).		

4.7 Diagnostic Tests

As shown in Table 5, many diagnostic tests were used to increase the robustness of the models. The findings showed that the models were unbiased, fit and consistent. In addition, the models were stationarity and integrated at the order I (0), as shown in Table 3. Based on the results of the Hausman test, FE was selected for Model 1 for the high-income countries, and RE was selected for Model 2 in the low-income countries. In addition, FGLS was run to overcome the problems of heteroskedasticity in all models and serial correlation in the results is shown in Table 5. Table 6 shows that the panels were homoscedastic and that there was no autocorrelation in the models.

5. DISCUSSION

Using multiple estimators, this study examined whether the grease the wheels and the sand the wheels hypotheses were valid in 14 low- and high-income countries. The main conclusion behind the sand the wheels hypothesis is that corruption leads to various kinds of economic distortions that hinder financial development. Méon and Sekkat (2005) supported this view by restricting the sand the wheels hypothesis to countries with bad governance. The significant negative results for GDP and corruption confirmed the sand the wheels hypothesis.

The study's findings revealed the nature of the relationship between the quality of governance and corruption, and the results differed as the negative estimates of the corruption variables became generally positive, and the role of the quality of governance reflected those results. Other variables may affect the relationship between corruption and financial development; for example, the rule of law and the competence of governments enhance the grease the wheels hypothesis (Méon & Sekkat, 2005). Meanwhile, the effect of corruption on GDP gives a reason for a certain growth under maximize growth level of quality of governments, then the corruption shifts from beneficial to detrimental. Méndez and Sepúlveda (2006) identified a non-monotonic relationship between corruption and development and asserted that corruption supports development when the quality of governance is low, supporting the grease the wheels hypothesis.

In addition, corruption simultaneously affects the accumulation of capital and attracts the grease the wheels hypothesis; However, the presence of a government efficiency variable makes choosing a theory difficult. Greasing the wheels occurs more often in countries with lower quality, especially with regard to the GDP, than explains that governance must work well for corruption to show rational economic results. In general, corruption exists in most countries in different proportions, cannot be prohibited and may be beneficial in different aspects. Therefore, countries must address the pre-existing distortions that led to the existence of corruption, such as developing legislation and government efficiency, and thus, countries work to attract the grease the wheels hypothesis.

The analysis of corruption is complicated because it can be simultaneously useful and harmful to companies and businessmen, depending on its form and type. If we assume that bribery is an example of corruption, then facilitating the obtaining of a building permit may differ significantly from bribery in order to avoid taxes. For example, an entrepreneur may try to facilitate the establishment of a project to avoid wasting time and promoting growth or submit a fixed bid for a government contract to rebuild the infrastructure of the state to address significant shortcomings at the system level, avoid costly corrections and reduce competition.

Even if most countries support the grease the wheels hypothesis, it is important to bear in mind that corruption has harmful and asymmetric effects. Furthermore, it will likely weaken beneficial collective social norms and increase economic distortions.

6. CONCLUSION AND POLICY IMPLICATIONS

According to Mauro's (1995) seminal paper, the greases the wheels versus sands the wheels debate largely confirmed the latter theory, because most debaters described the negative effects of corruption. However, Dreher and Gassebner (2013) revived the grease the wheels theory by showing that corruption can be beneficial when government regulations are excessive. This theory has gained more support for growth and enhanced the benefits of corruption.

This chapter has shown that an increase in corruption control leads to a decrease in financial development under highly effective governments in high-income countries, supporting the grease the wheels hypothesis and the beneficial effects of corruption. In contrast, this chapter has also shown that an increase in corruption control leads to an increase in financial development under ineffective governments in low-income countries. Therefore, for low-income countries, we rejected the grease the wheels hypothesis in favour of the sand the wheels hypothesis. It is found that a weak or inefficient government tends to worsen the negative impact of corruption on financial development, increasing the need for corruption control in order to achieve growth. Furthermore, government efficiency levels affect play a prominent role in whether countries encourage corruption. However, economic variables are no less important in interactions with corruption systems in countries.

A main implication of the corruption analysis in this study is that sophisticated modelling requires the accumulation of physical capital. This may be explained by the accumulation of human and social capital or improvements in aggregate government efficiency, which affect decision-making in economic sectors. Another important implication of this chapter is the need for governments to focus on enhancing transparency in all economic, financial, industrial, tourism and service sectors in order to gain confidence at the local and foreign levels and attract investors. In addition, governments should remove trade barriers and encourage the private sector to work in an integrated manner with the public sector in order to inject a spirit of social cooperation into their dealings, reject private interests and increase international cooperation. Meanwhile, since governments should adopt effective international competition standards to promote international trade and economic openness, there is a growing interest among policy-makers, civil society and government officials to identify the factors that affect corruption in developed and developing economies. This is especially crucial because corruption affects all aspects of life in society as well as economic development and political and social stability. The banking system should aim to stimulate the effectiveness of flexible credit policies with regard to interest rates on loans, improve the ease of doing business, and create more economic policies for the private sector in order to achieve sustainable economic growth capable of increasing the level of financial development.

The main limitation of this chapter is that it reveals an indirect relationship between corruption perception and financial development, as the dataset does not provide evidence of the effect of sub-economic sectors. Another limitation is the short time period under analysis due to the lack of availability of a corruption series for a longer period of time. In the future, we plan to conduct an in-depth analysis of the channels of corruption and growth and take advantage of improvements in those measures and the availability of data for a longer timeframe. In addition, future research could explain corruption and financial markets.

Note: The seven high-income countries were Australia, Iceland, Israel, Romania, the Czech Republic, Uruguay and the United States. The seven low-income countries were the Gambia, Madagascar, Mozambique, Rwanda, Sierra Leone, Tajikistan and Uganda.

DECLARATION

The author declares that the manuscript follows ethical standards and there are no potential conflicts of interest with respect to the research, authorship and/or publication of this chapter.

DISCLAIMER

The contents and views of this chapter are expressed by the author in his personal capacity. It is not necessary for the Editor and the Publisher to agree with these viewpoints, and they are not responsible for any duty of care in this regard.

ACKNOWLEDGMENT

The author extends sincere gratitude to

• The Editor and the International Editorial Advisory Board (IEAB) of this book who initially desk reviewed, arranged a rigorous double/triple blind review process, and conducted a thorough, minute, and critical final review before accepting the chapter for publication.

• All anonymous reviewers who provided very constructive feedbacks for thorough revision, improvement, extension, and fine tuning of the chapter.

• All colleagues, assistants and well-wishers who assisted the authors to complete this task.

REFERENCES

Ades, A., & di Tella, R. (1999). Rents, competition, and corruption. *The American Economic Review*, *89*(4), 982–993. doi:10.1257/aer.89.4.982

Adsera, A., Boix, C., & Payne, M. (2003). Are you being served? Political accountability and quality of government. *Journal of Law Economics and Organization*, *19*(2), 445–490. doi:10.1093/jleo/ewg017

Ahmad, Z., & Saleem, A. (2014). Impact of governance on human development. *Pakistan Journal of Commerce and Social Sciences*, *8*(3), 612–628.

Aidt, T. (2009). Corruption, institutions, and economic development. *Oxford Review of Economic Policy*, *25*(2), 271–291. doi:10.1093/oxrep/grp012

Anwar, S., & Nguyen, L. (2010). Foreign direct investment and economic growth in Vietnam. *Asia Pacific Business Review*, *16*(1-2), 183–202. doi:10.1080/10438590802511031

Bailey, D. H. (1966). The effects of corruption in a developing nation. *The Western Political Quarterly*, *19*(4), 719–732. doi:10.1177/106591296601900410

Baltagi, B. H. (2012). *Econometric Analysis of Panel Data*. Wiley.

Bardhan, P. (2002). *Corruption and development: A review of issues*. Routledge.

Beck, P. J., & Maher, M. W. (1986). A comparison of bribery and bidding in thin markets. *Economics Letters*, *20*(1), 1–5. doi:10.1016/0165-1765(86)90068-6

Beekman, G., Bulte, E., & Nillesen, E. (2013). Corruption and economic activity: Micro level evidence from rural Liberia. *European Journal of Political Economy*, *30*, 70–79. doi:10.1016/j.ejpoleco.2013.01.005

Bologna, J., & Ross, A. (2015). Corruption and entrepreneurship: Evidence from Brazilian municipalities. *Public Choice*, *165*(1-2), 59–77. doi:10.100711127-015-0292-5

Bologna Pavlik, J. (2018). Corruption: The good, the bad, and the uncertain. *Review of Development Economics*, *22*(1), 311–332. doi:10.1111/rode.12343

Brunetti, A., & Weder, B. (1998). Investment and institutional uncertainty: A comparative study of different uncertainty measures. *Weltwirtschaftliches Archiv*, *134*(3), 513–533. doi:10.1007/BF02707928

Budsaratragoona, P., & Jitmaneerojb, B. (2020). A critique on the corruption perceptions index: An interdisciplinary approach. *Socio-Economic Planning Sciences*, *70*, 100768. doi:10.1016/j.seps.2019.100768

Campante, F., Chor, D., & Do, Q. A. (2009). Instability and the incentives for corruption. *Economics and Politics*, *21*(1), 42–92. doi:10.1111/j.1468-0343.2008.00335.x

Campos, J. E., Lien, D., & Pradhan, S. (1999). The impact of corruption on investment: Predictability matters. *World Development*, *27*(6), 1059–1067. doi:10.1016/S0305-750X(99)00040-6

Chen, S., Hassan, M. S., Latif, A., Rafay, A., Mahmood, H., & Xu, X. (2023, June). Investigating resource curse/blessing hypothesis: An empirical insight from Luxembourg, the Netherlands, and Portugal economies. *Resources Policy*, *83*, 103647. doi:10.1016/j.resourpol.2023.103647

Coleman, J. (1990). *Foundations of social theory*. Harvard University Press.

De Hoyos, R. E., & Sarafidis, V. (2006). Testing for cross-sectional dependence in panel-data models. *The Stata Journal*, *6*(4), 482–496. doi:10.1177/1536867X0600600403

Dincer, O. (2019). Does corruption slow down innovation? Evidence from a cointegrated panel of U.S. states. *European Journal of Political Economy*, *56*, 1–10. doi:10.1016/j.ejpoleco.2018.06.001

Dreher, A., & Gassebner, M. (2013). Greasing the wheels? The impact of regulations and corruption on firm entry. *Public Choice*, *155*(3), 413–432. doi:10.100711127-011-9871-2

Drury, C., Krieckhaus, J., & Lusztig, M. (2006). Corruption, democracy, and economic growth. *International Political Science Review*, *27*(2), 121–136. doi:10.1177/0192512106061423

Ehrlich, I., & Lui, F. (1999). Bureaucratic corruption and endogenous economic growth. *Journal of Political Economy*, *107*(6), 270–293. doi:10.1086/250111

Ellis, J., Smith, J., & White, R. (2020). Corruption and corporate innovation. *Journal of Financial and Quantitative Analysis*, *55*(7), 2124–2149. doi:10.1017/S0022109019000735

Evans, R. H. (1996). An analysis of criterion variable reliability in conjoint analysis. *Perceptual and Motor Skills*, *84*(3), 988–990. doi:10.2466/pms.1996.82.3.988

Fisman, R., & Svensson, J. (2007). Are corruption and taxation really harmful to growth? Firm level evidence. *Journal of Development Economics*, *83*(1), 63–75. doi:10.1016/j.jdeveco.2005.09.009

Ghoneim, A. F., & Ezzat, A. M. (2016). Growth and corruption in Arab countries: What type of relationship connects them? *Journal of Economics and International Finance*, *8*(5), 44–55. doi:10.5897/JEIF2015.0675

Giordano, C., & Lopez-Garcia, P. (2018). Is corruption efficiency-enhancing? A case study of the central and eastern European region. *European Journal of Comparative Economics*, *15*(1), 119–164.

Goedhuys, M., Mohnen, P., & Taha, T. (2016). Corruption, innovation and firm growth: Firm-level evidence from Egypt and Tunisia. *Eurasian Business Review*, *6*(3), 299–322. doi:10.100740821-016-0062-4

Hanousek, J., & Kochanova, A. (2016). Bribery environments and firm performance: Evidence from CEE countries. *European Journal of Political Economy*, *43*, 14–28. doi:10.1016/j.ejpoleco.2016.02.002

Haydaroğlu, C. (2016). Corruption, Institutions and Economic Growth in Sub-Saharan Africa. *International Journal of Economic Research, 7*, 14–26.

Hsiao, C. (2007). Panel data analysis-advantages and challenges. *Test, 16*(1), 1–22. doi:10.100711749-007-0046-x

Huntington, S. P. (1968). *Political order in changing societies*. Yale University Press.

Im, K. S., Pesaran, M. H., & Shin, Y. (2003). Testing for unit roots in heterogeneous panels. *Journal of Econometrics, 115*(1), 53–74. doi:10.1016/S0304-4076(03)00092-7

Iwasaki, I., & Suzuki, T. (2012). The determinants of corruption in transition economies. *Economics Letters, 114*(1), 54–60. doi:10.1016/j.econlet.2011.08.016

Kaufmann, D., & Wei, S. J. (1999). *Does "grease money" speed up the wheels of commerce?* (NBER Working Paper No. 7093). The National Bureau of Economic Research.

Ko, K., & Samajdar, A. (2010). Evaluation of international corruption indexes: Should we believe them or not? *The Social Science Journal, 47*(3), 508–540. doi:10.1016/j.soscij.2010.03.001

Kunieda, T., Okada, K., & Shibata, A. (2014). Corruption, capital account liberalization and economic growth: Theory and evidence. *Inter Economics, 139*, 80–108. doi:10.1016/j.inteco.2014.03.001

Lambsdorff, J. G. (2003). How corruption affects persistent capital flows. *Economics of Governance, 4*(3), 229–243. doi:10.100710101-002-0060-0

Lee, C. C., Wang, C. W., & Ho, S. J. (2020). Country governance, corruption, and the likelihood of firms' innovation. *Economic Modelling, 92*, 326–338. doi:10.1016/j.econmod.2020.01.013

Levi, M. (2006). Why we need a new theory of government. *Perspectives on Politics, 4*(1), 5–19. doi:10.1017/S1537592706060038

Levine, R. (1997). Financial development and economic growth: Views and agenda. *Journal of Economic Literature, 35*(2), 688–726.

Levine, R. (2005). Finance and growth: Theory and evidence. In Handbook Of Economic Growth, 1, 865–934.

Leys, C. (1965). What is the problem about corruption? *The Journal of Modern African Studies, 3*(2), 215–230. doi:10.1017/S0022278X00023636

Lien, D. H. D. (1986). A note on competitive bribery games. *Economics Letters, 22*(4), 337–341. doi:10.1016/0165-1765(86)90093-5

Lui, F. T. (1985). An equilibrium queuing model of bribery. *Journal of Political Economy, 93*(4), 760–781. doi:10.1086/261329

Martins, L., Cerdeira, J., & Teixeira, A. A. C. (2020). Does corruption boost or harm firm's' performance in developing and emerging economies? A firm-level study. *World Economy, 43*(8), 2119–2152. doi:10.1111/twec.12966

Mauro, P. (1995). Corruption and growth. *The Quarterly Journal of Economics*, *110*(3), 681–712. doi:10.2307/2946696

Mauro, P. (1998). Corruption and the composition of government expenditure. *Journal of Public Economics*, *69*(2), 263–279. doi:10.1016/S0047-2727(98)00025-5

Méndez, F., & Facundo, S. (2006). Corruption, growth and political regimes: Cross-country evidence. *European Journal of Political Economy*, *22*(1), 82–98. doi:10.1016/j.ejpoleco.2005.04.005

Mendoza, R., Lim, R., & Lopez, A. O. (2015). Grease or sand in the wheels of commerce? Firm level evidence on corruption and SMES. *Journal of International Development*, *27*(4), 415–439. doi:10.1002/jid.3077

Méon, P. G., & Sekkat, K. (2005). Does corruption grease or sand the wheels of growth? *Public Choice*, *122*(1), 69–97. doi:10.100711127-005-3988-0

Méon, P. G., & Weill, L. (2010). Is corruption an efficient grease? *World Development*, *38*(3), 244–259. doi:10.1016/j.worlddev.2009.06.004

Mo, P. H. (2001). Corruption and economic growth. *Journal of Comparative Economics*, *29*(1), 66–79. doi:10.1006/jcec.2000.1703

Özbaran, H. (2003). Yolsuzluk ve bu alanda mücadele eden uluslararası örgütler ve birimler. *Sayıştay Dergisi*, *50*(51), 17–34.

Park, B., & Khanoi, O. (2017). How does the globalization of firms affect corruption in developing economies? *Journal of Korea Trade*, *21*(3), 256–270. doi:10.1108/JKT-02-2017-0022

Pellegrini, L., & Gerlagh, R. (2006). Corruption, democracy, and environmental policy: An empirical contribution to the debate. *Journal of Environment & Development*, *15*(3), 332–354. doi:10.1177/1070496506290960

Pluskota, A. (2020). The Impact of corruption on economic growth and innovation in an economy in developed European countries. *Annales Universitatis Mariae Curie-Skło-Dowska, Sectio H – Oeconomia*, *54*(2), 77–87. doi:10.17951/h.2020.54.2.77-87

Rafay, A. (Ed.). (2023). *Concepts, Cases, and Regulations in Financial Fraud and Corruption*. IGI Global., doi:10.4018/978-1-6684-5007-9

Rafay, A., & Gilani, U. J. (2016). Banking Competition and Stability: Evidence from Inter-continental Markets. *DLSU Business and Economics Review*, *25*(2), 24–40.

Rodríguez-Pose, A., & Di Cataldo, M. (2015). Quality of government and innovative performance in the regions of Europe. *Journal of Economic Geography*, *15*(4), 673–706. doi:10.1093/jeg/lbu023

Rose-Ackerman, S. (2009). Governance and Corruption. In L. Bjorn (Ed.), *Global Crises, Global Solutions*. Cambridge University Press.

Saha, S., & Sen, K. (2021). The corruption–growth relationship: Does the political regime matter? *Journal of Institutional Economics*, *17*(2), 243–266. doi:10.1017/S1744137420000375

Scully, W. G. (2002). Economic freedom, government policy, and the trade-off between equity and economic growth. *Public Choice*, *113*(1-2), 77–96. doi:10.1023/A:1020308831424

Shafiu Ibrahim Abdullahi, S. I., Shuaibu, M., Yusufu, M., Shehu, K. K., & Rafay, A. (2023). Economic Growth, Financial Development and Bank Failure: The Case of Corruption in Nigeria. In A. Rafay (Ed.), *Concepts, Cases, and Regulations in Financial Fraud and Corruption* (pp. 144–163). IGI Global., doi:10.4018/978-1-6684-5007-9.ch006

Shahbaz, M., & Rahman, M. (2012). The Dynamic of Financial Development, Imports, Foreign Direct Investment and Economic Growth: Cointegration and Causality Analysis in Pakistan. *Global Business Review*, *13*(2), 201–219. doi:10.1177/097215091201300202

Sharma, C., & Mitra, A. (2015). Corruption, governance and firm performance: Evidence from Indian enterprises. *Journal of Policy Modeling*, *37*(5), 835–851. doi:10.1016/j.jpolmod.2015.05.001

Shleifer, A., & Vishny, R. W. (1993). Corruption. *The Quarterly Journal of Economics*, *108*(3), 599–617. doi:10.2307/2118402

Shumetie, A., & Watabaji, M. D. (2019). Effect of corruption and political instability on enterprises' innovativeness in Ethiopia: Pooled data based. *Journal of Innovation and Entrepreneurship*, *8*(11), 1–19. doi:10.118613731-019-0107-x

Swaleheen, M. (2011). Economic Growth with Endogenous Corruption: An Empirical Study. *Public Choice*, *146*(1), 23–41. doi:10.100711127-009-9581-1

Swaleheen, M., & Stansel, D. (2007). Economic Freedom, Corruption, and Growth. *The Cato Journal*, *27*, 343–358.

Tanzi, V., & Davoodi, H. (1997). *Corruption, public investment, and growth* (Working Paper WP/97/139). International Monetary Fund.

Ünlü, H., & Ulusoy, M. K. (2021). Innovation and Corruption in Turkey: "Grease the Wheels" or "Sand the Wheels". In A. Rafay (Ed.), *Handbook of Research on Theory and Practice of Financial Crimes* (pp. 80–103). IGI Global., doi:10.4018/978-1-7998-5567-5.ch006

WDI. (2022). *World Development Indicators*. Retrieved from https://databank.worldbank.org/source/world-development-indicators

WGI. (2022). *Worldwide Governance Indicators*. Retrieved from http://info.worldbank.org/governance/wgi/

Wooldridge, J. M. (2010). *Econometric Analysis of Cross Section and Panel Data*. The MIT Press. Retrieved from https://mitpress.mit.edu/books/econometric-analysis-cross-section-and-panel-data-second-edition

World Bank. (2018). *The State of Social Safety Nets 2018*. Washington, DC: World Bank. Retrieved from https://www.worldbank.org/en/topic/socialprotectionandjobs/publication/ the-state-of-social-safety-nets-2018

Chapter 8
Examining the Link Between Corruption and Bank Credit:
The Case of Sub-Saharan Africa

Ibrahim Nandom Yakubu
https://orcid.org/0000-0003-4424-996X
University for Development Studies, Tamale, Ghana

Alhassan Bunyaminu
University of Professional Studies, Accra, Ghana

Alhassan Musah
https://orcid.org/0000-0002-4416-6526
University for Development Studies, Tamale, Ghana

ABSTRACT

This research examines the influence of corruption on the expansion of bank credit in Sub-Saharan Africa from 2000 to 2017. By utilizing the generalized method of moments (GMM) technique, the investigation reveals a significant positive correlation between corruption and bank credit. Additionally, the findings indicate that while stability in the banking sector leads to a decrease in bank credit, economic growth and inflation contribute significantly to the growth of bank credit. Based on these results, the study offers essential recommendations to foster integrity and responsible lending practices in the banking sector. It proposes that banks establish robust whistleblowing procedures, encouraging employees to promptly report any instances of corrupt transactions associated with credit advancement. Through the cultivation of a transparent and accountable culture, banks can effectively address and mitigate the adverse impacts of corruption on credit growth. Furthermore, the research advocates for the enforcement of strict non-price constraints to regulate lending practices.

DOI: 10.4018/978-1-6684-8587-3.ch008

INTRODUCTION

Finance is an integral part of every business regardless of its size. As firms grow, more capital is required to support both short and long-term operations (Imran & Nishat, 2013). Yet, there are obstacles most firms encounter in raising capital to undertake such activities (Yakubu *et al.*, 2020). Also, the decision to either employ debt or equity finance poses some challenges for firms (Baoko *et al.*, 2017). In the finance literature, there are two key theories explaining firms' methods of financing. First is the trade-off theory, which argues for an optimum capital structure for firms. It postulates that increasing the use of debt creates benefits for firms in the form of tax shields (Myers, 1977). The pecking order theory alternates the trade-off theory, which emphasizes that firms prioritize internal financing, and will resort to debt at the expense of equity when requiring external finance (Myers & Majluf, 1984). This theory posits a hierarchical sequence in which firms make their financing decisions, prioritizing internal resources before considering external debt. Among the external financing sources, bank credit is the most resorted financing option (Baoko *et al.*, 2017).

Bank credit availability is critical for boosting business activities, contributing significantly to economic growth particularly in developing economies and emerging markets (Imran & Nishat, 2013; Shafiu *et al.*, 2023). Literature has shown that banks' ability to advance credit is driven by several factors which are directly related to their activities. Notable among these factors include bank capital level, governance structure, risk level, etc. Other factors such as regulatory framework (Quagliariello, 2009), financial strength (Balazs *et al.*, 2006), and macroeconomic settings (Cottarelli *et al.*, 2005) to a large extent influence bank lending.

Given the boom-and-bust periods most economies encountered before and after the financial crisis which globally affected banking activities, research on the factors influencing bank credit advancement has gained much attention and has also become a contemporary theme in the banking literature.

Undoubtedly, research on bank credit determinants has growingly been in the direction of bank-specific variables and macroeconomic indicators. In the extant literature, several studies have appraised factors such as bank deposit, liquidity, and bank size (as bank-level variables) and economic growth (GDP), inflation, and exchange rate (as macroeconomic factors) to drive bank credit. The institutional environment plays a vital role in shaping a country's economic activities including the banking sector. Banks' willingness to supply credit can be largely predicted by the quality of institutions. The relationship between institutional factors and bank credit growth has however escaped the attention of researchers, presenting a yawning gap in the existing literature. Hence, this study seeks to fill this lacuna by critically assessing the effect of corruption on bank credit advancement. The study emphasizes corruption because of its inimical impact on economic activities, including bank operations, particularly the effectiveness of funds mobilization and disbursement. For firms, corruption exacerbates the cost of doing business (Baxamusa & Jalal, 2014). Despite attempts by governments in Africa to tackle corruption, the level of corruption in the region keeps escalating.

The contribution of this study is that it adds to the scanty attempts on the institutional quality-bank credit nexus with an emphasis on corruption.

The rest of the chapter is structured as follows. Section 2 gives an overview of corruption in Sub-Saharan Africa and Section 3 extensively looks at the literature review. The empirical methods and techniques are presented in Section 4. While Section 5 discusses the empirical findings, Section 6 concludes the study.

CORRUPTION IN SUB-SAHARAN AFRICA

Corruption is a major issue in Sub-Saharan Africa, impacting the region's economic, social, and political development. In the 2020 Corruption Perception Index by Transparency International, Sub-Saharan Africa was the second most corrupt region in the world, after Eastern Europe and Central Asia (Transparency International, 2021). According to the recent report published by Transparency International on January 31, 2023, Sub-Saharan Africa was ranked the lowest-scoring region in the 2022 Corruption Perception Index. With an average score of 32 out of 100, this region has been identified as having the highest levels of corruption in the world (Transparency International, 2023).

The prevalence of corruption in Sub-Saharan Africa can be attributed to various factors, including weak governance structures, lack of accountability and transparency, and poverty. In many cases, corrupt practices are facilitated by the absence of adequate legal frameworks and institutions to enforce them (Mbaku, 2015).

The impact of corruption on the region's economic development is particularly significant. Corruption can deter foreign investment, limit economic growth, and result in the misallocation of public resources (Rafay, 2023). The diversion of funds from public coffers to private accounts also undermines public service delivery, including in critical areas such as health and education (Rose-Ackerman, 2016).

Corruption also has social consequences, exacerbating poverty and inequality. Corrupt practices can lead to the enrichment of a few at the expense of the majority, further perpetuating a cycle of poverty and inequality. In some cases, corruption can also undermine social cohesion and stability, as people lose faith in the ability of the state to provide for their basic needs (Kaufmann *et al.*, 2011).

In addition to its economic and social impact, corruption also poses a threat to democratic governance in the region. Corrupt practices can undermine the legitimacy of governments and erode public trust in institutions. The concentration of power in the hands of a few can also lead to a breakdown in the rule of law, further entrenching corrupt practices (Mungiu-Pippidi, 2017).

For the banking sector in Sub-Saharan Africa, corruption is a pervasive issue. The African Development Bank states that banking sector corruption is a significant contributor to the region's weak financial systems, which limits access to credit for businesses and individuals (African Development Bank, 2018). The sector's high level of corruption is frequently linked to poor governance, inadequate regulation and supervision, and a lack of transparency (Asongu *et al.*, 2019).

Efforts to address corruption in Sub-Saharan Africa have been ongoing, but progress has been slow. Some of the strategies that have been used include strengthening legal frameworks, improving accountability and transparency, and promoting public participation. In addition, international efforts such as the United Nations Convention against Corruption have played a role in raising awareness and promoting anti-corruption measures.

LITERATURE REVIEW

Theoretical Background

Generally, the interest rate channel and the bank lending channel are the common channels by which central banks and monetary authorities implement monetary policies. An expansionary monetary policy for instance via the interest rate channel lowers interest rates which reduces the cost of capital with a further significant increase in spending and investment. On the other hand, via the bank lending channel, an expansionary monetary policy strategy raises the level of bank deposits as well as reserves, triggering growth in bank loans, and thus enhancing spending and investment (Rafay, Mohsan & Sadiq, 2017)

On theoretical grounds, this study dwells on the bank lending channel of monetary policy transmission. Bernanke and Blinder (1988) serve as one of the earlier advocates of the bank lending channel hypothesis. In contrast to the "money view" where bank loans and other debt instruments are considered as perfect substitutes, Bernanke and Blinder (1988) disregard the assumption of perfect substitutability between bank loans and debt instruments, particularly bonds. They developed a three-asset class model distinctively separating bank loans into three asset groups including money, intermediated loans, and bonds. Bernanke and Blinder (1988) argue that to ensure a distinct bank lending channel of monetary policy transmission, three critical conditions must hold. First, there should not be perfect substitutability between intermediated loans and bonds. Second, the supply of intermediated loans in the economy should be influenced by monetary authorities through reserve controls. Finally, prices must imperfectly adjust to prevent any monetary policy shock from being neutral.

Mishkin (1996) opined that the bank lending channel is focused on banks' distinctive role in dealing with information asymmetry and other related market imperfections in the financial system.

Arguably, the bank lending channel has proven its usefulness by distinguishing between the "lending view" and "credit rationing". According to the lending view, a policy tightening should trigger a decline in new credit supply and a proportionate increase in loan rates relative to the rates in the market. Consequently, the extent of the shift in credit supply will be greater than the shift in demand for credit. The credit rationing view on the other hand postulates that as policy tightening will lead to a decline in the volume of new bank loans, the rate on loans increases but typically less than the quoted market rates.

The core premise of the bank lending channel of monetary policy transmission is that bank deposit growth is directly influenced by monetary policy, and deposits account for a significant portion of loanable funds, thus impacting banks' lending behaviour. In view of this, bank deposits may be depleted by a tighter monetary policy, hence inhibiting banks' ability to lend.

Empirical Literature

Bank credit determinants over the last few decades have been a topic for empirical investigation in both advanced and emerging economies. Generally, the factors influencing bank lending behaviour are classified as supply-side and demand-side factors. In both individual and cross-country analyses, several studies have explored how these factors affect bank credit growth with inconclusive results. For instance, by employing quarterly data spanning 1980-1998, Hofmann (2004) analyzed the drivers of bank credit in 16 industrialized countries. Applying the Vector Autoregression technique, the results showed that real gross domestic product (GDP) in the presence of property prices positively and significantly explains bank credit while real interest rate negatively affects bank lending.

In a cross-sectional analysis, Balazs *et al.* (2007) investigated the factors determining bank credit using Central and Eastern European (CEE) nations. Relying on the Ordinary Least Squares (OLS) and the Mean Group (MG) techniques, the study established that domestic credit to the private sector in the sampled countries is driven by GDP per capita, financial liberalization, inflation, and housing prices.

With a sample of 38 emerging markets, Guo and Stepanyan (2011) assessed the dynamics of bank credit over the period 2002-2010. The study indicated that non-resident liabilities, economic growth, and inflation positively influence credit while the effect of deposit growth rate is negative.

Olusanya *et al.* (2012) established that while deposit growth rate, exchange rate, reserve ratio, and liquidity impact positively and significantly on bank loan advancement, lending rate and portfolio investments impede the loan growth of banks in Nigeria. In a related study, Ajayi and Atanda (2012) revealed that commercial banks' reserve ratio and annual exchange rate are significant factors enticing banks to advance loans in Nigeria.

By employing the Vector Error Correction Model (VECM) technique on quarterly data for the period 2001Q1-2011Q4, Shijaku and Kalluci (2013) found that bank credit in Albania is positively determined by economic growth and exchange rates. Domestic debt, non-performing loans, and lending rates on the other hand showed a negative effect on credit growth.

Using annual data covering the period 1971-2010, Imran and Nishat (2013) analyzed the factors impacting bank credit in Pakistan with a focus on supply-side factors. Adopting the Autoregressive Distributed Lag (ARDL) approach, the results argued that in addition to foreign liabilities and deposits, overall economic activity (GDP), monetary conditions, and exchange rates are significant bank credit determinants in Pakistan.

Assefa (2014) examined the factors determining the growth of bank credit in Ethiopia with time series data spanning 1978-2011. Based on the ARDL analysis, the study found that foreign liabilities with commercial banks, money supply, deposit growth, real lending rate, inflation, and economic activity (GDP) are the significant long-run factors driving credit growth in Ethiopia.

Relying on the VECM technique, Jegede (2014) investigated the impact of monetary policy variables on the lending behaviour of commercial banks in Nigeria over the period 1988-2008. The findings indicated that bank lending is negatively influenced by banks' liquidity level and money supply while exchange rate and banks' interest rate exert a positive effect on lending activities.

Employing individual bank-level data from 264 Sub-Saharan African banks covering the period 2000-2007, Amidu (2014) examined the factors determining bank lending. The study found that at the bank level, bank lending is positively and significantly impacted by efficiency, growth, and the size of banks. From the macroeconomic perspective, interest rate (an indicator of monetary policy) reduces credit growth whereas lending is positively and significantly induced by economic activity (GDP).

Akinlo and Oni (2015) empirically assessed the key factors affecting bank credit in Nigeria with data covering 1980-2010. The error correction model results showed that bank asset growth, money supply, and inflation have a positive significant influence on bank credit. They also noted that banks' reserve ratio and lending negatively affect banks' ability to lend.

Rabab'ah (2015) established that bank lending in Jordan is positively and significantly driven by the size of banks and the level of economic activity while non-performing loans, lending rate, and banks' liquidity ratio have a negative impact on bank lending.

Employing bank-level data within the categories of big and small, Abbasoglu *et al.* (2015) documented that central bank policy rate and macroprudential policies negatively affect Turkish banks' credit advancement.

Using the fixed effects model with data from 11 banks over the period 2004-2014, Ivanovic (2016) examined the factors affecting credit growth in Montenegro. The empirical results reported that economic growth, banks' deposit level, and solvency ratio have a positive significant influence on bank credit advancement. The findings further showed that non-performing loans negatively induce bank credit, and the effect is significant.

In examining bank credit drivers in Ghana, Baoko *et al.* (2017) applied the ARDL technique to time series data extending from 1970 to 2011. The study evidenced that deposits, bank assets, money supply, and bank lending rate are significant short- and long-term determinants of credit growth in Ghana.

Ebire and Ogunyinka (2018) tested whether the bank lending channel holds in Nigeria. Using the VECM technique with quarterly data covering from 2002Q1 to 2017Q1, the findings argued that bank loan growth is negatively and significantly influenced by lending rate, confirming the presence of bank lending channel of monetary policy transmission in Nigeria. Also, while bank capital showed a positive insignificant effect on loan growth, the study found borrowing rate to motivate bank loans positively and significantly.

Oyebowale (2020) analyzed the factors driving bank lending in Nigeria using the ARDL technique with annual data spanning 1961-2016. The study presented bank capital, loan-to-deposit ratio, money supply, and inflation as significant long-run determinants of loan growth. Aside from inflation, all the factors showed a positive relationship with bank credit.

In the context of Turkey, Unvan (2020) investigated the key drivers of credit growth using quarterly data which spanned from 2000Q1 to 2016Q4. Applying the ARDL technique, the study found that bank credit is significantly influenced by the efficiency of banks, banks' asset growth, deposits, money supply, and inflation in the long run. Dharmadasa (2021) demonstrated that money supply, the growth in non-performing loans, banks' lending rate, inflation rate, and efficiency ratio strongly influence bank credit in Sri Lanka.

In a time, series analysis via the error correction model (ECM), Pratama and Putri (2022) established that capital adequacy ratio and non-performing loans have a negative impact on bank credit, while gross domestic product and money supply have a positive effect on bank credit in Indonesia. Norawati *et al.* (2022) established a significant effect of third-party funds and operational costs on credit growth in Indonesia.

Utilizing data from Micro, Small, and Medium Enterprises in Nigeria, Olunuga (2022) found that bank credit supply is positively influenced by bank size and deposit volume. The author also noted that credit risk, liquidity ratio, and interest rate negatively affect bank credit.

In a recent study, Ndanshau and Semu (2023) examined the drivers of bank credit in Tanzania over the period 1991Q1 to 2019Q4 using the ARDL method. The study revealed that economic growth positively affects bank credit, while bank lending rates and inflation have the opposite effect.

From the review of the literature, it can be noted that banks' willingness to advance credit is motivated by bank-level factors and macroeconomic fundamentals. Also, most of the studies are based on individual countries with few considering panel analyses. Consequently, this study seeks to add to the few existing panel studies on the determinants of bank credit. Also, institutional factors as drivers of bank credit are given less attention in the empirical literature. This study further adds to bridging this lacuna in the bank credit determinants literature.

Table 1 presents the summary of the empirical studies on the factors determining bank credit growth.

Table 1. Summary of the empirical literature on the determinants of bank credit

Author(s)	*Country /Region*	*Methodology*	*Variables*	*Impact of Independent Variables on Bank Credit*
Hofmann (2004)	Industrialized Countries	Vector Autoregression (VAR)	*Dependent variable*: Real credit to the private sector (% of GDP) *Independent variables*: Real GDP, real interest rate, property prices.	Real GDP (+) Real interest rate (-) Property prices (+)
Balazs *et al.* (2006)	Central and Eastern European Countries	Dynamic OLS and Mean Group Estimator	*Dependent variable*: Domestic credit to the private sector *Independent variables*: GDP per capita, nominal interest rate, inflation, housing prices, financial sector liberalization, credit registries	GDP per capita (+) Inflation (-) Nominal interest rate (-) Financial liberalization (+) Housing prices (+)
Guo and Stepanyan (2011)	Emerging Economies	Panel Regression: Benchmark Specification	*Dependent variable*: Banking sector private credit (% of GDP) *Independent variables*: Domestic deposits, non-resident liability growth, GDP growth, inflation, federal fund rate	Non-resident liability growth (+) Domestic deposits (+) GDP growth (+) Inflation (+)
Olusanya *et al.* (2012)	Nigeria	Ordinary Least Squares and Error Correction Model (ECM)	*Dependent variable*: Loans and advances *Independent variables*: Deposits, exchange rate, lending rate, reserve ratio, investment portfolio, liquidity ratio	Deposits (+) Exchange rate (+) Lending rate (-) Reserve ratio (+) Investment portfolio (-) Liquidity ratio (+)
Shijaku and Kalluci (2013)	Albania	Vector Error Correction Model (VECM)	*Dependent variable*: Bank credit to the private sector (% of GDP) *Independent variables*: Real GDP, non-performing loans, domestic debt, deposits, lending rate, exchange rate	Non-performing loans (-) Deposits (+) Exchange rate (+) Domestic debt (-) Lending rate (-)

Continued on following page

Table 1. Continued

Author(s)	*Country /Region*	*Methodology*	*Variables*	*Impact of Independent Variables on Bank Credit*
Imran and Nishat (2013)	Pakistan	Autoregressive Distributed Lag (ARDL)	*Dependent variable*: Private credit *Independent variables*: Deposits (domestic), inflation, real GDP, foreign liabilities, money supply, money market rate, exchange rate	Long-run: Deposit (+) Inflation (+) Real GDP (+) Foreign liabilities (+) Money supply (+) Money market rate (+) Exchange rate (+) Short-run: Exchange rate (-)
Assefa (2014)	Ethiopia	Autoregressive Distributed Lag (ARDL)	*Dependent variable*: Bank credit to the private sector *Independent variables*: Broad money, deposits, reserve requirements, foreign liability, real GDP, lending rate, inflation	Long-run and short-run impact: Broad money (-) Deposits (+) Reserve requirements (+) Foreign liability (+) Real GDP (+) Lending rate (+) Inflation (+)
Jegede (2014)	Nigeria	Vector Error Correction Model (VECM)	*Dependent variable*: Bank loans and advances *Independent variables*: Exchange rate, bank interest rate, money supply, liquidity ratio	Exchange rate (+) Bank interest rate (+) Money supply (-) Liquidity ratio (-)
Amidu (2014)	Sub-Saharan Africa	Random Effects	*Dependent variable*: Bank credit to the private sector *Independent variables*: Bank-specific: Bank size, efficiency, liquidity, growth Macroeconomic: GDP growth, inflation	Bank size (+) Efficiency (+) Liquidity (-) Bank growth (+) GDP growth (+) Inflation (-)
Akinlo and Oni (2015)	Nigeria	Error Correction Model (ECM)	*Dependent variable*: Bank credit to the private sector *Independent variables*: Money supply, bank asset, inflation, reserve ratio, lending rate	Bank asset (+) Inflation (+) Money supply (+) Reserve ratio (-) Lending rate (-)

Continued on following page

Table 1. Continued

Author(s)	*Country /Region*	*Methodology*	*Variables*	*Impact of Independent Variables on Bank Credit*
Rabab'ah (2015)	Jordan	Ordinary Least Squares	*Dependent variable*: Ratio of credit facilities to total assets *Independent variables*: Liquidity ratio, deposit rate, non-performing loans, bank size, economic growth, inflation, window rate	Liquidity ratio (-) Non-performing loans (-) Deposit rate (+) Bank size (+) Economic growth (+) Inflation (-) Window rate (-)
Abbasoglu *et al.* (2015)	Turkey	Generalized Method of Moments (GMM)	*Dependent variable*: Bank loans *Independent variables*: Macroprudential policies, central bank policy rate	Macroprudential policies (-) Central bank policy rate (-)
Ivanovic (2016)	Montenegro	Fixed Effects	*Dependent variable*: Total loans *Independent variables*: Deposit growth, non-performing loans, GDP growth, solvency ratio, profitability (return on equity), inefficiency ratio, inflation	Deposit growth (+) Non-performing loans (+) GDP growth (+) Solvency ratio (+) Profitability (-) Inefficiency ratio (+) Inflation (+)
Baoko *et al.* (2017)	Ghana	Autoregressive Distributed Lag (ARDL)	*Dependent variable*: Bank credit to the private sector *Independent variables*: bank deposit, bank asset, lending rate, real GDP, inflation, broad money, real exchange rate	Long-run: Bank deposit (-) Bank asset (+) Lending rate (-) Real GDP (-) Inflation (-) Broad money (+) Real exchange rate (+)
Ebire and Ogunyinka (2018)	Nigeria	Vector Error Correction Model (VECM)	*Dependent variable*: Loan supply *Independent variables*: Bank capital, lending rate, real GDP, inflation	Bank capital (+) Lending rate (-) Real GDP (-) Inflation (+) Borrowing rate (+)

Continued on following page

Table 1. Continued

Author(s)	*Country /Region*	*Methodology*	*Variables*	*Impact of Independent Variables on Bank Credit*
Oyebowale (2020)	Nigeria	Autoregressive Distributed Lag (ARDL)	*Dependent variable:* Loans and advances *Independent variables*: broad money, bank capital, inflation, loan-to-deposit ratio	Loan to deposit ratio (+) Broad money (+) Bank capital (+) Inflation (-)
Unvan (2020)	Turkey	Autoregressive Distributed Lag (ARDL)	*Dependent variable*: Bank credit to the private sector *Independent variables*: bank deposit, efficiency, asset growth, financial access, inflation, broad money	Bank deposit (-) Bank efficiency (-) Asset growth (+) Financial access (+) Inflation (-) Broad money (+)
Norawati *et al.* (2022)	Indonesia	Multiple Regression	*Dependent variable:* Credit growth *Independent variables:* Third-party funds and Operating costs	Third-party funds (+) Operating costs (-)
Pratama and Putri (2022)	Indonesia	Error Correction Model (ECM)	*Dependent variable:* Total credit distribution of commercial banks *Independent variables:* Capital adequacy ratio, nonperforming loan, gross domestic product, inflation, interest rate, money supply	Capital adequacy ratio (-) Nonperforming loans (-) Gross domestic product (+) Money supply (+)
Ndanshau and Semu (2023)	Tanzania	Autoregressive Distributed Lag (ARDL)	*Dependent variable:* Bank credit to the private sector *Independent variables:* Lending rate, economic growth, inflation	Lending rate (-) Economic growth (+) Inflation (-)

METHODOLOGY

Data

The study employs a panel dataset of 33 Sub-Saharan African countries over the period 2000-2017. The availability of relevant data informed the selection of these countries. Data for the study are sourced from the Global Financial Development Database (GFDD), World Development Indicators (WDI), and World Governance Indicators (WGI) of the World Bank. The sample countries include Benin, Botswana,

Burkina Faso, Cameroon, Central African Republic, Chad, Congo Republic, Cote D'Ivoire, Equatorial Guinea, Gabon, Ghana, Guinea, Kenya, Lesotho, Madagascar, Malawi, Mali, Mauritania, Mauritius, Mozambique, Niger, Nigeria, Rwanda, Senegal, Seychelles, Sierra Leone, South Africa, Sudan, Swaziland, Tanzania, Togo, Uganda, and Zambia.

Selection and Description of Variables

For the dependent variable, private credit provided by domestic banks as a percentage of GDP is used as a proxy for bank credit (BC). This measure has been widely employed in the bank credit determinants literature (Balazs *et al.*, 2006; Guo & Stepanyan, 2011; Shijaku & Kalluci, 2013; Imran & Nishat, 2013; Assefa, 2014; Akinlo & Oni, 2015; Baoko *et al.*, 2017; Unvan, 2020). It captures the amount of credit provided to the private sector. This measure also unravels credit advanced to the private sector from the value of credit provided to governments and their agencies, as well as public enterprises. In addition, it precludes the credit central bank advances. The strength of this measure is that it provides an accurate representation of the actual volume of funds received by the private sector.

Turning to the independent variables, the literature review clearly established that bank credit is influenced by various factors which are mainly categorized as bank-level factors and macroeconomic indicators. In this study, corruption is the main independent variable. The study controls for the effect of bank stability, economic growth, and inflation. Corruption (CR) captures perceptions of the extent to which public power is exercised for private gain, including both petty and grand forms of corruption, as well as the "capture" of the state by elites and private interests. Corruption is scored from -2.5 to +2.5, where a higher score indicates a better outcome. Banks' z-score measures banking sector stability (BS). The z-score proxy describes the probability of default of a country's banking system (Yakubu & Musah, 2022). Economic growth (EG) is measured by real gross domestic product (GDP) per capita (constant US dollars). Inflation (INF) is gauged by consumer prices (annual percentages).

Model Specification

To empirically examine the impact of corruption on bank credit, the functional model is stated as follows:

$$Bank\ Credit = f\,(Corruption + Control\ factors) \qquad (1)$$

The study takes a panel approach which is basically specified as:

$$yit = \alpha + \beta \mathrm{x}it + vit + \varepsilon \mathrm{i}t \qquad (2)$$

where i *s*ignifies the country indices and t *i*ndicates the time dimension. y *r*epresents the dependent variable (bank credit) and x *d*enotes the independent factor and the control variables. ε is the error term and vit_{i}s the time-invariant country-specific effects. Based on the variables, equation (2) can be rewritten as:

$$\mathrm{B}Cit = \alpha + \beta 1\mathrm{Cr}it + \beta 2B\mathrm{Sit} + \beta 3\mathrm{EGit} + \beta 4INF\mathrm{it} + vit + \varepsilon it \qquad (3)$$

Analytical Approach

The dynamic system generalized method of moments (GMM) technique by Arellano and Bond (1991), modified by Arellano and Bover (1995) is applied in the data analysis. The GMM technique addresses the problem of endogeneity, unlike the traditional panel techniques such as the ordinary least squares (OLS). The problem with unobserved country-specific effects that are inherent in panel analysis is likewise resolved by the GMM technique (Yakubu, 2019). The fundamental concept of the GMM technique revolves around a set of population moment conditions, also referred to as orthogonality conditions (Bunyaminu et al., *2022*).

EMPIRICAL RESULTS

Descriptive Statistics

In Table 2, the results of the descriptive statistics showing the mean, maximum, minimum, and standard deviation of each variable are presented. Bank credit gauged by private credit provided by domestic banks as a percentage of GDP has a mean of 16.7% and ranged from 1.3% to 102.8%. The average corruption value is -0.555 with a maximum and minimum of 1.2 and -1.8 respectively. The estimated mean value of corruption reiterates the high level of corruption in the sampled countries. Bank stability has a mean of 11.2. While the average real GDP per capita is $2,263.7, the mean of inflation is 6.2% with a standard deviation of 6.7%.

Table 2. Descriptive Statistics

	BC	*CR*	*BS*	*EG*	*INF*
Mean	16.657	-0.555	11.252	2263.683	6.231
Maximum	102.758	1.217	44.413	22942.580	37.142
Minimum	1.320	-1.826	2.160	138.699	-9.616
Std. Dev.	16.269	0.590	5.969	3502.541	6.712

Correlation and Multicollinearity Analysis

To check the strength of the relationship among the independent variables, the correlation analysis is carried out, and the results are presented in Table 3. It is observed that the variables have low correlation coefficients. This suggests that they are weakly correlated and therefore, there is no problem of multicollinearity in this study. To justify this, the variance inflation factor (VIF) analysis is performed. Gujarati (2003) suggests that when the VIF is greater than 10 and the tolerance value is less than 0.10, multicollinearity is possible. From the analysis, however, the VIF values for the variables are less than 10, with tolerances greater than 0.10. Hence, it can be concluded that there is no multicollinearity among the variables.

Table 3. Correlation and variance inflation factor (VIF) analysis

	CR	BS	EG	INF	VIF	Tolerance (1/VIF)
CR	1.000				1.05	0.949
BS	-0.024	1.000			1.01	0.992
EG	0.223	0.079	1.000		1.07	0.939
INF	-0.005	0.012	-0.067	1.000	1.00	0.995

Regression Results

Table 4 presents the results of the regression estimation using the GMM technique. Regarding the model diagnostics, the p-value of the Wald test indicates that the model is significant at 1%. The validity of the instruments used in the model is justified by the probability value of the Hansen J test. The AR (1) and AR(2) tests reveal the absence of serial correlation in the model.

Table 4. GMM estimation results

Variables	GMM Estimates
BC_{t-1}	0.8992***
	(0.0000)
CR	1.0089***
	(0.0000)
BS	-0.0577***
	(0.0000)
EG	0.0005***
	(0.0000)
INF	0.0590***
	(0.0000)
Diagnostics	
Wald χ^2	197144.4
Wald χ^2 *p-value*	0.0000
AR (1) *p-value*	0.9991
AR (2) *p-value*	0.9968
J-statistic	25.2554
Prob(J-statistic)	0.6649
Number of Countries	33

*** denotes significance at 1% and values in parenthesis are p-values

From the regression estimates, the lag of bank credit (BC_{t-1}) indicates that bank credit has a self-reinforcing effect. This means that the growth in bank credit is significantly driven by its previous value. The findings show that corruption has a positive significant effect on bank credit growth. The interpretation is that bank lending to the private sector is stimulated by corruption. Banks are hesitant to lend to most private firms due to high information asymmetries and default rates, particularly in Africa where the default tendencies are high. However, inefficiencies coupled with self-interest typically lead bank officials to lend to clients with weak investments, raising credit risk. The positive impact of corruption on bank credit is not surprising given the fact that Sub-Saharan African countries have been continuously ranked among the most corrupt countries in the world by Transparency International.

Banking sector stability exerts a negative significant impact on bank credit. The implication is that in a less stable banking environment, regulators put stringent measures to curb non-performing loans or mitigate credit risk. This decreases banks' ability to advance loans to customers especially those with default tendencies or poor credit history.

Economic growth and bank credit are positively and significantly related. The finding suggests that when economic activities increase, the demand for bank loans also increases. For instance, an increase in economic activities allows businesses to expand production which requires more inputs. To finance such inputs, bank credit mostly serves as a key financing source.

It is observed that inflation positively influences bank credit growth, suggesting that in periods of high inflation the demand for bank loans increases. A plausible explanation for this relationship is that inflation increases production costs given the high prices of raw materials and other inputs. For firms to acquire such inputs, more capital is needed, and loans from banks will not be out of the financing options.

CONCLUSION

Corruption remains a significant challenge for emerging countries, particularly in Africa. It has a detrimental impact on economic activities, including the effectiveness of bank operations, which can lead to the misallocation of resources and poor performance of financial institutions. Tackling corruption requires a multi-faceted approach, including strengthening institutions, promoting transparency and accountability, and enhancing public awareness of the negative effects of corruption on society. This study examined the impact of corruption on bank credit growth in the case of Sub-Saharan Africa over the period 2000-2017. Applying the generalized method of moments (GMM) technique, the findings show that corruption increases bank lending in Sub-Saharan Africa. The study also notes that while banking sector stability reduces bank credit, economic growth and inflation drive bank credit positively.

RECOMMENDATIONS

The study makes some policy recommendations. Firstly, in order to curb corruption among bank officials, it is recommended that banks should establish effective whistleblowing procedures that mandate employees to report any instances of corrupt transactions related to credit advancement immediately. This would help to promote accountability and transparency within the banking sector. Secondly, the study recommends the implementation of strict non-price constraints, such as collateral conditions, to prevent unqualified individuals and firms from accessing credit. Such measures need to be closely monitored by the relevant authorities to ensure compliance and prevent any potential loopholes that corrupt actors may exploit. About the finding that banking sector stability reduces bank credit, policy recommendations should focus on measures that enhance the stability of the banking sector. This can be achieved through the implementation of measures such as adequate capitalization and regulation, effective supervision, and the establishment of deposit insurance schemes. Such measures can help reduce the risk of bank failures and ensure that banks have the necessary resources to extend credit to the private sector. Finally, given the finding that economic growth and inflation drive bank credit positively, policy recommendations should prioritize measures that foster sustainable economic growth and stability. To achieve this, policies should aim to encourage investment, job creation, and increased productivity. Additionally, policies that maintain stable and low levels of inflation can facilitate a favourable environment for borrowing and lending, which can, in turn, facilitate economic growth.

DIRECTIONS FOR FUTURE RESEARCH

This study provides valuable insights into the impact of corruption on bank credit growth in Sub-Saharan Africa. However, there is still much to be explored in this area, and future research could make significant contributions to the understanding of this relationship. First, future research could consider examining the impact of corruption on bank lending by grouping the countries based on their ranking on the corruption perception index. Second, the current study only examined the period 2000–2017, and it may be worthwhile to conduct similar analyses for more recent years. Additionally, while the study found that economic growth and inflation drive bank credit positively, it did not examine how these factors interact with corruption to affect bank lending. Thus, future research could investigate the joint impact of corruption, economic growth, and inflation on bank lending in Sub-Saharan Africa.

DECLARATION

The authors declare that the manuscript follows ethical standards and there are no potential conflicts of interest with respect to the research, authorship and/or publication of this chapter.

DISCLAIMER

The contents and views of this chapter are expressed by the authors in their personal capacities. It is not necessary for the Editor and the Publisher to agree with these viewpoints, and they are not responsible for any duty of care in this regard.

ACKNOWLEDGMENT

The authors extend sincere gratitude to

- The Editor and the International Editorial Advisory Board (IEAB) of this book, who initially desk reviewed, arranged a rigorous double/triple-blind review process, and conducted a thorough, minute, and critical final review before accepting the chapter for publication.
- All anonymous reviewers who provided very constructive feedback for thorough revision, improvement, extension, and fine-tuning of the chapter.

• All colleagues, assistants and well-wishers who assisted to complete this task.

REFERENCES

Abbasoglu, O. F., Ileri, S. G., & Mimir, Y. (2015). *Determinants of credit growth in Turkey: does size matter?* Central Bank of the Republic of Turkey. Retrieved from http://erf.org.eg/wp-content/uploads/2016/03/ERF_22nd-AC_Finance_Abbasog-Gen-Mimir.pdf

African Development Bank. (2018). *African economic outlook 2018: Macroeconomic performance and outlook*. African Development Bank Group.

Ajayi, F., & Atanda, A. (2012). Monetary policy and bank performance in Nigeria: A two-step cointegration approach. *African Journal of Science and Research, 9*(1), 462–476.

Akinlo, A. E., & Oni, I. O. (2015). Determinants of bank credit growth in Nigeria 1980-2010. *European Journal of Sustainable Development, 4*(1), 23–30. doi:10.14207/ejsd.2015.v4n1p23

Amidu, M. (2014). What Influences banks lending in Sub-Saharan Africa. *Journal of Emerging Market Finance, 13*(1), 1–42. doi:10.1177/0972652714534022

Arellano, M., & Bond, S. (1991). Some tests of specification for panel data: Monte Carlo evidence and an application to employment equations. *The Review of Economic Studies, 58*(2), 277–297. doi:10.2307/2297968

Arellano, M., & Bover, O. (1995). Another look at the instrumental variable estimation of error-components models. *Journal of Econometrics, 68*(1), 29–51. doi:10.1016/0304-4076(94)01642-D

Asongu, S., & Nwachukwu, J. (2018). Bank size, information sharing and financial access in Africa. *International Journal of Managerial Finance, 14*(2), 188–209. doi:10.1108/IJMF-08-2017-0179

Assefa, M. (2014). Determinants of growth in bank credit to the private sector in Ethiopia: A supply side approach. *Research Journal of Finance and Accounting, 5*(17), 90–102.

Balazs, E., Back, P., & Zumer, T. (2006). *Private-sector credit in Central & Eastern Europe: New (over) shooting stars?* (Working Paper No. 852). Michigan: William Davidson Institute.

Baoko, G., Acheampong, I. A., & Ibrahim, M. (2017). Determinants of bank credit in Ghana: A bounds-testing cointegration approach. *African Review of Economics and Finance, 9*(1), 33–61.

Baxamusa, M., & Jalal, A. (2014). The effects of corruption on capital structure: When does it matter? *Journal of Developing Areas, 48*(1), 315–335. doi:10.1353/jda.2014.0012

Bernanke, B., & Blinder, A. (1988). Credit, money and aggregate demand. *The American Economic Review, 78*(2), 435–439.

Bunyaminu, A., Mohammed, I., Yakubu, I. N., Shani, B., & Abukari, A. L. (2022). The effect of health expenditure on average life expectancy: Does government effectiveness play a moderating role? *International Journal of Health Governance, 27*(4), 365–377. doi:10.1108/IJHG-03-2022-0027

Cottarelli, C., Dell'Ariccia, G., & Vladkova-Hollar, I. (2005). Early birds, late risers, and sleeping beauties: Bank credit growth to the private sector in Central and Eastern Europe and in the Balkans. *Journal of Banking & Finance*, *29*(1), 83–104. doi:10.1016/j.jbankfin.2004.06.017

Dharmadasa, P. D. C. S. (2021). Short and long term determinants of bank credit growth in Sri Lanka. *South Asian Journal of Finance*, *1*(1), 1–15. doi:10.4038ajf.v1i1.24

Ebire, K., & Ogunyinka, S. (2018). Bank lending channel of monetary policy transmission mechanism in Nigeria. *IIARD International Journal of Banking and Finance Research*, *4*(2), 51–64.

Gujarati, D. (2003). Basic Econometrics. Fourth Edition. Singapura: McGraw-Hill.

Guo, K., & Stepanyan, V. (2011). *Determinants of bank credit in emerging market economies* (Working Paper No. 11–51). Washington D.C.: International Monetary Fund.

Hofmann, B. (2004). The determinants of bank credit in industrialized countries: Do property prices matter? *International Finance*, *7*(2), 203–234. doi:10.1111/j.1367-0271.2004.00136.x

Imran, K., & Nishat, M. (2013). Determinants of bank credit in Pakistan: A supply side approach. *Economic Modelling*, *35*, 384–390. doi:10.1016/j.econmod.2013.07.022

Ivanovic, M. (2016). Determinants of credit growth: The case of Montenegro. *Journal of Central Banking Theory and Practice*, *2*(2), 101–118. doi:10.1515/jcbtp-2016-0013

Jegede, C. (2014). Effects of monetary policy on the commercial banks' lending in Nigeria. *Review of Public Administration and Management*, *3*(5), 134–146.

Kaufmann, D., Kraay, A., & Mastruzzi, M. (2011). The worldwide governance indicators: Methodology and analytical issues. *Hague Journal on the Rule of Law*, *3*(2), 220–246. doi:10.1017/S1876404511200046

Mbaku, J. M. (2010). *Corruption in Africa: Causes, consequences, and cleanups*. Lexington Books.

Mishkin, F. (1996). The channels of monetary transmission: lessons for monetary policy. In *Banque de France-Universite Conference*. National Bureau of Economic Research. 10.3386/w5464

Mungiu-Pippidi, A. (2017). *The Quest for Good Governance: How Societies Develop Control of Corruption*. Cambridge University Press.

Myers, S. C. (1977). Determinants of corporate borrowing. *Journal of Financial Economics*, *5*(2), 147–175. doi:10.1016/0304-405X(77)90015-0

Myers, S. C., & Majluf, N. S. (1984). Corporate financing and investment decisions when firms have information that investors do not have. *Journal of Financial Economics*, *13*(2), 187–221. doi:10.1016/0304-405X(84)90023-0

Ndanshau, M. O., & Semu, A. M. (2023). Determinants of bank credit supply to the private sector in Tanzania. *African Journal of Economic Review*, *11*(2), 92–115.

Norawati, S., Zulher, Z., Kasmawati, K., & Ratnasih, C. (2022). The effectiveness of the determinants of banking credit growth. *Accounting*, *8*(3), 287–292. doi:10.5267/j.ac.2021.12.001

Olunuga, A. (2022). Determinants of bank lending and credit accessibility of micro, small and medium enterprises. *Journal of Business Science, 10*(3), 299–313. doi:10.22139/jobs.1093265

Olusanya, S., Oyebo, A., & Ohadebere, E. (2012). Determinants of lending behaviour of commercial bank: Evidence from Nigeria. A co-integration analysis (1975-2010). *Journal of the Humanities and Social Sciences, 5*(5), 71–80.

Oyebowale, A. Y. (2020). Determinants of bank lending in Nigeria. *Global Journal of Emerging Market Economies, 12*(3), 376–398. doi:10.1177/0974910120961573

Pratama, D. P. I., & Putri, P. I. (2022). Determinants of Bank Credit in Indonesia. *Indonesian Journal of Development Economics, 5*(3), 254–266.

Quagliariello, M. (2009). Macroeconomic uncertainty and banks' lending decisions: The case of Italy. *Applied Economics, 41*(3), 323–336. doi:10.1080/00036840601007286

Rabab'ah, M. (2015). Factors affecting the bank credit: An empirical study on the Jordanian commercial banks. *International Journal of Economics and Finance, 7*(5), 166–178. doi:10.5539/ijef.v7n5p166

Rafay, A. (Ed.). (2023). *Concepts, Cases, and Regulations in Financial Fraud and Corruption*. IGI Global., doi:10.4018/978-1-6684-5007-9

Rafay, A., Mohsan, T., & Sadiq, R. (2017). Structural Mix of Credit Portfolios in Islamic Banking System: Evidence from a South Asian Economy. In D. Mutum, M. M. Butt, & M. Rashid (Eds.), *Advances in Islamic Finance, Marketing, and Management: An Asian Perspective* (pp. 185–210). Emerald Group Publishing Limited., doi:10.1108/978-1-78635-899-820161010

Rose-Ackerman, S., & Palifka, B. J. (2016). *Corruption and government: Causes, consequences, and reform*. Cambridge university press. doi:10.1017/CBO9781139962933

Shafiu Ibrahim Abdullahi, S. I., Shuaibu, M., Yusufu, M., Shehu, K. K., & Rafay, A. (2023). Economic Growth, Financial Development and Bank Failure: The Case of Corruption in Nigeria. In A. Rafay (Ed.), *Concepts, Cases, and Regulations in Financial Fraud and Corruption* (pp. 144–163). IGI Global., doi:10.4018/978-1-6684-5007-9.ch006

Shijaku, G., & Kalluci, I. (2013). *Determinants of bank credit to the private sector: the case of Albania* (Working Paper No. 09/48). Albania: Bank of Albania.

Transparency International. (2021). *Corruption Perceptions Index 2020*. https://www.transparency.org/en/cpi/2020/index/nzl

Transparency International. (2023). *Corruption Perceptions Index 2022*. https://www.transparency.org/en/cpi/2022

Unvan, Y. A. (2020). Determinants of bank credit in Turkey: An autoregressive distributed lag (ARDL) approach. *Turkish Studies – Economics, Finance. Politics, 15*(1), 675–686.

Yakubu, I. N. (2019). Does corruption grease or sand the wheels of bank profitability in Ghana? *Cogent Economics & Finance, 7*(1), 1–12. doi:10.1080/23322039.2019.1701909

Yakubu, I. N., & Musah, A. (2022). The nexus between financial inclusion and bank profitability: A dynamic panel approach. *Journal of Sustainable Finance & Investment*, 1–14. doi:10.1080/20430795.2022.2105792

Yakubu, I. N., Sulemana, A. M., & Abdallah, I. (2020). Small and medium-sized enterprises financing. *Gading Journal for Social Sciences*, *23*(2), 1–8.

Chapter 9
Inconsistencies in the Disclosures of Discount Rates:
The Case of Financial Reporting in Portugal

Miguel Assunção
Instituto Politécnico de Lisboa, Portugal

Fábio Albuquerque
https://orcid.org/0000-0001-8877-9634
Instituto Politécnico de Lisboa, Portugal

ABSTRACT

The use of the discount rate within financial reporting deserves particular attention from international standard-setting bodies because it has achieved prominence over time. This chapter uses archival research as a method and content analysis as a technique to assess mandatory and voluntary disclosure levels related to discount rates. The consolidated accounts for the year 2020 of listed entities in Euronext Lisbon are the sources of information. The results show differences in mandatory and disclosure levels regarding IAS/IFRS under analysis. Disclosures related to discount rates have been assessed either as an incidental topic or from a limited-scope analysis. Therefore, understanding the proper set of items to be disclosed and the factors that explain its disclosure, aligned with the efforts to ensure its compliance by legal authorities, may reduce asymmetries and enhance transparency in entities' financial reporting.

INTRODUCTION

Paragraph (§) 1 of Chapter 5 of the Conceptual Framework issued by the International Accounting Standards Board (IASB) defines recognition as the process of capturing for inclusion in the statement of financial position or the statement(s) of financial performance an item that meets the definition of

DOI: 10.4018/978-1-6684-8587-3.ch009

one of the elements of financial statements (FS), which involves depicting the item in words and by a monetary amount and including that amount in one or more totals.

Next, in §1 of Chapter 6, it is explained that the elements recognized in FS are quantified in monetary terms, which requires the selection of a measurement basis. In this same chapter, the possible measurement basis is detailed, that is, the historical cost and the current value. The latter includes the fair value, the present value, and the current cost. One of the parameters widely used in the measurement basis designated by the current value is, precisely, the discount rate.

Whether in the measurement through present value or even using fair value as a measurement basis, the discount rate is a fundamental variable and can cause relevant impacts on the FS of the entities, depending on the amounts involved. This is corroborated by PwC (2018) when it advocates that the discount rate is a fundamental financial assumption in the valuation of various types of assets and liabilities. Then, changes in discount rates to be applied in the measurement of long-term assets and liabilities can lead to materially relevant differences in the recognized amounts.

The present value as a measurement basis for the current value has achieved relative prominence over time (Alberto & Lopes, 2010; He, 2020). According to Peasnell (1977), for some accounting experts, or even most, the present value is the ideal concept for determining an asset's value. Thus, Alberto and Lopes (2010) conclude that measurement or evaluation techniques based on the concept of present value have been widely used for different purposes, namely for project assessments, in the Finance field, or for the measurement of tangible fixed assets and intangible assets, provisions, post-employment benefits, financial instruments, among others, in the accounting area.

Discount rates are associated with the concept of current value through the time-value of money and associated uncertainties, as it is through the inclusion of a discount rate in the calculation that it seeks to obtain the best estimate of the current value of future inflows or outflows (§B13, IFRS 13). Discount rates are required or permitted in some International Accounting Standards (IAS) and International Financial Reporting Standards (IFRS). However, when the different standards are assessed, some inconsistencies regarding the definition can be seen, as well as the lack of objectivity in determining the discount rate to be applied. When standards are less explicit regarding their formulation, it creates an opportunity for discretion (IASB, 2019).

According to the IASB (2019), inconsistencies between the IAS and IFRS also occur regarding the disclosure requirements on the discount rates, which may cause a deterioration in the financial information quality. Further, it may result in a lack of the necessary information for decision-making from the users' perspective. For instance, Alberto and Lopes (2010) conclude that the information disclosed by the entities in their FS does not provide users with a comprehensive understanding of the process of calculating the discount rate and its inputs. The authors also pointed out relevant differences in the discount rates used in the measurement of assets or liabilities between the different entities, even if they have the same nature or approximately the same risk. Finally, based on a sensitivity analysis, they warn that small changes in the discount rates used significantly impact the entity's FS.

Thus, the complex and subjective choice of the discount rate to be used in the measurement of assets and liabilities can affect the companies' financial position and performance with users of these FS not being able to understand this process and its effects, leading to inadequate decision-making. This subject has also been assessed by different theories. Husmann and Schmidt (2008), Carlin and Finch (2009), and He *et al.* (2021), supported by the agency's theory, suggest that discount rates are selected based on the interests of managers, as they seek to maximize results for their shareholders.

The disclosure of complete and understandable information will allow users greater confidence in decision-making (Ball, 2006; Rafay, Yasser & Khalid, 2019). Through mandatory and voluntary disclosures, entities can present, explain and, above all, base the judgments formulated to determine the most appropriate discount rate for each asset or liability measurement (Meek *et al.*, 1995; Rafay, 2022). There is also evidence in the literature that disclosure levels differ according to the standards under analysis either in Portugal (Kasyan *et al.*, 2017) or in other countries (Alkababji, 2016; Glaum *et al.*, 2013; Paugam *et al.*, 2013; Fahad *et al.*, 2020). The decision to disclose or not disclose is complex since it requires judgment for each specific case and the weighting of the costs and benefits of following a certain option, especially when it comes to sensitive information (Saha & Rose, 2021; Sarquis *et al.*, 2021). In a subject such as the discount rate used to measure assets and liabilities, where high judgment is needed and there is also a multiplicity of input options, it seems only possible to base the choices on proper disclosure to avoid confusion (Oliveira *et al.*, 2006). Thus, this proposal for a chapter presents the following objectives: i) Identify the criteria defined in the different IFRS for the selection of discount rates to be used and the corresponding disclosure criteria; ii) Identify the level of disclosure of requirements related to discount rates used by entities listed in Portugal. The subject under analysis is assumed to be relevant due to the quantitative and qualitative impact that the selection of the discount rate can have on the performance of the entities, affecting the perception, opinion, and, finally, the decisions of all those interested parties in the entities FS (Alberto & Lopes, 2010; EY, 2016; PwC, 2018).

The study uses the archive research method and content analysis as a technique for collecting information, based on the consolidated reports of the entities listed in Euronext Lisbon, or more specifically, in the Portuguese Stock Index (PSI) All-Share Index. Mandatory and voluntary disclosures regarding discount rates were identified as variables of analysis, materialized through the content provided, implicitly or explicitly, in the standards identified by the IASB (2019) as more relevant in the measurement of present value when determining the current value. More specifically, the study will focus on four standards, namely IFRS 13 – Fair Value Measurement, IAS 19 – Employee Benefits, IAS 36 – Impairment of Assets, and IAS 37 – Provisions, Contingent Liabilities and Contingent Assets, including not only the mandatory disclosures provided for in those IAS and IFRS but also the voluntary items identified as relevant.

No studies were identified in Portugal or globally that assess the selection of the discount rate and the level of disclosure related to this matter in a broader perspective, i.e., covering the different assets and liabilities or different IAS and IFRS. However, there are studies on a particular standard alone (or some), such as IFRS 13 (Alkababji, 2016; Kasyan *et al.*, 2017), IAS 19 (Street & Gray, 2002; Ali *et al.*,2004; Tsalavoutas, 2011; Santos *et al*, 2014; Fahad *et al.*, 2020), IAS 36 (Tsalavoutas, 2011; Paugam *et al.*, 2013; Glaum *et al.* 2013; Santos *et al*, 2014) and IAS 37 (Alnaas & Rashid, 2018).

THE FINANCIAL REPORT AND MEASUREMENT ISSUES RELATED TO DISCOUNT RATES

The quality of financial information is essential since, as stated in the IAS 1 – Presentation of financial statements, the objective of the FS is to 'provide information about the financial position, financial performance and cash flows of an entity that is useful to a wide range of users in making economic decisions. » (IAS 1, §9). The increasing competitiveness of entities due to internationalization has led to an increase in the volume and complexity of transactions, becoming increasingly relevant and necessary for the comparability of financial information and accounting practices (Rosa, 2013). As a result of

IAS 1, the FS should provide a true and fair view that allows financial analyses, including comparisons amongst entities even if they are placed in different economic, social, and geographical environments.

Zeff (2014) states that after World War II each country had its own generally accepted accounting principles (GAAP). The increasing demands for international harmonization of accounting standards led to the introduction in 1973 of the International Accounting Standards Committee (IASC), an independent standard-setter body whose main design was to design internationally accepted accounting standards. The objective of harmonizing the financial information was, in turn, to ensure improvements in the transparency and comparability of the FS (Rafay, Sadiq & Ajmal, 2016) eliminating some existing accounting barriers and contributing to the proper functioning of capital markets. In 2001, the IASC gives way to the IASB, and from that date on, the standards published by the IASB are called IFRS, rather than the previous IAS published by the IASC.

Growing concerns about the harmonization of financial reporting published by entities were also reflected in the European Union, initially by issuing accounting directives on the annual and consolidated accounts seeking to achieve more comparable financial information between their Member States. Then, in 2002 this strategy was changed with the issuance of the European Commission (EC) Regulation No 1606/2002 of the European Parliament and the Council of 19 July 2002 which identified several entities that would adopt, mandatorily or optionally, the IAS and IFRS. Regulation 1606/2002 covered a mandatory scope (Art. 4) and an optional scope (Art. 5), thus leaving it up to the Member States to extend the universe of entities subject to the use of IAS and IFRS.

In Portugal, the scope of the IAS and IFRS for the entities referred to in Regulation No. 1606/2002 is currently in place in Decree-Law (DL) No. 158/2009, of July 13, republished by Decree-Law (DL) No. 98/2015, of June 2. According to this, all entities with securities issued for trading on a regulated market are now obliged to use the IAS and IFRS in the presentation of their consolidated accounts. Later, in the light of regulation of the Securities Market Commission (CMVM) No 11/2005 of 3 November, entities with securities issued for trading on a regulated market, but which were not obliged to draw up and present consolidated accounts, were also obliged to use these standards in their annual (individual) accounts from January 1, 2007. The adoption of IAS and IFRS in the consolidated accounts of the other entities was proposed as optional, provided that such FS were subject to legal certification of accounts. Finally, the entities included in the perimeter of groups whose parent company applies the IAS and IFRS consolidated FS, mandatorily or optionally, may also draw up their annual (individual) accounts under the IAS and IFRS. In such cases, it is required for entities a minimum period of IAS and IFRS application of three years.

The process of accounting harmonization has been questioned despite efforts to promote it, mainly because transactions and events can be accounted differently according to the applicable IAS and IFRS, which can provide, among other aspects, different measurement techniques, criteria, and assumptions to be used, as well as various inputs, to be incorporated (Maia & Martins, 2014). Consequently, the different claims of stakeholders can lead to different treatments concerning the recognition and measurement associated with each asset or liability, with potential impacts on the FS, depending on the choices made by preparers. The interests related to the disclosure of financial information may also differ between users and managers (Aguiar, 2018). In this sense, managers aim to maximize profits and present positive performances of their entities, while users of FS seek to obtain useful information for decision-making (Healy & Palepu, 2001). Furthermore, investors are interested in knowing the fair value as a requirement to assess the maximization of the value of their shares while other users such as banks, suppliers, customers, workers, or public institutions may have other information needs (Diana, 2009; Rafay & Farid, 2018).

The issues related to the measurement arise, for instance, when an asset or liability is initially recognized in the balance sheet, being necessary to assign a value, that is, measure it. Also, in the periods following the initial recognition, the entity shall identify and account for changes to be recognized in those assets or liabilities. For this, and according to §1 of Chapter 6 of the IASB (2018), the entities have the following measurement basis: historical cost and current value, the latter including fair value, present value, and current cost.

This research focuses on current value since on this measurement basis it can be incorporated a discount rate, a variable that is associated with the time value of money. According to the IASB (2018), the measurement basis designated as current value, which includes present value and fair value, can use techniques based on future cash flows for the initial or subsequent measurement of an asset or liability. These techniques incorporate a certain set of variables, including an estimate of the amount, the time in which it occurs, the uncertainty of future cash flows, as well as a discount rate that converts a future amount into its equivalent on the measurement date.

The time value of money is a core concept in finance. Typically, a certain amount of money is worth more today than the same amount that will be worth in the future, which is the idea behind the idea of the time value of money. The cash flow techniques date to the end of the 19th century, and their widespread practice dates to the 20th century, with Fibonacci as the first to demonstrate the mathematics of various discount periods and the emergence of a new abstract concept known as the time value of money (Blum & Thérond, 2019). Historically, however, the idea of time (present and future) value of money only emerged after the Renaissance (17th century), when probability and statistics were born, since accounting-based management prevailed (Nitzan & Bichler, 2009). Also, Peasnell (1977) indicates that the present value, as a relevant concept in the measurement basis which underlies the current value, has achieved some prominence over time. It also states that for some, or even for most accounting experts, the present value is the ideal concept for assessing the value of an asset.

Currently, it seems undeniable the importance of using the current value and its techniques, to measure assets or liabilities and, consequently, the selection of the discount rate. PwC (2018) confirms this view when it states that the discount rate is a fundamental financial assumption in the valuation of various types of non-financial assets and liabilities. Also, according to The PwC (2018), changes in discount rates to be applied in the measurement of long-term assets and liabilities can lead to materially relevant differences in the amounts recognized. Lopes (2007, cited by Alberto & Lopes, 2010)[1], in an analysis of the impact of a change in the discount rate on the value of use, concluded that, under normal circumstances, a 1% change in the discount rate corresponds to approximately a 5% change in the value of use. Aligned with this, EY (2016) indicates that the impact of deviations on the discount rate is significant. Generally, a reduction in the discount rate by one percentage point increases the provision for defined benefit obligations by 15% and vice versa.

Fahad *et al.* (2020) show, in a survey on the consequences of selecting the discount rate on liabilities related to defined contribution pension plans, that the average discount rate used by the entities was 3.96%, with the minimum to be 0.80% up to the maximum of 7.04% identified over the period covered by their research. The range of the rates used, on an annual basis, was 4.03% on average, i.e., twice the amplitude found by Billings *et al.* (2017, cited by Fahad *et al.*, 2020)[2] that used data from UK entities before 2010 as regards IAS 19. Another example can be observed by Andrews (2006, cited by Alberto and Lopes, 2010)[3], in a pioneering study whose sample was based on the entities of the Financial Times Stock Exchange (FTSE) 350 index, identified that the discount rates used ranged between 3% and 32%.

Despite the scant literature on the selection of discount rates opportunistically, and the consequent adverse impact on the reliability of financial information, the research by He *et al.* (2020) concluded that the discount rate can be also used in an abusive manner, aligned with the earning management theories. This conclusion was based on the use of discount rates to achieve projected earnings, increase the value of the entity, and maximize managers' bonuses. With no concrete and objective guidance and considering their significant impacts on the FS, a wide range of discount rates can be chosen in an abusive manner, manipulating the results of the entities (Alberto & Lopes, 2010).

As such, the subject under analysis in this research is assumed to be relevant due to the quantitative and qualitative impact that the selection of the discount rate may have on the financial position and performance of the entities, affecting the perception, opinion, and, finally, the decisions of all stakeholders in the FS of the entities under assessment.

The following section provides the framework of the IAS and IFRS identified by the IASB (2019) where the discount rate is assumed as a significant assumption in the measurement of present value when determining the current value basis of current value, along with disclosure requirements.

DISCOUNT RATES UNDER IAS AND IFRS

In this section, we examine the criteria to select and disclosures to be made in the matters related to discount rates under IAS and IFRS.

Discount rates are required or permitted by some IAS and IFRS. According to Blum and Thérond (2019), the discount rate is mentioned in twelve IAS and IFRS of the IASB, representing 21% of the IAS and 35% of the IFRS, namely:

- IAS 17 – Leases[4].
- IAS 19 - Employee benefits.
- IAS 26 - Accounting and reporting of retirement benefit plans.
- IAS 36 – Impairment of assets.
- IAS 37 - Provisions, contingent liabilities, and contingent assets.
- IAS 38 - Intangible assets.
- IFRS 4 - Insurance contracts[5];
- IFRS 5 - Non-current assets held for sale and discontinued operations.
- IFRS 9 - Financial instruments.
- IFRS 13 - Fair value measurement.
- IFRS 15 - Revenue from contracts with customers.
- IFRS 16 - Leases.

Several differences were found in research by IASB (2019) with the aim to assess the requirements provided in IAS and IFRS as regards the inputs to be used in the measurement of the current value of assets or liabilities. As an example, some IAS and IFRS require, while others permit, the use of different discount rates, but the reasons for those differences are unclear. Thauvron *et al.* (2022) found that the IFRS 13, IAS 19, and IAS 36 were identified as some of the main IAS and IFRS that require the use of discount rates in the measurement of assets or liabilities. In a more specific analysis, the IASB (2019) found IFRS 13, IAS 19, IAS 36, and IAS 37 as the main standards that use the present value measurement technique to determine the current value. Consequently, the IAS and IFRS in which the measurement basis is related to the historical cost, for example, IFRS 16 – Leases, were not assessed.

In the literature, several studies address a single IAS or IFRS, mainly associated with the asset or liability under assessment, namely IFRS 13 (Alkababji, 2016; Kasyan *et al.*, 2017), IAS 19 (Fahad *et al.*, 2020), IAS 37 (Alnaas & Rashid, 2018). For example, studies on several goodwill-related perspectives have been identified, which, consequently, examine more specifically the IAS 36 (namely, Paugam *et al.* 2013; Glaum *et al.*, 2013).

This research focuses on the four standards identified by the IASB (2019), namely the IFRS 13, IAS 19, IAS 36, and IAS 37, since they are mentioned as the most relevant in terms of measuring the present value to determine the current value and, consequently, the use of the discount rate as a fundamental financial assumption. From 2014 to 2017, the IASB (2019) study concluded that there are inconsistencies in the requirements related to the discount rates under the IAS and IFRS. These inconsistencies are essentially related to the types of inputs used in applying the present value technique or how the value of those inputs is determined. Other inconsistencies identified were related to the fact that different IAS and IFRS adopt different measurement basis since they were conceived at different times and with specific approaches. Such issues lead to an increase in the judgment and subjectivity levels, as well as the complexity and diversity in their use.

Table 1 shows the similarities and differences identified, either in terms of the measurement basis or inputs proposed within the different IAS and IFRS assessed by the IASB (2019).

Table 1. Summary of differences on measurement basis and inputs by IAS and IFRS

	IFRS 13	IAS 36	IAS 37	IAS 19
Nature	**assets or liabilities at fair value**	**non-financial assets**	**provisions**	**defined benefit obligations**
Measurement basis (explicit)	Yes	Yes	Yes	No
Measurement basis (clear)	Yes	Yes	No	No
Measurement basis (as described or inferred)	Fair value	Value in use	Amount to settle or transfer	Present value of the estimated expense
Measurement inputs include:				
Cash-flows estimates	Yes	Yes	Yes	Yes
Time value of money	Yes	Yes	Yes	Yes
Risk premium	Yes	Yes	Implicit	No
Liquidity	Yes	Yes	Unclear (not observable in practice)	Some
Own credit risk	Yes	N/A	Unclear	Some
Measurement inputs clear	Yes	Yes	No	No

Source: Withdrawn from IASB (2019, p. 12)

Regarding the divergences identified for discount rates, it is observed, for instance, that:

- According to **IAS 36,** the value in use shall be calculated using discount rates that reflect the best market assessments for the time value of money and these should be adjusted by the risks specific to the asset for which the future cash flow estimates have not been adjusted (IAS 36, §55).
- **Under IAS 37**, the discount rate (or rates) shall be a pre-tax rate (or rates) that reflect(s) current market assessments of the time value of money and the risks specific to the liability. The discount rate(s) shall not reflect risks for which future cash flow estimates have been adjusted (IAS 37, §47).
- However, under **IAS 19,** the discount rate must be determined by reference to market yields at the end of the reporting period for high-quality corporate bonds (IAS 19, §83).

Despite the possible difficulties associated with the existing differences, the literature on the subject does not argue that discount rates should be defined uniformly, but rather a more precise identification or definition of the criteria that should be at the basis of their selection (Eckel *et al.*, 2003; Thauvron *et al.*, 2022; Blum & Thérond, 2019, Husmann & Schmidt, 2008; Kvaal, 2010).

Corroborating the previous statement, Eckel *et al.* (2003) argue that the disclosure of the use of models using present value makes it essential to define an effective IAS or IFRS dedicated to the selection of a discount rate adapted to the specificity of each case. Accounting and financial reporting standards follow a case-by-case approach, sometimes making only recommendations on the discount rate to be used and, in other cases, being more incisive in the criteria for determining the rate. Still, according to Eckel *et al.* (2003), there are several potential problems with this situation, including the need for professional (partly unguided) judgment in the selection of rates, the lack of comparability of the resulting values between entities, and the lack of principles on which to base a choice in the case of a new application.

The literature on this subject recognizes a significant diversity of considerations about best practices in the selection of discount rates, sometimes dependent on the item (asset, liability, or the entity as a whole as the object of assessment).

In particular, the analysis carried out by Eckel *et al.* (2003) on this subject identified the following references proposed by other authors, namely:

- A rate adjusted to the risk, as proposed by Peasnell (1977, cited by Eckel *et al.*, 2003)[6]. The author proposes the use of a discount rate adjusted for the risk premium to reflect the risks to which a given entity is exposed, although it does not discuss the appropriate rate to be used by entities.
- The weighted average cost of capital, as proposed by Gamble and Cramer (1992, cited by Eckel *et al.*,2003)[7]. The authors debate the use of the discount as a tool to establish the present value of non-monetary financial assets and liabilities. In this context, and for the selection of the underlying discount rate, they conclude that the weighted average cost of capital (WACC) should be chosen given other alternatives, mainly because it minimizes the number of judgments that someone should make.
- The use of a pre-determined rate, indistinctly applied to all assets (15%) and liabilities (10%), as proposed by Weil (1990, cited by Eckel *et al.*,2003)[8].
- A discount rate based on an interest rate with no risk for individual items, under conditions of certainty, namely the risk-free interest rate, as proposed by Bodenhorn (1984, cited by Eckel *et al.*,2003)[9].

Another issue that is raised in determining the discount rate is whether a risk premium should be included. In this matter, Thauvron *et al.* (2022) indicate that one of the greatest advances in modern finance was the establishment of the method to calculate the discount rate according to the capital asset pricing model (CAPM), which defines the relationship between risk and return of an asset. According to CAPM, the expected rate of return of an asset is directly related to its non-diversifiable risk sensitivity. However, Blum and Thérond (2019), Husmann and Schmidt (2008), and Kvaal (2010) are aligned when they call into question CAPM as a reliable model for estimating the cost of equity by rejecting market rates as candidates for discount rates.

Husmann and Schmidt (2008), in turn, suggest Ross's model, known as Arbitrage Pricing Theory (APT), as a better substitute for CAPM, while Kvaal (2010) advocates consideration of the incremental borrowing rate. This disagreement may be related to homogeneity or heterogeneity of risks, making the incremental borrowing rate a good alternative to capture the entity's overall risk or to create a gap between the existing and future funding structure, respectively (Husmann & Schmidt, 2008).

Additionally, Blum and Thérond (2019) examined the IAS and IFRS with have explicit or implicit references to discount rates and concluded that, in some cases, these should be the result of an Internal Rate of Return (IRR), which implies the implicit solution used for cash flows series. In other cases, when the rate is a foresight parameter, discount rates assume several possibilities, which may be a market rate or a risk-free rate and may also capture different risk estimates. Sometimes, also according to those authors, the literature discusses the specific terms for those rates.

On the other hand, accounting and financial reporting standards may guide the selection and/or determination of the appropriate discount rate to be used for each asset or liability. In this sense, Blum and Thérond (2019) identify that IFRSs provide for the use of implied discount rates (IAS 17 and IFRS 16), market discount rates, or risk-free interest rates (IAS 19, IAS 36, IFRS 2, IFRS 4, IFRS 9 and IFRS 16) and discount rates that assumes risk-taking (IAS 36, IFRS 13 and IFRS 15).

Regarding IFRS 13, for instance, PwC (2015) and KPMG (2017) are aligned when they state that an entity, to determine the discount rate to be considered at level 3 of the fair value hierarchy, could select a model used to assess risk assets, namely CAPM. On the other hand, determining the value in use according to IAS 36 requires an estimate of the cost of capital, according to Kvaal (2010). The guidance from §A17 of IAS 36 recommends, as one of the three alternative starting points, the estimated weighted average cost of capital (WACC) based, for example, on CAPM. This starting point is following the state of the art in the theory of finance. Notwithstanding, and regarding the second alternative starting point, namely the incremental borrowing rate, opinions differ. Thus, while Husmann and Schmidt (2008) concluded that this option should be removed, Kvaal (2010) argues that this conclusion is based on a misunderstanding of what is meant by incremental loans and that the incremental indebtedness rate can be a useful approximation to the cost of capital in the CAPM model. However, it demonstrates that the wording of this IAS is not clear and, consequently, different interpretations would result in significant divergences, so its use is not recommended.

Based on the previous elements, it turns out that the selection of the appropriate discount rate is controversial, and the recommendations differ according to the type of assets or liabilities, but also the risks that are seeking to incorporate into the discount models. It is possible to infer that there is a high diversity of possible discount rates to be applied in the measurement of a given asset or liability, and there is no single rate to be incorporated into its valuation (Eckel *et al.*, 2003; Blum & Thérond, 2019). Additionally, the level of disclosure required by the IAS and IFRS regarding the present value and discount rate is not equivalent to all standards (IASB, 2019).

Table 2 identifies the differences between the disclosure requirements provided for in the four standards covered by this study. From table 2, it is observed in Table 2 that the disclosure of the rate itself is required in IAS 19, IAS 36, and IFRS 13, but not in IAS 37, and other inconsistencies are also identified concerning the disclosure requirements for information relating to the present value (IASB, 2019). Another example relates to the sensitivity analysis (quantitative), which is partially required in IAS 36 since §134 (f) only mentioned the need for disclosure "*if a reasonably possible change in a key assumption on which management has based its determination of the recoverable amount of the unit (group of units) would only cause the carrying amount of the unit (group units) exceeded their recoverable amount*". On the other hand, this information is mandatory in IFRS 13 and IAS 19, while IAS 37 does not require its disclosure at all.

Table 2. Summary of differences as regards disclosure requirements by IAS and IFRS

	IFRS 13 (level 3)	**IAS 19**	**IAS 36**	**IAS 37**
Disclosure requirements in IFRS 13 for level 3 measurements:				
Description of valuation technique and inputs used	Yes	Depends on	Yes	No
Quantitative information about significant unobservable inputs	Yes	Yes	Yes	No
Changes to valuation technique and reasons	Yes	IAS 8	IAS 8	IAS 8
Reconciliation from the opening to closing balance	Yes	Yes	Not applicable	Yes
Unrealized gains/losses recognized in profit or loss	Yes	Not applicable	Yes	Yes
Description of valuation processes and policies	Yes	No	No	No
Sensitivity analysis to unobservable inputs (narrative)	Yes	Yes	No	Yes
Sensitivity analysis to a reasonable change in assumptions (quantitative)	Yes	Yes	Partly	No
Method for calculating a reasonable possible change in assumptions	Yes	Yes	No	No
Disclosure requirements in IAS and IFRS other than IFRS 13				
Discount rate used	-	Yes	Yes	No
Effect of unwinding of discount	-	Yes	Not applicable	Yes
Effect of change in the discount rate	-	Yes	Not applicable	Yes

Source: Withdrawn from IASB (2019, p. 14)

The following subsection aims to present the specific IAS and IFRS under assessment in this research, namely those identified as more relevant by the IASB (2019) in the measurement of the present value to determine the current value.

Discount Rates Under IFRS 13

IFRS 13 was published in May 2011 and defines fair value, establishes a framework for fair value measurement, and requires disclosure of fair value measurements. This IFRS defines fair value as (§2, IFRS

13) "*the price at which an orderly transaction to sell the asset or to transfer the liability would take place between market participants at the measurement date under current market conditions*".

According to Kunz (2015), IFRS 13 aims to increase consistency and reduce complexity by presenting an accurate definition of fair value and a single source for measurement purposes and disclosures required. To increase the coherence and comparability of fair value measurement and related disclosures, this standard establishes a three-level hierarchy that allows classifying the data to be used in fair value measurement techniques.

At the first level, the data used are quoted prices of assets or liabilities in active markets to which the entity has access to the date of measurement with no adjustments. At the second level, the data used is those other than the quoted prices included in the first level, directly or indirectly observable for the asset or liability. Finally, the third level includes non-observable data to measure assets or liabilities.

IFRS 13 provides for three measurement techniques, namely the market-based approach, the cost-based approach, and, finally, the income-based approach.

The market-based approach is a measurement technique that seeks to estimate fair value using one or more methods that compare the asset with similar assets/liabilities that have been traded on the market at a relatively recent time. The cost-based approach is a measurement technique based on the substitution principle, i.e., it reflects the value that would be required at present to replace a particular asset with another equivalent. The income-based approach is a valuation technique that converts the expected value of future cash flows into a current single value, i.e., a discounted value.

The use of the discount rate is fundamentally part of the fair value measurement using the yield approach and, consequently, using level 3 data. For this level of data, IFRS 13 requires a set of disclosures, which identify the following requirements more directly related to the measurement technique and the discount rate:

- The evaluation techniques and data used to develop these measurements (§91(a)).
- In the case of fair value measurements classified at level 3 of the fair value hierarchy, the entity shall provide quantitative about the significant unobservable inputs used in the fair value measurement (§93 d)).
- A reconciliation from the opening to closing balance (§93(e)).
- A narrative description of the sensitivity of the fair value measurement to changes in unobservable inputs if a change in those inputs to a different amount might result in a significantly higher or lower fair value measurement (§93, (h) i)).

Discount Rates Under IAS 19

IAS 19, originally published by the IASC in June 1983 and reissued by the IASB in June 2011 (with subsequent amendments), aims to establish the accounting regulation for the accounting and disclosure of employee benefits. This standard includes, among others, post-employment benefits, such as retirement benefits and other long-term employee benefits, including long-term paid absences or long-term disability benefits.

One of the most relevant financial actuarial assumptions for estimating pension plan liabilities is the discount rate. The discount rate reflects the time value of money, but not the actuarial or investment risk. Furthermore, the discount rate does not reflect the specific credit risk of the entity borne by the entity's creditors, nor does it reflect the risk that future experience may differ from actuarial assumptions.

According to §66 of IAS 19, the ultimate cost of a defined benefit plan may be influenced by many variables. The ultimate cost of the plan is uncertain, and this uncertainty is likely to persist over a long period. In the same paragraph, it is also mentioned that actuarial assumptions are the best estimates of the entity of the variables that will determine the final cost of providing post-employment benefits, distinguishing demographic assumptions about the future characteristics of current and former employees and financial assumptions, which include the discount rate. On the latter, IAS 19 in §83 indicates that the rate used to discount post-employment benefit obligations (both funded and unfunded) shall be determined by reference to market yields at the end of the reporting period on high-quality corporate bonds. In countries where there is no deep market in such bonds, the market yields (at the end of the reporting period) on government bonds shall be used. The currency and term of the corporate bonds or government bonds shall be consistent with the currency and estimated term of the post-employment benefit obligations.

Additionally, in §86 of IAS 19, it is detailed that in some cases, there may be no deep market in bonds with a sufficiently long maturity to match the estimated maturity of all the benefit payments. In such cases, an entity uses current market rates of the appropriate term to discount shorter-term payments and estimates the discount rate for longer maturities by extrapolating current market rates along the yield curve.

Also under the IAS 19 standard, the disclosure requirements are established most directly related to the measurement technique and the discount rate:

- A reconciliation from the opening to the closing balance (§140).
- The present value of the defined benefit obligation (§140. ii) (a)).
- The significant actuarial assumptions used to determine the present value of the defined benefit obligation (§144).
- A sensitivity analysis for each significant actuarial assumption as of the end of the reporting period (§145(a)).

Discount Rates Under IAS 36

IAS 36, originally published by the IASC in June 1998 and reissued by the IASB in March 2004 (with subsequent amendments), prescribes the procedures that an entity applies to ensure that its assets are booked for no more than their recoverable amount and the necessary disclosures.

Following §1 of IAS 36, an asset is carried at more than its recoverable amount if the asset's carrying amount exceeds the amount to be recovered through its use or sale. If this is the case, the asset is described as impaired, and the IAS requires the entity to recognize an impairment loss. According to this §55 of this standard, the discount rate should be a pre-tax rate that reflects current market assessments of the time value of money and the risks specific to the asset for which the future cash flow estimates have not been *adjusted. In §56 of IAS 36, it is stated that this rate is estimated from the rate implicit in current market transactions for similar assets or from the weighted average cost of capital of a listed entity that has a single asset (or a portfolio of assets) similar in terms of service potential and risks to the asset under review. However, the discount rate(s) used to measure an asset's value in use shall not reflect risks for which the future cash flow estimates have been adjusted. Otherwise, the effect of some assumptions will be double counted.

§A17 of IAS 36 presents additional guidance for the selection of the appropriate discount rate since here it is suggested as a starting point in making such an estimate, the entity might consider the following rates:

a) The entity's weighted average cost of capital determined using techniques such as the CAPM;
b) The entity's incremental borrowing rate; and
c) Other market borrowing rates.

Thus, the recognition of impairment losses and reversals of previously recognized impairment losses often requires the formulation of complex exercises to estimate the recoverable amount of the asset. For this reason, IAS 36 determines a very extensive and explicit disclosure of the procedures and assumptions used for the development of this estimate, where the following requirements are identified more directly related to the measurement technique and the discount rate:

- The amount of impairment losses recognized in profit or loss during the period, or the reversals of impairment losses recognized in profit or loss during the period (§126(a) and (b)).
- The recoverable amount of the asset (the cash-generating unit) and whether the recoverable amount of the asset (cash-generating unit) is its fair value less costs of disposal or its value in use (§130 e).
- A description of the valuation technique(s) used to measure fair value less costs of disposal (§130, ii, f).
- The key assumptions, including the discount rate, are used to measure fair value less costs of disposal (§130, iii, f).
- The discount rate, if the recoverable amount is value in use, the discount rate(s) used in the current estimate and previous estimate (if any) of value in use (§130(g)).
- The assumptions used to determine the recoverable amount of assets (cash-generating units) during the period. (§132).
- The recoverable amount of the unit (group of units) is based on the value in use or if the fair value less costs of disposal is measured using discounted cash flow projections, the period over which management has projected cash flows, and the growth rate used to extrapolate cash flow projections (§134 (iii) and iv) of point d) and §134 (iii) and iv), €).

Discount Rates Under IAS 37

Originally issued by the IASC in September 1998, IAS 37 was adopted by the IASB in April 2001 (with subsequent amendments) to ensure that recognition criteria and measurement basis are appropriate to provisions, and contingent assets and liabilities and that sufficient information is disclosed in the notes, to allow users to understand their nature, timing, and amount.

Paragraph 45 of IAS 37 states that where the effect of the time value of money is material, the amount of a provision shall be the present value of the expenditures expected to be required to settle the obligation. §46 of IAS 37 adds that provisions are therefore discounted when the effect is material and Paragraph 47 of the same details that the discount rate (or rates) shall be a pre-tax rate (or rates) that reflect(s) current market assessments of the time value of money and the risks specific to the liability.

IAS 37 regarding measurement-related disclosures requires the following:

- A reconciliation of the opening balance and closing balance, in so far as it indicates that the carrying amount at the beginning and the end of the period (§84(a)) shall be disclosed, the additional provisions made in the period, including increases to existing provisions (§84(b)), the amounts used (i.e., incurred and charged against the provision) during the period (§84 (c)) and unused amounts reversed during the period (§84(d));
- The increase during the period in the discounted amount arising from the passage of time and the effect of any change in the discount rate (§84(e)).

Following the presentation of the contents on discount rates within IAS and IFRS under assessment in this research, the next section is dedicated to presenting the empirical analysis developed for this chapter.

EMPIRICAL ANALYSIS

This section aims to assess mandatory and voluntary disclosure levels related to discount rates through a set of IAS and IFRS previously selected, from which this matter appears relevant for the present value estimates. For this purpose, this section is divided into two subsections. The first provides the methodological approach to the result analysis, also including the sources, population, and reference year for the analysis as well as the items and variables that will be used to assess the data. Following, the second one presents the findings.

Methodology

The research method used in this study is file research, and the data is analyzed from an approach based on content analysis, based on consolidated reports and accounts of entities listed in Euronext's Portuguese Stock Index (PSI) All-Share Index Lisbon.

There are different types of approaches to content analysis. Beattie *et al.* (2004) identify various forms of content analysis and divide them into two categories: subjective (analyst evaluations) and semi-objective (studies through disclosure index, thematic content analysis, readability studies, and linguistic analysis).

This work falls into the category of semi-objective techniques, more precisely in the set of studies that use the indexes of disclosure. According to Romero (1991, cited by Silva, 2015)[10], content analysis is a controlled and systematic count, not an impressionist observation process, and therefore quantitative aspect is a technique designed to obtain descriptive data on content variables.

This study initially used the identification of listed entities, on December 31, 2020, in the Portuguese Stock Index (PSI) All-Share Index of Euronext Lisbon. This choice can be explained by the public availability of consolidated accounts and reports by those entities. Access to information was obtained by consulting the Euronext Lisbon webpage. However, entities that did not report consolidated accounts for the year 2020. Also, Pharol SGPS SA and Lisgráfica were also excluded because they did not have any observable element relevant to this study. It should be mentioned that the Porto SAD and Sporting SAD entities were not excluded, despite presenting accounts concerning June 30, since the reference date of the annual reports does not present itself as a relevant constraint in terms of the objectives defined for this study. Thus, after the selection criteria mentioned above, 5 entities were excluded, and the study population was limited to the 33 entities that are part of the PSI All-Share Index.

Table 3 shows the entities included in this study, with an indication of the industry in which they are framed, based on the Industry Classification Benchmark (ICB).

Table 3. PSI All-Share Index entities and industry

Entity code	Entity	Industry (ICB classification)	ICB code
ALSS	Altri SGPS SA	Basic Materials	55
BCP	Banco Comercial Português	Financials	30
SLBEN	Benfica SAD	Consumer Discretionary	40
CFN	Cofina	Consumer Discretionary	40
CORA	Corticeira Amorim	Industrials	50
CTT	CTT Correios de Portugal SA	Industrials	50
EDP	EDP Energias de Portugal SA	Utilities	65
EDPR	EDP Renováveis	Utilities	65
ESON	Estoril Sol	Consumer Discretionary	40
FLEXD	Flexdeal	Financials	30
GALP	Galp Energia	Energy	60
GLINT	Glintt	Technology	10
IBS	Ibersol Reg	Consumer Discretionary	40
GPA	Imobiliaria Construtora Grão-para	Consumer Discretionary	40
IMPA	Impresa	Consumer Discretionary	40
INA	Inapa	Basic Materials	55
JMT	Jerónimo Martins SGPS	Consumer Staples	45
MARTI	Martifer	Industrials	50
MCP	Media Capital	Telecommunications	15
MOTA	Mota Engil SGPS	Industrials	50
NOS	Nos SGPS	Telecommunications	15
NBA	Novabase	Technology	10
FCPP	Porto SAD	Consumer Discretionary	40
RAMA	Ramada Investimentos e Indústria	Basic Materials	55
RENE	Ren Redes Energeticas Nacionais SGPS	Utilities	65
SEM	Semapa	Basic Materials	55
SONI	Sonae Indústria	Industrials	50
YSO	Sonae SGPS	Consumer Staples	45
SNC	Sonaecom	Telecommunications	15
SPSO	Sporting SAD	Consumer Discretionary	40
TDSA	Teixeira Duarte	Industrials	50
SCT	Toyota Caetano	Industrials	50
VAF	VAA-Vista Alegre	Consumer Discretionary	40

Source: Authors' Compilation

As a metric to measure the levels of disclosure of the different entities which comprise the sample, information disclosure indexes (IDI) composed of several items were computed. The IDI was developed based on the studies of Street and Gray (2002), Ali *et al.* (2004), Tsalavoutas (2011), and Matiş *et al.* (2013). Those indexes constitute objective assessment elements, and it is not associated with the quality of the report overall, but with the level of transparency instead, assessed by the amount of information disclosed (Urquiza *et al.*, 2009).

The IDI proposed in this investigation consists of unweighted indices, i.e., it is assumed that all items have the same degree of importance for stakeholders. This assumption is supported by Owusu-Ansah (1998), Street and Gray (2002), Ali et al. (2004), and Marques (2015), who considered that weighted IDI is too persuaded by subjective factors since the weighting proposed for each element varies depending on the analyst. Cooke (1989, cited by Dasgupta, 2003)[11] argues that assigning weights to disclosure items is irrelevant because entities that tend to be better at disclosing "less important information" also tend to be better at disclosing "more important information". Additionally, Dasgupta (2003) also reached similar results for weighted and non-weighted indices, not finding significant differences between them.

Thus, the mandatory disclosure (MDI), voluntary (VDI), and total (TDI) indexes have been developed. In the first case (MDI), the disclosure requirements relating to the discount rates provided for in each of the IAS and IFRS proposed for this study were included. In the second (VDI), only voluntary disclosure items related to the same subject were included. The latter, finally, results from the full consideration of the elements included in the MDI and the VDI. Regarding voluntary disclosures, the inclusion of items foreseen as mandatory in some of the IAS and IFRS, but not foreseen in others, stand out. Additionally, items not provided for in the standards were included, given that they have been already disclosed by a still-expressive set of entities, based on the shreds of evidence gathered during data collection.

Thus, a disclosure checklist was built, based on the literature review that identified the items according to their mandatory or voluntary characteristics, as shown in Table 4.

Table 4. MDI and VDI disclosure checklist by IAS and IFRS

IAS and IFRS and item type		Item Description	Source
IFRS 13 - TDI items	1	The evaluation technique	a) § 91
	2	The discount rate: for the fair value measurements classified at level 3 of the hierarchy, the entity shall provide quantitative information on the significant non-observable data used in fair value measurement	d) § 93
	3	Reconciliations: reconciliation between the start and end balances	(e) § 93
	4	The estimated expected cash flow - data used to develop these measurements	a) § 91
	5	A narrative description of the sensitivity of fair value measurement to changes in unobservable data if a change of this data to a different value can result in measurement at a fair value significantly higher or lower.	h) i. § 93
IAS 19 - MDI Items	2	The discount rate: within the framework of significant actuarial assumptions to determine the present value of the defined benefit obligation.	§ 144
	3	Reconciliations: reconciliation between the start and end balances	§ 140
	4	The present value of the defined benefit obligation	a) ii. § 140
	5	A sensitivity analysis for each significant actuarial assumption at the end of the reporting period	a) § 145
IAS 19 - VDI Items	1	The evaluation technique	
	7	Disclosure on the rating for the discount rate	§ 83
	8	Disclosure on the use of a rate for reference to high-quality obligations of entities relating to the discount rate	§ 83
	9	Disclosure of the deadline or extrapolation to the deadline consistent with the estimated post-employment benefit obligations as a guarantee of consistency with the deadlines for discount rates	§ 83
IAS 36 - MDI Items	1	The valuation technique: description of the valuation technique used to measure fair value minus disposal costs	f) ii. § 130
	2	The discount rate: under the key assumptions used to measure fair value minus disposal costs, which includes the discount rate	f) iii. § 130
	4	The recoverable amount of the asset or cash-generating unit (CGU) and whether that recoverable amount of the asset or CGU represents its fair value less the costs of disposal or its value in use	(e) § 130
IAS 36 - VDI Items	3	Reconciliations: reconciliation between the start and end balances	
	5	An analysis of sensitivity to the main assumptions used.	
	9	Disclosure of the discount rate used for each CGU	
IAS 37 - MDI Items	3	Reconciliations: reconciliation between the start and end balances	a) § 84
	6	The entity discloses the effects of the change in the discount rate - the unwinding effect.	(e) § 84
IAS 37 - VDI Items	1	The evaluation technique	
	2	The discount rate used	
	4	The estimated expected cash flow	
	5	An analysis of sensitivity to the main assumptions used.	

For each item under analysis, the value "1" was assigned if the information is disclosed appropriately. In cases where disclosure is not following the requirements defined in the study, the value "0" was assigned. Furthermore, for cases where the item analyzed did not apply to the specific reality of that entity, the codification "NA" was attributed and this information was not computed in the indexes, in line with the Owusu-Ansah proposal (1998). This coding proposal indicates that entities should not be penalized for not making a particular item available when it does not apply to the reality in which they are inserted. Given those different items can be assessed for the same entity and some of the points under consideration may be applied differently to each entity, the number of requirements to be met by each entity will be unique and distinct from the other ones (Owusu-Ansah, 1998).

In this sense, the XDI for each entity can be obtained through the relationship between the total items disclosed by the entity and the number of items computed as applicable to the reality of the entity (Owusu-Ansah, 1998), as presented in the following expression:

$$XDI = \frac{\sum_{i=1}^{m} di}{\sum_{i=1}^{n} dp} \quad (1)$$

Where:

X = mandatory (M), voluntary (V), or total (T), as appropriate.
d = "1" when the element is disclosed and "0" otherwise.
m = number of items disclosed.
n = number of items susceptible to disclosure.
i = observed disclosures.
p = total disclosures that can be observed.

Based on Table 4, three global indices were computed that do not distinguish between the IAS and IFRS under assessment, which aims to evaluate the generalized compliance of mandatory disclosures (MDI), voluntary (VDI), and total (TDI) by entities selected for this study.

Findings

Through the proposed items and disclosure indexes it became possible to synthesize, and thus understand, the level of dissemination of the mandatory and voluntary items made by the selected entities, in global terms and for the different IAS and IFRS under assessment in this research.

To this end, the consolidated reports of the 33 entities were assessed, which resulted in a total of 89 observations (asset or liability items) distributed by the different IAS and IFRS under assessment, as shown in Table 5. The lowest number of liability observations was under IAS 37 (only 11%).

Table 5. Number of observations by IAS and IFRS

IAS and IFRS	Number of observations	As a percentage
IFRS 13	31	35
IAS 19	20	22
IAS 36	28	31
IAS 37	10	11
Total	**89**	**100**

Table 6 shows the average levels of disclosure identified for the various mandatory and voluntary items that are part of the TDI, which are relatively different across IAS and IFRS for the period under assessment.

Through an item analysis, it is possible to observe that, overall, the items related to evaluation techniques (item 1) and reconciliation of balances (item 3), either as a mandatory requirement or as voluntary disclosure, have higher average disclosure rates (greater than 75%). It is worthwhile to mention that it is for IFRS 13 that the smallest values for these items are observed, with 81% for item 1 and 77% for item 3. For other IAS and IFRS, the figures exceed 90%, reaching 100% in some cases.

The disclosure of discount rates used (item 2) reaches significant values concerning IAS 19 and IAS 36, reaching 100% in the first case. Although with lower levels (between 75% and 80%), these standards also stand out in the disclosure of a sensitivity analysis involving the main assumptions used in the evaluation (item 5). At issue, IAS and IFRS are more directly related to items of liabilities and assets, respectively, but have, as a similarity, the fact that they are often included in all matters involving the need for a higher level of estimates or critical assumptions.

As the topic specifically relates to liabilities, it is also in IAS 19, together with IAS 37, that the reference amounts in the valuation carried out (item 4) are presented as a disclosure item made by all entities.

Finally, and as regards the specific voluntary disclosures for some of the IAS and IFRS under assessment, we highlight the disclosure of the discount rates used for the CGU under evaluation under IAS 36, which reaches 86%.

Table 6. Mandatory (M) and voluntary (V) items by IAS and IFRS

Item	Description (overview)	IFRS 13	IAS 19	IAS 36	IAS 37
1	Evaluation technique used	81% (M)	100% (V)	100% (M)	90% (V)
2	Discount rates	61% (M)	100% (M)	96% (M)	20% (V)
3	Reconciliation of balances	77% (M)	95% (M)	96% (V)	100% (M)
4	Reference amounts in the valuation	39% (M)	100% (M)	14% (O)	100% (V)
5	Sensitivity analysis	32% (M)	80% (M)	75% (V)	0% (V)
6	Unwinding effect				30% (M)
7	Rating		30% (V)		
8	High-quality obligations		55% (V)		
9	Deadline information		25% (V)		
10	Discount rate for CGU			86% (V)	

Through analysis by IAS and IFRS, it is observed that, under **IFRS 13,** the results of mandatory disclosures related to the measurement of assets demonstrate that entities comply at a higher level with the disclosure of the technique used in the measurement, with a disclosure level of 81% (item 1). The following is, with a level of 77%, the disclosure regarding the reconciliation between the initial balance and the final balance (item 3). It is also verified that the sensitivity analysis (item 5) was only presented by less than one-third of the entities (32% disclose this information). Regarding disclosures related to the discount rates used (item 2), there is a level of 61% while the estimated expected cash flow (item 4) reaches a level of 39%.

As regards **IAS 19,** and regarding liabilities related to pension plan liabilities, there is a tendency toward a high level of disclosure of mandatory disclosure items, especially the disclosure of the discount rate and the present value of the defined benefit obligation (items 2 and 4, respectively).

In both cases, it was possible to obtain a disclosure level of 100%. Also, the reconciliation of opening and closing balances (item 3) has a high level of disclosure, at 95%. This is followed by the sensitivity analysis for each significant actuarial assumption at the end of the reporting period (item 5), disclosed by 80% of the analyzed entities that have this type of liability.

Regarding voluntary items, the technique used to estimate the responsibilities with post-employment benefits (item 1) obtained a disclosure level of 100%. Conversely, the remaining items obtained significantly lower levels. Thus, and with the second-highest level of disclosure, it is verified that 55% of the entities under analysis disclose information about the use of a rate by reference to the high-quality obligations of companies (item 8). Regarding the discount rate, it is verified that only 30% present information regarding the rating in their report and accounts (item 7). Finally, only 25% of the entities under review disclose information about the deadline or extrapolation to the deadline consistent with the estimated term of post-employment benefit obligations (item 8).

Concerning **IAS 36,** a 100% level of disclosure was identified concerning the mandatory disclosure of a description of the evaluation technique used (item 1). Next, and with 96%, two items are identified, namely, the level of mandatory disclosure of one of the main key assumptions used to measure fair value, i.e., the discount rate (item 2), as well as, regarding voluntary disclosures, the reconciliation of the opening balance and final balance, having in this item number 3 obtained a disclosure level of 96%.

Also, in the scope of voluntary disclosures, information on the discount rate used to measure each asset or CGU was set at 86% (item 10). Among the items with an expressive level of disclosure in this context is also the analysis of sensitivity to the main assumptions used, performed by 75% of the entities under assessment (item 5).

Finally, and returning to the mandatory disclosures, and with a lower level of disclosure than the other items of IAS 36, the item relating to the disclosure of the recoverable amount of the asset (of the CGU) is identified, and whether this recoverable amount of the asset (CGU) represents its fair value less the costs to disposal or its value in use (item 4), with a disclosure level of only 14%.

As for the mandatory disclosures provided **for in IAS 37,** it was found that all entities have a reconciliation of the opening and closing balances (item 3). The same is observed concerning the voluntary disclosure of the estimated expected cash flow (item 4). Also in this context, the disclosure of the evaluation technique presents an increasing level of disclosure, setting itself at 90% (item 1). The remaining items, mandatory or voluntary, are already far from these values.

Thus, it is observed that only 30% of the entities under analysis disclose the effects of the change in the discount rate (item 6) and 20% disclose the information about the discount rate used in the discount of provisions (item 2), the first being a mandatory item and the second a voluntary item. Finally, regarding voluntary items, no entity disclosed a sensitivity analysis of the main assumptions used (item 5).

After assessing the different items that make up the disclosure indexes, Table 7 presents the overall results obtained for the different indices (TDI, MDI, and VDI), either according to each of the IAS and IFRS or for the total entities included in this study.

Table 7. Descriptive statistics of variables

Variable	IAS and IFRS	N	Minimum	Maximum	Average	Standard deviation
TDI	IFRS 13	31	0.000	1.000	0.581	0.289
TDI	IAS 19	20	0.500	1.000	0.731	0.174
MDI	IAS 19	20	0.750	1.000	0.938	0.108
VDI	IAS 19	20	0.250	1.000	0.525	0.305
TDI	IAS 36	28	0.333	1.000	0.780	0.141
MDI	IAS 36	28	0.333	1.000	0.702	0.136
VDI	IAS 36	28	0.333	1.000	0.857	0.208
TDI	IAS 37	10	0.333	0.833	0.567	0.153
MDI	IAS 37	10	0.500	1.000	0.650	0.229
VDI	IAS 37	10	0.250	0.750	0.525	0.135
TDI	All	33	0.400	0.909	0.679	0.139
MDI	All	33	0.400	1.000	0.697	0.155
VDI	All	31	0.250	1.000	0.682	0.218

From the results obtained, it is possible to conclude that the entities disclose, on average, 67.9% of the disclosure items analyzed. By detail, the disclosure of mandatory items reaches 69.7%, a slightly higher level. For items with a voluntary nature, however, the levels of disclosure do not deviate significantly from these values, with an average value of 68.2%.

Comparing MDI with VDI, it is possible to see that the lowest minimum values are identifiable for the second (VDI), for both the total or by each IAS and IFRS under assessment. However, it is for the MDI that the average value has the highest values, except for the items that integrate this index for IAS 36.

Through analysis by IAS and IFRS, there is a lower level of disclosure compared to IFRS 13 and IAS 37, with an average level of 58.1% and 56.7%, respectively. Additionally, it is also for IFRS 13 that the highest value for the standard deviation is observed.

In the opposite direction, IAS 19 and IAS 36, with higher average levels of disclosure, are around 73.1% and 78%, respectively. It should be highlighted that, under IAS 19, the highest average value in the comparison between MDI and VDI is due to the former, a situation opposite to what is the case for IAS 36.

It is important to note the still significant amplitude (difference between maximum and minimum) in each of the calculated indices, with the lowest observable value for the IAS 19 (25 percentage points). For this index, it should be noted that all entities had a result of more than 75% and some reach 100%. On the other hand, the TDI for IFRS 13 is at its greatest extent, and it should be noted that an entity does not comply with this IFRS.

Thus, in the light of the classification proposed by Samaha and Stapleton (2008), it can be affirmed that the level of overall disclosure of the entities subject to this study is part of the so-called intermediate level of disclosure, considering this classification values that are in the range between 60% and 79%. There is also a differentiated treatment by the entities for mandatory or voluntary disclosures within the framework of each of those IAS and IFRS. Despite the difficulty of drawing up differences with previous studies, due to differences in terms in terms of methodology, period, or sample, it is possible to identify as a common point the divergences in the levels of disclosure according to the subject under analysis, that is, according to the different IAS and IFRS assessed.

The results are thus in line with Tsalavoutas's (2011) conclusions, which found, in a more cross-sectional study on the subject, differences between the levels of disclosure for IAS 19, IAS 36, and IAS 37. It also corroborates, from another perspective, the divergences between the levels of disclosure identified and the different studies that used, individually, the same IAS and IFRS proposed in this study, namely for IFRS 13 (Matiş *et al.*, 2013; Kasyan *et al.*, 2017), IAS 19 (Street & Gray, 2002); IAS 36 (Glaum *et al.*, 2013; Paugam *et al.*, 2013) and IAS 37 (Alnaas & Rashid, 2018).

To obtain more robust conclusions regarding the differences identified for disclosure levels, Table 8 presents the Kruskal Wallis test result, comparing the different indices (TDI, MDI, and VDI) between the various standards under analysis.

Table 8. Kruskal-Wallis Test

Variable	IAS and IFRS	N	Average post
TDI	IFRS 13	31	34.94
	IAS 19	20	49.60
	IAS 36	28	57.96
	IAS 37	10	30.70
MDI	IFRS 13	31	32.94
	IAS 19	20	70.13
	IAS 36	28	43.89
	IAS 37	10	35.25
VDI	IAS 19	20	20.55
	IAS 36	28	39.18
	IAS 37	10	20.30
Test statistics			
	MDI	**VDI**	**TDI**
H de Kruskal-Wallis	28.59	19.31	15.70
Df	3	2	3
Significance level	0.000	0.000	0.001

It should be stressed that the test was not performed for the VDI whenever IFRS 13 is involved in the analysis, since no voluntary disclosure items have been identified concerning that IFRS.

The Kruskal Wallis test results corroborate the results already presented, observing statistically significant differences between the different IAS and IFRS to the disclosures made by the entities for each of the indexes under assessment. The Mann-Whitney U test provides a more detailed comparison of the differences between the different IAS and IFRS and the indexes assessed. Then, Table 9 shows the significance levels obtained for this test between the various comparisons made.

Table 9. Mann-Whitney Test U

	Sig significance. (2 sided)					
	IFRS 13 vs. IAS 19	**IFRS 13 vs. IAS 36**	**IFRS 13 vs. IAS 37**	**IAS 19 vs. IAS 36**	**IAS 19 vs. IAS 37**	**IAS 36 vs. IAS 37**
TDI	0.043	0.001	0.988	0.177	0.024	0.002
MDI	0.000	0.024	0.560	0.000	0.005	0.070
VDI	NA	NA	NA	0.000	0.559	0.000

Differences statistically significant are confirmed from this test between the indices considering the different analyses performed, with the following exceptions: between IFRS 13 and IAS 37 (for TDI and MDI), between IAS 19 and IAS 36 (only for TDI), and between IAS 19 and IAS 37 (VDI only).

CONCLUSION

The results obtained show that, in average terms, about 68% of the mandatory and voluntary disclosure requirements are met by all entities in the period analyzed, reaching a slightly higher level when it comes to mandatory requirements (70%). Detailing the results, as a rule, there is a lower level of disclosure compared to IFRS 13 (58%) and IAS 37 (57%) compared to IAS 19 (73%) and IAS 36 (78%).

Thus, intermediate disclosure levels (between 60% and 79%) were identified in this context from a global perspective. However, these figures may be lower or higher depending on the subject matter in question and the mandatory or voluntary nature of the disclosure. Such differences can be explained, in the light of the results obtained, either by the material importance of the item or by its nature. It is for IAS 19 and IAS 36, which are often reported by entities as standards whose content proves to be judgment and critical estimates, that the specific item relating to the discount rates is the most disclosed. In the first case, full disclosure was reinforced by compliance with mandatory requirements, and, in the second case, some of the voluntary requirements were absent in the IAS concerned.

Thus, the conclusions of this study point out the need for further clarification by standard-setting bodies in general and the IASB regarding the elements to be disclosed in matters relating to discount rates, such as the definition of what should be the practice in the selection of the rate to be used or the level of expedients used in its formulation.

It was also found that voluntary disclosures can take on a relevant complementary role by closing information gaps that are not properly specified in the standards.

Significant differences are identified between the indices in the different analyses made with the following exceptions, namely between IFRS 13 and IAS 37 (for TDI and MDI), between IAS 36 and IAS 37 (MDI only), and between IAS 19 and IAS 37 (VDI only). Thus, it is concluded that, overall, the existence of some significant differences between the IAS and IFRS regarding the levels of disclosure observed for the listed entities in Portugal. Consequently, it is possible to see the existence of evidence of divergences in this area of disclosure for entities located in the same jurisdiction, identifying this element as a contribution from this research.

This study contributes to the literature through the cross-sectional analysis of the proposed subject.

It is therefore intended that the conclusions of this study contribute to the need for further clarification by standard-setting bodies in general and the IASB regarding the elements to be disclosed in matters relating to disclosure rates. This includes, inter alia, the definition of what should be practiced in selecting the discount rate to be used or at the level of expedients used in its formulation.

FUTURE RESEARCH DIRECTIONS

The research technique adopted with a limitation of this work is identified since content analysis presents a high degree of subjectivity, which weighs the care and methodological concerns adopted. One of the initial difficulties in defining the dependent variable associated with voluntary disclosures was precisely the identification of the characteristics to be observed in the reports and accounts on this subject, due to the lack of specific literature related to disclosures related to discount rates. In this context, it is important to mention the need for further studies in this area that can contribute to the reduction of subjectivity inherent in the methodological options followed in this research.

Other opportunities for future research may be the inclusion of listed entities in other European countries, different sectors, or, further, the use of a longer period, regardless of the maintenance of the proposal for the cross-cutting analysis of the subject followed in this investigation. Such studies could allow for a more comprehensive view of the differences over time, in the treatment given to disclosures related to the discount rate between countries, sectors, and, of course, IAS and IFRS. This last aspect will allow more direct comparisons with the results obtained in this study. They can also identify the factors that explain the highest levels of disclosure, in the light of existing theories.

DECLARATION

The authors declare that the manuscript follows ethical standards and there are no potential conflicts of interest with respect to the research, authorship and/or publication of this chapter.

DISCLAIMER

The contents and views of this chapter are expressed by the authors in their personal capacities. It is not necessary for the Editor and the Publisher to agree with these viewpoints, and they are not responsible for any duty of care in this regard.

ACKNOWLEDGMENT

The authors extend sincere gratitude to

• The Editor and the International Editorial Advisory Board (IEAB) of this book who initially desk reviewed, arranged a rigorous double/triple blind review process, and conducted a thorough, minute, and critical final review before accepting the chapter for publication.

• All anonymous reviewers who provided very constructive feedbacks for thorough revision, improvement, extension, and fine tuning of the chapter.

• All colleagues, assistants and well-wishers who assisted to complete this task.

REFERENCES

Aguiar, Y. (2018). Índice de conformidade da divulgação de informação no âmbito da IAS 37 - Análise a sociedades cotadas em quatro mercados bolsistas europeus no ano de 2016. Master Thesis in Accounting, Instituto Universitário de Lisboa - ISCTE Business School.

Alberto, F., & Lopes, J. (2010). A utilização do valor de uso nas empresas do PSI 20. *Revista de la Asociación Española de Contabilidade y Administración de Empresas, 91*, 4–6. Retrieved from http://hdl.handle.net/10198/2732

Ali, M. J., Ahmed, K., & Henry, D. (2004). Disclosure compliance with national accounting. *Accounting and Business Research, 34*(3), 183–199. doi:10.1080/00014788.2004.9729963

Alkababji, M. (April, 2016). The extent of compliance with disclosure requirements for fair value measurements (IFRS-13): a study on the annual reports of Palestinian corporations. *European Journal of Accounting, Auditing and Finance Research, 4*(4), 65–88. Retrieved from https://www.eajournals.org/keywords/ifrs-13/

Alnaas, A., & Rashid, A. (2019). Firm characteristics and compliance with IAS/IFRS: Evidence from North African companies. *Journal of Financial Reporting and Accounting, 17*(3), 383–410. doi:10.1108/JFRA-06-2018-0052

Ball, R. (2006). International Financial Reporting Standards (IFRS): Pros and cons for investors. *Accounting and Business Research, 36*(1), 5–27. https://papers.ssrn.com/sol3/papers.cfm?abstract_id=929561. doi:10.1080/00014788.2006.9730040

Beattie, V., Mclnnes, B., & Fearnley, S. (2004). A methodology for analyzing and evaluating narratives in annual reports: A comprehensive descriptive profile and metrics for disclosure quality attributes. *Accounting Forum, 28*(3), 205–236. doi:10.1016/j.accfor.2004.07.001

Blum, V., & Thérond, P. (2019). Discount rate in accounting: How practitioners depart the IFRS Maze towards the end of determinism in accounting. *Autorité des Normes Comptables*. Retrieved from https://EconPapers.repec.org/RePEc:hal:journl:hal-03283265

Carlin, T., & Finch, N. (2009). Discount rates in disarray evidence on flawed goodwill impairment testing. *Australian Accounting Review, 19*(4), 326–336. doi:10.1111/j.1835-2561.2009.00069.x

Dasgupta, M. (2003). A study of company characteristics associated with financial disclosure practices in India. Dissertação de mestrado em Contabilidade. Perth: Edith Cowan Univeristy.

Diana, C. I. (2009). Historical cost versus fair value. *Annals of Faculty of Economics, 3*(1), 860–865. https://EconPapers.repec.org/RePEc:ora:journl:v:3:y:2009:i:1:p:860-865

Eckel, L., Fortin, S., & Fisher, K. (2003). The choice of discount rate for external reporting purposes: Considerations for standard setting. *Accounting Forum, 27*(1), 28–59. doi:10.1111/1467-6303.00095

EY. (2016). *Accounting treatment of social benefits with a view to financial reporting requirements under the future EPSAS*. Retrieved from https://circabc.europa.eu/sd/a/992fbb51-d3ce-4cef-be2d-90af9c42f664/Issue%20Paper%20on%20Social%20Benefits.pdf

Fahad, N., Ma, N., & Scott, T. (2020). The consequences of discount rate selection for defined benefit liabilities. *Journal of Contemporary Accounting & Economics, 16*(1), 1–16. doi:10.1016/j.jcae.2020.100184

Glaum, M. S., Street, D., & Vogel, S. (2013). Compliance with IFRS 3 and IAS 36-required disclosures across 17 European countries: Company- and country-level determinants. *Accounting and Business Research, 43*(3), 163–204. doi:10.1080/00014788.2012.711131

He, L. (2020). Discount rate behaviour in fair value reporting. *Journal of Behavioral and Experimental Finance, 28*, 100386. doi:10.1016/j.jbef.2020.100386

He, L., Wright, S., & Evans, E. (2021). The impact of managerial discretion on fair value information in the Australian agricultural sector. *Accounting and Finance, 61*(S1), 1897–1930. doi:10.1111/acfi.12647

Healy, P., & Palepu, K. (2001). Information asymmetry, corporate disclosure, and the capital markets: A review of the empirical disclosure literature. *Journal of Accounting and Economics, 31*(1-3), 405–440. doi:10.1016/S0165-4101(01)00018-0

Husmann, S., & Schmidt, M. (2008). The discount rate: A note on IAS 36. *Accounting in Europe, 5*(1), 49–62. doi:10.1080/17449480802088762

IASB. (2018). *Conceptual framework for financial reporting*. London: IFRS Foundation. Retrieved from https://www.ifrs.org/content/dam/ifrs/publications/pdf-standards/english/2021/issued/part-a/conceptual-framework-for-financial-reporting.pdf

IASB. (2019). Discount rates in IFRS standards. London: IFRS Foundation. Retrieved from https://cdn.ifrs.org/content/dam/ifrs/project/discount-rates/project-summary.pdf

Kasyan, A., Santos, P. G. D., Pinho, C., & Pinto, V. (2017). Disclosure of fair value measurement techniques of financial instruments: Study applied to the Portuguese banking sector according to IFRS 7. *International Review of Management and Business Research, 6*(4), 1453–1468.

KPMG. (2017). Fair value measurement - Questions and answers US GAAP and IFRS. Retrieved from https://assets.kpmg/content/dam/kpmg/xx/pdf/2017/12/fair-value-qa-2017.pdf

Kunz, B. (2015). The scope of disclosures of fair value measurement methods of financial instruments in financial statements of banks listed on the Warsaw stock exchange. *Research Papers of the Wroclaw University of Economics / Prace Naukowe Uniwersytetu Ekonomicznego we Wroclawiu*(381),158–176. https://doi:10.15611/pn.2015.381.12

Kvaal, E. (2010). The discount rate of IAS 36 – A comment. *Accounting in Europe*, *7*(1), 87–95. doi:10.1080/17449480.2010.485378

Maia, D., & Martins, P. (2014). Internacional Financial Reporting Standards - IFRS: Percepção dos profissionais de contabilidade sobre a nova contabilidade e o impacto dessa na controladoria. *Revista de Contabilidade do Mestrado em Ciências Contábeis da UERJ*, *19*(1), 42–57. doi:10.12979/8191

Marques, C. (2015). Provisões e Contingências - Análise das divulgações das entidades do PSI20. Master thesis in Accounting and Finance, Universidade de Coimbra - Faculdade de Economia.

Matiş, D., Damian, M. I., & Bonaci, C. G. (2013). Fair value measurement disclosures: Particularities in the context of listed companies and European funding. *Annales Universitatis Apulensis Series Oeconomica*, *15*(1), 40–53. doi:10.29302/oeconomica.2013.15.1.3

Meek, G., Roberts, C., & Gray, S. (1995). Factors influencing voluntary annual report disclosures by U.S., U.K and continental European multinational corporations. *Journal of International Business Studies*, *26*(3), 555–572. https://www.jstor.org/stable/155561. doi:10.1057/palgrave.jibs.8490186

Nitzan, J., & Bichler, S. (2009). *Capital as power - A study of order and creorder*. Routledge. doi:10.4324/9780203876329

Oliveira, L., Rodrigues, L., & Craig, R. (2006). Firm-specific determinants of intangibles reporting: Evidence from the Portuguese stock market. *Journal of Human Resource Costing & Accounting*, *10*(1), 11–33. doi:10.1108/14013380610672657

Owusu-Ansah, S. (1998). The impact of corporate attributes on the extent of mandatory disclosure and reporting by listed companies in Zimbabwe. *The International Journal of Accounting*, *33*(5), 605–631. doi:10.1016/S0020-7063(98)90015-2

Paugam, L., Ramond, O., Husson, B., Philippe, H., & Casta, J. F. (2013). Risque d'estimation, coût du capital et communication des tests de dépréciation. *Finance Contrôle Stratégie*, *16*(1). Advance online publication. doi:10.4000/fcs.1260

Peasnell, K. (1977). The present value concept in financial reporting. *Journal of Business Finance & Accounting*, *4*(2), 153–168. doi:10.1111/j.1468-5957.1977.tb00702.x

PwC. (2015). *A look at current financial reporting issues - IFRS 13 disclosure requirements - questions and answers*. Retrieved from https://www.PwC.co.za/en/assets/pdf/indepth-ifrs-13-questions-and-answers-march-2015.pdf

PwC. (2018). *Applying discount rates under the future European Public Sector Accounting Standards (EPSAS)*. Retrieved from https://circabc.europa.eu/sd/a/12a99051-5c46-4dc4-add5-d6464877ed3f/Issue%20paper%20on%20applying%20discount%20rates.pdf

Rafay, A. (2022). Related party disclosures in financial reporting for Islamic banks. *Journal of Islamic Accounting and Business Research*, *13*(7), 997–1017. doi:10.1108/JIABR-03-2020-0066

Rafay, A., & Farid, S. (2018). Shariah Supervisory Board Report (SSBR) in Islamic Banks: An experimental study of Investors' perception and behaviour. *International Journal of Islamic and Middle Eastern Finance and Management*, *11*(2), 274–296. doi:10.1108/IMEFM-07-2017-0180

Rafay, A., Sadiq, R., & Ajmal, M. M. (2016). The effect of IAS-24 disclosures on governance mechanisms and ownership structures in Pakistan. *Lahore Journal of Business*, *5*(1), 15–36. doi:10.35536/ljb.2016.v5.i1.a2

Rafay, A., Yasser, F., & Khalid, Z. (2019). Revaluation of Non-Current assets under IAS-16: Possibility of any managerial inducement - Evidence from a South Asian economy. *DLSU Business and Economics Review*, *29*(1), 93–105.

Rosa, S. (2013). *A importância da informação financeira nas PME: mensuração do ativo fixo tangível.* Tese de Doutoramento. Especialidade de Economia da Empresa, Universidade Autónoma de Lisboa.

Saha, A., & Bose, S. (2021). Do IFRS disclosure requirements reduce the cost of capital? Evidence from Australia. *Accounting and Finance*, *61*(3), 4669–4701. doi:10.1111/acfi.12744

Samaha, K., & Stapleton, P. (2008). Compliance with International Accounting Standards in a national context: Some empirical evidence from the Cairo and Alexandria Stock Exchanges. *Afro-Asian Journal of Finance and Accounting*, *1*(1), 40–66. doi:10.1504/AAJFA.2008.016890

Santos, E. S., Ponte, V. M., & Mapurunga, P. V. (2014). Adoção obrigatória do IFRS no Brasil (2010): Índice de conformidade das empresas com a divulgação requerida e alguns fatores explicativos. *Revista Contabilidade & Finanças*, *25*(65), 161–176. doi:10.1590/S1519-70772014000200006

Sarquis, R., Santos, A., Lourenço, I., & Braunbeck, G. (2021). Joint venture investments: An analysis of the level of compliance with the disclosure requirements of IFRS 12. *Journal of International Financial Management & Accounting*, *32*(2), 207–232. doi:10.1111/jifm.12130

Street, D., & Gray, S. (2002). Factors influencing the extent of corporate compliance with International Accounting Standards: Summary of a research monograph. *Journal of International Accounting, Auditing & Taxation*, *11*(1), 51–76. doi:10.1016/S1061-9518(02)00054-X

Thauvron, A., Astolfi, P., & Desban, M. (2022). Valuation and discount rates under IFRS: Does a size premium exist on the French market? *Accounting Auditing Control*, *28*(4), 101–141.

Tsalavoutas, I. (2011). Transition to IFRS and compliance with mandatory disclosure requirements: What is the signal? *Advances in Accounting*, *27*(2), 390–405. doi:10.1016/j.adiac.2011.08.006

Urquiza, F., Navarro, M., & Trombetta, M. (2009). Disclosure indices design: Does it make a difference? *Revista de Contabilidad*, *12*(2), 253–277. doi:10.1016/S1138-4891(09)70008-1

Zeff, S. A. (2014). A Evolução do IASC para o IASB e os Desafios Enfrentados. *Revista Contabilidade & Finanças*, *25*(spe), 300–320. doi:10.1590/1808-057x201400040

ADDITIONAL READING

Decreto-Lei n.º 158/2009. (2009, de 13 de julho). Ministério das Finanças e da Administração Pública. D.R. n.º 133/2009. Série I. 4375–4384. Retrieved from https://dre.pt/dre/detalhe/Decreto-Lei/158-2009-492428

Decreto-Lei n.º 35/2005. (2005, de 17 de fevereiro). Ministério das Finanças e da Administração Pública. D.R. n.º 34/2005. Série I-A. 1186–1200. Retrieved from https://dre.pt/dre/detalhe/Decreto-Lei/35-2005-605330

Decreto-Lei n.º 98/2015. (2015, de 2 de junho). Ministério das Finanças. D.R. n.º 106/2015. Série I. 3470–3493. Retrieved from https://dre.pt/dre/detalhe/decreto-Lei/98-2015-67356342

Gollier, C., & Hammitt, J. K. (2014). The long-run discount rate controversy. *Annual Review of Resource Economics*, *6*(1), 273–295. doi:10.1146/annurev-resource-100913-012516

Groom, B., Hepburn, C., Koundouri, P., & Pearce, D. (2005). Declining discount rates: The long and the short of it. *Environmental and Resource Economics*, *32*(4), 445–493. doi:10.100710640-005-4681-y

Haga, J., Ittonen, K., Tronnes, P. C., & Wong, L. (2018). Is earnings management sensitive to discount rates? *Journal of Accounting Literature*, *41*(1), 75–88. doi:10.1016/j.acclit.2018.03.001

Penman, S. H., & Yehuda, N. (2019). A matter of principle: Accounting reports convey both cash-flow news and discount-rate news. *Management Science*, *65*(12), 5584–5602. doi:10.1287/mnsc.2018.3187

Regulamento (CE) n.º 1126/2008 da Comissão. (2008, November 3). Retrieved from https://eur-lex.europa.eu/legal-content/PT/TXT/?uri=CELEX%3A02008R1126-20160101

Regulamento (CE) n.º 1606/2002 do Parlamento Europeu e do Conselho. (2002, de 19 de julho). Retrieved from https://eur-lex.europa.eu/legal-content/PT/TXT/?uri=celex%3A32002R1606

Regulamento da Comissão do Mercado de Valores Mobiliários n.º 11/2005. (de 3 de novembro). Retrieved from https://www.cmvm.pt/pt/legislacao/legislacaonacional/Regulamentos/pages /reg.2005 _11.aspx

Ronen, J. (2021). The discount rate used in the current expected credit loss standard creates accounting losses where there are no economic losses. *Journal of Accounting, Auditing & Finance*, 0148558X211034959. https://doi.org/ doi:10.1177/0148558X211034959

KEY TERMS AND DEFINITIONS

Current value: Current value measures provide monetary information about assets, liabilities and related income and expenses, using information updated to reflect conditions at the measurement date. Because of the updating, current values of assets and liabilities reflect changes, since the previous measurement date, in estimates of cash flows and other factors reflected in those current values. Unlike historical cost, the current value of an asset or liability is not derived, even in part, from the price of the transaction or other event that gave rise to the asset or liability. Current value measurement basis include: (a) fair value; (b) value in use for assets and fulfilment value for liabilities; and (c) current cost.

Current cost: The current cost of an asset is the cost of an equivalent asset at the measurement date, comprising the consideration that would be paid at the measurement date plus the transaction costs that would be incurred at that date.

Fair value: Fair value is the price that would be received to sell an asset, or paid to transfer a liability, in an orderly transaction between market participants at the measurement date.

Fulfilment value: Fulfilment value is the present value of the cash, or other economic resources, that an entity expects to be obliged to transfer as it fulfils a liability.

Measure: The result of applying a measurement basis to an asset or liability and related income and expenses.

Measurement basis: An identified feature—for example, historical cost, fair value or fulfilment value—of an item being measured.

Recognition: The process of capturing for inclusion in the statement of financial position or the statement(s) of financial performance an item that meets the definition of one of the elements of financial statements—an asset, a liability, equity, income or expenses. Recognition involves depicting the item in one of those statements—either alone or in aggregation with other items—in words and by a monetary amount and including that amount in one or more totals in that statement.

Value in use: Value in use is the present value of the cash flows, or other economic benefits, that an entity expects to derive from the use of an asset and from its ultimate disposal.

ENDNOTES

1 Lopes, J. C. (2007). *The reliability of the Capital Assets Pricing Model in the process of accounting measurement-An empirical study applied to dotcom companies* (Doctoral dissertation). Universidade Autónoma de Madrid, Madrid, Spain.

2 Billings, M., O'Brien, C., Woods, M., & Vencappa, D. (2017). Discretion in accounting for pensions under IAS 19: using the "magic telescope"? *Accounting and Business Research, 47*(2), 123–143.

3 Andrews, R. (2006) *Impairment of assets: measurement without disclosure?* London, The Association of Chartered Certified Accountants.

4 IFRS 16 was issued in January 2016 entering into force for reporting periods initiated from (or later of) January 1, 2019, overriding IAS 17.

5 IFRS 17 was issued in March 2017 entering into force for reporting periods initiated (or later of) from January 1, 2023, overriding IFRS 4.

6 Peasnell, K.V. (1977). The present value concept in financial reporting. *Journal of Business Finance and Accounting 4*(2), 153–168.

7 Gamble, G., & Cramer, J. (1992). The role of present value in the measurement and recording of nonmonetary financial assets and liabilities: an examination. *Accounting Horizons, 6*(4), 32–41.

8 Weil, R. (1990). Role of the time value of money in financial reporting. *Accounting Horizons, 4*(4), 47–67.

9 Bodenhorn, D. (1984). Balance sheet items as the present value of future cash flows. *Journal of Business Finance and Accounting 11*(4), 493–510.

10 Romero, A. (1991) *Content analysis methodology.* Lisbon: Portuguese Catholic University. ISBN - 972-9430-13-6

11 Cooke, T. E. (1989) *Disclosure in the corporate annual reports of Swedish companies. Accounting and Business Research, 19*(74), 113–124.

Chapter 10
Occupational Fraud in the Highly Regulated Banking Industry:
The Case of India

M. Beemamol
https://orcid.org/0000-0001-5481-9351
Pondicherry University, India

ABSTRACT

Banking has witnessed a significant surge in occupational fraud globally, establishing it as the most impacted industry. Similarly, the banking industry in India has also experienced a rise in fraudulent activities perpetrated by bank officials. This chapter aims to investigate five notable cases of high-value occupational fraud committed by top management personnel in Indian banks. Multiple contributing factors have been identified, including greed, social comparison, corrupt ideology, lack of ethics and morality, a sense of entitlement and ego, hubris, and a hyper-competitive culture. These factors played a pivotal role in enticing top management to exploit fraud opportunities and collaborate with other bank employees and corporate borrowers for personal gain. The prevalence of collusive fraud within the banking sector is an alarming trend that jeopardizes the industry's integrity, potentially foreshadowing its decline. The findings of this study establish a robust foundation for future empirical research and provide valuable insights to enrich the existing body of literature.

INTRODUCTION

How did the sector with the highest regulations end up being the one most susceptible to occupational fraud[1]? According to the Association of Certified Fraud Examiners (ACFE), the financial and banking sectors are the biggest global victims of occupational fraud (ACFE, 2020a). Occupational fraud is the use of one's line of work for personal benefit. The ACFE has broadly classified occupational fraud as asset misappropriation[2], corruption[3], and financial statement fraud[4]. Occupational fraud is a severe ill-

DOI: 10.4018/978-1-6684-8587-3.ch010

ness that may spread across the business via growing connivance. Once it starts, it will last for a very long period. Finding the source and beginning rhizome medication before it expands is the only way to stop it. It will grow and become worse when the cause is not identified. As per the special research of the "ACFE Report to the Nations in 2020 on Banking and Financial Services," the loss and number of cases vary in different regions around the world; Sub-Saharan Africa had the highest median loss with ₹1.398 crore and followed by Asia-Pacific and the Middle East and North Africa, with losses of ₹1.234 crore. The average loss in Southern Asia (Afghanistan, Bangladesh, India, Nepal, Pakistan, and Sri Lanka) is ₹0.822 crore. The fragility of internal controls is the root cause of occupational fraud, and the weaknesses in internal controls include the ability to bypass already-in-place measures and a lack of management monitoring (ACFE, 2020a).

Although occupational fraud occurs more often in banks and other financial institutions, the median loss was less. The number of frauds perpetrated by owners and executives was less, but the damages were more significant. The statistics show that younger criminals with a median age of 35 caused less damage to the organisation than elderly perpetrators while considering the age of the offenders. When looking at fraud by gender, men committed 71 percent of the crimes, and their median loss was twice that of women offenders. The organisation might suffer greater damage from collusion[5] among the culprits than fraud alone. When examining the criminals' behavioural red flags[6], it discovered that 87% of the offenders had one or more of the following characteristics: living above one's means, money troubles, strong, unusual connections with customers, divorce or family issues, impatience, suspiciousness, or defensiveness (ACFE, 2020a).

As the custodian of public funds, the banks' misuse of that money will have an impact on the whole financial system and the economy (Rafay, 2023). Occupational fraud is becoming more prevalent in the Indian banking industry, and it is high time to take decisive action to prevent the problem from worsening and damaging the whole financial system. Recently, the Indian banking industry has witnessed an increase in corporate advance fraud, which has been exacerbated by collusion between corporate borrowers and bank executives. There are two distinct forms of high-value fraud that are evident in banking in India: 1) fraud perpetrated by corporate borrowers; and 2) fraud conducted by senior management. The fraud instances involving the Industrial Credit and Investment Corporation of India (ICICI) Bank, Yes Bank, Punjab National Bank (PNB), Industrial Development Bank of India (IDBI) Bank, and Punjab & Maharashtra Co-operative Bank Limited (PMC) Bank are suitable examples of high-value occupational frauds. Despite a surge in fraud committed by corporate borrowers, this was the first time in the history of the Indian banking industry to witness a failure of the tone at the top in the private, public and Co-operative banks in a short interval. The five significant cases in the field of behavioural forensics are discussed in this chapter. Although each instance has a unique stimulus, the opportunity to perpetrate fraud has been found as the common denominator.

In the case of Yes Bank, the co-founder and ex-Chief Executive Officer (CEO) of Yes Bank, Rana Kapoor, has committed corruption by colluding with the promoters of Dewan Housing Finance Ltd. (DHFL) and other corporate borrowers by approving loans and receiving kickbacks; asset misappropriation by diverting funds to shell companies and financial statement fraud by underreporting the Non-Performing Assets (NPAs) and cooking of balance sheets (Press Trust of India, 2022a; Ramchandani & Jethwani, 2021; Sharma & Aggarwal, 2022). In contravention of the Banking Regulation Act, Reserve Bank of India (RBI) instructions, and the bank's credit policy, Chanda Kochhar, the former CEO and Managing Director (MD) of the ICICI bank (the second-largest private bank in India), approved credit facilities totalling ₹3,250 crore to the Videocon Group firms promoted by Dhoot. As the kickback for this, Dhoot invested ₹64 crores in Nupower Renewables, which was owned by Chanda Kochhar's husband, Deepak (Das, 2023; Livemint, 2022).

Furthermore, the second-largest Public Sector Bank (PSB), PNB, was defrauded by the diamond tycoon Nirav Modi and his uncle Mehul Choksi through forged Letters of Undertaking (LoUs) to siphon off ₹14,000 crore through collusion with some of its officers, including a former deputy general manager of PNB, Gokulnath Shetty. Additionally, Usha Ananthasubramanian, the former CEO of PNB, was aware of the methods used in these frauds but didn't take any meaningful corrective action in her capacity as the executive leader of the bank. She also gave her subordinates permission to use the RBI guidelines without taking any further action (Business Standard, 2019; Press Trust of India, 2022b). Further, in the IDBI bank, 15 officials were involved in the loan fraud of 600 cr., including the former Chairman, MD and CEO, and former Deputy Managing Director (Sharma, 2018; Press Trust of India, 2021b). In addition, Waryam, the former chairman of Punjab & Maharashtra Co-operative Bank (PMC Bank), and Joy Thomas, the bank's managing director, conspired to fraudulently sanction loans for Rakesh Wadhawan and his son Sarang, directors of the Housing Development & Infrastructure Limited (HDIL) group, and they hid all NPAs connected to HDIL for a very long time through ghost accounts (Press Trust of India, 2021a; Singh, 2019).

A question that always comes is, "How can a senior executive from a highly regulated sector perpetrate substantial fraud?" How can they steal public funds when they are the custodians of such funds? Do they adhere to strict regulations? Through the thorough literature review, it is identified that certain factors exist for the prevalence of these frauds. This research tried to accomplish the following research questions and the objectives of the study.

RESEARCH QUESTIONS

What are the reasons for the failure of the tone at the top in the banking industry in India? How serious is the current scenario of the banking industry in India?

OBJECTIVES

1. To identify the characteristics of the perpetrators and determine the factors that influence the occurrence of fraud in the banking industry in India.
2. To know the current level of fraudulent activities in the banking industry in India with the ABC model.

To find the answer to the questions and accomplish these objectives, this study uses the ABC model, proposed by Ramamoorti, Morrison & Koletar (2009), to analyse the stage of the Indian banking sector. The ABC approach categorises fraud into bad apples, bad bushels, and bad crops. The "bad apple" is an individual who commits fraud, the "bad bushel" is collusive fraud, in which top executives combine to commit fraud, and the "bad crop" is social and cultural elements that influence fraud susceptibility. In addition to the ABC model, this study included pertinent theories of white-collar crime[7] to help readers to understand the factors of fraud. Following is the arrangement of the remaining sections: The second part evaluates the range of literature about the theoretical and industrial background. The third section presents the research methodology. The analysis of the instances is covered in the fourth section, and the discussion of the ABC model is included in the fifth section. The implications are covered in the sixth section, and the research is concluded in the seventh section.

LITERATURE REVIEW

Theoretical Background

The term "white-collar crime" was first used by Sutherland (1940). He was the first one to combine criminal acts by upper-class white-collar people with finance and commercial activities. He defined a white-collar criminal as a sophisticated individual who primarily breaches "delegated or implied trust." He contends that the social position of a professional fosters a culture of respect and fear (Dorminey *et al.*, 2012; Sutherland, 1940, 1945). For several reasons, white-collar crimes were less evident than violent ones. For example, the public's burden of suffering may be stretched over a longer time frame, more people may have participated in the act, and the victims may be harder to locate and poorly organised (Dorminey *et al.*, 2012; Sutherland, 1945). Donald R. Cressey, a criminology doctoral candidate who started researching embezzlement behaviour, was being supervised by Sutherland (Dorminey *et al.*, 2012). Cressey observed similarities among inmates incarcerated for white-collar crimes. Cressey (1950), (1953) proposed three conditions for criminal breaches of trust in light of his observations: (1) a financial issue that cannot be shared; (2) understanding how a particular business operates and having the opportunity to break the trust; and (3) a person's capacity to change how they see themselves such that breaking this trust does not seem to them to be criminality. According to Cressey's (1950) theory, to occur fraud, each of the three conditions perceived pressure, perceived opportunity, and rationalization—must be met (Cressey, 1950, 1953; Dorminey *et al.*, 2012). Now it is known as the "Fraud Triangle" (Wells, 2001).

The driving force behind the crime is perceived pressure brought on by an unshareable financial issue. Due to their view of the societal stigma of admitting such a problem, a person may decide that a problem is unshareable. Further, a strong feeling of vanity or ego may keep someone from asking for assistance or disclosing their issue. Perceived opportunity is when there is a managerial vulnerability and, more significantly, there is little chance of getting detected. In order to take advantage of a perceived opportunity, one must be able to do it covertly. Rationalization is an effort to lessen a person's cognitive dissonance (Dorminey *et al.*, 2012; Ramamoorti, 2008; Ramamoorti, Morrison & Koletar 2009). According to Cressey (1950), (1953), those who perpetrate fraud like to stay in their moral comfort zones. As a result, the fraudster attempts to defend the fraudulent conduct before the initial fraudulent deed, at least inwardly. Albrecht, Howe & Romney (1984) thought that fraud was hard to foresee and challenging to characterise those who commit occupational fraud. Derived from their research findings, they developed the fraud scale that depends on the two elements of the Fraud Triangle, pressure and opportunity but substitutes personal integrity for rationalization (Albrecht, Howe & Romney, 1984; Dorminey *et al.*, 2012). According to Wolfe and Hermanson (2004), the Fraud Triangle might be improved by taking capability into account, which would help to prevent fraud because no fraud can happen without the capacity to take advantage of control flaws to conduct and cover up the fraud act.

To define the traits of white-collar crime, Albrecht, Albrecht & Albrecht (2006) proposed the Triangle of Fraud Action or Elements of Fraud. The three attributes of the Triangle of Fraud Action are the act, concealment, and conversion. The act depicts how the deception was carried out and how it was done;

concealment means to cover up deceitful conduct, and the action of converting illicit profits into something the offender may use in a manner that looks to be legal is known as conversion (Albrecht, Albrecht & Albrecht, 2006; Dorminey *et al.*, 2012). For the examination and classification of fraud, Ramamoorti, Morrison and Koletar (2009) suggested the ABC model: a bad Apple, a bad Bushel, and a bad Crop. According to Kranacher & Riley (2019), the acronym MICE which stands for money, ideology, coercion, and ego—might be a more useful way of categorising and elaborating on fraud offenders' motivations.

Ideological motivators explain their ability to commit fraud or theft in order to further some envisioned larger good that is in line with their views (ideology). When someone is coerced into participating in a fraud scheme against their choice, they may later become whistleblowers. Ego may also be a driving force behind fraud since individuals often do not want to lose their status or influence in front of their communities or family. Social pressure can be a solid motive to commit fraudulent acts just to keep their ego. It gives experts a wider context in which to think about the risk of fraud. Crowe Horwath altered the Fraud Diamond with the variable "arrogance" by highlighting the fraud perpetrated by CEO and Chief Financial Officer (CFO) or more enormous financial crimes. When someone feels that internal restrictions do not directly apply to them, they have arrogance, which is an attitude of superiority, entitlement, or avarice (Marks, 2012).

According to Kassem & Higson (2012), it is crucial for auditors to take into account all fraud models in order to comprehend why fraud happens. They advocate for the integration of all the aforementioned models: Fraud Triangle, Fraud Diamond, Fraud Scale, and MICE model into a single model known as "the New Fraud Triangle Model", which also takes into account the motive, opportunity, integrity, and fraudster's capability. Vousinas (2019) created the SCORE model, also known as the fraud hexagon, which consists of the variables: stimulus, capability, collusion, opportunity, rationalization, and ego. Vousinas also added the variable collusion by arguing that it is a key component in many sophisticated and expensive frauds and financial (white-collar) crimes. Saluja, Aggarwal & Mittal (2021) modified the Fraud Triangle with the variable "Integrity" in the context of the case of India, mentioned that integrity influences the prevention of fraud, and proposed the model "Fraud Square". The aforementioned theories outline the elements of white-collar crime, and some of them have been empirically examined and validated to assist fraud examiners in spotting fraud as early as possible. In the context of fraud in the banking industry in India, this study focuses on the ABC model.

Bad Apple, Bad Bushel, and Bad Crop Syndrome: The ABCs of White-collar Crime.

Ramamoorti, Morrison & Koletar (2009) proposed the ABC theory by incorporating the behavioural sciences elements, psychology and sociology with the accounting for fraud detection (Khan & Amoozegar, 2022). Numerous academics (Albrecht, Howe & Romney, 1984; Cressey, 1950; Dorminey *et al.*, 2012; Kranacher & Riley, 2019; Marks, 2012; Saluja, Aggarwal & Mittal, 2021; Vousinas, 2019; Wolfe & Hermanson, 2004) have attempted to use criminological and psychological elements in accounting for the detection of financial fraud. But, Ramamoorti, Morrison & Koletar (2009) tried to develop a taxonomy for white-collar crime or C-Suite, which helps to classify frauds. ABC paradigm enables fraud to be classified as an individual (bad apple), collusive (bad bushel), or cultural and social forces that foster fraud (bad crop).

The question of "Why did the good person commit fraud?" may be the most confusing of all for fraud researchers. Understanding why individuals alter their ideas is necessary to comprehend why a person who is a good citizen in all other spheres of their life chooses to conduct fraud. Which circumstances apply? What methods do they use to achieve so?

The bad Apple features the characteristics and personality traits of the white-collar criminal. Each fraudster is different in their characteristics and personality traits and the modus operandi of the crime. Reversal Theory is a psychological theory of personality, behaviour, and emotions. It emphasises the dynamic elements of everyday human life to explain how someone often switches across psychological conditions, reflecting their motivational style and the significance they place on a specific circumstance at a particular moment (Ramamoorti, Morrison and Koletar, 2009). According to Ramamoorti, Morrison and Koletar (2009), the individual, or bad apple, will be between the ages of 45 and 55, have a university degree, have worked for the business for ten to fifteen years, and have a spotless record.

Seriously, was the apple bad? Or was it good at first?

The archetypal fraudster is often portrayed as a first-time offender, a middle-aged, well-educated, trustworthy professional in a place of authority, and as someone who has contributed to society and is therefore seen favourably by others (Dorminey *et al.*, 2012; Ramamoorti, Morrison & Koletar, 2009). The Fraud Triangle postulates that the offender suffers from a non-shareable issue based on financial deficiencies, and when this condition is combined with an opportunity and a rationalization, a virtuous person who would generally behave honourably commits fraud. This individual may be described as an accidental fraudster. Despite the fraud act, it is assumed that the unintentional fraudster, who is a nice, virtuous individual under ordinary situations, would never contemplate stealing, breaking felony laws, or harming others. Once the suspected culprit is found, the family, friends, coworkers, and other concerned citizens will be astonished and horrified by their purported actions (Dorminey *et al.*, 2012).

Predator fraudsters are serial offenders who are less likely to hold leadership roles, have lower levels of education, and prefer to prey on smaller businesses rather than publicly traded enterprises. Predators are fraudsters who have previously committed fraud, but their schemes are often more expensive, and there is some indication that their schemes are more likely to entail asset misappropriation or corruption (Hermanson, Ramamoorti & Riley, 2017; Rafay, 2021a). Predators are more equipped to cope with auditors and other monitoring mechanisms because they are well-organised, use more intricate concealing techniques, and are better structured (Kranacher & Riley, 2019). Finally, since opportunity is the predator's primary concern, a risk analysis focused on pressure and rationalization is doubtful to uncover predatory plans. Ramamoorti *et al.* (2013) best referred to the predatory fraudster as a "malignant bad apple," in contrast, the situational fraudster as a "benign bad apple", indicating the shift from accidental fraudster to predator fraudster.

"One bad apple can spoil the bunch."

The term "bad bushel" alludes to collusive fraud, which occurs when management people collude to commit fraud. The "bad bushel" refers to team interaction and interactions among senior management employees that often encourage fraud. The bad bushels argue that some group dynamics attract or assist fraud, which may be demonstrated through collusive fraud (Ramamoorti, Morrison & Koletar, 2009). Collusive fraud poses a serious danger to anti-fraud initiatives. As a result, the anti-fraud field concentrates particularly on possible collusion-related domains. Collusion partners might include persons working for the same organisation, individuals working for different organisations, or individuals working for several organisations. They often operate in many areas, including local, state, federal, and worldwide (Dorminey *et al.*, 2012). Internal controls typically fail when collusion is present (AICPA, 2005). The primary internal control of the division of tasks divides the ownership, reporting, and authorisation activities to ensure that one person does not manage all parts of an operation. AICPA (2005) and Rezaee

& Riley (2010) both make the observation that proactive fraud detection also entails a proactive look for collusion. Journal entries, estimations, and odd or noteworthy transactions are all subject to dynamic search scrutiny.

The term "bad crop" indicates a lack of a strong "tone at the top" that stresses the legitimacy and ethics of all acts, either at the organisational or community levels and which gradually penetrates the company, as well as culture and value. The "bad crop syndrome" may potentially affect an entire sector of the economy (Ramamoorti, Morrison & Koletar, 2009). The notion of the bad crop denotes a lack of morality at the top of the company, which is ubiquitous across the organisation and perhaps culture and society (Dorminey *et al.*, 2012). According to the notion, one individual creates a strong unit, which creates a complete historical and cultural aspect. The bad apple may produce a bad bushel and bad crop. In some cases, the chance of becoming a bad apple, bad bushel or bad crop either or is possible. In Bernie Madoff's case, was he a bad apple or a bad bushel? (Ramamoorti, Morrison & Koletar, 2009). The subprime lending crisis of 2007-2008, in which banks collectively and aggressively extended loans to assure higher profits, is an example of a 'bad crop' in which a mindset of incompetence and selfishness penetrated the financial systems, resulting in billions of dollars in losses (Desai, 2020). The NPA crises in banks in India is a significant problem and one of the most notable instances of a "bad crop" in which the financial institutions were infected by a culture of excessive greed and corruption, resulting in losses of crores of rupees (Desai, 2020; Saluja, Aggarwal & Mittal, 2021). According to Ramamoorti (2008), it's critical to understand the psychological underpinnings of what motivates employees to commit fraud. Nevertheless, since employees operate in an environment, the business's organisational culture does have an impact on how they behave because they have an impact on the organisation.

History of Banking Frauds in India

The first bank in India, The Bank of Hindustan, was founded in 1870. Bank of Calcutta, Bank of Bombay, and Bank of Madras were established later under the Presidency Bank's Act of 1876, which laid the groundwork for modern banking in India. The RBI Act was approved in 1934, and the RBI was established as an apex organisation with little government control. In 1949, the Banking Regulations Act was enacted, and this rule gave power to the government over RBI. The statute gave the RBI broad authority to oversee and manage banks. The Act also gave control over granting licences and the right to perform audits to the RBI. (Goyal & Joshi, 2012). Based on the RBI 2023 annual report, 12 PSBs, 22 private sector banks, 46 foreign banks, 56 regional rural banks, 1485 urban co-operative banks, and 96,000 rural co-operative banks make up the Indian banking system.

In 2022, the banking industry's total assets, including public and private sector banks, rose to ₹21,970,495 crore. Both the public and private banking sectors had total assets of ₹7,611,912 crore and ₹13,120,664 crore, accordingly. Bank credit increased at a Compounded Annual Growth Rate (CAGR) of 0.62 percent from Fiscal Year (FY)16 to FY22. Total credit provided as of FY22 increased to ₹12,608,842 crore. The deposits grew at a CAGR of 10.92% from FY16 to FY22, reaching ₹17,444,738 crore by FY22. During the 1800s, there was a rise in financial fraud in the banking industry in India. Beginning in 1840, the East India Company established the Presidency Bank of Bombay (PBB). It was steady and conservatively operated until the middle of the 1850s. Due to inflated balance sheets and accounting fraud, PBB collapsed in 1861 (Agrawal, 2018). PNB fraud is another noteworthy scam that victimised the banking industry. Rajendra Sethia, a businessman from India who lived in London, was accused of defrauding three Indian banks with countless millions in 1986.

RBI commented on this fraud: "*The fraud in PNB is a case of operational risk arising on account of delinquent behaviour by one or more employees of the bank and failure of internal controls*" (Agrawal, 2018; Chawla, 1986).

The other notable case was the Harshad Mehta case, where he defrauded the SBI and other banks in the 1990s. Likewise, Ketan Parekh defrauded the banks in 1999 with the same modus operandi (Ghosh & Bagheri, 2006). These cases caused the banking industry a colossal loss. But still, fraud cases are increasing, with different types. In 1996, the banking industry witnessed a failure of tone at the top; the Indian Bank Chairman and Managing Director (CMD), along with 20 bank officials including the Chief General Manager, Zonal Manager and the Branch Manager of the bank, colluded with the corporate borrower, and the bank lost ₹5.51 crore (The New Indian Express, 2019).

Further, banks often become the victim of corporate fraud by corporate borrowers like Vijay Mallya, Nirav Modi, DHFL, and ABG Shipyard (Murthy & Gopalkrishnan, 2022). The long list of fraud is still continuing in the banking industry in India (Appendices I & II), and the pattern of fraud committed by corporate borrowers and the top management is repeating, but fraud detection is becoming still slower. Many top managements fell for the corruption, receiving kickbacks or quid pro quo; some notable cases are Syndicate Bank, Yes Bank, ICICI Bank, SBI, and PNB frauds. These fraud cases show that banks in India are vulnerable to many risks (Pande & Prakash, 2019).

The fraud system in the Indian banking industry starts with the aggressive lending by banks to its corporate borrowers to achieve their competitive targets among the banks and also to confirm the collusion with corporate borrowers, which leads to higher NPAs and frauds in India (Gangwani, 2021; Murthy & Gopalkrishnan, 2022; Singh *et al.*, 2016). Due to these reasons, in recent times, there was a positive correlation visible in the Indian banking sector; when the NPAs increased, and the number of corporate advances frauds also increased (Murthy & Gopalkrishnan, 2022; C. Singh *et al.*, 2016). The number of frauds and their volume is also rising in the banking Industry in India (Singh *et al.*, 2016). It was clear that the modus operandi of the fraud committed by the corporate borrowers is experiencing again, but the actions from the regulators are still delayed. Recently, the Central Bureau of Investigation (CBI) has started to study the modus operandi to prevent the occurrence of financial fraud by considering the top 53 financial frauds that happened in India.

According to the RBI annual report 2022–2023, banks saw the highest number of frauds in the digital payment category during the FY. There was a 49 percent reduction in the amount involved in the total frauds reported during FY2023 over FY2022. The number of frauds climbed from 3075 in 2021–2022 to 3405 in 2022–2023 at the PSB, although the total amount involved declined. The private sector bank had similar fluctuations in the number of frauds, which went from 5332 in 2021–2022 to 8932 in 2022-23. Additionally, there has been a rise in the number of frauds recorded under the category of "advances", with a drop in the losses sustained. In the banking industry in India, substantial fraud mostly takes the form of two types. 1) Fraud committed by the corporate borrower; 2) fraud by top management. Due to the high incidence of fraud in the banking industry, it is crucial to look into its origins and gauge the sector's health.

METHODOLOGY

Numerous academics have conducted studies to determine the causes of occupational fraud or white-collar crime (Nakitende *et al.*, 2021) and the traits of the fraudster in different nations under various circumstances in various industries, which are covered in the evaluation of the literature. To accomplish the aforementioned objectives and provide a solution to the research question, this study uses the case study analysis method after determining the relevance of the study from the current situation of the banking sector in India. This study has chosen five occupational fraud cases from the top private, public, and co-operative banks in India because they were the outcome of the failure of the tone at the top. Additionally, this essay provides some insight into the kinds of occupational fraud committed by top management and its causes. Moreover, using the ABC model, this research identifies the variables that contributed to the deception visible in these five situations and highlights the traits shared by all of them and contributed to the prevalence of occupational fraud in the banking sector in India.

CASE ANALYSIS: FAILURE OF TONE AT THE TOP IN THE BANKING INDUSTRY

Case 1: ICICI Bank Fraud

Profile of the Offender

In 1984, Chanda Kochhar began her career working for ICICI Bank as a management trainee. Over time, she advanced to become one of the core members of the bank. She has a business administration master's degree and a bachelor's degree in commerce (Dey, 2022; Roy, 2022). She served as the bank's CFO from 2007 to 2009 before being named MD and CEO in 2009. She was the bank's first female CEO; when the banking industry was mostly seen as male-dominated, she was often listed as one of the top Indian women bankers. Kochar's contribution to the banking industry earned Kochar the Padma Bhushan Award (the third-highest civilian award in India) in 2011 (Dey, 2022; Roy, 2022). She ranked 40th in the Forbes List of powerful women in 2016 and fifth in Powerful Women in Finance in 2017 (Forbes, 2016, 2017). She was 48 years old when she committed fraudulent activities and left ICICI Bank in 2018 (Dey, 2022; Roy, 2022).

Profile of the Bank

ICICI was founded in 1955 at the initiative of the World Bank, the Govt. of India, and leaders from Indian business. ICICI Bank was founded in 1994 as part of the ICICI collective (ICICI Bank.Com: About Us I History, n.d.). It was the second-largest and the largest private bank in India Parameswar, Dhir & Dhir, 2017). Based on the BT-KPMG Best Banks and Fintech Survey 2022, ICICI Bank was selected as the best bank of the year and the best bank in innovation (Adhikari, 2023). For the quarter that ended 31st March 2023, ICICI Bank Ltd. announced a 30 percent increase in standalone net profit at ₹9,122 crore on the strength of enhanced net interest income and strong loan growth. It posted an independent net profit of ₹7,029 crore at the same time last year. The gross NPA ratio of ICICI Bank decreased from 3.6 percent to 2.81 percent during the year, reflecting an improvement in asset quality. A rise from ₹1,069 crore to ₹1,620 crore was recorded in provisions and contingencies. The Tier-1 capital adequacy ratio was 17.60 percent, and the total capital adequacy ratio was 18.34 percent (Jagannath, 2023).

The Case

Arvind Gupta, a whistleblower, uncovered the loan fraud. In 2018, he addressed a message to the Prime Minister's Office (PMO). In the email, he alleged that a pay-for-play agreement existed between ICICI Bank (headed by Chanda Kochar) and Videocon CEO Venugopal Dhoot. Mr Arvind Gupta's main charge was that ICICI Bank sanctioned a loan of ₹600 Crore (approx. value) for the benefit of the Videocon corporation when Chanda Kochar was the authorising board's chairperson. According to Gupta, Venugopal Dhoot handed over ownership of NuPower Renewables to Deepak Kochar (Chanda Kochar's husband) for ₹64 crore due to the loan sanction. Gupta claims that this is only one example of Chanda Kochar's deception. As a result of this loan occurrence, ICICI Bank faced significant losses due to bad debts. After deliberating about the letter for a year, the government directed federal agencies to begin an inquiry. The CBI and the Enforcement Directorate (ED) filed First Information Reports (FIRs) following preliminary investigations. According to the CBI charge sheet, under Kochhar, ICICI Bank sanctioned loans to Videocon Group and others later designated as NPAs and caused losses to the bank and unlawful benefits to the borrowers and accused (ET Online, 2022).

The fraudulent activities started after granting loans between 2009 and 2012, and they manipulated the books of accounts from 2016 to 2019. In 2017, the loan accounts were declared as NPA and in 2019, the CBI registered the case of fraudulent activities against the perpetrator (Murthy & Gopalkrishnan, 2022). After working for 25 years at a bank, the offender approved a loan for kickbacks in 2009, and the transaction was only discovered nine years later. For a whole year, neither the government nor the regulator did anything. The perpetrator, the former CEO of the ICICI bank, colluded with the corporate borrower and engaged in illegal behaviour, including collecting bribes in exchange for authorising the loan, end ended up in corruption (ACFE, 2020b). In addition to the corruption, this case exhibits financial statement fraud and asset misappropriation (ACFE, 2020b). Underreporting of NPA, fund theft, money laundering (Rafay 2021b), incorrect asset categorisation, noncompliance with regulatory requirements, falsification of accounts, and poor credit judgments were all present (Murthy & Gopalkrishnan, 2022). The stimulus to conduct the fraud was to get funding for the husband's business which came out of her "corrupt ideology", "greediness", "arrogance", and "lack of ethics" with the external collusion. As the CEO of the bank, Kochar had the opportunity to identify the loopholes in the regulations in the weak corporate governance and internal controls and misuse them in the way Kochar benefits. Kochar concealed these fraudulent acts by falsification of accounts and underreporting of NPA. This case shows the presence of external collusion; when considering the bank and the industry, this case falls under the category of "bad apple".

Case 2: Yes Bank Fraud Case

Profile of the Offender

Rana Kapoor founded Yes Bank at the age of 46 out of his passion, determination, and drive for success (Srinivas, 2009). Although Yes Bank was established at a later stage in Rana Kapoor's career, the groundwork for it had already been laid. This was evident from Rana Kapoor's career trajectory. To get his MBA, he attended Rutgers University in 1979. Working as an intern in the IT division of City Bank in New York during his MBA studies gave Kapoor his initial experience in the banking sector. Kapoor's idea to construct a comparable structure in India was motivated by the flash and grandeur of banking in the major metropolis. However, he needed some experience initially; thus, he spent 15 years travelling around Asia as a junior banker for Bank of America before taking over the outright company (Karnik, 2017). In 2004, he obtained a banking licence and founded Yes Bank (Srinivas, 2009). According to Forbes List, he was the 100th richest man in India in 2017 and 1756th billionaires globally (Forbes, 2018).

Profile of the Bank

Yes Bank, founded in 2004 by Rana Kapoor and the late Ashok Kapur, is a modern banking institution (NDTV Profit, 2023). In August 2004, Yes Bank established its first branch in Mumbai. A year later, it entered the capital market with an Initial Public Offering (IPO), generating over ₹300 crore (Karnik, 2017). The bank's success narrative implied that every shareholder, investor, and client said "resoundingly YES" to Rana Kapoor's idea. And it was this confidence from diverse stakeholders that fuelled Yes Bank's rapid expansion throughout the board in the banking industry. The same might be seen in the fantastic trend of a bank that won several awards between 2008 and 2016. In fact, one of the Top 500 Banking Brands was Yes Bank, the fifth-largest private sector bank in India. (Yes Bank, 2016). The Yes Bank got the "Business Innovator Award" from the Asian Business Leadership Forum (ABLF) in 2014 in honour of its rapid development as India's fourth-largest private sector bank (Press Trust of India, 2014). Further, in FY23, Yes Bank recorded an increase in standalone assets. The total assets of the bank were ₹2.919 crore in FY 2022–2023, an increase of almost 11.49 percent over the ₹2.618 crore in FY22. Yes Bank was also able to record an increase in net cash brought in by operational operations in the most recent FY. Also announced, the net cash flow from operational operations was ₹25,626.01 crore, an 8.47% increase over the prior year.

The Case

On 5th March 2020, RBI imposed a moratorium on Yes Bank as a result of the fraudulent activities that happened in the bank. The case started when Kapoor sanctioned ₹400 crores to Avantha Group as lease rent in 2016, and in 2017, the company defaulted, and the account became stressed. The bank hid the default account, and it didn't appear in the books of the bank. Yes Bank purchased debentures from DHFL between April and June 2019 for 3,700 crores. Consequently, the money was given to DHFL. DHFL then provided DOIT Urban Ventures Pvt Ltd (DUVPL) with a loan of 600 crore rupees (an entity beneficially owned by Rana Kapoor and his family). The investigation also showed that Yes Bank had purchased the aforementioned short-term DHFL debentures using public funds, and DHFL has not yet repaid them. On the other hand, DHFL complied with Rana Kapoor by providing his beneficially owned firm, DUVPL, with the so-called loan of 600 crores without sufficient security. It was said that the loans provided to the business run by Kapoor's family served as a cover for the whole operation (Press Trust of India, 2022).

The research has shown that a loan of 600 crores was made on subpar properties with a merger value of 39.68 crores, and by taking into account the transition of those properties from agricultural land to residential property, an inflated value of 735 crores was displayed, it said. It has also been revealed that Yes Bank had invested in DHFL shortly before the approval of these loans. The charge sheet shows a criminal conspiracy between Rana Kapoor, Kapil, and Dheeraj Wadhawan to get a loan by pledging grossly overpriced assets. It further states that DUVPL had no operational or running businesses when the loan application was made. DUVPL may not be able to make payments given its current business activity and income since it has no economic activity and is thus not currently producing any income. This blatantly exposes a quid pro quo situation. Additionally, Yes Bank has also approved a loan of 750 crore for the construction of M/s Belief Realtors Private Limited's Bandra Reclamation Project in Mumbai, which is beneficially owned by the Wadhawans. According to an investigation, the Wadhawans siphoned off the entire money issued to M/s Belief Realtors by stacking it via their shell businesses and never used it for the intended purpose (Press Trust of India, 2022).

From 2014 to 2019, Yes Bank was lending aggressively, and in 2017, RBI noticed lapses in governance practices (Murthy & Gopalkrishnan, 2022). Bank reported ₹748.98 crore as their NPA in 2016, but RBI has ascertained the actual NPA ₹4925.68 crore and detected the variation in the financial reporting of Yes Bank. In this case, it is also visible that the perpetrator has committed financial statement fraud by overstating financial statements to manifest the organisation's financial strength. He has allegedly diverted ₹2185 crore to Morgan credit private limited, which is one of the holding companies of Yes Bank and which falls under the cash scheme of Asset misappropriation. Here, the ex-CEO has colluded with the promoters of DHFL, Kapil Wadhawan and Dheeraj Wadhawan and perpetrated corruption. The RBI did not permit the founder of the "most coveted new bank" to lead the organisation he founded. The regulator listed three grounds for not letting Rana Kapoor remain as MD & CEO of Yes Bank: "weak compliance culture in Yes Bank," "weak governance in Yes Bank," and "wrong asset classification" (Rai, 2018). The stimulus that led to the fraud was to get funding for the family business, which came out of his "corrupt ideology", "high-competitive culture", "greediness", "arrogance", and "lack of ethics" with external collusion. ED mentioned that "There is no doubt about the fact that Rana Kapoor has misused his official position to gain undue financial benefit for him and his family members,". Based on the fraudulent activities of the case and its absence of internal collusion, this case falls under the category of "bad apple".

However, I continue to have a question: How can someone who built his dream into reality could commit fraud with their own dream? Was it really a dream? Or was it a scheme to siphon off public funds? However, it is always commendable to consider Yes Bank's contribution to the Indian economy from the standpoint of contemporary banking.

Case 3: PMC Bank

This instance paints a picture of internal and external collusion to commit bank fraud. In further cases, the profile of the offender is not included since several bank employees are implicated in the fraud.

Profile of the Bank

Having barely ₹0.164 crore in capital and a sole branch, PMC Bank started operations on 13th February 1984 in a tiny room in Sion, Mumbai. Over the course of more than 35 years, PMC Bank expanded to become a multi-state scheduled urban co-operative bank with 137 branches and activities in the states of Delhi, Madhya Pradesh, Gujarat, Maharashtra, Goa, and Karnataka (Gupta, 2021). The bank said in its annual report that it had a net profit of ₹99.69 crore in 2018–19. When compared to public-sector banks, the bank performed well, with gross non-performing assets (NPAs) amounting to 3.76 percent (or ₹315 crore) of loans (₹8,383 crore) (Business Standard, 2020).

The Case

In September 2019, the five-page confession statement by Joy K Thomas, MD and CEO of PMC (one of India's ten largest co-operative banks) regarding the gross discrepancies, connivance, and fraud in PMC Bank's banking activities from 2008 onwards. The RBI acted quickly, imposing restrictions on ordinary banking activity and limiting withdrawals to a certain amount. With a 73 percent commitment to a single borrower, HDIL & related entities, who were also facing insolvency proceedings, and complete recovery was nearly unattainable. When it comes to the entire amount of the bank fraud, it was ₹4,355 crore. The bank's overall NPA has now reached 73 percent. The PMC Bank reportedly privileged the owners of HDIL by granting them passcode of "masked accounts." It was discovered that about 21,049 bank accounts were formed under false names to hide 44 loan accounts. To conceal these loan accounts, the bank's software was also modified, with this financial fraud and the scheme was uncovered by a group of female PMC bank credit department employees. These employees informed the RBI of their knowledge of the phantom accounts (H. Singh, 2019). The actual fraud goes like this, the HDIL started defaulting during 2011-2013, and from 2014, the PMC failed to classify as NPA hide this with ghost accounts (Murthy & Gopalkrishnan, 2022). The confession letter revealed how PMC Bank and HDIL had been favouring one another since 2008 on a "quid pro quo" basis. When PMC Bank was having financial difficulties, the Wadhawan family and the HDIL promoters came to the bank's aid, invested money in the institution, and prevented the bank from going bankrupt.

Joy K Thomas quoted, "In 1986–87, just two years later PMC Bank started operations, it was on the verge of closure when the second-generation Wadhawans', Rajesh Kumar Wadhawan and Rakesh Kumar Wadhawan parked big volume of deposits into the bank to help the bank build its credibility among depositors. Similarly, in 2004, Wadhawans deposited more than ₹164.573 crores in PMC Bank so that it could recover from a liquidity crunch" (Dugal, 2019).

The Wadhawans, specifically HDIL and its group companies, were patrons of PMC Bank, and a total of 15 bank officials were directly involved in this fraud, which shows the lack of ethical culture, corporate governance, and internal control. The management override and collusion are also the other reasons for the fraud. It was also notable that the former Chairman and MD & CEO perpetrated this out of their ideology, hubris and quid pro quo. The perpetrators have committed large-value occupational fraud and concealed it by creating ghost accounts. This case is a perfect example of internal and external collusion involving fraudulent activities, which led the bank to a "bad bushel".

Case 4: Punjab National Bank

Profile of the Bank

When Punjab was under the British, particularly following its acquisition in 1849, it had tremendous growth that gave birth to a new educated class. One of the most important aspirations of this emerging class was to establish a Swadeshi Bank with Indian capital and administration from all facets of the Indian population. According to Lala Lajpat Rai, the concept was initially proposed by Rai Mool Raj of the Arya Samaj, who had long cherished the notion that Indians need to establish their own national bank (PNB, 2023a). The first Swadeshi bank in India, PNB, began operations on 12th April 1895 in Lahore with a working capital of ₹20,000 and an authorised capital of ₹0.02 crore. The Bank was the first bank solely run by Indians with Indian capital, and it was founded in the spirit of nationalism. In the lengthy history of the Bank, PNB has merged or amalgamated with nine banks. On 1st April 2020, PNB merged with the Oriental Bank of Commerce and the United Bank of India and Rose to the position of the second-largest bank in the nation (PNB, 2023b). According to the FY 2023 report, PNB is one of the biggest PSBs in the country, with a Global Gross Business of 21,65,844 Crore. With a 43.0 percent share, the Bank continues to retain its strength in low-cost CASA deposits. The bank's main priorities have been quality business development, recovery, and stopping new shortfalls. In FY23, PNB reported net interest income of ₹34,492 crore, an increase of 20.2%, as well as operational and net profits of ₹22,529 and ₹2,507 crore, respectively.

The Case

PNB, India's second most significant PSB, revealed a fraud of ₹11,400 crore conducted by one of the world's wealthiest diamond traders, Nirav Modi, on 14th February 2018. He is ranked 85th on Forbes' 2017 list of India's most affluent individuals (Forbes India, 2016). From 2007 to 2014, he took loans from various banks and in 2015, the account was declared NPA by PNB (Murthy & Gopalkrishnan, 2022). Nirav Modi organised and carried out the scheme with the help of Gokulnath Shetty, the Deputy Manager of the PNB Mumbai branch, and employee Manoj Kharat (Choudhary, 2018). Modi and his uncle, Mehul Choksi, conspired with these two individuals. They had enabled the issuing of unlawful LOUs to Modi and his firm without following protocol. The LOU is a financial instrument used to address a bank's customer's short-term credit needs. Under LOU, the bank lets the consumer borrow money from an overseas branch of another bank in India. PNB did not follow the authorised protocol for issuing an LOU to its customer Nirav Modi, which facilitated the fraud. The post-scam has damaged PNB shares by vanishing their market cap worth.

Additionally, Usha Ananthasubramanian, the former CEO of PNB, was aware of the methods used in these frauds but took no meaningful corrective action in her capacity as the executive leader of the bank. She also gave her subordinates permission to use the RBI guidelines without taking any further action (Sahgai, 2018). In the case of PNB, the deputy manager and clerk colluded with the corporate borrower and did fraudulent activities under the awareness of the ex-CEO Usha Ananthasubramanian. Modi reportedly received more than six years of assistance from two junior employees at a bank branch. They skirted the restrictions on employee transfers that place a time limit on how long they may work at a single branch. Therefore, they broke fundamental laws intended to stop borrower-lender collusion. It is visible that there was an external and internal collusion to perpetrate the fraud. Here, both bank officials misused their official position for their personal benefit. The fraud was committed, and long-term concealment was made possible by internal and external collusions. This case was like the custodian of public money helped the thieves to loot it and hide it. The collusion pushed the bank to the category of the "bad bushel".

Case 5: IDBI BANK

Profile of the Bank

IDBI was established as a development financial institution on 1st July 1964, by notice dated 22nd June, according to the Industrial Development Bank of India Act 1964. On 3rd October 2006, IDBI and the United Western Bank Ltd. (UWB), a Satara-based private sector bank merger, went into force (IDBI,

2019). Due to higher net interest margins, private sector lender IDBI Bank's net profit for the quarter ending March 2023 increased by 64% to ₹1,133 crore. The lender achieved a record-breaking net profit of ₹3,645 crore, or 49% higher than ₹2,439 crore for FY22. In addition, its Net Interest Income (NII) climbed by 35% to ₹3,280 crore in Q4 FY23 from ₹2,420 crore in the corresponding quarter of FY22. When compared to the ₹2,925 crore recorded in the December quarter of FY23, NII is up 13% consecutively (Das, 2023). The government's first initiative for banking sector privatisation in India is the sale of IDBI Bank. The government had anticipated that the sale of their 60.72 percent interest in IDBI Bank (Press Trust of India, 2023) in the first half of FY24 would fetch at least ₹32918.2 crore (Livemint, 2023).

The Case

The ₹600 loan scam involving IDBI bank is a notable example of how its senior executives robbed their bank. The 15 bank officials involved in this fraud, including "MS Raghavan, then CMD of IDBI, B K Batra, then DMD of IDBI, MO Rego, then DMD of IDBI and now serving MD and CEO of Syndicate Bank, PA Shenoy, then independent director at of IDBI, S Ravi, then independent director of IDBI, Niladkerpe, then independent director of IDBI, K Biju George, then and current GM of IDBI, Manoj Alex, then regional manager of IDBI and currently DGM of IDBI, Venka Krishnan, then and current GM of IDBI, Subrata Gupta, then CGM of IDBI and serving ED of IDBI, Vinney Kumar, then ED of IDBI, G Suneel Babu, then DGM IDBI and current GM of IDBI, B Rabrinathanath, then ED of IDBI and GM Yadwadkar, then ED now DMD of IDBI Bank and Kishore Kharat, then CMD of IDBI and now current MD and CEO of Indian Bank, Chennai"(Pandey, 2018).

One of Sivasankaran's companies, Win Wind Oy (WWO), with headquarters in Finland, received a loan of ₹322 crore from IDBI Bank in October 2010. Three years after the loan was made, the firm filed for bankruptcy. Another business led by Sivasankaran, Axcel Sunshine, domiciled in the British Virgin Islands, received a loan from IDBI in the amount of ₹523 crore in February 2014. It has been claimed that WWO and other group firms' dues were paid illegally using the financing that Axcel Sunshine had obtained. It was further alleged that the loans were given to the aforementioned companies by the IDBI Bank at its highest decision-making level, which included senior most management and even independent directors, in violation of the set principles, directions, and processes, leading to the relaxation or complete disregard of several terms. IDBI Bank acknowledged the loan given to Axcel Sunshine, which became an NPA in December 2015, in a notification issued to the exchanges. The whole loan has been utilised to pay off other loans' obligations. In August 2016, the bank started collection procedures to recoup debts owed by the borrower (Pandey, 2018).

Top CBI officials claim that the bank never requested to file a complaint on this issue. The accused utilised the help of high-ranking IDBI Bank employees to cheat the bank of ₹600 crore. This is the failure of corporate governance and is visible from the inclusion of 15 bank executives, including the present CEOs of other PSBs, independent directors, and other bank officials in the fraud. This indicates that the Indian banking industry is moving towards the "bad crop" from the "bad bushel". The ultimate reason is the weak regulatory system, corporate governance, lack of professionalism, internal control, and ethical culture. The top executives of the banks are engaging in these kinds of fraudulent activities as the result of "corrupt ideology", "hubris", and "greediness".

Though one point is certain, the cases demonstrate that the corporate governance standards in the banking industry are inadequate to avoid such types of fraud and conflict of interest when a large amount of public money is involved, both in the form of stock and debt. The guardians of public funds themselves plundered and harmed India's whole banking sector. As bank management becomes complicit in fraudulent operations, it implies inadequate corporate governance procedures, a lack of regulatory intervention, evergreening of loans[8], poor loan follow-up, and a lack of due diligence. The instances mentioned earlier were carried out in collaboration with corporate advances borrowers. As a result, the incidents are instances of "bad bushels." However, if regulators do not take any action to prevent it, it may affect the ethical culture of the entire bank and may lead to other bank officials and employees committing more fraudulent activities, which will kill the whole banking system and become the "bad crop" like the subprime loan crisis in 2007-2008.

DISCUSSION

ABC Theory

Ramamoorti, Morrison and Koletar (2009) proposed the classification of the white-collar crime/C-suites with the ABC taxonomy. This research created a visual representation of the model based on the analysis of the five cases. The authors categorised the fraud into three types: bad apples, bad bushels, and bad crops. The "bad apple" is an individual who commits fraud, the "bad bushel" is collusive fraud, in which top execs combine to commit fraud, and the "bad crop" is social and cultural elements that influence fraud susceptibility (Ramamoorti, Morrison & Koletar, 2009). The study categorised and presented a vivid image that reflects the seriousness of the fraud situation in the organisation (Figure 1). Each circle depicts a different kind of fraud, with the yellow circle for the "bad apple." As the fraud perpetrated by an individual is a "bad apple," it will cost the company less than the "bad bushel." Consequently, the specific deception is indicated using the colour yellow and a little circle. These occurrences demonstrate that the fraudsters like Chanda Kochar and Rana Kapoor of the ICICI and Yes Bank institutions, respectively, did not collude with internal individuals to commit the fraud. Therefore, these instances are considered as a "bad apple."

Further, the second circle represents the "bad bushel" or collusive deception. The level of fraud in the company is higher when compared to bad apples but lower compared to bad crops. As a result, collusive or group fraud in the organisation is indicated with the colour orange and a medium-sized circle. There was internal and external collusion with a larger number of bank officials in the commission of fraud in instances like PMC, PNB, and IDBI. Nearly all instances fell under the category of "bad crop." According to Ramamoorti, Morrison and Koletar (2009), If a company is involved in a fraud case, including significant collusion, it can be considered a "bad crop." Here, we may either think of a "bad bushel" or "bad crop." The third circle depicts the widespread, highly sophisticated scams that afflicted the sector with internal collusion and failure of the tone at the top. In addition to using the ABC taxonomy, this study determined the stimuli and opportunities for the fraudster. This research refers to the urge to commit fraud as a stimulus (or incentive), and it may be both financial and non-financial in character (Vousinas, 2019). Opportunity is the notion that there is a managerial vulnerability and, more significantly, that there is little chance of getting detected (Dorminey *et al.*, 2012).

Eight triggers were selected from these five incidents that were the main drivers of large-value occupations fraud in these banks. But in addition to these triggers, another familiar stimulus was "money." The eight stimuli are Social/ Status Comparisons Ramamoorti, Morrison & Koletar, 2009): A social comparison is when a person compares some aspects of themselves to those of others to comprehend better who and how that differ from them (Buunk & Gibbons, 2007). Greediness (Ramamoorti, Morrison & Koletar, 2009): an unhealthy craving for money. Corrupt ideology ((Desai, 2020; Kranacher & Riley, 2019): the ideology of corruption "receiving a bribe is normal" India is in the 85th position in the Corruption Perception Index report (The Indian Express, 2022). The ideology of corruption, which begins with the clerk and extends to top management, is the cause of increased bank fraud in India.

There is a sense of entitlement and Inflated Ego (Desai, 2020; Kranacher & Riley, 2019) in some individuals. Narcissistic individuals have a strong feeling of entitlement and a profusion of egocentric tendencies, "the world revolves around me," and "'I'm better than anyone else"(Cohn, 2015). Hyper-competitive culture (Desai, 2020; Ramamoorti, Morrison & Koletar, 2009): "I want to win". In banking, lending aggressively without following regulatory guidance is an act of hyper-competitive culture. Hubris (Ramamoorti, Morrison & Koletar, 2009; Sharma & Aggarwal, 2022): leadership overconfidence and arrogance are features of hubris, or hubris syndrome, which are often shown by those in positions of authority and have a harmful impact on both individuals and organisations and abuse of entrenched authority by influencing business decisions for one's personal gain (Sharma & Aggarwal, 2022). Example: Mr Kapoor lent aggressively without considering any credit rating requirements to succeed in the fiercely competitive banking industry and achieve early development. Absence of Ethics and Morality (Rose *et al.*, 2021): These perpetrators ran these banks for years without regard for the morals or ethics of utilising public funds; instead, they abused them for their benefit.

The perpetrators committed the fraud due to the availability of opportunities in the banking industry. The opportunities were a weak regulatory system (Gupta & Gupta, 2015), delayed action (Gupta & Gupta, 2015), lack of professionalism (Gupta & Gupta, 2015; Singh *et al.*, 2016), weak corporate governance (Gupta & Gupta, 2015), Weak ethical culture (Desai, 2020; Murthy & Gopalkrishnan, 2022), management override (Desai, 2020), lack of due diligence (Gupta & Gupta, 2015), blame game (Gupta & Gupta, 2015; Singh *et al.*, 2016), ineffective monitoring (Gupta & Gupta, 2015; Singh *et al.*, 2016) and evergreening of loans (Murthy & Gopalkrishnan, 2022). When the opportunities were available due to the absence of regulatory or government interference, the offenders were so skilled at spotting it when these stimuli appeared, and they were able to perpetrate fraud for an extended period without being discovered abusing their official authority.

As a consequence of the surge in frauds performed by the top management by colluding with internal bank employees and external corporate borrowers and the banking sector in India is heading towards the "bad crop." When there are stimuli, the top management has the capacity to see opportunities for fraud and perpetrate it; the number of frauds and their costs rise, which has an impact on the whole financial system. This can be the result of a "bad apple" producing a "bad crop," which will spell the end of India's banking sector (Figure 2). When frauds rise, and the RBI takes longer to intervene, people will begin to believe that they won't get detected if they commit fraud as well. This assumption might result in an increase in fraud in the banking sector and, ultimately, the collapse of the whole system. If the government and regulator take the appropriate steps for the early discovery and prevention of fraudulent activity in the banking sector, this might avert the sector's collapse.

Figure 1. ABC Model: A Taxonomy of Fraud
(Ramamoorti et al., 2013)
Note: Author developed this pictorial presentation of the model

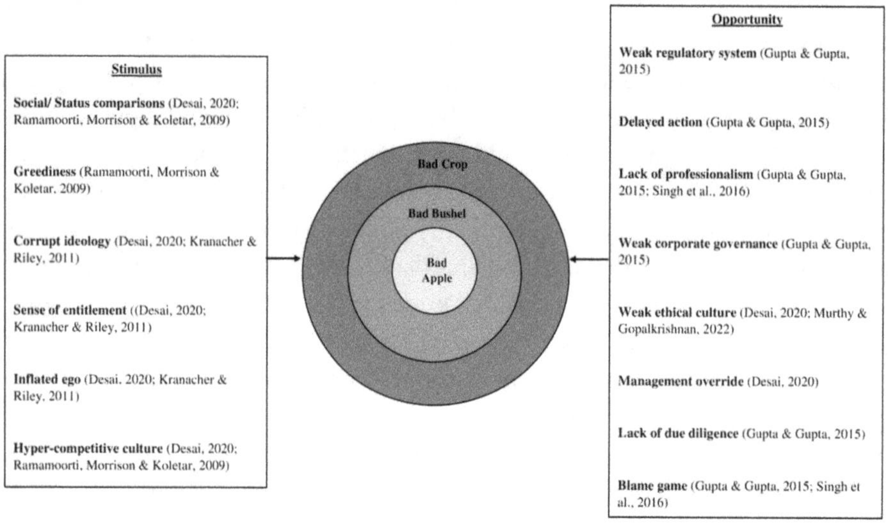

Figure 2. The transition of fraud in the banking industry in India
Source: Author created

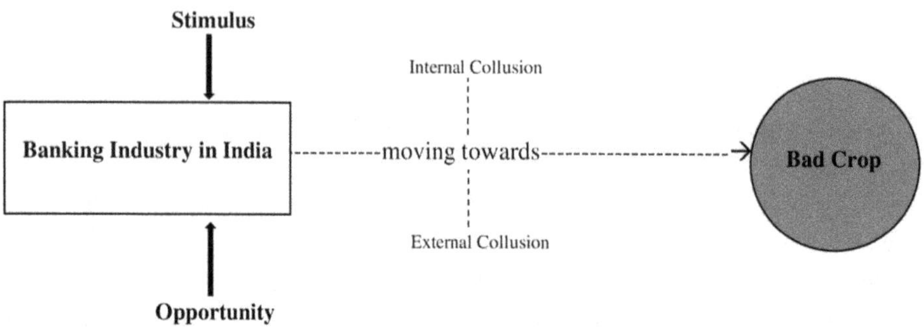

Collusion and Management Override in the Banking Industry in India

Two of the most serious dangers to anti-fraud measures are collusive fraud and managerial override. As a result, the anti-fraud industry has to concentrate on potential areas of collusion or managerial override (ACFE, 2020b; Dorminey *et al.*, 2012). Collusion may essentially be divided into two categories: internal and external collusion. There are three types of internal collusion that may be distinguished: 1) among management, 2) among employees, and (3) between management and employees (Figure 3). The financial values associated with fraud losses dramatically increase when collusion is involved; the fraudulent behaviour that was discovered in the financial industry made it obvious. In the instances of

Yes Bank and ICICI Bank, external collusion and management override was evident, which resulted in the issuing of loans to ineligible parties without following RBI requirements in return for bribery. Individual predators may inflict significant losses, but when those predators act in collusion with others, the harm may be severe and far more ubiquitous.

Figure 3. Types of Collusion
Source: Author created

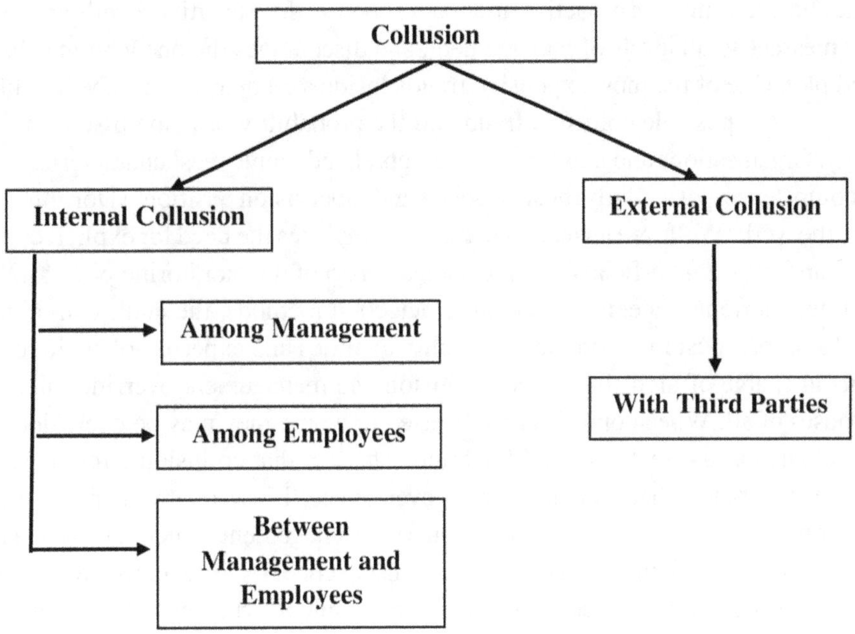

However, in the instances of PMC Bank, PNB, and IDBI Bank, the bank officials defrauded the bank by conspiring with both internal and external parties. It made it possible for the bank executives to hide the fraud for an extended period without being discovered. They were able to bypass internal safeguards and engage in management override due to their involvement in both collusions. Internal controls typically fail when collusion is present (AICPA, 2005). The primary internal control of the division of tasks ensures that no one person controls every transaction component and divides the custody, auditing, and authorisation activities. In the PNB instance, the employee and the deputy manager avoided the standard employee transfer and, later, internal control, and they persisted in their collusion for more than six years.

Along with having the ability to foresee upper management's potential for deception, in 2013, RBI gave power to the CEO of the bank, the Audit Committee of the Board, and, in the case of significant value fraud, the Special Committee of the Board, to be in charge of the bank's fraud risk management, monitoring, and investigative functions. RBI also added that it is crucial that the Audit Committee of the Board, the Special Committee of the Board, and CMDs/ CEOs work on creating effective fraud risk management systems and risk reduction strategies. This amounted to opening the door for the thief or giving him the key. After 2013, the incidence of fraud perpetrated by senior management Rose (refer to aforementioned case studies). Although internal measures cannot prevent collusive fraud and financial crime, they could aid in the detection of such practices (Dorminey *et al.*, 2012). It was very hard to stop since collusion was a component of all fraud. However, the regulator's complicity in the deception was not immediately detectable. Even when a whistleblower came out, the government and regulator often remained silent. For instance, they delayed the ICICI bank fraud investigation for over a year.

Many advise the audit committee to tackle management override and collusive fraud in a proactive manner due to the possibility of its occurrence and the considerable risk it poses. Collusive management fraud must be prevented and detected by actively looking for fraudulent techniques. In other circumstances, the information and governance framework required for more reliable detection may not exist (Dorminey *et al.*, 2012). The audit committee's proactive approach supports the executive level's anti-fraud attitude, provides a good message to all levels of management, and discourages the one who may be considering a collusive fraud plot. One of the most expensive frauds inside a company would be less likely to occur as a result of the view of possible collusive fraud and the probability of being discovered from such a proactive strategy. Organisations and auditors must comprehend employees' characteristics and skills to concentrate on competence, particularly those in power and supervision positions (Dorminey *et al.*, 2012).

Additionally, the work (Wolfe & Hermanson, 2004) exemplifies the need for explicit consideration of senior executives and important officials' competencies as part of the monitoring process. When preparing audits, creating deterrent strategies, or creating detection methods, the audit committee, company accountants, and auditors must focus on the personality qualities and expertise of senior executives and other individuals in charge of high-risk areas. Collusion and management override might be the most severe fraud exposes of all. When controls are subverted or where they may be overridden by management must be evaluated as a direct potential for fraud. The fact that collusion circumvents controls to create the possibility of fraud, whereas management override nullifies a control in a particular situation, is a crucial difference in this case. In the latter scenario, management effectively self-reports that no fraud occurred and covers up their wrongdoing as a consequence. Consequently, these components of the control environment must be the focus of any risk assessment, whether for audit risk or fraud risk (Dorminey *et al.*, 2012).

Based on the RBI annual report 2023, they have taken some initiatives to prevent fraud; under the theme 'Prevention and Mitigation of Financial Frauds', six entities have been selected for testing, and the entities commenced testing their products in February 2023. The entities are testing various products, including risk-based authentication solutions, an early warning system for credit monitoring and fraud identification using internal and external data (RBI, 2023).

IMPLICATIONS

Regulatory Implications

The result of this study opens a pathway to understanding the current state of the banking industry in India in the occurrence of fraud perpetrated by the tone of the banks. It anticipates that regulators, government, and policymakers will undertake steps that will improve the anti-fraud measure and ethical culture in the banking sector more practically than keeping in the annual reports. This study aspires that the regulator will address the opportunity side factors such as weak regulatory system, delayed action, lack of professionalism, lack of due diligence, blame game and ineffective monitoring to mitigate the fraudulent activities in the banking industry. Additionally, there should be serious monitoring and proper regulation for the loan process and avoidance of evergreening of loans. Taking a systematic and appropriate regulation in the view of professional scepticism can reduce the anticipated losses on the occurrence of fraud. In addition, this study has significance for the development of the regulations and standards for due diligence, professionalism, fraud detection, effective monitoring, good governance, and mandated forensic audit, which can help to control the fraudulent activities committed by the management in the banking industry for protecting the industry from falling into the "bad crop".

Managerial Implications

Along with the regulatory implications, the governance implications also have significance in the mitigation of fraud in the banking industry. As the factors such as lack of professionalism, weak corporate governance, lack of internal control, weak ethical culture and management override create the opportunity to commit fraud in the banks. The Bank must take the initiative to build good management to work professionally with good governance and internal control. It is also vital to create an ethical culture and ensure practice in the bank to avoid the occurrence of fraud.

CONCLUSION

This study used the ABC approach to analyse five high-value incidents of occupational fraud committed by banks' top executives and discovered the stimuli and opportunities that encouraged the offenders to engage in fraudulent activity at the bank. Despite the various modus operandi, the inadequate regulatory framework, inefficient due diligence, subpar corporate governance, delayed action, lack of professionalism, blame game evergreening of loans and ineffective monitoring were the causes of the high-value occupational frauds. After using the ABC model to analyse the problem, it is observed that when senior management conspires with other bank officials and corporate borrowers to commit fraud, the effect of the fraud becomes more severe. Consequently, the banks are being pushed in the direction of "bad crop". Moving towards "bad crop" is the symptom of the collapse of the entire banking industry in the economy. The reasons for the perpetration of frauds were 1) greed, social comparison, corrupt ideology, lack of ethics and morality, sense of entitlement and ego, hubris and hyper-competitive culture; 2) collusion between the bank officials and the corporate borrowers resulting out of the weak regulatory system and poor corporate governance practices in the banks which created the opportunity for the fraudulent actions led the banks from "bad bushels" to "bad crop". And it is high time to take action to prevent the banks from going towards bad crops.

The regulator must consider the situation as the need of the hour and build new viable and robust regulations to build due diligence, good governance, ethics and integrity in the organisation with a proper system to undergo the loan sanctioning and disbursement to the corporate borrowers by avoiding opportunities to commit fraud by bank officials colluding with the borrowers. Additionally, when collusion is present, implement proactive auditing measures for the early discovery and prevention of fraud. Since this research did not experimentally evaluate the stimuli and opportunities to confirm it, it has the same limitations as any other study. Future studies may experimentally verify the elements that motivate perpetrators and classify the intensity of fraud in the banking industry with the ABC model for the taxonomy of fraud.

DECLARATION

The author declares that the manuscript follows ethical standards and there are no potential conflicts of interest with respect to the research, authorship and/or publication of this chapter.

DISCLAIMER

The contents and views of this chapter are expressed by the author in her personal capacity. It is not necessary for the Editor and the Publisher to agree with these viewpoints, and they are not responsible for any duty of care in this regard.

ACKNOWLEDGMENT

The author extends sincere gratitude to

- The Editor and the International Editorial Advisory Board (IEAB) of this book, who initially desk reviewed, arranged a rigorous double/triple-blind review process, and conducted a thorough, minute, and critical final review before accepting the chapter for publication.
- All anonymous reviewers who provided very constructive feedback for thorough revision, improvement, extension, and fine-tuning of the chapter.
- All colleagues, assistants and well-wishers who assisted to complete this task.

REFERENCES

ACFE. (2020). *Report to the nations: 2020 global study on occupational fraud and abuse - Banking and financial service edition*. Retrieved from https://legacy.acfe.com/report-to-the-nations/2020/docs/RTTN-Banking-Financial.pdf

ACFE. (2020b). *Report to the nations - The global study on occupational fraud and abuse*. Retrieved from https://legacy.acfe.com/report-to-the-nations/2020/

Adhikari, A. (2023a). How India's banking sector is staging a strong comeback. *Business Today*. Retrieved from https://www.businesstoday.in/interactive/longread/how-india-s-banking-sector-is-staging-a-strong-comeback-232-19-01-2023

Agrawal, A. (2018, February 24). Banking crises: An Indian history. *Mint*. Retrieved from https://www.livemint.com/Sundayapp/fjheowjLjiFNsGcjzVZXsO/Banking-crises-An-Indian-history.html

AICPA. (2005). *Management override of internal controls: the Achilles' heel of fraud prevention: The audit committee and oversight of financial reporting*. Retrieved from https://us.aicpa.org/content/dam/aicpa/forthepublic/auditcommitteeeffectiveness/downloadabledocuments/achilles_heel.pdf

Albrecht, S., Howe, K., & Romney, M. (1984). *Deterring fraud: The internal auditor's perspective*. Institute of Internal Auditors.

Albrecht, W. S., Albrecht, C. C., & Albrecht, C. O. (2006). *Fraud examination*. Thomson South-Western.

Business Standard. (2019). *What is PNB scam? | PNB fraud case*. Retrieved from https://www.business-standard.com/about/what-is-pnb-scam

Business Standard. (2020). *What is PMC bank crisis? PMC bank case. Business Standard*. Retrieved from https://www.business-standard.com/about/what-is-pmc-bank-crisis

Buunk, A. P., & Gibbons, F. X. (2007). Social comparison: The end of a theory and the emergence of a field. *Organizational Behavior and Human Decision Processes, 102*(1), 3–21. doi:10.1016/j.obhdp.2006.09.007

Chawla, P. (1986, March 31). Rajendra Sethia bank fraud case: Delhi HC quashes PNB official Amarjit Singh's dismissal. *India Today*. Retrieved from https://www.indiatoday.in/magazine/economy/story/19860331-rajendra-sethia-bank-fraud-case-delhi-hc-quashes-pnb-official-amarjit-singh-dismissal-800745-1986-03-30

Choudhary, S. (2018). PNB scam: 2 bank officials, Nirav Modi's company executive arrested by CBI. *Business Standard*. Retrieved from https://www.business-standard.com/article/finance/cbi-arrests-2-pnb-officials-1-executive-of-niravi-s-cos-in-bank-fraud-case-118021700228_1.html

Cohn, S. (2015, November 6). The Greed report: American ego — the common thread in the biggest scams. *CNBC*. Retrieved from https://www.cnbc.com/2015/11/06/the-greed-report-american-ego--the-common-thread-in-the-biggest-scams.html

Cressey, D. R. (1950). The criminal violation of financial trust. *American Sociological Association, 15*(6), 738–743. https://www.jstor.org/stable/2086606

Cressey, D. R. (1953). *Other people's money; A study of the social psychology of embezzlement*. Free Press.

Das, B. (2023, April 29). IDBI bank Q4 results: Net profit rises 64%, dividend of Rs 1 per share announced. *Business Today*. Retrieved from https://www.businesstoday.in/industry/banks/story/idbi-bank-q4-results-net-profit-rises-64-dividend-of-rs-1per-share-announced-379394-2023-04-29

Das, B. (2023, June 29). ICICI Bank loan fraud case: Chanda Kochhar, husband bought flat, worth Rs 5.3 crore, for just Rs 11 lakh, CBI tells court. *Business Today*. Retrieved from https://www.businesstoday.in/latest/corporate/story/icici-bank-loan-fraud-case-chanda-kochhar-husband-bought-flat-worth-rs-53-crore-for-just-rs-11-lakh-cbi-tells-court-387183-2023-06-27

Desai, N. (2020). Understanding the theoretical underpinnings of corporate fraud. *Vikalpa, 45*(1), 25–31. doi:10.1177/0256090920917789

Dey, P. (2022, December 27). ICICI Loan Fraud Case Explained: Journey of Chanda Kochhar from being the first woman CEO of an Indian bank to going behind bars. *Zee Business*. Retrieved from https://www.zeebiz.com/india/news-icici-loan-fraud-case-explained-journey-of-chanda-kochhar-from-being-the-first-woman-ceo-of-an-indian-bank-to-going-behind-bars-214730

Dorminey, J., Fleming, A. S., Kranacher, M. J., & Riley, R. A. Jr. (2012). The evolution of fraud theory. *Issues in Accounting Education, 27*(2), 555–579. doi:10.2308/iace-50131

Dugal, I. (2019, October 1). Confession letter of PMC Bank's former MD: The story of a decades-long relationship gone wrong. *BQ Prime*. Retrieved from https://www.bqprime.com/business/confession-letter-of-pmc-banks-former-md-the-story-of-a-decades-long-relationship-gone-wrong

Forbes. (2016). *Chanda Kochhar-Profile*. Retrieved from https://www.forbes.com/profile/chanda-kochhar/?sh=59e7fb25674c

Forbes. (2017, November 1). No. 5: Chanda Kochhar -Power women: Most powerful women in finance. Retrieved from https://www.forbes.com/pictures/ 59f4ea1ca7ea436b47b47be6/ no-5-chanda-kochhar/?sh=5217f8a22b8f Forbes. (2018). *Rana Kapoor*. https://www.forbes.com/profile/rana-kapoor/?sh=7275f1213efd

Forbes India. (2016). *Nirav Modi - Forbes India Magazine*. Retrieved from https://www.forbesindia.com/richprofile2016/nirav-modi/1557/141

Gangwani, M. (2021). Suitability of forensic accounting in uncovering bank frauds in India: An opinion survey. *Journal of Financial Crime*, *28*(1), 284–299. doi:10.1108/JFC-07-2020-0126

Ghosh, S., & Bagheri, M. (2006). The Ketan Parekh fraud and supervisory lapses of the Reserve Bank of India (RBI): A case study. *Journal of Financial Crime*, *13*(1), 107–124. doi:10.1108/13590790610641279

Goyal, K. A., & Joshi, V. (2012). Indian banking industry: Challenges and opportunities. [IJBRM]. *International Journal of Business Research and Management*, *3*(1), 18–28.

Gupta, A. (2021). The Devil's laugh at corporate governance: The case of Punjab and Maharashtra Co-operative Bank (PMC Bank) India. *Indian Journal of Corporate Governance*, *14*(2), 248–267. doi:10.1177/09746862211047315

Gupta, P. K., & Gupta, S. (2015). Corporate frauds in India - Perceptions and emerging issues. *Journal of Financial Crime*, *22*(1), 79–103. doi:10.1108/JFC-07-2013-0045

Hermanson, D. R., Justice, S. E., Ramamoorti, S., & Riley, R. A. Jr. (2017). Unique characteristics of predator frauds. *Journal of Financial Accounting Research*, *2*(1), A31–A48. doi:10.2308/jfar-51747

ICICI. (n.d.). *ICICI Bank: About us | History*. Retrieved from https://www.icicibank.com/about-us/history

IDBI. (2019). *Information on the constitution of IDBI*. Retrieved from https://www.idbibank.in/pdf/BriefHistoryofIDBI.pdf

Jagannath, J. (2023, April 22). ICICI Bank Q4 results: Net profit rises 30% to Rs 9,122 cr; lender declares Rs 8 dividend. *Business Today*. Retrieved from https://www.businesstoday.in/industry/banks/story/icici-bank-q4-results-net-profit-rises-30-to-rs-9122-cr-378445-2023-04-22

Karnik, M. (2017, January 23). Once an intern at Citibank, Yes Bank's Rana Kapoor is now India's newest banking billionaire. *Quartz*. Retrieved from https://qz.com/india/891891/once-an-intern-at-citibank-yes-banks-rana-kapoor-is-now-indias-newest-banking-billionaire

Kassem, R., & Higson, A. (2012). The new Fraud Triangle model. *Journal of Emerging Trends in Economics and Management Science*, *3*(3), 191–195.

Khan, M. M., & Amoozegar, A. (2022). Effect of corporate and shariah governance on prevention of frauds in banking sector of Pakistan: Mediating role of compliance audit. [Ziran Kexue yu Gongcheng Jishu Ban]. *Tianjin Daxue Xuebao, 55*(2), 160–176. doi:10.17605/OSF.IO/MXU8K

Kranacher, M. J., & Riley, R. A. (2019). *Forensic accounting and fraud examination*. John Wiley & Sons.

Livemint. (2022, December 26). ICICI Bank loan fraud case: Why has the CBI arrested Videocon's Venugopal Dhoot? *Mint*. Retrieved from https://www.livemint.com/news/india/icici-bank-loan-fraud-case-the-arrest-of-videocon-founder-venugopal-dhoot-and-cbi-custody-of-chanda-kochhar-11672036632789.html

Livemint. (2023, March 17). IDBI Bank privatisation on track, says DIPAM Secretary. *Mint*. Retrieved from https://www.livemint.com/news/india/idbi-bank-privatisation-on-track-says-dipam-secretary-11679039514740.html

Marks, J. (2012). The Mind behind the fraudsters crime: Key behavioral and environmental elements discussion leader. *Crowe Horwath LLP*. Retrieved from https://www.fraudconference.com/uploadedFiles/Fraud_Conference/Content/Course-Materials/presentations/23rd/ppt/10C-Jonathan-Marks.pdf

Murthy, N., & Gopalkrishnan, S. (2022). Creating a nexus between dark triad personalities, Non-Performing Assets, Corporate Governance and frauds in the Indian banking sector. *Journal of Financial Crime, 30*(4), 859–876. doi:10.1108/JFC-05-2022-0097

Nakitende, M. G., Rafay, A., & Waseem, M. (2021). Frauds in Business Organizations: A Comprehensive Overview. In A. Rafay (Ed.), *Handbook of Research on Theory and Practice of Financial Crimes* (pp. 21–38). IGI Global., doi:10.4018/978-1-7998-5567-5.ch002

Online, E. T. (2022, December 26). Loan fraud case: CBI arrests Videocon CEO Venugopal Dhoot. *The Economic Times*. Retrieved from https://economictimes.indiatimes.com/news/india/loan-fraud-case-cbi-arrests-videocon-ceo-venugopal-dhoot/articleshow/96510207.cms?from=mdr

Pande, S., & Prakash, M. V. (2019). Case study on scam in Indian banking industry (Nirav Modi). *Pramana Research Journal, 9*(6), 626–630. https://www.pramanaresearch.org/gallery/prj-p1051.pdf

Pandey, M. (2018, April 26). Rs 600 crore loan fraud: How top bankers helped in looting IDBI bank. *India Today*. Retrieved from https://www.indiatoday.in/india/story/rs-600-crore-loan-fraud-how-top-bankers-helped-in-looting-idbi-bank-1221074-2018-04-26

Parameswar, N., Dhir, S., & Dhir, S. (2017). Banking on innovation, innovation in Banking at ICICI Bank. *Global Business and Organizational Excellence, 36*(2), 6–16. doi:10.1002/joe.21765

PNB. (2023a). Origin. *Punjab National Bank*. Retrieved from https://www.pnbindia.in/origin-of-PNB.html

PNB. (2023b). Profile. *Punjab National Bank*. Retrieved from https://www.pnbindia.in/profile.html

Press Trust of India. (2014, December 16). Yes Bank chief Rana Kapoor awarded 'Business Innovator Award'. *The Economic Times*. Retrieved from https://economictimes.indiatimes.com/news/company/corporate-trends/yes-bank-chief-rana-kapoor-awarded-business-innovator-award/articleshow/45534475.cms?from=mdr

Press Trust of India. (2021a, September 2). PMC Bank: PMC bank fraud: Enforcement Directorate attaches HDIL group's shares worth Rs 233 crore. *The Economic Times*. Retrieved from https://economictimes.indiatimes.com/industry/banking/finance/banking /pmc-bank-fraud-enforcement-directorate-attaches-hdil-groups-shares-worth-rs-233-crore/articleshow/85868445.cms?from=mdr

Press Trust of India. (2021b, December 7). Sivasankaran, serving and retired top officials of IDBI Bank booked by CBI in ₹600-cr loan fraud. *The Hindu Business Line*. Retrieved from https://www.thehindu-businessline.com/info-tech/sivasankaran-serving-and-retired-top-officials-of-idbi-bank-booked-by-cbi-in-600-cr-loan-fraud/article23687454.ece

Press Trust of India. (2022a, April 23). Rs 5,000-Crore fraud by Yes Bank's Rana Kapoor, Wadhawans: probe agency. *NDTV*. Retrieved from https://www.ndtv.com/india-news/yes-bank-fraud-rs-5-000-crore-fraud-by-yes-banks-rana-kapoor-wadhawans-probe-agency-2913012

Press Trust of India. (2022b, November 9). Explainer: How Nirav Modi cheated PNB of Rs 14,000 crore through fraudulent LoUs. *The Economic Times*. Retrieved from https://economictimes.indiatimes.com/news/india/explainer-how-nirav-modi-cheated-pnb-of-rs-14000-crore-through-fraudulent-lous/articleshow/95410291.cms?from=mdr

Press Trust of India. (2023, June 11). FY24 to be golden year for Punjab National Bank: MD. *The Economic Times*. Retrieved from https://economictimes.indiatimes.com/industry/banking/finance/banking/fy24-to-be-golden-year-for-punjab-national-bank-md/articleshow/100917556.cms?from=mdr

Profit, N. D. T. V. (2023). *Yes Bank Ltd.: Reports, company history, director's report, chairman's speech, auditor's report of Yes Bank*. Retrieved from https://www.ndtv.com/business/stock/yes-bank-ltd_yesbank/reports

Rafay, A. (Ed.). (2021a). *HandBook of Research on Theory and Practice of Financial Crimes*. IGI Global., doi:10.4018/978-1-7998-5567-5

Rafay, A. (Ed.). (2021b). *Money Laundering and Terrorism Financing in Global Financial Systems*. IGI Global., doi:10.4018/978-1-7998-8758-4

Rafay, A. (Ed.). (2023). *Concepts, Cases, and Regulations in Financial Fraud and Corruption*. IGI Global., doi:10.4018/978-1-6684-5007-9

Rai, N. (2018). Yes Bank: 3 reasons cited by RBI for sacking Rana Kapoor as CEO and now his board seat in jeopardy. *The Economic Times*. Retrieved from https://economictimes.indiatimes.com/industry/banking/finance/banking/3-reasons-cited-by-rbi-for-sacking-rana-kapoor-as-ceo-and-now-his-board-seat-in-jeopardy/articleshow/65904385.cms?from=mdr

Ramamoorti, S. (2008). The psychology and sociology of fraud: Integrating the behavioral sciences component in to fraud and Forensic Accounting curricula. *Issues in Accounting Education*, *23*(4), 521–533. doi:10.2308/iace.2008.23.4.521

Ramamoorti, S., Morrison, D., & Koletar, J. W. (2009). Bringing freud to fraud: Understanding the state-of-mind of the C-level suite/white collar offender through "ABC" analysis. Institute for Fraud Prevention (IFP), West Virginia University.

Ramamoorti, S., Morrison, D. E., Koletar, J. W., & Pope, K. R. (2013). *ABC's of behavioral forensics: Applying psychology to financial fraud prevention and detection*. Wiley. doi:10.1002/9781118740422

Ramchandani, K., & Jethwani, K. (2021). Yes bank: An untold story. *Emerald Emerging Markets Case Studies*, *11*(1), 1–37. doi:10.1108/EEMCS-04-2020-0123

RBI. (2023). Annual Report 2022-23. *Reserve Bank of India*. Retrieved from https://rbidocs.rbi.org.in/rdocs/AnnualReport/PDFs/0ANNUALREPORT20222322A548270D6140D998AA20E8207075E4.PDF

Rezaee, Z., & Riley, R. (2010). *Financial statement fraud prevention and detection*. John Wiley&Sons, Inc.

Rose, A. M., Rose, J. M., Suh, I., Thibodeau, J., Linke, K., & Norman, C. S. (2021). Why financial executives do bad things: The effects of the slippery slope and tone at the top on misreporting behavior. *Journal of Business Ethics*, *174*(2), 291–309. doi:10.100710551-020-04609-y

Roy, D. (2022, December 24). Chanda Kochhar biography, career, husband, fraud, education, net worth, age, height and more. *Indias Magazine*. https://indiasmagazine.in/chanda-kochhar-biography/

Sahgai, R. (2018). PNB Fraud: Former MD of PNB was aware of Nirav Modi fraud, says CBI. *Economic Times*. Retrieved from https://economictimes.indiatimes.com/industry/banking/finance/banking/former-md-of-pnb-was-aware-of-nirav-modi-fraud-says-cbi/articleshow/64260412.cms?from=mdr

Saluja, S., Aggarwal, A., & Mittal, A. (2021). Understanding the fraud theories and advancing with integrity model. *Journal of Financial Crime*, *29*(4), 1318–1328. doi:10.1108/JFC-07-2021-0163

Sharma, M. (2018, April 27). IDBI Bank fraud: CBI books former Aircel promoter Sivasankaran, top bankers for Rs 600-crore loan scam. *Business Today*. Retrieved from https://www.businesstoday.in/industry/banks/story/idbi-bank-fraud-aircel-promoter-sivasankaran-arrested-cbi-600-crore-loan-104148-2018-04-27

Sharma, N. J., & Aggarwal, D. (2022). Yes Bank fraud: Examining the softer underbelly of the fraud from a behavioral model. *Journal of Financial Accounting Research*, *7*(1), 133–150. doi:10.2308/JFAR-2021-022

Singh, C., Pattanayak, D., Dixit, D. S., Antony, K., Agarwala, M., Kant, R., Mukunda, S., Nayak, S., Makked, S., Singh, T., & Mathur, V. (2016). *Frauds in the Indian banking industry* (Working Paper No. 505). IIMB. Retrieved from https://www.iimb.ac.in/sites/default/files/2018-07/WP_No._505.pdf

Singh, H. (2019). PMC Bank fraud case: Full detail of the bank fraud. *Jagran Josh*. Retrieved from https://www.jagranjosh.com/general-knowledge/pmc-bank-fraud-case-1570456027-1

Srinivas, A. (2009, February 5). How to be a 'Yes' man. *Business Today*. Retrieved from https://www.businesstoday.in/magazine/new-business/story/how-to-be-a-yes-man-244278-2009-01-21

Sutherland, E. H. (1940). White-Collar Criminality. *American Sociological Review*, *5*(1), 1–12. doi:10.2307/2083937

Sutherland, E. H. (1945). Is 'White Collar Crime' Crime? *American Sociological Review*, *10*(2), 132–139. doi:10.2307/2085628

The Indian Express. (2022, January 26). India ranks 85 in Transparency International's corruption index. Retrieved from https://indianexpress.com/article/india/india-ranks-85-in-transparency-internationals-corruption-index-7741760/

The New Indian Express. (2019, June 12). Former chairman of Indian Bank gets 3-yr jail in fraud case. *The New Indian Express*. Retrieved from https://www.newindianexpress.com/cities/chennai/2019/jun/12/former-chairman-of-indian-bank-gets-3-yr-jail-in-fraud-case-1989137.html

Vousinas, G. L. (2019). Advancing theory of fraud: The S.C.O.R.E. model. *Journal of Financial Crime, 26*(1), 372–381. doi:10.1108/JFC-12-2017-0128

Wells, J. T. (2001). Why employees commit fraud. *Journal of Accountancy, 191*(2), 89.

Wolfe, D. T., & Hermanson, D. R. (2004). The Fraud Diamond: Considering the four elements of fraud. *The CPA Journal, 12*(74), 38–42.

Yes Bank. (2016, February 26). Yes bank has ranked top 500 global banking brands list by the banker. Retrieved from://www.yesbank.in/about-us/media/press-releases-details/3000000212277-copy-of-press-release-list-item-feb-15-16-02

ENDNOTES

1 **Occupational fraud** is the misuse of one's profession for personal benefits.

2 **Asset misappropriation** is a strategy when a worker steals resources belonging to the employer

3 **Corruption** is a strategy when an employee breaches their obligation to the company by using their influence in a commercial transaction for personal gain, whether direct or indirect.

4 **Financial statement fraud** is a strategy in which a worker purposefully falsifies or omits vital information from the company's financial reports.

5 **Collusion** is an agreement among individuals to work together covertly or criminally to mislead or defraud.

6 **Red flag** is a collection of events that deviate from the ordinary or are unique in some way. It is a hint that something is unusual and may need to be looked into further.

7 **White-collar crime** perpetrated by someone of high social standing while engaged in their line of work.

8 **Evergreening of loan** is a technique used to disguise the real condition of NPAs or bad loans by giving new or additional loans to borrowers who are unable to repay their current debts.

APPENDIX

Table 1. Fraud reported in different areas of operation

(Amount in ₹ crore)

Area of Operation	2020-21		2021-22		2022-23	
	Number of Frauds	Amount Involved	Number of Frauds	Amount Involved	Number of Frauds	Amount Involved
1	2	3	4	5	6	7
Advances	3,476	1,30,990	3,833	57,733	4,109	28,792
	(47.4)	(99.0)	(42.2)	(96.5)	(30.4)	(95.2)
Off-balance Sheet	23	535	21	1077	14	296
	(0.3)	(0.4)	(0.2)	(1.7)	(0.1)	(1.0)
Forex Transactions	4	129	7	7	13	12
	-	(0.1)	(0.1)	-	(0.1)	-
Card/Internet	2,545	119	3,596	155	6,659	276
	(34.7)	(0.1)	(39.5)	(0.3)	(49.2)	(0.9)
Deposits	504	434	471	493	652	258
	(6.9)	(0.3)	(5.2)	(0.8)	(4.8)	(0.9)
Inter-Branch Accounts	2	-	3	2	3	-
	-	-	-	-	-	-
Cash	329	39	649	93	1470	158
	(4.5)	-	(7.1)	(0.2)	(10.9)	(0.5)
Cheques/DDs, *etc.*	163	85	201	158	118	25
	(2.2)	(0.1)	(2.2)	(0.3)	(0.9)	(0.1)
Clearing Accounts	14	4	16	1	18	3
	(0.2)	-	(0.2)	-	(0.1)	-
Others	278	54	300	100	474	432
	(3.8)	-	(3.3)	(0.2)	(3.5)	(1.4)
Total	**7,338**	**1,32,389**	**9,097**	**59,819**	**13,530**	**30,252**
	(100.0)	**(100.0)**	**(100.0)**	**(100.0)**	**(100.0)**	**(100.0)**

- : Nil/Negligible.
Note: 1. Figures in parentheses represent the percentage share of the total.
2. Refer to footnotes 2-5 of Table VI.2.
Source: RBI Supervisory Returns.

Table 2. Fraud reported in different groups of banks

(Amount in ₹ crore)

Bank Group/Institution	2020-21		2021-22		2022-23	
	Number of Frauds	Amount Involved	Number of Frauds	Amount Involved	Number of Frauds	Amount Involved
1	2	3	4	5	6	7
Public Sector Banks	2,888	77,879	3,075	40,015	3,405	21,125
	(39.4)	(58.8)	(33.8)	(66.9)	(25.2)	(69.8)
Private Sector Banks	3,705	45,515	5,332	17,387	8,932	8,727
	(50.5)	(34.4)	(58.6)	(29.1)	(66.0)	(28.9)
Foreign Banks	519	3110	494	1,206	804	292
	(7.1)	(2.4)	(5.5)	(2.0)	(5.9)	(1.0)
Financial Institutions	22	5853	9	1,178	9	70
	(0.3)	(4.4)	(0.1)	(2.0)	(0.1)	(0.2)
Small Finance Banks	114	30	155	30	312	31
	(1.5)	-	(1.7)	-	(2.3)	(0.1)
Payments Banks	88	2	30	1	68	7
	(1.2)	-	(0.3)	-	(0.5)	-
Local Area Banks	2	-	2	2	-	-
	-	-	-	-	-	-
Total	**7,338**	**1,32,389**	**9,097**	**59,819**	**13,530**	**30,252**
	(100.0)	**(100.0)**	**(100.0)**	**(100.0)**	**(100.0)**	**(100.0)**

- : Nil/Negligible.
Note: 1. Figures in parentheses represent the percentage share of the total.
2. Data are in respect of frauds of ₹1 lakh and above reported during the period.
3. The figures reported by banks and financial institutions are subject to changes based on revisions filed by them.
4. Frauds reported in a year could have occurred several years prior to year of reporting.
5. Amounts involved reported do not reflect the amount of loss incurred. Depending on recoveries, the loss incurred gets reduced. Further, the entire amount involved is not necessarily diverted.
Source: RBI Supervisory Returns.

Chapter 11
The Effect of Corruption Perception on Foreign Direct Investment:
The Case of Latin America

Thiago Ferreira
Universidade Federal de Viçosa, Brazil

Viviani Silva Lirio
Universidade Federal de Viçosa, Brazil

Felippe Clemente
https://orcid.org/0000-0003-3465-9711
Universidade de Lisboa, Portugal

Tayo Oke
Afe Babalola University, Nigeria

ABSTRACT

Economists have been studying the effects of corruption on a variety of economic variables, like growth, inequality and innovation. This chapter investigates the impact of Transparency International's Corruption Perception Index (CPI) on the inflows of Foreign Direct Investment to Latin American Countries for the period 2012-2019. The choice of the period is due to the new methodology of the CPI which allows for comparisons between time periods. A panel data model is employed to investigate whether corruption "grease the wheels" or "sand the wheels" of FDI. Results show that the CPI exerts no influence on the inflows of FDI, at least for this time period and sample. The chapter also considered the criticism raised by Heywood (2017), who criticizes the very use of measures of perception of corruption as valid parameters to analyze the role of corruption on economic outcomes.

DOI: 10.4018/978-1-6684-8587-3.ch011

INTRODUCTION

Corruption is a worldwide problem. According to the World Economic Forum[1], in 2018 the costs of corruption amounted to 3.6 billion dollars. No doubt, this is a significant figure and merits some attention. Indeed, economists have been studying the effects of corruption on a variety of economic variables, like growth, inequality and innovation. For example, Dincer (2019) estimates a panel data model for 48 American states and finds that corruption has a negative impact on innovation. A few years earlier, Gupta, Davoodi & Alonso-Terme (2002) analyzed cross-sectional data for various countries and found a significant positive association between corruption and inequality, showing that this is still a topic with an open space for discussion.

As for growth, in an influential paper, Mauro (1995) shows that corruption negatively impacts economic growth, with a substantial reduction in investment. This result is confirmed in Mo (2001), Méon and Sekkat (2005). In this last study, the authors contrast two different hypotheses, the "grease the wheels" hypothesis and the "sand the wheels" hypothesis. The former hypothesis refers to the possibility that corruption might be beneficial for economic growth. The later hypothesis to the standard interpretation that corruption degrades economic performance. The reasoning behind the "grease the wheels" effect is that corruption arises when institutions are inefficient, therefore, corruption acts as a mechanism to compensate for sluggish public sector functioning (Rafay, 2023). Some works have provided evidence for the "grease the wheels" hypothesis, such as Dreher and Gassebner (2013), Méon and Weill (2010). But as Ugur (2013), Gründler and Potrafke (2019) have pointed out, the general empirical findings are pointing towards the "sand the wheels" effect of corruption.

If corruption is detrimental to growth, especially through depressing investments, this notion may be carried out to establish whether corruption cuts back the incentive to invest abroad. In particular, for emerging economies, foreign capital can be a crucial factor to relax the constraints imposed by inadequate levels of internal savings. As it is documented, for example in Calderon, Chong & Loayza (2000), Kandil and Greene (2002), Yurdakul and Ucar (2015), current account deficits are associated with economic growth. A current account deficit implies a surplus in the capital account, an inflow of capital from abroad to finance an increase in investments.

Since market-oriented reforms have taken place in the 1990s, an increase in capital flows is observed toward Latin American countries. However, as Edwards *et al.* (1999) indicate in a historical description of capital flows to Latin America, inflows of capital have been unstable, from being a target of intense inflows of capital in the first half of the 1990s to periods of instability and crisis in the second half. Given these instabilities, the determinants of capital flows to emerging market economies have been a subject of great interest to researchers.

In fact, the behavior of international capital flows is not entirely understood since Lucas (1990) posed the question as to why doesn't capital flow naturally from rich to poor countries. It is expected, according to traditional economic theory that capital would flow from places where it is relatively abundant to places where it is relatively scarce, until the equalization of marginal returns on capital. However, this is not what is observed in the empirical literature.

Since this chapter focuses on foreign direct investment (FDI), the determinants of FDI are looked into, which are different from other types of capital flows. Speaking broadly, international capital flows usually follow a push-pull pattern. That is, there are specific factors that lead to an inflow of foreign capital into a given country. The push factors are external factors that increase the inflow of foreign capital into a country. The pull factors are internal factors which increase the inflow of foreign capital into a country. Using this framework, certain pull factors may be chosen that increase the inflows of FDI toward emerging market economies.

The OLI framework put forth by Dunning (1980) is a popular framework for analyzing FDI attractiveness. It is based on the idea that a firm, which spreads its economic activities to different countries, does so because it must yield advantages that would not be possible otherwise. Markusen and Maskus (2002) present two diverse types of internationalization of production: horizontal and vertical. Horizontal internationalization posits that a firm simply replicates its activities in foreign countries, while vertical internationalization posits that firms seek to lower their costs by dividing their production processes into countries where specific production factors are abundant, and therefore, cheaper.

This study is about the effects of corruption on FDI. Whether "grease the wheels" or "sand the wheels" aspects of corruption dominate FDI as well as if corruption is a significant (negative or positive) "pull" factor to attract FDI from abroad. There exists already some literature that relates capital flows to corruption. For example, Wei (2000) studies the effect of corruption on capital flows for a large panel of developed and developing countries, his findings are that corruption affects most severely foreign direct investment, altering the structure of capital flows to corrupt countries. Egger and Winner (2005) also employ a model based on panel data for 73 countries to study solely the effect of corruption on FDI and show that corruption has a positive impact on FDI, contributing to the "grease the wheels" hypothesis. Al-Sadig (2009) finds two different effects, for cross-sectional data it is estimated a negative impact of corruption on FDI. While for panel data, corruption is not so much of a problem if the quality of institutions is adequate.

Lambsdorff (2003) focuses on an aggregate measure of capital flows and finds that corruption deters capital inflows for a cross-section of several countries. The author goes further and decomposes corruption into several components to investigate possible channels of influence. In that study, government stability and civil liberties exert a negative influence on capital flows while an index of law and order exerts a positive influence, and the bureaucratic quality shows mixed results across different regressions. There have been studies linking institutional quality to capital flows in emerging market economists, like Alfaro *et al.* (2008) who argues that institutional quality fully explains the so-called "Lucas Paradox". Azémar and Desbordes (2013) confirm that institutional quality is important but cannot fully explain capital flow patterns. More recently Arya, Banerjee and Cavoli (2019) also confirm that institutional quality is of relevance in explaining the amount of capital flows, particularly focusing on emerging market economies.

Jalil, Qureshi & Feridun (2016) finds that corruption can improve the flows of FDI to developing countries in Asia and Africa while negatively impacting FDI to Latin American countries. Qureshi *et al.* (2021) using a panel VAR model finds that corruption acts differently in developed and developing countries. Corruption can boost FDI in developing countries and lower FDI in developed countries.

In this study, Latin American countries are focused, mainly on two reasons: Firstly, foreign direct investment, as we've stated, can be an important driver for the growth and development of this region. Secondly, Latin America has been historically a region where weak institutions and even a lack of democracy altogether have been present. Weak institutions and lack of governance (Rafay, Sadiq & Ajmal, 2016) are fertile grounds for the emergence of corrupt behavior. This is evidenced by the recent corruption scandals, particularly in Brazil, and the same is true for other countries as well (Rotberg, 2019).

Thus, this research contributes to the ongoing debate over the effects of corruption on foreign direct investment. It does so by focusing specifically on Latin American countries and by exploiting the fact that one of the main measures of corruption utilized in empirical studies, the corruption perception index

(CPI), has undergone a methodological shift in which year-to-year comparisons are possible. So, studies prior to 2012 were not so reliable given that it is only after 2012 that the index allows for comparability each year.

CONCEPTUAL FRAMEWORK

As mentioned in the introduction, this study is concerned with the effect of corruption on capital inflows. The conceptual apparatus which will aid in fulfilling the objectives of this study are the "push-pull" framework for analyzing capital flows coupled with the "grease the wheels" vs "sand the wheels" effect of corruption. As per available information so far, there is no model that fully worked for these two phenomena. Hence, in this section, these two notions are exposed in detail and then a possible link is described between them, namely, how can corruption influence the amount of capital flows.

Corruption

Within the scope of economic theory, corruption is usually framed in terms of a Principal-Agent problem, where the agent is a public official and the principal is a higher public official or a more abstract entity such as the "public interest." Framed in this way, the principal delegates a task to the agent which takes an action, but since the action taken by the agent is costly or difficult to observe by the principal, the agent defects his task and acts according to his own private benefit, as described by Lambsdorff (2007). Framed in this way, it is clear that when institutions are inefficient in detecting "defective" behavior on the part of the agent, corruption can occur. Bribery, extortion and embezzlement all fall within the Principal-Agent model where the actions taken by the agents are not monitored properly.

Aside from theoretical consideration a way of actually measuring corruption is necessary. The most popular measure of corruption is the Corruption Perception Index (CPI). As Lambsdorff (2007) explains, it is a composite index that considers surveys conducted with experts, businesspeople and risk agencies. It gives, however, a subjective measure of corruption, that is, it is a perceived, not actual, measure of corruption.

However, this theoretical apparatus has been subject to criticism. Heywood (2017), for example, comments that the economic framework to describe corruption is too abstract. Hence, the literature so far has been incapable of providing useful policy advice to curb corruption. The same author also criticizes the CPI index. Corruption cannot be measured as a single number given that it is a multidimensional problem, arising and manifesting itself in several different ways. Anyhow, despite criticism, the Principal-Agent approach and the CPI are still the dominant way of analyzing these issues.

"Grease the wheels" vs "sand the wheels" Hypothesis

The difference between the "grease the wheels" and "sand the wheels" hypotheses is about the efficiency-enhancing or damaging effects of corruption. The point of departure for both views is the bad quality of governance, a situation where corrupt behavior makes itself most present.

The "grease the wheels" effect at first may seem counterintuitive, but upon closer inspection, it is a hypothesis worth considering (Ünlü & Ulusoy, 2021). The central argument is that corruption compensates, speeds up slow processes and even enhances the allocation of resources. That happens because, for example, paying bribes can be considered a price mechanism of sorts. Lui (1985) develops a model where customers form a queue to be served by arrival time. In that context, bribes are used to gain a better position in the queue, and that leads to an increase in efficiency, in the sense that those who wish to minimize their waiting time in the queue can do so by paying the price. Beck and Mahler (1986) compare bribery to a competitive auction model and reach the conclusion that both are equivalent. That is, corrupt public officials accepting bribes is fundamentally the same as a good being auctioned off to the highest bidder. There is literature, although, less formal that makes the case for the "grease the wheels" hypothesis (Huntington, 2006; Leff, 1964).

The "sand the wheels" effect takes the opposite stance, the main argument being that public officials create further impediments, purposefully slowing bureaucratic processes and granting special privileges in exchange for bribes or any sort of personal gain. Shleifer and Vishny (1993) show that corruption reduces the level of output when permits and licenses function as complementary goods. In that setting, if officials have any monopoly power in granting the licenses, corruption degrades economic performance. So, it is a theoretical model highlighting how malfunctioning institutions lead to corruption which in turn leads to inefficient outcomes. As it is already mentioned in the introduction, the empirical literature suggests that the "sand the wheels" hypothesis is more prevalent. However, it is possible to notice that the effect of corruption is dependent on the structure of the incentives involved and there is no unanimous answer. It is likely that corruption "greasing" or "sanding the wheels" is a case-by-case phenomenon and how that magnifies to a macroeconomic level has not been theoretically resolved.

The OLI Framework and Determinants of FDI

Foreign direct investment is defined as a firm establishing long-term production activities or the purchase of assets entailing managerial control over a firm in a foreign country. As such, its study has been developed as a subset of the general theory of international trade. Trade theory focuses on developing models to explain patterns of international trade of goods among countries. Issues like relative factor abundance, tariffs and returns to scale help explain why two countries might trade with each other and why there are gains from trade. The trade that occurs through FDI is the so-called intra-firm trade, that is, trade occurring within a firm.

Two countries trade with each other because it confers a benefit for both of them, likewise a firm choose to establish itself in a different country if that confers some sort of advantage in comparison to just exporting its goods abroad. There are two types of intra-firm trade, and hence FDI: horizontal and vertical. Horizontal trade occurs when a firm decides to produce the same good on a plant located in a foreign country. Vertical trade occurs when the production process breaks up in a chain where part of the process happens in a foreign country.

Now it is possible to observe why the decision of a firm to internationalize its production is related to trade theory. If, for example, a country has a significant market for a product of a given foreign firm, but the country imposes significant costs through tariffs, that firm might choose to engage in horizontal FDI, for it might be advantageous to establish a production plant abroad than to export to that country. But as Krugman, Obstfeld and Melitz (2018) explain, that decision is related to increasing returns. If there are increasing returns to scale, breaking up the production process into several low-producing plants might not be profitable, there is what is called a proximity-concentration trade, which relates the cost to export and the cost to build a plant abroad.

Vertical FDI also exhibits a trade-off between fixed cost and per-unit cost. The decision to engage in vertical FDI relates to factor endowments present in the foreign country: lower wages, a specific natural resource, technology or managerial skills which would make it advantageous to split the production activity among different countries.

To encapsulate the decisions of a firm to become a Multinational Enterprise (MNE) the OLI framework was developed by Dunning (1980). It has become a popular way to analyze strategic decisions by a firm engaging in FDI. As explained by Gandolfo and Trionfetti (2014), a firm must possess three advantages in order to become an MNE:

a) Ownership advantages: it refers to what is called knowledge capital, like managerial skills, human capital, patents, a trademark or reputation. Those assets can be easily transferred across countries at a low cost.
b) Location advantages: it refers to geographical advantages that the host country might possess. Usually, those are due to lower costs of inputs, like lower wages. It could also be a strategy to avoid trade barriers as already explained.
c) Internalization advantages: it refers to the benefit of keeping that knowledge-based asset internal to the firm, as opposed to simply licensing the product to a third party. If a firm would like to keep greater control of the production process, it must be that sharing its knowledge with other firms might diminish the value of the product or the firm in general.

Consistent with the OLI framework, Blonigen (2005) provides a survey of the empirical literature on the determinants of FDI. Firstly, FDI might be responsive to exchange rates. The argument is that an appreciation of the currency of the source country would increase the wealth of a firm with a stronger currency vis-à-vis a firm with a weak currency and that would generate an advantage for the foreign firm. Currency depreciation also lowers asset prices and thus could also attract more FDI. The tax rate is also a significant variable that determines FDI, the obvious argument being that higher taxes discourage FDI.

Institutions also seem to be a relevant determinant of FDI. When institutions don't provide enough protection for assets, expropriation risk is present. When markets are not well-functioning and infrastructure is poorly developed, profitability is compromised leading to a decrease in FDI.

Trade openness can also impact the level of investments by foreign firms. If countries impose restricting tariffs, a foreign firm might feel compelled to install a production facility to avoid dealing with the extra tariffs' costs. But it is important to notice that tariffs might encourage horizontal FDI and discourage vertical FDI. For vertical FDI, the extra costs to import inputs from other stages of the production process could be an impediment. So, it is likely that the effect of trade protection is contingent on the type of FDI a source country receives.

Other variables that were shown to be relevant in attracting FDI are GDP, as it measures the market size and possible economies of scale. Human capital, as a certain level of labor skill, might be necessary to make use of modern technologies, and macroeconomic fundamentals, since a stable macroeconomic environment is beneficial for business activities. The determinants of FDI are widely discussed by Nonnenberg and Mendonça (2005), Blonigen (2005), Sánchez-Martín, De Arc & Escribano (2014), Amal, Tomio & Raboch (2010).

METHODOLOGICAL PROCEEDINGS, DATA AND TREATMENT

To assess the effect that corruption perception might have on FDI for Latin American countries, 14 Latin American countries are selected from the period 2012-2019. The choice of this period is due to the methodological change carried out by Transparency International which was already mentioned. So, there is a panel data set with N = 14 and T = 8. Panel data models are used when a panel data structure is present.

One of the main virtues of panel data models is the ability to control individual heterogeneity. A panel data model can be formalized as:

$$\begin{aligned} &y_{it} = x_{it}'\beta_{it} + z_i a + u_{it}, \\ &u_{it} \sim IID\left(0, \sigma_u^2\right) \\ &i = 1, 2, 3, \ldots, N \\ &t = 1, 2, 3, \ldots, T \end{aligned} \quad (1)$$

Where:

y_{it}= independent variables observe for cross-sectional unit "i" at time "t";
x_{it}= vector of covariates;
z_i= vector of specific characteristics for cross-sectional unit "i";
u_{it}= error term for cross-sectional unit "i" at the time "t";

The assumptions one makes about the vector z_i are crucially important for panel data models. There are three main cases to consider:

I - z_i is constant;
II - z_i is correlated with the vector of covariates
III - z_i is uncorrelated with the vector of covariates but is a random variable.

If condition I holds, then one estimates a Pooled regression model, using simple ordinary least squares. If condition II holds, then a fixed effects model is to be estimated. If condition III holds, then the random effects model is estimated. This study will not go into the details of the derivation and properties of the estimators of each model. The interested reader is referred to Greene (2011).

Table 1 presents the variables, gives a description of them and refers to the relevant sources:

Table 1. Variables and sources

Variable	Description	Source
FDI	The Inflow of foreign direct investment as a percentage of GDP	World Bank
CPI	Corruption Perception Index. This variable is a measure of the corruption level of a given country	Transparency International
Gdpgrowth	GDP growth rate of a given country	World Bank
Tradeopen	A measure of trade openness, which consists of the sum of imports and exports divided by the GDP	World Bank
Education	Mean years of education. This variable is a proxy for the level of the human capital of a given country	United Nations Development Program
Taxrate	Tax revenue as a percentage of GDP. This is a proxy for the tax burden of a given country	World Bank
Naturalres	Total rents of natural resources (oil, land and forestry) as a percentage of GDP	World Bank
Exchange	Real effective exchange rate	World Bank
Econfreedom	Economic freedom index. This is a proxy for institutional quality and a business-friendly environment	Heritage Foundation
Usint	United State interest rate. This is a proxy for world interest rates.	IMF
Inflation	Inflation is measured by the consumer price index of a given country. This is the proxy for country risk, and also macroeconomic stability.	World Bank
Usgrowth	United States growth rate. This is a proxy for the world's growth rate.	World Bank

The choice of variables is based on what was presented in section 2.3, given the model structure given in (1). Following is the Equation:

$$FDI_{it} = \beta_0 + \beta_1 CPI_{it} + \beta_2 GDPgrowth_{it-1} + \beta_3 Tradeopen_{it-1} + \beta_4 Education_{it} + \beta_5 Taxrate_{it}$$
$$+ \beta_6 Naturalres_{it} + \beta_7 Exchange_{it} + \beta_8 Econfreedom_{it} + \beta_9 Usint_{it} + \beta_{10} Inflation + \beta_{11} Usgrowth_{it} + u_{it} \quad (2)$$

The lagged variables in (2) are to guard against potential endogeneity from these variables. This is the same approach adopted by Egger and Winner (2005).

ESTIMATION RESULTS AND DISCUSSION

One cannot decide beforehand which model to adopt, whether pooled, fixed or random effects are the most adequate. Although intuition can show which sort of unobserved characteristics are being dealt with (common for all units, differing or random), it is necessary to test which model is the best for this particular sample. The Hausman test is a popular statistical procedure to decide between the random effects or the fixed effect model. If the null hypothesis cannot be rejected, the random effects models is preferable due to consistency (Greene, 2011)

By using the Hausman Test, a statistic of 2417.4 is generated with a p-value of 0, thus, the null hypothesis is rejected that the estimates of the random effects model are consistent. Table 2 provides an

F-test for differing group intercepts which also rejected the null hypothesis for the pool ability of the model, leading the authors to use the fixed effects model for this sampled data.

Table 2 presented the results of the estimation adopting a fixed effects model.

Table 2. Fixed Effects Model A and B Independent variable: FDI (%GDP)

Model	Fixed Effects ACoefficients	Std. Error(p-value)	Fixed Effects BCoefficients	Std. Error(p-value)
Constant	−2.58178	18.1015(0.8901)	9.24558	9.33239(0.3508)
CPI	0.0233374	0.0980652(0.8179)	0.0234972	0.0939639(0.8088)
GDPgrowth	0.178563	0.0745806(0.0436)**	0.196551	0.0725567(0.0267)**
Tradeopen	0.0714808	0.0271192(0.0299)**	0.0591562	0.0298634(0.0829)*
Education	0.986219	1.35341(0.4870)		
Naturalres	0.0429019	0.143347(0.7723)		
Taxrate	−0.928224	0.183132(0.0010)***	−0.902820	0.222624(0.0037)***
Usint	−0.550950	0.222171(0.0381)**	−0.318965	0.142841(0.0560)*
Inflation	−0.197915	0.113261(0.1187)		
Exchange	−0.0959658	0.0308506(0.0144)**		0.0225077(0.0065)***
Econfreedom	0.259537	0.0782271(0.0106)**	0.182679	0.111430(0.1398)
Usgrowth	0.298955	0.320208(0.3778)		
LSDV R-Squared	0.8536		0.8408	
Schwarz Criterion	246.51		235.20	
F-test(common intercept)	2.6391	(0.03404)	9.05781	(1.7941e-005)

Source: Authors' Calculation

As is possible to observe in Table 2, two models A and B are estimated. This is due to the fact that several variables turned out to be not statistically significant, including the main explanatory variable, the corruption perception index. So, a more parsimonious model is tested dropping those insignificant variables, but the CPI index is kept.

Ignoring the statistical insignificance of the variables, it is found that all variables turn out to have coefficients with the expected sign. A positive CPI index reminds that a higher score index implies a smaller corruption perception, which means that a one-point increase in the CPI index accounts for a 0.02% increase in the FDI/GDP ratio. This result is consistent with the "sand the wheels" hypothesis and is in line with Wei (2000), Habib and Zurawicki (2002), Bénassy-Quéré, Coupet & Mayer (2007), Al-Sadig (2009). Other insignificant variables were education, the proxy for human capital, the presence of natural resources and inflation, the proxy for country risk. It may be argued that since the panel consists of very few time periods, those variables could represent long-term relationships, so a greater number of periods would be necessary to adequately evaluate the relevance of those variables. Those variables also had the expected sign, indicating that higher inflation, which is a sign of higher risk, has a negative impact on FDI, the presence of natural resources positively impacts FDI and so does the level of human capital.

Turning to the variables which have shown statistical significance, it is observed that GDP growth positively impacts FDI. This is the measure of an increase in the size of a market, signaling higher profitability. The tax rate, a measure of the tax burden of a country, shows to be negatively associated with FDI. The level of the exchange rate, which is the only variable with an ambiguous expected sign turns out to be negative, indicating that an appreciation of the local currency has a negative impact on FDI, this is consistent with the narrative that an appreciation of the host country exchange rate makes the assets in these countries relatively more expensive and thus decreasing the level of FDI.

For model A, the economic freedom index, which approximates institutional quality and a business-friendly environment was statistically significant. This is interesting and promising since like the CPI, this index is a composite measure of several factors, including control of corruption. One could argue then, that corruption by itself is not explanatory but only becomes important when bundled with other factors like protection of property rights, financial freedom, and so on (Kapuria-Foreman, 2008; Azman-Saini, 2010)

Finally, for model A still, the US interest rate is shown to be negatively associated with FDI, which means that liquidity and credit effects are relevant for firms deciding to engage in FDI. It would be perhaps now interesting to give a more charitable view towards Heywood (2017) when he argues that single measures and rankings of corruption could possibly be an inadequate manner of seeing the issue. If this model is correct, and the perception of corruption as measured by the CPI does not bear much influence on the decisions of firms to invest in a foreign country it could be that corruption is actually a more complex and nuanced phenomenon than a single index is capable of capturing.

What was assumed implicitly is that the CPI index could, as a single measure, give an adequate description of corruption. But which description could that be? As Heywood (2017) explains, the definition of corruption as "abuse of entrusted power for private gain" is an all-encompassing term that fits several diverse kinds of behaviors. At this level of abstraction, it is hard to pin down how corruption is actually underlying the mechanics of the interaction of private and public spheres. It is sometimes believed that corruption imposes a cost to investors, and the higher the cost, the less they would be inclined to make long-term investments in a country, then it is likely that the cost is attached to a specific type of corrupt behavior. Could a single measure capture that cost? Sometimes yes, and sometimes no, apparently. As the same author mentions, this very abstract notion of what corruption is, and entails, could be what lies behind the contradictory findings of the empirical literature, sometimes finding a negative effect of corruption and sometimes finding a positive effect of corruption, and in this case, a non-significant effect.

Another source of possible criticism of corruption indexes is that they focus on perceptions of corruption, not actual corruption. This notion opens an avenue for stereotypical measures of corruption, as Heywood (2015) suggests. For example, corruption perception indexes are correlated with variables such as economic development, freedom of the press, state of democracy and so on, but do not correlate well with actual cases of experiences of corruption (Heywood, 2015). So, it could be that, for example, a country has a high perception level of corruption without actually imposing relevant costs or risk on a given firm, and vice-versa. Is there any reason a company would quantify risks and costs based on someone else perception? It is possible that the individual experience of corruption is the key variable, not a perception by third parties of it. There is also a different problem, for example, in Brazil up to 2014 the CPI index fluctuated between 43 and 42. After 2014, a major corruption scandal emerged. The "*lava jato*" operation exposed a major corruption scheme, and in addition to that, the recently reelected president Dilma Rousseff faced an impeachment process that succeeded in forcing her out of office. At the same time, the CPI index for Brazil decreased to 37/35 score points. So, exposing corruption scandals could increase the perception of corruption. But isn't it a fact that discoveries of corrupt behavior are a signal that corruption is being front fully faced and thus becoming more costly to be corrupt so that corruption is being disincentivized? This is an indication that perception of corruption could actually measure an inverse relationship at times with actual corruption. It is possible that corruption perception indexes actually provide a sterile number for policymakers and private investors.

No doubt, corruption is still a critical issue, and most probably has significant real effects on the development and performance of countries. But the inability to reach definite conclusions about a subject is a sign that new perspectives might be adequate to be called upon.

CONCLUSION

This study it was analyzed the relationship between Transparency International's Corruption Perception Index and the inflow of Foreign Direct Investment toward Latin American Countries between 2012 and 2019. The choice of the time period was due to the fact that the methodological shift of the CPI index made it comparable across periods. In an effort to contribute to the ongoing literature to provide evidence on the relationship between corruption (measures of it) and important variables for the development of emerging market economies, which is theoretically ambiguous, and hence calls for more empirical validation, the two main different views are contrasted on the effect of corruption on economic outcomes, the "grease the wheels" and "sand the wheels" hypothesis. The former advocates that corruption can facilitate economic efficiency by overcoming sluggish and inefficient institutions, the latter has the opposite view, that corruption takes advantage of the inefficient institution, creates further impediments and raises costs for private agents.

To empirically model the relationship between foreign direct investment and corruption, the most popular framework is used to analyze determinants of FDI, with corruption being one of the determinants, Dunning's OLI or eclectic paradigms. Due to data across time periods for several cross-sectional units, a panel data structure is suitable. After common tests for which panel data model to adopt the fixed effect model is chosen.

Results confirmed some results of the existing literature, variables like trade openness, GDP growth and the level of the exchange rate were statistically significant. Variables like the presence of natural resources, human capital, inflation, and external output growth are less so, albeit having the expected sign according to the theory and the previous literature. The United States interest rate, a proxy for world interest rates has shown to be significant for one of these models, which could be an indicator that external liquidity has an impact on FDI. Another interesting finding is that the index of economic freedom has been significant, meaning that less corruption could be important when bundled with other institutional factors.

Much evidence may not be provided that the corruption perception index has any significant effect on FDI. Although this study is severely constrained by a small sample, it is argued that the effect of corruption on FDI (or any other economic variable) could be badly framed if one uses a single measure of corruption. Corruption is likely to be a multidimensional complex phenomenon that cannot be adequately captured by a single index and hence the current controversy between the "sand the wheels" and "grease the wheels" is not likely to be resolved, with some studies pointing to negative effects while others point to positive effects, and of course ours which do not find any strong evidence at all to any direction.

Given inconclusive findings related to the effect of corruption perception on FDI, it is important to consider the criticism discussed by Heywood (2015, 2017) regarding the measures of corruption perception. The criticisms are due to methodological limitations and the significance of such measures. The first problem is a problem of aggregation, a single parameter could not fully capture the multidimensional aspects of corruption, its various forms and its changing nature. The second criticism reflects the aspects of it being a measure of corruption perception, not a measure of actual corruption. Perceptions can lead to stereotypical and even negative correlations with actual levels of corruption and therefore can lead to empirical unpredictable effects and even no effects. Indexes of perception are thus likely not to be an adequate measure for policymakers and investors.

Based on the finding, the authors of this chapter agree with Heywood (2015) that is in general difficult to prescribe policies based on corruption perception measures. The inconclusive findings do not support with much weight that "climbing" the corruption perception rank would yield advantages such as more foreign direct investment. How corruption is even defined, its scope and multidimensional nature seem to be relevant for policy purposes.

A final comment would be that, if one is still interested in pursuing this line of research, which is an established one, it is fully recognized that, then more finely-grained data should be adopted. Corruption possibly acts on a case-by-case basis, so that firm-level data could be more adequate. Still, the issue is not simple, possibly getting conclusive results are far away and a better methodological grounding is called for, this is the final message the authors would like to mention.

DECLARATION

The authors declare that the manuscript follows ethical standards and there are no potential conflicts of interest with respect to the research, authorship and/or publication of this chapter.

DISCLAIMER

The contents and views of this chapter are expressed by the authors in their personal capacities. It is not necessary for the Editor and the Publisher to agree with these viewpoints, and they are not responsible for any duty of care in this regard.

ACKNOWLEDGMENT

The authors extend sincere gratitude to

- The Editor and the International Editorial Advisory Board (IEAB) of this book who initially desk reviewed, arranged a rigorous double/triple blind review process, and conducted a thorough, minute, and critical final review before accepting the chapter for publication.
- All anonymous reviewers who provided very constructive feedbacks for thorough revision, improvement, extension, and fine tuning of the chapter.
- All colleagues, assistants and well-wishers who assisted to complete this task.

REFERENCES

Al-Sadig, A. (2009). The effects of corruption on FDI inflows. *The Cato Journal*, *29*(2), 267.

Alfaro, L., Kalemli-Ozcan, S., & Volosovych, V. (2008). Why doesn't capital flow from rich to poor countries? An empirical investigation. *The Review of Economics and Statistics*, *90*(2), 347–368. doi:10.1162/rest.90.2.347

Amal, M., Tomio, B. T., & Raboch, H. (2010). Determinants of foreign direct investment in Latin America. *GCG: Revista de DGobalización. Competitividad y Gobernabilidad*, *4*(3), 116–133.

Arya, V., Banerjee, R., & Cavoli, T. (2019). Capital flows to Asia and Latin America: Does institutional quality matter? *World Economy*, *42*(7), 2039–2069. doi:10.1111/twec.12783

Azémar, C., & Desbordes, R. (2013). Has the Lucas Paradox been fully explained? *Economics Letters*, *121*(2), 183–187. doi:10.1016/j.econlet.2013.07.025

Azman-Saini, W. N. W., Baharumshah, A. Z., & Law, S. H. (2010). Foreign direct investment, economic freedom and economic growth: International evidence. *Economic Modelling*, *27*(5), 1079–1089. doi:10.1016/j.econmod.2010.04.001

Beck, P. J., & Maher, M. W. (1986). A comparison of bribery and bidding in thin markets. *Economics Letters*, *20*(1), 1–5. doi:10.1016/0165-1765(86)90068-6

Bénassy-Quéré, A., Coupet, M., & Mayer, T. (2007). Institutional determinants of foreign direct investment. *World Economy*, *30*(5), 764–782. doi:10.1111/j.1467-9701.2007.01022.x

Blonigen, B. A. (2005). A review of the empirical literature on FDI determinants. *Atlantic Economic Journal*, *33*(4), 383–403. doi:10.100711293-005-2868-9

Calderon, C., Chong, A., & Loayza, N. (2000). *Determinants of current account deficits in developing countries*. World bank., Retrieved from https://openknowledge.worldbank.org/handle/10986/19825

Dincer, O. (2019). Does corruption slow down innovation? Evidence from a cointegrated panel of US states. *European Journal of Political Economy*, *56*, 1–10. doi:10.1016/j.ejpoleco.2018.06.001

Dreher, A., & Gassebner, M. (2013). Greasing the wheels? The impact of regulations and corruption on firm entry. *Public Choice*, *155*(3), 413–432. doi:10.100711127-011-9871-2

Dunning, J. H. (1980). Toward an eclectic theory of international production: Some empirical tests. *Journal of International Business Studies*, *11*(1), 9–31. doi:10.1057/palgrave.jibs.8490593

Edwards, S., Diaz, F. G., & Fraga, A. (1999). Capital flows to Latin America. In *International Capital Flows* (pp. 5–56). University of Chicago Press.

Egger, P., & Winner, H. (2005). Evidence on corruption as an incentive for foreign direct investment. *European Journal of Political Economy*, *21*(4), 932–952. doi:10.1016/j.ejpoleco.2005.01.002

Gandolfo, G., & Trionfetti, F. (2014). *International Trade Theory and Policy*. Springer. doi:10.1007/978-3-642-37314-5

Greene, W. H. (2011). *Econometric analysis*. Pearson Education.

Gründler, K., & Potrafke, N. (2019). Corruption and economic growth: New empirical evidence. *European Journal of Political Economy, 60*, 101810. doi:10.1016/j.ejpoleco.2019.08.001

Gupta, S., Davoodi, H., & Alonso-Terme, R. (2002). Does corruption affect income inequality and poverty? *Economics of Governance, 3*(1), 23–45. doi:10.1007101010100039

Habib, M., & Zurawicki, L. (2002). Corruption and foreign direct investment. *Journal of International Business Studies, 33*(2), 291–307. doi:10.1057/palgrave.jibs.8491017

Heywood, P. (Ed.). (2015). *Routledge handbook of political corruption*. Routledge.

Heywood, P. M.Paul M. Heywood. (2017). Rethinking corruption: Hocus-pocus, locus and focus. *Slavonic and East European Review, 95*(1), 21–48. doi:10.5699laveasteurorev2.95.1.0021

Huntington, S. P. (2006). *Political order in changing societies*. Yale University Press.

Jalil, A., Qureshi, A., & Feridun, M. (2016). Is corruption good or bad for FDI? Empirical evidence from Asia, Africa and Latin America. *Panoeconomicus, 63*(3), 259–271. doi:10.2298/PAN1603259J

Kandil, M., & Greene, J. E. (2002). The impact of cyclical factors on the US balance of payments (IMF Working Paper No. 02/45). International Monetary Fund.

Kapuria-Foreman, V. (2007). Economic freedom and foreign direct investment in developing countries. *Journal of Developing Areas*, 143–154.

Krugman, P. R., Obstfeld, M., & Melitz, M. (2018). *International Economics: Theory and Policy*. Pearson Education Limited.

Lambsdorff, J. G. (2003). How corruption affects persistent capital flows. *Economics of Governance, 4*(3), 229–243. doi:10.100710101-002-0060-0

Lambsdorff, J. G. (2007). *The institutional economics of corruption and reform: Theory, evidence and policy*. Cambridge university press. doi:10.1017/CBO9780511492617

Leff, N. H. (1964). Economic development through bureaucratic corruption. *The American Behavioral Scientist, 8*(3), 8–14. doi:10.1177/000276426400800303

Lucas, R. E. (1990). Why doesn't capital flow from rich to poor countries? *The American Economic Review, 80*(2), 92–96.

Lui, F. T. (1985). An equilibrium queuing model of bribery. *Journal of Political Economy, 93*(4), 760–781. doi:10.1086/261329

Markusen, J. R., & Maskus, K. E. (2002). Discriminating among alternative theories of the multinational enterprise. *Review of International Economics, 10*(4), 694–707. doi:10.1111/1467-9396.00359

Mauro, P. (1995). Corruption and growth. *The Quarterly Journal of Economics, 110*(3), 681–712. doi:10.2307/2946696

Méon, P. G., & Sekkat, K. (2005). Does corruption grease or sand the wheels of growth? *Public Choice*, *122*(1), 69–97. doi:10.100711127-005-3988-0

Méon, P. G., & Weill, L. (2010). Is corruption an efficient grease? *World Development*, *38*(3), 244–259. doi:10.1016/j.worlddev.2009.06.004

Mo, P. H. (2001). Corruption and economic growth. *Journal of Comparative Economics*, *29*(1), 66–79. doi:10.1006/jcec.2000.1703

Nonnenberg, M. J. B., & Mendonça, M. J. C. D. (2005). Determinantes dos investimentos diretos externos em países em desenvolvimento. *Estudos Econômicos*, *35*(4), 631–655. doi:10.1590/S0101-41612005000400002

Qureshi, F., Qureshi, S., Vo, X. V., & Junejo, I. (2021). Revisiting the nexus among foreign direct investment, corruption and growth in developing and developed markets. *Borsa Istanbul Review*, *21*(1), 80–91. doi:10.1016/j.bir.2020.08.001

Rafay, A. (Ed.). (2023). *Concepts, Cases, and Regulations in Financial Fraud and Corruption*. IGI Global., doi:10.4018/978-1-6684-5007-9

Rafay, A., Sadiq, R., & Ajmal, M. M. (2016). The Effect of IAS-24 Disclosures on Governance Mechanisms and Ownership Structures in Pakistan. *Lahore Journal of Business*, *5*(1), 15–36. doi:10.35536/ljb.2016.v5.i1.a2

Rotberg, R. I. (2019). The Corruption of Latin America. In *Corruption in Latin America* (pp. 1–25). Springer.

Sánchez-Martín, M. E., De Arce, R., & Escribano, G. (2014). Do changes in the rules of the game affect FDI flows in Latin America? A look at the macroeconomic, institutional and regional integration determinants of FDI. *European Journal of Political Economy*, *34*, 279–299. doi:10.1016/j.ejpoleco.2014.02.001

Shleifer, A., & Vishny, R. W. (1993). Corruption. *The Quarterly Journal of Economics*, *108*(3), 599–617. doi:10.2307/2118402

Ugur, M. (2014). Corruption's direct effects on per-capita income growth: A meta-analysis. *Journal of Economic Surveys*, *28*(3), 472–490. doi:10.1111/joes.12035

Ünlü, H., & Ulusoy, M. K. (2021). Innovation and Corruption in Turkey: "Grease the Wheels" or "Sand the Wheels". In A. Rafay (Ed.), *Handbook of Research on Theory and Practice of Financial Crimes* (pp. 80–103). IGI Global., doi:10.4018/978-1-7998-5567-5.ch006

Wei, S. J., & Shleifer, A. (2000). Local corruption and global capital flows. *Brookings Papers on Economic Activity*, *2000*(2), 303–354. doi:10.1353/eca.2000.0021

Yurdakul, F., & Ucar, B. (2015). The relationship between current deficit and economic growth: An empirical study on Turkey. *Procedia Economics and Finance*, *26*, 101–108. doi:10.1016/S2212-5671(15)00885-0

ENDNOTE

1 https://www.weforum.org/agenda/2018/12/the-global-economy-loses-3-6-trillion-to-corruption-each-year-says-u-n

Chapter 12
The Political Economy of Corruption:
The Case of Lebanon

Fatih Kırşanlı
Yozgat Bozok University, Turkey

ABSTRACT

Lebanon is facing one of the most acute socioeconomic and political crises in history. While it was the financial center during the 1950s, 60s, and early 70s with its sophisticated banking sector, the civil war between 1975 and 1990 demolished this position. Beginning from 1990 until 2019, the Lebanese economy was slowly dragged into an economic collapse with depreciated Lebanese lira against foreign currencies, which was the preferred monetary policy. This chapter focuses on this collapse and the so-called Ponzi scheme, organized by the Lebanese central and commercial banks. It elucidates the leading cause of the issues (e.g., financial engineering, Beirut Explosion, political deadlock, economic turmoil), namely rampant corruption, from the perspective of political economy. It also discusses foreign interventions, the dominance of Hezbollah, and terror financing issues. Lastly, it sheds light on future research by providing policy recommendations for the Lebanese political economy.

INTRODUCTION

Lebanon is facing a severe socioeconomic and political crisis. A large share of the population is struggling with poverty, unemployment, inflation, and debt (Baumann, 2019; Daher, 2022). The provision of fundamental basic needs is absent. Even though there is massive dissatisfaction and unhappiness with the current system, it does not alter the political status quo because of the Lebanese-specific political and economic traits. The sectarian political structure where the power is distributed among certain sects (e.g., the President is a Maronite Christian, the Speaker of the Parliament is a Shi'a Muslim, and the Prime Minister is a Sunni Muslim) led to political deadlocks and turmoil that exacerbated the country's economic issues because of self-perpetuating rent-seeking mechanisms among the sects (Salti & Chaaban, 2010).

DOI: 10.4018/978-1-6684-8587-3.ch012

Lebanon was known as the Switzerland of the Middle East during the 1950s, 1960s, and early 1970s (Ricour-Brasseur, 2021). Under the leadership of two brothers, Raymond, and Pierre Eddé, bankers were politicians who understood the future of finance. The renaissance of economies under financialization, the 1956 Secrecy Law, and the Association of Banks in Lebanon (ABL) in 1959 were introduced. The two masterpieces made Lebanon the capital of financial elites (Safieddine, 2019). The Banking Secrecy Law, which kept all financial transactions clandestine, was critical since it provided an institutional base for the banker's position in the system. In addition, establishing ABL, a powerful bankers' lobby, steadily increased the capital elite's political influence. The last move needed to prove Lebanon's complete independence after 1943 was establishing Banque du Liban (BDL), a central bank founded in 1964 (Safieddine, 2019). Lebanon was the financial hub of the Middle East and North Africa (MENA) and was envisioned as the epicenter of banking and tourism (Morakabati, 2013). While many neighboring countries possess natural resources, Lebanon does not have this advantage (Springborg, 2020). The Eddé brothers and their colleagues articulated a plan where the region would deposit money in Lebanon. It worked perfectly from the 1950s until the mid-1960s. It was again reinvigorated in the early 1970s with the Gulf states oil boom until conflict and civil war hit the country in 1975 (Safieddine, 2019). The civil war was mainly caused by the instabilities of the neighboring countries, which ignited hatred between various ethnic groups. Interventions by countries such as Syria and Israel aggravated the internal tribulations. Lebanon suffered a long-lasting conflict until the 1989 Taif Agreement, also known as the National Reconciliation Accord, provided a political normalization and the end of the civil strife.

Even though the system created under the Secrecy Law worked until the early 1970s, sectarianism created a rent-seeking mechanism where elite capture, nepotism, and corruption increased between sects in Lebanon. Sectarian politics has existed in Lebanon since its independence in 1943, but the civil war worsened the conflicts. After losing its position as the hub of finance in the MENA region, fifteen years of internal war increased the political havoc, bringing economic destruction. Hezbollah, the Shi'a militia group, was founded in southern Lebanon in 1982 during the war (Daher, 2019). Since then, Hezbollah has been active in the country economically by providing financial help in the south (e.g., building schools, helping hospitals, providing humanitarian aid, providing electrification, and supporting agricultural production) and politically by participating in the Lebanese parliament and at the ministerial level. The loss of economic significance, followed by civil war and an unstable political environment continued with financial engineering under the BDL.

The financial engineering system built under Chairman Riad T. Salameh, hired by Rafic Hariri in 1993, depreciated the Lebanese currency by more than 90% in the black market. Currency depreciation melted away people's savings and accelerated the economic upheaval (e.g., inflation over 150%, unemployment above 40%) intensified by the pandemic (The WB, 2022). Moreover, the 2020 Beirut chemical explosion compounded colossal economic struggles, costing the Lebanese economy an estimated $8 billion loss, according to the World Bank (The WB, 2020). On top of that, commodity prices rose following the start of the Russia-Ukraine war in 2022. The fight further accelerated economic impediments because Lebanon imports 78% of its wheat from Ukraine and Russia (Yazbeck *et al.*, 2022). The course of the Russian invasion will be decisive for the Lebanese economy, at least in the short and medium runs.

Corruption is one of the major the root causes of all evils (Rafay, 2023). The primary determinant of these massive issues in Lebanon is the prevalent corruption in political and bureaucratic fields that prevents socioeconomic development. Income disparities, inflation, unemployment, debt, and sectarian politics opened the way for illegal activities and escalated corruption further (Cortés & Kéchichian, 2020). According to the 2022 report by Transparency International, the leading institute in corruption whose scores vary between 0 and 100 (higher scores represent less corruption), Lebanon received 24 out of 100, ranking it 150th among 180 countries (TI, 2022). Lebanon's corruption score has decreased (become more corrupt) since 2012 from 30 out of 100, except in 2022. Regarding corruption's cost to the Lebanese economy, a report written by a private company and commissioned by the United Nations Center for International Crime Prevention (UNCICP) illustrates that Lebanon loses $1.5 billion annually due to political and bureaucratic corruption at all levels of government (Abdelnour, 2001). Considering other direct and indirect adverse effects of corruption on Lebanon's productivity, investment, economic growth (Farida & Ahmadi-Esfahani, 2006), and other macroeconomic variables, corruption is a deadly phenomenon.

Terror financing can be one of the adverse consequences of corruption and other illegal activities (Rafay, 2021). Due to sectarian politics, Lebanon is implicitly open to terrorism, which needs channels for funding terror activities. In this regard, the Shi'a militia group Hezbollah can sustain its existence through illegal activities, including embezzlement, arms deals, gas and fuel smuggling, and illegal fundraising.[1] According to statistics, Hezbollah has $100 million in annual revenue, provided by the Iranian regime directly and by other international networks of funds from the Middle East, Asia, Latin America, Europe, and the United States (Goldberg, 2002). Hezbollah's role is crucial as it increased its voting power from 5% and 6% during the 1990s to approximately 20% in the last election, May 2022, although losing the majority (Laila *et al.*, 2022). Hezbollah is still significant in the Lebanese parliament in terms of the member of parliaments (MPs) and the number of ministries.

In this vein, this paper investigates the political economy of corruption in Lebanon as seen through the lenses of the 2019 financial engineering collapse, sectarian politics, and the 2020 Beirut chemical explosion being the apex of corruption. It is crucial to analyze the political economy with a comparative methodology of before and after the financial engineering crisis, which caused intense harm to ordinary citizens due to the Lebanese government's indebtedness and people's struggle to afford basic needs. Also, sectarian politics is the key to intertwined social, political, and economic issues; thus, it should be part of the investigation. Lastly, the 2020 Beirut explosion, the pinnacle of corruption in Lebanon, explains the collapse of the entire system in the eyes of ordinary citizens. Hence, the analysis of financial engineering, sectarian politics, and the Beirut explosion provides a framework for the outcomes of the Lebanese political economy before and after these three issues. To the best of our knowledge, this type of political economy analysis from the perspectives of these three phenomena has not been previously investigated in the literature.

The chapter first analyzes the channels behind being the region's financial hub and its repercussions, then examines how Lebanon lost its financial significance and the outcomes of that loss. Next, the chapter investigates how financial engineering started in 1993 and collapsed in 2019, bringing extreme economic costs to Lebanese society. It continues with Hezbollah's role in Lebanese political and economic life, linking Hezbollah's activities with corruption. Finally, the chapter touches upon how conditions worsened after the 2020 Beirut explosion. The sections are as follows: Lebanon—the financial hub of the Middle East and North Africa; financial engineering and collapse; sectarian politics and Hezbollah's role; Beirut explosion—the zenith of corruption; and lastly, discussion and conclusion.

LEBANON: THE FINANCIAL HUB OF THE MIDDLE EAST AND NORTH AFRICA

In order to understand how Lebanon became the financial hub of the MENA region during the 1950s through the mid-1960s (i.e., until the Arab nationalist movements and Intra Bank's 1966 bankruptcy), comprehending the Eddé brothers' role is important. Raymond and Pierre Eddé were bankers and politicians who were the architects of the banking system in Lebanon after independence. The younger brother, Pierre, was the first manager of Bank Beirut Riyadh, one of the banks funded by the Gulf resources, which wanted to dominate the Lebanese market (Safieddine, 2019). Raymond won a parliamentary seat in 1951, followed by Pierre's election in 1953. Pursuing their political benefits, they created the Secrecy Law (1956) and founded ABL (1959). These two institutions initiated the success story of Lebanon as a financial hub of the region. The Secrecy Law's advantage for those who had investments in the Lebanese banking system was that money resources and how cash flow was created would never be questioned (Serhan *et al.*, 2016). Illegal cash flow was allowed. On the other hand, ABL, the first of its kind in the Arab world, was founded to provide professional cooperation, support, and solidarity between its members in financial defense mechanisms and to collaborate in public and private institutions (Safieddine, 2019).

The system under the Secrecy Law and ABL thrived in Lebanon until the mid-1960s when Arab nationalism—Nasserism—spread among the Arab nations. Starting from the mid-1960s, the liaison role of the Lebanese banking sector between the Gulf and the West eroded through a lack of available credits and foreign exchange rate instability (Safieddine, 2019). Western countries were dealing with Gulf money by themselves rather than considering Lebanon as a middleman and facing pro-Arab movements around the 1950s and 1960s, where nation-states controlled economies (Safieddine, 2019). A central bank was needed for a *laissez-faire* economic system, and BDL was founded in 1963 to establish the complete economic independence of the Lebanese economy. The President of Lebanon at the time, Fuad Chehab, explicitly drew a line between the state and banking system when BDL's constitution was declared. The roles of the state and the central bank in economic decisions were identified. BDL was stabilizing Lebanon's financial system and liaising between the state and International Financial Institutions (IFIs). Arab nationalism increased the conflict between Saudi King Faysal and Lebanon's so-called pro-Nasser stand. This was when Lebanon started to lose its central position in the MENA; Gulf money was taken out of Lebanese banks, especially with the bankruptcy of Intra in 1966 (Cobham & Dibeh, 2009).

During the 1970s, when the Arab oil boom began, attempts were made to reinvigorate Lebanon's financial position. Although it was successful for a short period that stopped in 1975 when the civil war started. During the civil war, a new set of actors, leaders of militias, and new contractor elite with close links to the Gulf countries entered the economic scene. The banking system continued to be essential for creating and distributing rents between these groups, as were the reconstruction and the real estate sectors. Lastly, the government continued to distribute rents through the service ministries. However, the sectarian rent-seeking mechanisms entered a different phase when the civil war ended with the Taif Agreement in 1989. The new phase, the three-decades-long financial-engineering period under Riad T. Salameh, continued until 2019 when the so-called Ponzi scheme system could not move forward.

FINANCIAL ENGINEERING AND ITS COLLAPSE

After two years following the end of the civil war, Rafic Hariri became the prime minister. He hired Riad T. Salameh, his portfolio manager (when Salameh was working for Merrill Lynch), as the governor of

BDL in 1993 (Dib, 2020). Salameh has been the governor of BDL since then. In 1993, BDL initiated a new financial mechanism. In this financial engineering, BDL pegged the Lebanese lira to the US dollar in 1997, and it has been protected through high interest on deposits. Back then, this idea was praised by many as stabilizing the Lebanese economy. The system has been implemented by paying high-interest rates to commercial banks to fund state expenditures, generating a vicious cycle where the Lebanese government spends from the funds at BDL, which borrows from commercial banks with higher interest rates.

In 2015, economic problems worsened due to increasing debts and higher interest to cover government expenses. From 2019 onwards, the so-called Ponzi scheme of financial engineering collapsed, and the Lebanese government could not pay the interest debt to commercial banks (Khalife *et al.*, 2022). Moreover, alternative exchange rates had been utilized in the black market due to hyperinflation. While the pegged rate continued to be 15,000, the black-market rates exceeded 75,000 Lebanese lira per US dollar. After 2019, the government could not even afford the necessities of society due to being in enormous debt and hyperinflation, which created a political predicament and prompted extensive street protests.

The system was not sustainable and survived the last 30 years with the help of internal and external capital elites. Nevertheless, when the financial engineering of BDL increased the foreign exchange reserves to $30 billion in 2016 from $3 billion in 2008, the government continued to borrow higher interest rates from commercial banks, which also funded the central bank with higher-than-average interest rates. This system continued until 2019 when it became impossible to move forward. But the rent-seeking mechanism and relations could be traced by looking at the distribution of economic rent in the banking sector. The banking sector is historically the center of economic activity in Lebanon and amassed a staggering amount of $176 billion of consolidated assets (350% of GDP) in 2014 (Chaaban, 2016).

The Ponzi scheme caused debt levels to reach unbearable levels. This episode illustrates the main political-economic problems of the country that led to the current crisis. The civil war changed the parameters of the country, the idea of Lebanon as a tourism and banking hub could no longer be sustained, and a reconfiguration of Lebanon to more productive sectors was necessary to have an economically sovereign state. Political actors do not offer any vision for the country's long-term prospects but compete to increase their share of the pie. The unsustainability of this economic regime was evident for an extended period, but none of the political actors objected to this system as there was a close link between financial elites and politicians. An empirical study illustrates that individuals closely linked to politicians control 43% of commercial banking sector assets in Lebanon (Chaaban, 2016). Eighteen out of twenty banks (concentrating on banks with more than $1 billion assets) have close ties to political elites. Four out of the top ten banks have crony capital shares, more than 70%. Eight families control 29% of total banking sector shares, which is $7.3 billion in equity (Chaaban, 2016). This crony capitalism brings political clientelism, rent-seeking opportunities, and higher default risk (Khwaja & Mian, 2005; Dinc, 2005; Morck *et al.*, 2011).

The financial engineering conundrum stemmed from a game between capital and political elites who ruled the system for the last three decades. Capital elites are the people who enjoy their position through their financial capabilities. In contrast, political elites use their reputations and higher authority positions in social interactions (Vucetic, 2011). The former control all pharmaceutical, oil and gas, cement, and asphalt companies in Lebanon. According to Cortés and Kéchichian (2020), five companies control 50% of the pharmaceutical market, while seven companies control 60% of the fuel and fuel-relevant products, and a single company monopolizes 95% of the gas market. Three and four companies manage the asphalt and cement markets. Fuel companies import three to four times the needs of the Lebanese economy and then illegally smuggle the remaining product to Syria through Hezbollah, which operates the fuel market under the Assad regime (Cortés & Kéchichian, 2020).

Eventually, extensive street protests began toward the end of 2019, when the Lebanese people protested against the corrupt regime (Kraidy, 2019). More than two million people went to the street complaining about the living standards and existing political system (Cortés and Kéchichian, 2019). Corruption was the primary motivating factor of the protests as a sectarian system justified political and bureaucratic corruption (Cortés & Kéchichian, 2019). In this vein, Leenders (2012) agrees that there existed mechanisms in the realms of political and economic spheres of Lebanon that stimulated corrupt behaviors and spread them through the political and bureaucratic fields of Lebanese society. Deep-rooted corruption helped many individuals benefit from profits from such a system (Leenders, 2012).

In the midst of corrupt elites, a new model that takes social justice into its core is required in order to restore the Lebanese economy to its previous position, which can be achieved with a progressive tax reform that charges higher salaries and wealth with more taxes (Assouad, 2021). Assouad (2021) thinks that tax reform can solve inequality, poverty, and unemployment problems and support the fundamental needs of Lebanese society. Inequality levels have reached unprecedented levels in Lebanon. For example, 1% of the population gets 25% of the national income on average, whereas the bottom 50% of the population receives less than 10% on average since 2005. Along with income inequalities, wealth inequality has also risen. The top 10% of the population gets 70% of the total wealth in Lebanon, and the middle and lower classes have less chance of upward mobility (Assouad, 2023).

Similarly, 78% of the population lives below the poverty level, and over 30% of the labor force is unemployed (Chehayeb, 2021). Hence, reforms under the new economic model with tax reforms will help to lower these inequalities and the collapsed system can be reinvigorated. Nevertheless, the role of sectarian politics and the Hezbollah militia group should be considered, primarily affecting Lebanon's political and economic spheres.

SECTARIAN POLITICS AND THE ROLE OF HEZBOLLAH

After its independence in 1943, Lebanon made a constitutional change and opted for a confessional political system, a type of consociationalism in which power is distributed among religious sects (Salamey, 2009). The Lebanese system remained the backbone of political sectarianism after the 1989 Taif Agreement. This confessional system and the recent history of conflict played a role in political fragmentation and its chaotic nature. The geopolitical situation where the country has been thrust between Israel and Syria has exacerbated the problems. Since the 1970s, Lebanon has been importing unrest from the conflicts of these countries, and politics continue to be oppressed under the larger geopolitical fight.

The political economy of Lebanon is closely related to the geopolitical balance between Syria, Iran, Israel, the United States, and the Gulf countries. Between the 1990 and 2000s, the political scene was characterized by an implicit deal between the Syria and United States-Saudi Arabia axis, and Rafic Hariri was the embodiment of the agreement. After the deteriorating relations between Syria and the United States in the 2000s, this system started to destruct. Historically, this situation formed the background of Hezbollah's prominence in the political scene, which signified the dominance of Syria and Iran in Lebanon. In the last twenty years, there has been a gradual increase in the predominance of Hezbollah to the point where it achieved a more powerful military presence than the Lebanese Armed Forces (LAB). The country's top generals are paid less than the entry-level Hezbollah and ISIS fighters with the depreciation of the Lebanese lira against the dollar in recent years. Even though the Hezbollah-led coalition lost its majority in parliament in the last election, May 2022, Hezbollah still plays an essential role in Lebanon's political economy (Daher, 2020).

Lebanon's effort to rebuild its economy under Rafiq Hariri after the civil war was internationally supported and mainly backed by Saudi Arabia and the Western block. Hariri became Prime Minister in 1992 to oversee this economic reconstruction program. However, Syria became suspicious as it sought to influence Lebanese politics following some Lebanese allies who blamed Hariri for the Lebanese economic performance (Nizameddin, 2006). Hariri wanted to privatize the state sector to eliminate corruption and attract foreign direct investment (FDI), which was incompatible with Syrian hegemony. Other factors caused Syria's disapproval of Lebanon, including Hariri's Western stance, Syria's security in Lebanon, and the financial interests of the Ba'ath regime in the Lebanese economy. However, the efforts of Hariri toward economic liberalization and the long-term goals to alleviate state-driven corruption were immovable and demonstrated the weaknesses of the post-Taif political order (Nizameddin, 2006). Hariri's stance on clearing the state of corruption and attracting foreign direct investment through political stability and economic liberalization clashed with Syria's determination to be the decision-maker in Lebanese politics. This clash continued until Hariri's assassination (Rudner, 2010).

After Rafic Hariri's assassination in 2005, Hezbollah created the March 8 alliance with the support of Michel Aoun's Free Patriotic Movement (FPM) and weaker allies. After the Lebanon-Israel war, Hezbollah tightened its grip on the state. The March 14 alliance, a coalition of political parties and independents with an anti-Syrian stance could not stem this trend and has a more fractured base with a leadership problem. From 2008 until 2019, Hezbollah enjoyed veto power in the cabinet, controlling over a third plus one of all ministerial positions. On top of that, Hezbollah uses its hybrid status by operating outside of the state. Therefore, Hezbollah benefits from all the profits without paying the costs of society's dissatisfaction by casting itself as an outsider against the clash of economic elites who exploit the Lebanese people. The economic situation in this period could be portrayed as a stalemate between Hezbollah, its patrons Iran and Syria, and economic elites. Hezbollah did not take over the state but kept its dual status as a tool. Hezbollah did not try to block rival groups from continuing their rent-seeking activities, and the banking sector is one of the best examples of that (Daher, 2016).

When financial engineering collapsed in 2019, conditions changed for every sect, including Hezbollah. Sectarianism has brought prevalent corruption to Lebanon since 1943, as each denomination saw its members benefit from the current system and abused the power. This corruption in political and bureaucratic areas increased the insolvency risk of issues in Lebanon. Facing these risks, Hezbollah financed its expenses through different channels, although this is what the militia group has been doing since its initiation in 1982.

Technically, militia groups do not usually open bank accounts under their institution names, especially in the West (Levitt, 2002). Nevertheless, Hezbollah operates openly and has accounts in its own or other known names. Further, Hezbollah funds itself through gold and diamond smuggling, which is found in several areas, including the Democratic Republic of Congo (Levitt, 2002). Also, the banking sector is the funding channel of Hezbollah. For example, Al-Madina Bank in Lebanon was the vehicle of the criminal activities of Hezbollah. If a financial institution does not ask questions, a fake person can be employed at a bank for illegal money transfers or bank account openings, such as in the Lebanese Canadian Bank. The financial activities of Hezbollah can be easily sustained. Although some banks can be cautious about transactions that may raise red flags, they can still miss some operations, as occurred just before 9/11 (Freeman & Ruehsen, 2013).

A clear example of corruption and terror financing happened in 2003 with Al-Madina Bank and its subsidiary United Credit Bank (UCB). Their clandestine and illegal transactions caused the bank's collapse and loss of funds. When the two Lebanese-Saudi brothers bought the bank in 1984, Rana Qoleilat became the executive assistant who had the full authority to give orders to the brothers' lawyer about the transactions made on their behalf (Freeman & Ruehsen, 2013). According to accusations, Mrs. Qoleilat illegally transferred funds to Saddam Hussein's regime in Iraq and to Russian mafia groups and made agreements with diamond dealers. More importantly for the context of this chapter, Rana Qoleilat made transactions with the arms dealer for Hezbollah. She also made transactions that funded Syrian politicians and generals when Syria occupied Lebanon. When all these Ponzi schemes (another Ponzi scheme in Lebanon after financial engineering under BDL and commercial banks) collapsed, the bank's owners lost US $1.5 billion (Freeman & Ruehsen, 2013). Even though the bank owners lost a considerable amount of money, thanks to the funds of the Iranian government and international fundraisers Hezbollah has a $100 million yearly budget (Goldberg, 2002).

As aforementioned, the Lebanese Canadian Bank was also accused of financing Hezbollah at numerous levels. Active accounts in the bank laundered money and sent commissions to Hezbollah. The bank employed several employees who worked for the militia group's terror financing right under the eye of the bank's staff. These employees helped bring massive amounts of cash from the airport and deposited it into the closest LCB branch (Freeman & Ruehsen, 2013).

In summary, Hezbollah has three primary sources: military assistance from Iran and Syria; enforcement of extra fees on local businesses in Lebanon and Beqaa Valley; and funds through the Shi'a diaspora in the Middle East, Asia, Europe, North and South America, and West Africa (Levitt, 2002; Daher, 2016). Their methods include money laundering through financial systems, as mentioned above in the examples of Al-Madina, UCB, and the Lebanese Canadian Banks; informal payment transfer networks (e.g., *hawala*); luxury jewelry smuggling; and drugs. Thus, closer surveillance of state institutions in the financial system, ports, and airports is needed to control terror financing. Nonetheless, a key question is how this should be accomplished and whether criminal transactions will be eliminated in a fragile institutional environment like Lebanon (Rudner, 2010). One of the most critical incidents that illustrate what weak institutions and especially rampant corruption can cause is the 2020 Beirut chemical blast.

BEIRUT EXPLOSION: THE ZENITH OF CORRUPTION

The 2020 Beirut chemical explosion was primarily an outcome of corrupt politics and economics. Over two hundred people were reported dead, more than six thousand were injured, and total property damage was over $8 billion (The WB, 2020). Due to the substantial impact, Cyprus, Israel, Palestine, Turkey, Syria, and some European countries physically felt the results of the explosion (Nassar & Nastacă, 2021).

The blast raised questions about sectarian politics and corruption (Nakhoul, 2020; Fakih & Majzoub, 2021). Regardless of which party was responsible, widespread corruption was the central dynamic behind the explosion. The blast increased the economic burden considering the port handles about 90% of imports and 10% of exports by weight (Baff & Azzi, 2021), and created other political crises inside the country. After the explosion, the international community reacted and assisted Lebanon. To prevent further corruption, Transparency International collaborating with the Lebanese Transparency Association, the American University of Beirut, and Issam Fares Institute for Public Policy, launched "The Beirut Blast Recovery and Reconstruction Monitor" program. The monitor aimed to compile data and measure the transparency and accountability of international donations (TI, 2020). However, it may be less likely to resolve this incident with local authorities as there have been mysterious deaths and disappearances of prominent people.

When Reuters investigated the incident, it discovered that the first signals of the explosion came in 2014, three months after a ship came from Georgia. Colonel Joseph Skaf, who mysteriously died in 2017, was the head of the anti-narcotics and money laundering division (Nakhoul *et al.*, 2020). He stated in a letter that the ship was carrying ammonium nitrate, which jeopardized public life. He urged the authorities to move the ship away from the dock and to surveil. After the explosion incident, a telecom employee who was a photographer was assassinated when preparing to take his daughters to kindergarten. It was questioned whether this cold-blooded killing recorded on camera was related to the explosion as murderers took the photographer's phone, which was found a few days later.

The corruption scandals did not end with this murder case. In December 2020, a retired customs officer was assassinated in his home, and the Ministry of Interior denied the connection of this killing with the Beirut explosion (Taha, 2020). Reuters investigated whether there is a connection between these assassinations, the explosion, and politicians, including Hezbollah. These politicians are either board members or managers or shareholders in line companies. In addition, since Beirut is an important and busy port, it has lost billions of dollars of payments through smuggling, theft, and missing invoicing (Cortés & Kéchichian, 2020). The explosion showed the pinnacle of corruption in Lebanon and proved how capital and political elites rebutted functioning institutions and made Lebanon a nonfunctioning state.

DISCUSSION AND CONCLUSION

Lebanon has had enormous socioeconomic and political problems since 2019. Prevalent corruption, power greed, clientelism, and networking between Christians, Sunnis, and Shi'as generated an excessive burden on the state budget. Ethnic and religious heterogeneity as well as incompetence in the administration of economic affairs pushed Lebanon to the edge of bankruptcy. Financial engineering, sectarian politics, and the Beirut explosion suppressed internal consensus and prevented effective policies.

Starting from the deadlock in the political system and continuing with financial engineering catastrophes led by BDL, the institutional quality of Lebanon has seen one of the lowest levels in its history. Corruption, political instability, defunctionalization of the government, and potential bankruptcy generate a grim picture for the Lebanese people. The Lebanese people are dissatisfied with the current political atmosphere and the economic scene, simulating further brain drain, which would be a massive blow to the economy's long-term prospects.

Bribery and illegal behavior cannot increase bureaucratic effectiveness and institutional quality. Lebanon needs political and economic structural reforms, which require substantial funding, patience, and, most importantly, political determination. The complex circumstances continue to produce a vicious cycle where political problems feed economic complexities and create corruption. Since the Taif Agreement, prevalent corruption has restrained Lebanon's political consensus and long-term development.

Even though Riad Salameh was considered the mastermind behind the collapsed so-called Ponzi scheme (Majed & Salman, 2019), where wealthy people and commercial banks earned extra rents at the expense of the state budget, all of the political actors were complicit. In all cases, a reconfiguration of the financial system is inevitable after this collapse. Hence, implementing a new economic paradigm such as tax reform (Assouad, 2021) should be considered to alleviate unemployment, inflation, poverty, and the debt trap.

Along with existing institutional issues, the country's sectarian politics gave rise to Hezbollah, a Shi'a militia group that continues in power due to its primarily illegal financial transactions and operations in other countries outside the Middle East. Hezbollah is active in Latin America, Europe, and the United States, raising millions of dollars annually to fund its activities. These funds and financial stability have given Hezbollah political power and dominance amid Lebanon's crisis for the last three decades. The political rise of Hezbollah helped it to increase its votes and to have a more significant number of members of parliaments and ministries in the country. However, it lost its majority in the last election.

Sectarian politics influence Hezbollah, which increases its influence by helping ordinary Lebanese people by providing health, infrastructure, transportation, education, and humanitarian assistance. Its terror financing channels also increase Hezbollah's life span, further influencing the Lebanese political economy. The financial engineering planned and orchestrated by the Lebanese central bank and commercial banks (political influence is also extensive in the Ponzi scheme due to politicians' close affiliation with commercial bank authorities) sought benefits for only political and financial elites. This accelerated the political and economic rise of Hezbollah, and Hezbollah used these channels to its benefit.

Lastly, the Beirut explosion in 2020 was the tipping point of these adverse incidents. According to some, Hezbollah was responsible for the Beirut explosion and tried to remove the case's judge, Tarek Bitar, from duty, although this attempt has been unsuccessful so far (Katerji, 2021). Regardless of who was responsible for the blast, which cost around $8 billion, it proves the Lebanese government's poor institutional quality and incapability (Hafez, 2009). Moreover, an unstable political atmosphere creates a conflict every several years when there is no consensus between the sects. This perpetuates the corrupt transactions within each religious denomination, as the system is based on a rent-seeking mechanism that fosters corruption and hampers economic development (Hafez, 2009).

Improving institutional quality, eliminating corruption, and finding a consensus within the sects through conventional wisdom may solve Lebanon's political deadlock and turmoil in the long run. However, international help is required to alleviate the dominance of Hezbollah in Lebanese politics, which is due to Hezbollah's financially stable position. Otherwise, Lebanon, where almost 80% of the population lives below poverty levels, will soon be a failed state. Due to all these reasons, it was essential to make the comparative political economy analysis of the Lebanese case considering the three important determinants (financial engineering, the role of Hezbollah, and the Beirut explosion) as the causes of tumultuous times. Therefore, the contribution of this chapter guides to pursue more research about Lebanon in the future.

DECLARATION

The author declares that the manuscript follows ethical standards and there are no potential conflicts of interest with respect to the research, authorship and/or publication of this chapter.

DISCLAIMER

The contents and views of this chapter are expressed by the author in his personal capacity. It is not necessary for the Editor and the Publisher to agree with these viewpoints, and they are not responsible for any duty of care in this regard.

ACKNOWLEDGMENT

The author extends sincere gratitude to

• The Editor and the International Editorial Advisory Board (IEAB) of this book, who initially desk reviewed, arranged a rigorous double/triple-blind review process, and conducted a thorough, minute, and critical final review before accepting the chapter for publication.

• All anonymous reviewers who provided very constructive feedback for thorough revision, improvement, extension, and fine-tuning of the chapter.

• All colleagues, assistants and well-wishers who assisted to complete this task.

REFERENCES

Abdelnour, Z. (2001). The three faces of corruption in Lebanon. *Middle East Intelligence Bulletin, 3*(2). Retrieved from https://www.meforum.org/meib/articles/0102_12.htm

Assouad, L. (2021). *Lebanon's political economy: From predatory to self-devouring* (Working Paper). Washington, DC: Carnegie Middle East Center.

Assouad, L. (2023). Rethinking the Lebanese economic miracle: The extreme concentration of income and wealth in Lebanon, 2005–2014. *Journal of Development Economics*, *161*, 103003. doi:10.1016/j.jdeveco.2022.103003

Baff, S., & Azzi, A. (2021, August 20). *Port of Beirut: Analysis and prospects*. BlomInvest Bank. Retrieved from https://blog.blominvestbank.com/wp-content/uploads/2021/08/ Port-of-Beirut-Analysis-and-Prospects.pdf

Baumann, H. (2019). The Causes, nature, and effect of the current crisis of Lebanese capitalism. *Nationalism & Ethnic Politics*, *25*(1), 61–77. doi:10.1080/13537113.2019.1565178

Chaaban, J. (2016). I've got the power: Mapping connections between Lebanon's banking sector and the ruling class. In I. Diwan, A. Malik, & I, Atiyas (Eds.) Crony Capitalism in the Middle East: Business and Politics from Liberalization in the Middle East (pp. 330–343). Oxford: Oxford University Press. doi:10.1093/oso/9780198799870.003.0013

Chehayeb, K. (2021, October 1). UN urges Lebanon to implement reforms as extreme poverty grows. *Aljazeera*. Retrieved from https://www.aljazeera.com/news/2021/10/1/un-lebanon-reforms-extreme-poverty-economic-crisis#:~:text=According%20to%20the%20UN's%20Emergency,%2C%20sanitation%2C%20and%20child%20protection.

Cobham, D. P., & Dibeh, G. (Eds.). (2009). *Monetary policy and central banking in the Middle East and North Africa*. Routledge. doi:10.4324/9780203884553

Cortés, F. S. B., & Kéchichian, J. A. (2019). *Does corruption benefit compromised societies? The case of Lebanon*. Middle East Institute.

Cortés, F. S. B., & Kéchichian, J. A. (2020). The practice of corruption in Lebanon. *Middle East Policy, 27*(4), 119–135. doi:10.1111/mepo.12530

Daher, A. (2019). *Hezbollah: Mobilisation and power* (H. W. Randolph, Trans.). Oxford University Press. doi:10.1093/oso/9780190495893.001.0001

Daher, J. (2016). *Hezbollah: The political economy of Lebanon's Party of God*. Pluto Press. doi:10.2307/j.ctt1gk07vx

Daher, J. (2020). Hezbollah, neoliberalism and political economy. *Politics and Religion, 13*(4), 719–747. doi:10.1017/S1755048320000218

Daher, J. (2022). *Lebanon: How the post war's political economy led to the current economic and social crisis*. San Domenico di Fiesole: European University Institute. Retrieved from https://data.europa.eu/doi/10.2870/824020

Dib, K. (2020). Predator neoliberalism. *Contemporary Arab Affairs, 13*(1), 3–22. doi:10.1525/caa.2020.13.1.3

Dinc, I. (2005). Politicians and banks: Political influences on government-owned banks in emerging markets. *Journal of Financial Economics, 77*(2), 453–479. doi:10.1016/j.jfineco.2004.06.011

Fakih, L., & Majzoub, A. (2021, August 3). *"They killed us from the inside": An investigation into the August 4 Beirut blast*. Human Rights Watch. Retrieved from https://www.hrw.org/report/2021/08/03/they-killed-us-inside/investigation-august-4-beirut-blast

Farida, M., & Ahmadi-Esfahani, F. Z. (2006). *Corruption and economic growth in Lebanon*. Paper presented in Australian Agricultural and Resource Economics Society 52nd Annual Conference.

Freeman, M., & Ruehsen, M. (2013, August). Terrorism financing methods. *Perspectives on Terrorism, 7*(4), 5–26. https://www.universiteitleiden.nl/binaries/content/assets/customsites/perspectives-on-terrorism/2013/issue-4/terrorism-financing-methods-an-overview--michael-freeman-and-moyara-ruehsen.pdf

Goldberg, J. (2002). In the party of God. *The New Yorker*. Retrieved from https://www.newyorker.com/magazine/2002/10/28/in-the-party-of-god-2

Hafez, Z. (2009). The culture of rent, factionalism, and corruption: A political economy of rent in the Arab World. *Contemporary Arab Affairs, 2*(3), 458–480. doi:10.1080/17550910903034989

Katerji, O. (2021, October 25). *Hezbollah has no choice but escalation*. FP. Retrieved from https://foreignpolicy.com/2021/10/25/hezbollah-escalation-lebanon-beirut-port-blast-amal-movement/

Khalife, D., Yammine, J., & El Bazi, T. (2022). How to put the collapsed Lebanese banking sector on the right track? *The Arab Economics and Business Journal, 14*(1), 31–46. doi:10.38039/2214-4625.1007

Khwaja, A. I., & Mian, A. (2005). Do lenders favor politically connected firms? rent provision in an emerging financial market. *The Quarterly Journal of Economics, 120*(4), 1371–1411. doi:10.1162/003355305775097524

Kraidy, M. M. (2019). The Lebanese rise up against a failed system. *Current History (New York, N.Y.), 118*(812), 361–363. doi:10.1525/curh.2019.118.812.361

Laila, B., Azhari, T., Gebeily, M., & Perry, T. (2022, May 17). *Lebanon's Hezbollah, allies likely to lose parliamentary majority*. Reuters. Retrieved from https://www.reuters.com/world/middle-east/anti-hezbollah-lebanese-forces-party-says-it-has-won-least-20-seats-2022-05-16/

Leenders, R. (2012). *Spoils of truce: Corruption and state-building in postwar Lebanon*. Cornell University Press.

Levitt, M. A. (2002). The Political economy of Middle East terrorism. *Middle East Review of International Affairs, 6*(4), 49–65.

Majed, R., & Salman, L. (2019). Lebanon's thawra. *Middle East Report (New York, N.Y.), 292*(3), 6–9.

Morakabati, Y. (2013). Tourism in the Middle East: Conflicts, crises and economic diversification, some critical issues. *International Journal of Tourism Research, 15*(4), 375–387. doi:10.1002/jtr.1882

Morck, R., Yavuz, M. D., & Yeung, B. (2011). Banking system control, capital allocation, and economy performance. *Journal of Financial Economics, 100*(2), 264–283. doi:10.1016/j.jfineco.2010.12.004

Nakhoul, S. (2020, August 5). *Initial investigations point to negligence as cause of Beirut blast*. Retrieved from https://www.reuters.com/article/us-lebanon-security-blast-warehouse-idUSKCN2511G7

Nakhoul, S., Francis, E., & Georgy, M. (2020). *In Beirut port, all of Lebanon's ills are laid bare*. Retrieved from https://www.reuters.com/article/uk-lebanon-crisis-port-insight-idAFKBN27D1JF

Nassar, C. K., & Nastacă, C. (2021). The Beirut port explosion: Social, urban and economic impact. *Theoretical and Empirical Researches in Urban Management, 16*(3), 42–52.

Nizameddin, T. (2006). The political economy of Lebanon under Rafiq Hariri: An interpretation. *The Middle East Journal, 60*(1), 95–114. doi:10.3751/60.1.15

Rafay, A. (Ed.). (2021). *Money Laundering and Terrorism Financing in Global Financial Systems*. IGI Global., doi:10.4018/978-1-7998-8758-4

Rafay, A. (Ed.). (2023). *Concepts, Cases, and Regulations in Financial Fraud and Corruption*. IGI Global., doi:10.4018/978-1-6684-5007-9

Ricour-Brasseur, J. (2021, December 24). Lebanon: From Switzerland of the Middle East to modern-day dystopia. *Middle East Eye*. Retrieved from https://www.middleeasteye.net/opinion/lebanon-switzerland-middle-east-modern-day-dystopia

Rudner, M. (2010). Hizbullah terrorism finance: Fund-raising and money-laundering. *Studies in Conflict and Terrorism, 33*(8), 700–715. doi:10.1080/1057610X.2010.494169

Safieddine, H. (2019). *Banking on the state: The financial foundations of Lebanon.* Stanford University Press.

Salamey, I. (2009). Failing consociationalism in Lebanon and integrative options. *International Journal of Peace Studies, 14*(2), 83–105.

Salti, N., & Chaaban, J. (2010). The Role of Sectarianism, in the Allocation of Public Expenditure in Postwar Lebanon. *International Journal of Middle East Studies, 42*(4), 637–655. doi:10.1017/S0020743810000851

Serhan, C., Mikhael, S., & Warrak, S. E. (2016). Anti-Money laundering rules and the future of banking secrecy laws: Evidence from Lebanon. *International Finance and Banking, 3*(2), 148–161. doi:10.5296/ifb.v3i2.10165

Springborg, R. (2020). *Political Economies of the Middle East and North Africa.* Polity Press.

Taha, R. (2020, December 05). *Beirut Blast: Mystery over murder of two customs colonels killed three years apart.* Alarabiya News. Retrieved from https://english.alarabiya.net/News/middle-east/2020/12/05/Beirut-Blast-Mystery-over-murder-of-two-customs-colonels-killed-three-years-apart

The WB. (2020, August 31). *Decisive action and change needed to reform and rebuild a better Lebanon.* The World Bank. Retrieved from https://www.worldbank.org/en/news/press-release/2020/08/30/beirut-explosion-decisive-action-and-change-needed-to-reform-and-rebuild-a-better-lebanon

The WB. (2022, November 23). *Lebanon Economic Monitor: Time for an Equitable Banking Resolution.* The World Bank. Retrieved from https://www.worldbank.org/en/country/lebanon/publication/lebanon-economic-monitor-fall-2022-time-for-an-equitable-banking-resolution

TI. (2020). *The Beirut blast recovery and reconstruction monitor.* Transparency International. Retrieved from https://www.transparency.org/en/press/the-beirut-blast-recovery-and-reconstruction-monitor

TI. (2022). *Corruption perceptions index.* Transparency International. Retrieved from https://images.transparencycdn.org/images/Report_CPI2022_English.pdf

Vucetic, S. (2011). *The Anglosphere: A genealogy of a racialized identity in international relations.* Stanford University Press. doi:10.1515/9780804777698

Yazbeck, N., Mansour, R., Salame, H., Chahine, N. B., & Hoteit, M. (2022). The Ukraine–Russia war is deepening food insecurity, unhealthy dietary patterns and the lack of dietary diversity in Lebanon: Prevalence, correlates and findings from a national cross-sectional study. *Nutrients, 14*(17), 3504. doi:10.3390/nu14173504 PMID:36079761

ADDITIONAL READING

Alarabiya News. (2022, May 12). *Lebanon jobless rate almost triples since crisis.* Retrieved from https://english.alarabiya.net/News/middle-east/2022/05/12/Lebanon-jobless-rate-almost-triples-since-crisis-Survey

Wittig, T. (2009). Terrorist finance: Asking the right questions. *Politics*, *29*(2), 145–153. doi:10.1111/j.1467-9256.2009.01350.x

ENDNOTE

1 Australia, Canada, Egypt, Israel, the Netherlands, the United Kingdom, and the United States recognize Hezbollah as a terrorist organization (Rudner, 2010)

Compilation of References

Abbasoglu, O. F., Ileri, S. G., & Mimir, Y. (2015). *Determinants of credit growth in Turkey: does size matter?* Central Bank of the Republic of Turkey. Retrieved from http://erf.org.eg/wp-content/uploads/2016/03/ERF_22nd-AC_Finance_Abbasog-Gen-Mimir.pdf

Abdelnour, Z. (2001). The three faces of corruption in Lebanon. *Middle East Intelligence Bulletin, 3*(2). Retrieved from https://www.meforum.org/meib/articles/0102_l2.htm

ABM. (1934). Corporations: Duty of director to stockholder on stock exchange sales. *Michigan Law Review, 32*(5), 678–685. doi:10.2307/1280999

Abor, J., & Quartey, P. (2010). Issues in SME development in Ghana and South Africa. *International Research Journal of Finance and Economics, 39*(6), 218–228.

Acemoglu, D., & Robinson, J. A. (2012). *Why Nations Fail.* Crown Business.

ACFE. (2020). *Report to the nations: 2020 global study on occupational fraud and abuse - Banking and financial service edition.* Retrieved from https://legacy.acfe.com/report-to-the-nations/2020/docs/RTTN-Banking-Financial.pdf

ACFE. (2020b). *Report to the nations - The global study on occupational fraud and abuse.* Retrieved from https://legacy.acfe.com/report-to-the-nations/2020/

Ades, A., & di Tella, R. (1999). Rents, competition, and corruption. *The American Economic Review, 89*(4), 982–993. doi:10.1257/aer.89.4.982

Adhikari, A. (2023a). How India's banking sector is staging a strong comeback. *Business Today.* Retrieved from https://www.businesstoday.in/interactive/longread/how-india-s-banking-sector-is-staging-a-strong-comeback-232-19-01-2023

Adsera, A., Boix, C., & Payne, M. (2003). Are you being served? Political accountability and quality of government. *Journal of Law Economics and Organization, 19*(2), 445–490. doi:10.1093/jleo/ewg017

Adusei, M. (2016). Does entrepreneurship promote economic growth in Africa? *African Development Review, 28*(2), 201–214. doi:10.1111/1467-8268.12190

African Development Bank. (2018). *African economic outlook 2018: Macroeconomic performance and outlook.* African Development Bank Group.

Agoba, A. M., Abor, J. Y., Osei, K., Sa-Aadu, J., Amoah, B., & Dzeha, G. C. O. (2019). Central Bank independence, elections and fiscal policy in Africa: Examining the moderating role of political institutions. *International Journal of Emerging Markets, 14*(5), 809–830. doi:10.1108/IJOEM-08-2018-0423

Agrawal, A. (2018, February 24). Banking crises: An Indian history. *Mint.* Retrieved from https://www.livemint.com/Sundayapp/fjheowjLjiFNsGcjzVZXsO/Banking-crises-An-Indian-history.html

Aguiar, Y. (2018). Índice de conformidade da divulgação de informação no âmbito da IAS 37 - Análise a sociedades cotadas em quatro mercados bolsistas europeus no ano de 2016. Master Thesis in Accounting, Instituto Universitário de Lisboa - ISCTE Business School.

Ahmad, Z., & Saleem, A. (2014). Impact of governance on human development. *Pakistan Journal of Commerce and Social Sciences*, *8*(3), 612–628.

AICPA. (2005). *Management override of internal controls: the Achilles' heel of fraud prevention: The audit committee and oversight of financial reporting*. Retrieved from https://us.aicpa.org/content/dam/aicpa/forthepublic/auditcommitteeeffectiveness/downloadabledocuments/achilles_heel.pdf

Aidt, T. (2009). Corruption, institutions, and economic development. *Oxford Review of Economic Policy*, *25*(2), 271–291. doi:10.1093/oxrep/grp012

Ainslie, E. K. (2006). Indicting corporations revisited: Lessons of the Arthur Andersen prosecution. *The American Criminal Law Review*, *43*, 107–125.

Ainsworth, R. T. (2006). *Carousel fraud in the EU: A digital VAT solution* (Working Paper No. 06-23). Boston University School of Law. Retrieved from https://papers.ssrn.com/sol3/papers.cfm?abstract_id=924189

Ainsworth, R. T. (2009). *The morphing of MTIC fraud: VAT fraud infects tradable CO_2 permits* (Working Paper No. 09-35). Boston University School of Law. Retrieved from https://papers.ssrn.com/sol3/papers.cfm?abstract_id=1443279

Ainsworth, R. T. (2010). *VoIP MTIC - The Italian job (Operazione 'Phuncards-Broker')*. (Working Paper No. 10-09). Boston University School of Law. Retrieved from https://papers.ssrn.com/sol3/papers.cfm?abstract_id=1596608

Ajayi, F., & Atanda, A. (2012). Monetary policy and bank performance in Nigeria: A two-step cointegration approach. *African Journal of Science and Research*, *9*(1), 462–476.

Ajide, F. M. (2020). Infrastructure and Entrepreneurship: Evidence from Africa. *Journal of Developmental Entrepreneurship*, *2*(1), 1–20.

Ajide, F. M., & Dada, J. T. (2023). Poverty, entrepreneurship, and economic growth in Africa. *Poverty & Public Policy*, *15*(2), 1–28. doi:10.1002/pop4.368

Ajide, F. M., & Ojeyinka, T. A. (2022). Financial development and entrepreneurship: Insights from Africa. *Journal of Financial Regulation and Compliance*, *30*(5), 596–617. doi:10.1108/JFRC-09-2021-0079

Ajide, F. M., & Osinubi, T. T. (2020). Foreign aid and entrepreneurship in Africa: The role of remittances and institutional quality. *Economic Change and Restructuring*, *55*(1), 193–224. doi:10.100710644-020-09305-5

Ajide, F. M., Osinubi, T. T., & Dada, J. T. (2021). Economic Globalization, Entrepreneurship, and Inclusive Growth in Africa. *Journal of Economic Integration*, *36*(4), 689–717. doi:10.11130/jei.2021.36.4.689

Ajide, F. M., & Soyemi, K. A. (2022). Oil Rent, entrepreneurial start-ups, and institutional quality: Insights from African oil-rich countries. *Entrepreneurial Business and Economics Review*, *10*(1), 35–49. doi:10.15678/EBER.2022.100103

Akinlo, A. E., & Oni, I. O. (2015). Determinants of bank credit growth in Nigeria 1980-2010. *European Journal of Sustainable Development*, *4*(1), 23–30. doi:10.14207/ejsd.2015.v4n1p23

Alberto, F., & Lopes, J. (2010). A utilização do valor de uso nas empresas do PSI 20. *Revista de la Asociación Española de Contabilidade y Administración de Empresas, 91*, 4–6. Retrieved from http://hdl.handle.net/10198/2732

Albrecht, S., Howe, K., & Romney, M. (1984). *Deterring fraud: The internal auditor's perspective*. Institute of Internal Auditors.

Albrecht, W. S., Albrecht, C. C., & Albrecht, C. O. (2006). *Fraud examination*. Thomson South-Western.

Alemika, E. E. (2013). *The impact of organized crime on governance in West Africa*. Friedrich Ebert-Stiftung.

Alfaro, L., Kalemli-Ozcan, S., & Volosovych, V. (2008). Why doesn't capital flow from rich to poor countries? An empirical investigation. *The Review of Economics and Statistics*, *90*(2), 347–368. doi:10.1162/rest.90.2.347

Ali, M. J., Ahmed, K., & Henry, D. (2004). Disclosure compliance with national accounting. *Accounting and Business Research*, *34*(3), 183–199. doi:10.1080/00014788.2004.9729963

Alkababji, M. (April, 2016). The extent of compliance with disclosure requirements for fair value measurements (IFRS-13): a study on the annual reports of Palestinian corporations. *European Journal of Accounting, Auditing and Finance Research*, *4*(4), 65–88. Retrieved from https://www.eajournals.org/keywords/ifrs-13/

Alnaas, A., & Rashid, A. (2019). Firm characteristics and compliance with IAS/IFRS: Evidence from North African companies. *Journal of Financial Reporting and Accounting*, *17*(3), 383–410. doi:10.1108/JFRA-06-2018-0052

Al-Sadig, A. (2009). The effects of corruption on FDI inflows. *The Cato Journal*, *29*(2), 267.

Amal, M., Tomio, B. T., & Raboch, H. (2010). Determinants of foreign direct investment in Latin America. *GCG: Revista de DGobalización. Competitividad y Gobernabilidad*, *4*(3), 116–133.

Amereller, F. (1995). Hintergru¨nde des ''Islamic banking. *Schriften zum Internationalen Recht, 71.*

Amidu, M. (2014). What Influences banks lending in Sub-Saharan Africa. *Journal of Emerging Market Finance*, *13*(1), 1–42. doi:10.1177/0972652714534022

Amjad, M. M., Arshed, N., & Anwar, M. A. (2021). Money Laundering and Institutional Quality: The Case of Developing Countries. In A. Rafay (Ed.), *Money Laundering and Terrorism Financing in Global Financial Systems* (pp. 91–107). IGI Global., doi:10.4018/978-1-7998-8758-4.ch004

Analytics Insight. (2022, January 23). *Cryptocurrency in India: Demographic survey of the domestic cryptocurrency market*. Retrieved from https://www.analyticsinsight.net/cryptocurrency-in-india-demographic-survey-of-the-domestic-cryptocurrency-market/

Anginer, D., Narayanan, M. P., Schipani, C. A., & Seyhun, H. N. (2012). Should size matter when regulating firms? implications from backdating of executive options. *New York University Journal of Legislation and Public Policy*, *15*, 1–44.

Anwar, S., & Nguyen, L. (2010). Foreign direct investment and economic growth in Vietnam. *Asia Pacific Business Review*, *16*(1-2), 183–202. doi:10.1080/10438590802511031

Arellano, M., & Bond, S. (1991). Some tests of specification for panel data: Monte Carlo evidence and an application to employment equations. *The Review of Economic Studies*, *58*(2), 277–297. doi:10.2307/2297968

Arellano, M., & Bover, O. (1995). Another look at the instrumental variable estimation of error-components models. *Journal of Econometrics*, *68*(1), 29–51. doi:10.1016/0304-4076(94)01642-D

Arping, S., & Sautner, Z. (2013). Did SOX section 404 make firms less opaque? Evidence from cross-listed firms. *Contemporary Accounting Research*, *30*(3), 1133–1165. doi:10.1111/j.1911-3846.2012.01188.x

Arya, V., Banerjee, R., & Cavoli, T. (2019). Capital flows to Asia and Latin America: Does institutional quality matter? *World Economy*, *42*(7), 2039–2069. doi:10.1111/twec.12783

Asongu, S. A., & Tchamyou, V. S. (2015). The impact of entrepreneurship on knowledge economy in Africa. *Journal of Entrepreneurship in Emerging Economies*, *8*(1), 101–131. doi:10.1108/JEEE-08-2015-0045

Asongu, S., & Nwachukwu, J. (2018). Bank size, information sharing and financial access in Africa. *International Journal of Managerial Finance*, *14*(2), 188–209. doi:10.1108/IJMF-08-2017-0179

Assefa, M. (2014). Determinants of growth in bank credit to the private sector in Ethiopia: A supply side approach. *Research Journal of Finance and Accounting*, *5*(17), 90–102.

Assouad, L. (2021). *Lebanon's political economy: From predatory to self-devouring* (Working Paper). Washington, DC: Carnegie Middle East Center.

Assouad, L. (2023). Rethinking the Lebanese economic miracle: The extreme concentration of income and wealth in Lebanon, 2005–2014. *Journal of Development Economics*, *161*, 103003. doi:10.1016/j.jdeveco.2022.103003

Audretsch, D. B., Heger, D., & Veith, T. (2015). Infrastructure and entrepreneurship. *Small Business Economics*, *44*(2), 219–230. doi:10.100711187-014-9600-6

Azémar, C., & Desbordes, R. (2013). Has the Lucas Paradox been fully explained? *Economics Letters*, *121*(2), 183–187. doi:10.1016/j.econlet.2013.07.025

Azman-Saini, W. N. W., Baharumshah, A. Z., & Law, S. H. (2010). Foreign direct investment, economic freedom and economic growth: International evidence. *Economic Modelling*, *27*(5), 1079–1089. doi:10.1016/j.econmod.2010.04.001

Babajide, A., Lawal, A., Asaleye, A., Okafor, T., & Osuma, G. (2020). Financial stability and entrepreneurship development in sub-Sahara Africa: Implications for sustainable development goals. *Cogent Social Sciences*, *6*(1), 1798330. do i:10.1080/23311886.2020.1798330

Baff, S., & Azzi, A. (2021, August 20). *Port of Beirut: Analysis and prospects*. BlomInvest Bank. Retrieved from https://blog.blominvestbank.com/wp-content/uploads/2021/08/ Port-of-Beirut-Analysis-and-Prospects.pdf

Bailey, D. H. (1966). The effects of corruption in a developing nation. *The Western Political Quarterly*, *19*(4), 719–732. doi:10.1177/106591296601900410

Balazs, E., Back, P., & Zumer, T. (2006). *Private-sector credit in Central & Eastern Europe: New (over) shooting stars?* (Working Paper No. 852). Michigan: William Davidson Institute.

Baldwin, F. N. Jr. (2004). The financing of terror in the age of the internet: Willful blindness, greed or a political statement? *Journal of Money Laundering and Control*, *8*(2), 127–158. doi:10.1108/13685200510621154

Ball, K., Canhoto, A. I., Daniel, E., Dibb, S., Meadows, M., & Spiller, K. (2015). *The private security state? Surveillance, consumer data and the war on terror*. Copenhagen Business School Press.

Ball, R. (2006). International Financial Reporting Standards (IFRS): Pros and cons for investors. *Accounting and Business Research*, *36*(1), 5–27. https://papers.ssrn.com/sol3/papers.cfm?abstract_id=929561. doi:10.1080/00014788.2006.9730040

Baltagi, B. H. (2012). *Econometric Analysis of Panel Data*. Wiley.

Baoko, G., Acheampong, I. A., & Ibrahim, M. (2017). Determinants of bank credit in Ghana: A bounds-testing cointegration approach. *African Review of Economics and Finance*, *9*(1), 33–61.

Bardhan, P. (2002). *Corruption and development: A review of issues*. Routledge.

Bartlett, R. P. (2009). Going private but staying public: Reexamining the effect of Sarbanes-Oxley on Firms' Going Private Decisions. *The University of Chicago Law Review. University of Chicago. Law School*, *76*, 7–44.

Bartov, E., & Cohen, D. A. (2009). The "Numbers Game" in the pre- and post-Sarbanes Oxley Eras. *Journal of Accounting, Auditing & Finance*, *24*(4), 505–534. doi:10.1177/0148558X0902400401

Basu, S. (1997). The conservatism principle and the asymmetric timeliness of earnings. *Journal of Accounting and Economics*, *24*(1), 3–37. doi:10.1016/S0165-4101(97)00014-1

Baumann, H. (2019). The Causes, nature, and effect of the current crisis of Lebanese capitalism. *Nationalism & Ethnic Politics*, *25*(1), 61–77. doi:10.1080/13537113.2019.1565178

Baumol, W. J. (1996). Entrepreneurship: Productive, unproductive, and destructive. *Journal of Business Venturing*, *11*(1), 3–22. doi:10.1016/0883-9026(94)00014-X

Baxamusa, M., & Jalal, A. (2014). The effects of corruption on capital structure: When does it matter? *Journal of Developing Areas*, *48*(1), 315–335. doi:10.1353/jda.2014.0012

Beattie, V., Mclnnes, B., & Fearnley, S. (2004). A methodology for analyzing and evaluating narratives in annual reports: A comprehensive descriptive profile and metrics for disclosure quality attributes. *Accounting Forum*, *28*(3), 205–236. doi:10.1016/j.accfor.2004.07.001

Becker, G. (1968). Crime and punishment: An economic approach. *Journal of Political Economy*, *76*(2), 169–217. doi:10.1086/259394

Beck, N., & Katz, J. N. (1995). What to do (and not to do) with time-series cross-section data. *The American Political Science Review*, *89*(3), 634–647. doi:10.2307/2082979

Beck, P. J., & Maher, M. W. (1986). A comparison of bribery and bidding in thin markets. *Economics Letters*, *20*(1), 1–5. doi:10.1016/0165-1765(86)90068-6

Beebeejaun, A., Gunputh, R., & Rafay, A. (2023). Base Erosion and Profit Shifting (BEPS) in International Taxation System: The Case of Mauritius in the light of OECD/G20 initiatives. In A. Rafay (Ed.), *Concepts, Cases, and Regulations in Financial Fraud and Corruption* (pp. 259–277). IGI Global., doi:10.4018/978-1-6684-5007-9.ch011

Beekman, G., Bulte, E., & Nillesen, E. (2013). Corruption and economic activity: Micro level evidence from rural Liberia. *European Journal of Political Economy*, *30*, 70–79. doi:10.1016/j.ejpoleco.2013.01.005

Bénassy-Quéré, A., Coupet, M., & Mayer, T. (2007). Institutional determinants of foreign direct investment. *World Economy*, *30*(5), 764–782. doi:10.1111/j.1467-9701.2007.01022.x

Bernanke, B., & Blinder, A. (1988). Credit, money and aggregate demand. *The American Economic Review*, *78*(2), 435–439.

Blonigen, B. A. (2005). A review of the empirical literature on FDI determinants. *Atlantic Economic Journal*, *33*(4), 383–403. doi:10.100711293-005-2868-9

Blum, V., & Thérond, P. (2019). Discount rate in accounting: How practitioners depart the IFRS Maze towards the end of determinism in accounting. *Autorité des Normes Comptables*. Retrieved from https://EconPapers.repec.org/RePEc:hal:journl:hal-03283265

Boland, J. C. (1985). *Wall Street's Insiders: How You Can Profit with the Smart Money* (1st ed.). Morrow.

Bologna Pavlik, J. (2018). Corruption: The good, the bad, and the uncertain. *Review of Development Economics*, *22*(1), 311–332. doi:10.1111/rode.12343

Bologna, J., & Ross, A. (2015). Corruption and entrepreneurship: Evidence from Brazilian municipalities. *Public Choice*, *165*(1-2), 59–77. doi:10.100711127-015-0292-5

Bova, F., Minutti-Meza, M., Richardson, G., & Vyas, D. (2014). The Sarbanes-Oxley Act and exit strategies of private firms. *Contemporary Accounting Research*, *31*(3), 818–850. doi:10.1111/1911-3846.12049

Braml, M. T., & Felbermayr, G. J. (2019). What do we really know about the transatlantic current account? *CESifo Economic Studies*, *65*(3), 255–274. doi:10.1093/cesifo/ifz012

Braml, M. T., & Felbermayr, G. J. (2022). The EU self-surplus puzzle: An indication of VAT fraud? *International Tax and Public Finance*, *29*(5), 1075–1097. doi:10.100710797-021-09713-x

Brochet, F. (2010). Information content of insider trades before and after the Sarbanes Oxley Act. *The Accounting Review*, *85*(2), 419–446. doi:10.2308/accr.2010.85.2.419

Brunetti, A., & Weder, B. (1998). Investment and institutional uncertainty: A comparative study of different uncertainty measures. *Weltwirtschaftliches Archiv*, *134*(3), 513–533. doi:10.1007/BF02707928

Budsaratragoona, P., & Jitmaneerojb, B. (2020). A critique on the corruption perceptions index: An interdisciplinary approach. *Socio-Economic Planning Sciences*, *70*, 100768. doi:10.1016/j.seps.2019.100768

Bunyaminu, A., Mohammed, I., Yakubu, I. N., Shani, B., & Abukari, A. L. (2022). The effect of health expenditure on average life expectancy: Does government effectiveness play a moderating role? *International Journal of Health Governance*, *27*(4), 365–377. doi:10.1108/IJHG-03-2022-0027

Bureau, B. I. (2022, June 21). Crypto scammers have reportedly stolen Rs. 1000 crore off Indian users by posing as fake exchanges. *Business Insider India*. Retrieved from https://www.businessinsider.in/cryptocurrency/news/indian-investors-may-have-lost-almost-1000-crore-in-crypto-scam-according-to-a-new-report/articleshow/92358876.cms

Business Standard. (2019). *What is PNB scam? | PNB fraud case*. Retrieved from https://www.business-standard.com/about/what-is-pnb-scam

Business Standard. (2020). *What is PMC bank crisis? PMC bank case. Business Standard.* Retrieved from https://www.business-standard.com/about/what-is-pmc-bank-crisis

Buunk, A. P., & Gibbons, F. X. (2007). Social comparison: The end of a theory and the emergence of a field. *Organizational Behavior and Human Decision Processes*, *102*(1), 3–21. doi:10.1016/j.obhdp.2006.09.007

Cahan, S. F., & Zhang, W. (2006). After Enron: Auditor conservatism and ex-Andersen clients. *The Accounting Review*, *81*(1), 49–82. doi:10.2308/accr.2006.81.1.49

Calderon, C., Chong, A., & Loayza, N. (2000). *Determinants of current account deficits in developing countries*. World bank., Retrieved from https://openknowledge.worldbank.org/handle/10986/19825

Campante, F., Chor, D., & Do, Q. A. (2009). Instability and the incentives for corruption. *Economics and Politics*, *21*(1), 42–92. doi:10.1111/j.1468-0343.2008.00335.x

Campbell, L. (2018). Dirty cash (money talks): 4AMLD and the money laundering regulations. *Criminal Law Review (London, England)*, *2*, 102–122.

Campos, J. E., Lien, D., & Pradhan, S. (1999). The impact of corruption on investment: Predictability matters. *World Development*, *27*(6), 1059–1067. doi:10.1016/S0305-750X(99)00040-6

Canhoto, I. A. (2021). Leveraging machine learning in the global fight against money laundering and terrorism financing: An affordances perspective. *Journal of Business Research*, *131*, 441–452. doi:10.1016/j.jbusres.2020.10.012 PMID:33100427

Carlin, T., & Finch, N. (2009). Discount rates in disarray evidence on flawed goodwill impairment testing. *Australian Accounting Review*, *19*(4), 326–336. doi:10.1111/j.1835-2561.2009.00069.x

CBSL. (2018). *Public awareness on virtual currencies in Sri Lanka.* Colombo: Central Bank of Sri Lanka. Retrieved from doi:https://www.cbsl.gov.lk/en/news/public-awareness-on-virtual-currencies-in-sri-lanka

Chaaban, J. (2016). I've got the power: Mapping connections between Lebanon's banking sector and the ruling class. In I. Diwan, A. Malik, & I, Atiyas (Eds.) Crony Capitalism in the Middle East: Business and Politics from Liberalization in the Middle East (pp. 330–343). Oxford: Oxford University Press. doi:10.1093/oso/9780198799870.003.0013

Chambers, D., & O'Reilly, C. (2021). The economic theory of regulation and inequality. *Public Choice, 193*(1-2), 63–78. doi:10.100711127-021-00922-w

Chaney, P. K., & Philipich, K. L. (2002). Shredded reputation: The cost of audit failure. *Journal of Accounting Research, 40*(4), 1221–1245. doi:10.1111/1475-679X.00087

Chaochharia, V., & Grinstein, Y. (2007). Corporate governance and firm value: The impact of the 2002 governance rules. *The Journal of Finance, 62*(4), 1789–1825. doi:10.1111/j.1540-6261.2007.01257.x

Chawla, P. (1986, March 31). Rajendra Sethia bank fraud case: Delhi HC quashes PNB official Amarjit Singh's dismissal. *India Today*. Retrieved from https://www.indiatoday.in/magazine/economy/story/19860331-rajendra-sethia-bank-fraud-case-delhi-hc-quashes-pnb-official-amarjit-singh-dismissal-800745-1986-03-30

Chehayeb, K. (2021, October 1). UN urges Lebanon to implement reforms as extreme poverty grows. *Aljazeera*. Retrieved from https://www.aljazeera.com/news/2021/10/1/un-lebanon-reforms-extreme-poverty-economic-crisis#:~:text=According%20to%20the%20UN's%20Emergency, %2C %20sanitation%2C%20and%20child%20protection.

Chen, S., Hassan, M. S., Latif, A., Rafay, A., Mahmood, H., & Xu, X. (2023, June). Investigating resource curse/blessing hypothesis: An empirical insight from Luxembourg, the Netherlands, and Portugal economies. *Resources Policy, 83*, 103647. doi:10.1016/j.resourpol.2023.103647

Chesson, A., Marilyn, T., & Haynes, J. (2018). *Asymmetries in trade data: Diving deeper into UK bilateral trade data.* Office for National Statistics. Retrieved from https://backup.ons.gov.uk/wp-content/uploads/sites/3/2018/01/Asymmetries-in-trade-data-diving-deeper-into-UK-bilateral-trade-data.pdf

Chi, W. (2004). The effect of the Enron-Andersen affair on audit pricing. SSRN *Electronic Journal. 886. https://doi.org/* doi:10.2139/ssrn.614884

Choudhary, S. (2018). PNB scam: 2 bank officials, Nirav Modi's company executive arrested by CBI. *Business Standard.* Retrieved from https://www.business-standard.com/article/finance/cbi-arrests-2-pnb-officials-1-executive-of-niravi-s-cos-in-bank-fraud-case-118021700228_1.html

Christensen, J. (2012). The hidden trillions: Secrecy, corruption, and the offshore interface. *Crime, Law, and Social Change, 57*(3), 325–343. doi:10.100710611-011-9347-9

CIS. (2013). *Croatia in figures 2013.* Croatian Institute of Statistics Retrieved from https://podaci.dzs.hr/media/w4jo4fmk/croinfig_2013.pdf

CIS. (2014). *Croatia in figures 2014.* Croatian Institute of Statistics Retrieved from https://podaci.dzs.hr/media/h40htohq/croinfig_2014.pdf

Coates, J. C., & Srinivasan, S. (2014). SOX after ten years: A multidisciplinary review. *Accounting Horizons, 28*(3), 627–671. doi:10.2308/acch-50759

Cobham, D. P., & Dibeh, G. (Eds.). (2009). *Monetary policy and central banking in the Middle East and North Africa.* Routledge. doi:10.4324/9780203884553

Cohen, D. A., Dey, A., & Lys, T. Z. (2008). Real and accrual-based earnings management in the pre- and post-Sarbanes Oxley periods. *The Accounting Review, 83*(3), 757–787. doi:10.2308/accr.2008.83.3.757

Cohn, S. (2015, November 6). The Greed report: American ego — the common thread in the biggest scams. *CNBC*. Retrieved from https://www.cnbc.com/2015/11/06/the-greed-report-american-ego--the-common-thread-in-the-biggest-scams.html

Coleman, J. (1990). *Foundations of social theory*. Harvard University Press.

Conti, R., & Broverman, A. (2022, June 13). What is an NFT? Non-fungible tokens explained. *Forbes Advisor*. Retrieved from https://www.forbes.com/advisor/ca/investing/cryptocurrency/nft-non-fungible-token/

Cortés, F. S. B., & Kéchichian, J. A. (2019). *Does corruption benefit compromised societies? The case of Lebanon*. Middle East Institute.

Cortés, F. S. B., & Kéchichian, J. A. (2020). The practice of corruption in Lebanon. *Middle East Policy, 27*(4), 119–135. doi:10.1111/mepo.12530

Cottarelli, C., Dell'Ariccia, G., & Vladkova-Hollar, I. (2005). Early birds, late risers, and sleeping beauties: Bank credit growth to the private sector in Central and Eastern Europe and in the Balkans. *Journal of Banking & Finance, 29*(1), 83–104. doi:10.1016/j.jbankfin.2004.06.017

Coulibaly, S. K., Erbao, C., & Mekongcho, M. T. (2017). Economic globalization, entrepreneurship, and development. *Technological Forecasting and Social Change, 127*(C), 271–280.

Countryeconomy.com. (2022). *Sovereigns ratings list*. Retrieved from https://countryeconomy.com/ratings

Cowen, D. J. (2000). The first bank of the United States and the securities market crash of 1792. *The Journal of Economic History, 60*(4), 1041–1060. doi:10.1017/S002205070002636X

Cressey, D. R. (1950). The criminal violation of financial trust. *American Sociological Association, 15*(6), 738–743. https://www.jstor.org/stable/2086606

Cressey, D. R. (1953). *Other people's money; A study of the social psychology of embezzlement*. Free Press.

Daher, J. (2022). *Lebanon: How the post war's political economy led to the current economic and social crisis*. San Domenico di Fiesole: European University Institute. Retrieved from https://data.europa.eu/doi/10.2870/824020

Daher, A. (2019). *Hezbollah: Mobilisation and power* (H. W. Randolph, Trans.). Oxford University Press. doi:10.1093/oso/9780190495893.001.0001

Daher, J. (2016). *Hezbollah: The political economy of Lebanon's Party of God*. Pluto Press. doi:10.2307/j.ctt1gk07vx

Daher, J. (2020). Hezbollah, neoliberalism and political economy. *Politics and Religion, 13*(4), 719–747. doi:10.1017/S1755048320000218

Daily News. (2022). *Illegal assets investigation division nabs suspect linked to drug dealer*. The Associated Newspapers of Ceylon Ltd.

Daniel, N. D., Denis, D. J., & Naveen, L. (2008). Do firms manage earnings to meet dividend thresholds? *Journal of Accounting and Economics, 45*(1), 2–26. doi:10.1016/j.jacceco.2007.11.002

Das, B. (2023, April 29). IDBI bank Q4 results: Net profit rises 64%, dividend of Rs 1 per share announced. *Business Today*. Retrieved from https://www.businesstoday.in/industry/banks/story/idbi-bank-q4-results-net-profit-rises-64-dividend-of-rs-1per-share-announced-379394-2023-04-29

Das, B. (2023, June 29). ICICI Bank loan fraud case: Chanda Kochhar, husband bought flat, worth Rs 5.3 crore, for just Rs 11 lakh, CBI tells court. *Business Today*. Retrieved from https://www.businesstoday.in/latest/corporate/story/icici-bank-loan-fraud-case-chanda-kochhar-husband-bought-flat-worth-rs-53-crore-for-just-rs-11-lakh-cbi-tells-court-387183-2023-06-27

Dasgupta, M. (2003). A study of company characteristics associated with financial disclosure practices in India. Dissertação de mestrado em Contabilidade. Perth: Edith Cowan Univeristy.

De Hoyos, R. E., & Sarafidis, V. (2006). Testing for cross-sectional dependence in panel-data models. *The Stata Journal*, *6*(4), 482–496. doi:10.1177/1536867X0600600403

DeAngelo, L. E. (1981). Auditor size and audit quality. *Journal of Accounting and Economics*, *3*(3), 183–199. doi:10.1016/0165-4101(81)90002-1

DeFond, M. L., & Lennox, C. S. (2011). The effect of SOX on small auditor exits and audit quality. *Journal of Accounting and Economics*, *52*(1), 21–40. doi:10.1016/j.jacceco.2011.03.002

Department of Census and Statistics. (2020). *Sri Lanka labour force survey*. Department of Census and Statistics.

Desai, H., Rajgopal, S., & Yu, J. J. (2016). Were information intermediaries sensitive to the financial statement-based leading indicators of bank distress prior to the financial crisis? *Contemporary Accounting Research*, *33*(2), 576–606. doi:10.1111/1911-3846.12161

Desai, N. (2020). Understanding the theoretical underpinnings of corporate fraud. *Vikalpa*, *45*(1), 25–31. doi:10.1177/0256090920917789

Dey, P. (2022, December 27). ICICI Loan Fraud Case Explained: Journey of Chanda Kochhar from being the first woman CEO of an Indian bank to going behind bars. *Zee Business*. Retrieved from https://www.zeebiz.com/india/news-icici-loan-fraud-case-explained-journey-of-chanda-kochhar-from-being-the-first-woman-ceo-of-an-indian-bank-to-going-behind-bars-214730

Dey, P., & Kumar, H. (2022, January 28). 30% rise in money laundering activity in crypto in 2021. *Outlook*. Retrieved from https://www.outlookindia.com/business/30-rise-in-money-laundering-activity-in-crypto-in-2021-finds-study-news-48007

Dharmadasa, P. D. C. S. (2021). Short and long term determinants of bank credit growth in Sri Lanka. *South Asian Journal of Finance*, *1*(1), 1–15. doi:10.4038ajf.v1i1.24

Diana, C. I. (2009). Historical cost versus fair value. *Annals of Faculty of Economics*, *3*(1), 860–865. https://EconPapers.repec.org/RePEc:ora:journl:v:3:y:2009:i:1:p:860-865

Dib, K. (2020). Predator neoliberalism. *Contemporary Arab Affairs*, *13*(1), 3–22. doi:10.1525/caa.2020.13.1.3

Dincer, O. (2019). Does corruption slow down innovation? Evidence from a cointegrated panel of U.S. states. *European Journal of Political Economy*, *56*, 1–10. doi:10.1016/j.ejpoleco.2018.06.001

Dinc, I. (2005). Politicians and banks: Political influences on government-owned banks in emerging markets. *Journal of Financial Economics*, *77*(2), 453–479. doi:10.1016/j.jfineco.2004.06.011

Dirks v. SEC, 463 US 646 (1983).

Djankov, S., McLiesh, C., & Ramalho, R. M. (2006). Regulation and growth. *Economics Letters*, *92*(3), 395–401. doi:10.1016/j.econlet.2006.03.021

DOJ. (2018). *Monrovia man found guilty in 'Hawala' scheme to move money for international drug trafficking organizations, included drug cartels.* California: US Department of Justice. Retrieved from https://www.justice.gov/usao-cdca/pr/monrovia-man-found-guilty-hawala-scheme-move-money-international-drug-trafficking

Doogar, R., Sougiannis, T., & Xie, H. (2003). *The impairment of auditor credibility: Stock market evidence from the Enron-Andersen saga* (Working paper). University of Illinois at Urbana-Champaign.

Dorminey, J., Fleming, A. S., Kranacher, M. J., & Riley, R. A. Jr. (2012). The evolution of fraud theory. *Issues in Accounting Education*, *27*(2), 555–579. doi:10.2308/iace-50131

Dreher, A., & Gassebner, M. (2013). Greasing the Wheels? The Impact of Regulations and Corruption on Firm Entry. *Public Choice*, *155*(3-4), 413–432. doi:10.100711127-011-9871-2

Drury, C., Krieckhaus, J., & Lusztig, M. (2006). Corruption, democracy, and economic growth. *International Political Science Review*, *27*(2), 121–136. doi:10.1177/0192512106061423

Dugal, I. (2019, October 1). Confession letter of PMC Bank's former MD: The story of a decades-long relationship gone wrong. *BQ Prime*. Retrieved from https://www.bqprime.com/business/confession-letter-of-pmc-banks-former-md-the-story-of-a-decades-long-relationship-gone-wrong

Dunning, J. H. (1980). Toward an eclectic theory of international production: Some empirical tests. *Journal of International Business Studies*, *11*(1), 9–31. doi:10.1057/palgrave.jibs.8490593

Dutta, N., & Meierrieks, D. (2021). Financial development and entrepreneurship. *International Review of Economics & Finance*, *73*, 114–126. doi:10.1016/j.iref.2021.01.002

Dyck, A., Morse, A., & Zingales, L. (2010). Who blows the whistle on corporate fraud? *The Journal of Finance*, *65*(6), 2213–2253. doi:10.1111/j.1540-6261.2010.01614.x

Ebire, K., & Ogunyinka, S. (2018). Bank lending channel of monetary policy transmission mechanism in Nigeria. *IIARD International Journal of Banking and Finance Research*, *4*(2), 51–64.

Eckel, L., Fortin, S., & Fisher, K. (2003). The choice of discount rate for external reporting purposes: Considerations for standard setting. *Accounting Forum*, *27*(1), 28–59. doi:10.1111/1467-6303.00095

Edwards, S., Diaz, F. G., & Fraga, A. (1999). Capital flows to Latin America. In *International Capital Flows* (pp. 5–56). University of Chicago Press.

Egger, P., & Winner, H. (2005). Evidence on corruption as an incentive for foreign direct investment. *European Journal of Political Economy*, *21*(4), 932–952. doi:10.1016/j.ejpoleco.2005.01.002

Ehrlich, I., & Lui, F. (1999). Bureaucratic corruption and endogenous economic growth. *Journal of Political Economy*, *107*(6), 270–293. doi:10.1086/250111

Ellis, J., Smith, J., & White, R. (2020). Corruption and corporate innovation. *Journal of Financial and Quantitative Analysis*, *55*(7), 2124–2149. doi:10.1017/S0022109019000735

Engel, E., Hayes, R. M., & Wang, X. (2007). The Sarbanes Oxley Act and firms' going private decisions. *Journal of Accounting and Economics*, *44*(1-2), 116–145. doi:10.1016/j.jacceco.2006.07.002

Europol. (2009). Review of Europol 2009. Retrieved from https://data.europa.eu/data/datasets?catalog=europol&show catalogdetails=true&locale=hr

Evans, R. H. (1996). An analysis of criterion variable reliability in conjoint analysis. *Perceptual and Motor Skills*, *84*(3), 988–990. doi:10.2466/pms.1996.82.3.988

EY. (2016). *Accounting treatment of social benefits with a view to financial reporting requirements under the future EPSAS*. Retrieved from https://circabc.europa.eu/sd/a/992fbb51-d3ce-4cef-be2d-90af9c42f664/Issue%20Paper%20on%20Social%20Benefits.pdf

Fahad, N., Ma, N., & Scott, T. (2020). The consequences of discount rate selection for defined benefit liabilities. *Journal of Contemporary Accounting & Economics*, *16*(1), 1–16. doi:10.1016/j.jcae.2020.100184

Fakih, L., & Majzoub, A. (2021, August 3). *"They killed us from the inside": An investigation into the August 4 Beirut blast*. Human Rights Watch. Retrieved from https://www.hrw.org/report/2021/08/03/they-killed-us-inside/investigation-august-4-beirut-blast

Farida, M., & Ahmadi-Esfahani, F. Z. (2006). *Corruption and economic growth in Lebanon*. Paper presented in Australian Agricultural and Resource Economics Society 52nd Annual Conference.

FATF. (2022). *Mutual Evaluations*. Financial Action Task Force. Retrieved from https://www.fatf-gafi.org/publications/mutualevaluations/?hf=10&b=0&s=desc(fatf_releasedate)

Feenstra, R. C., Hai, W., Woo, W. T., & Yao, S. (1999). Discrepancies in international data: An application to China-Hong Kong Entrepôt trade. *The American Economic Review*, *89*(2), 338–343. doi:10.1257/aer.89.2.338

Feldman, E. R. (2006). A basic quantification of the competitive implications of the demise of Arthur Andersen. *Review of Industrial Organization*, *29*(3), 193–212. doi:10.100711151-006-9117-5

Ferede, E. (2021). Entrepreneurship and personal income tax: Evidence from Canadian provinces. *Small Business Economics*, *56*(4), 1765–1781. doi:10.100711187-019-00226-w

Finzer, D. (2021, September 15). Announcement: our commitment to the OpenSea community. *OpenSea Blog*. Retrieved from https://opensea.io/blog/announcements/employee-information-use-at-opensea/

Firth, M. (1990). Auditor reputation: The impact of critical reports issued by government inspectors. *The RAND Journal of Economics*, *21*(3), 374–387. doi:10.2307/2555615

Fisman, R., & Svensson, J. (2007). Are corruption and taxation really harmful to growth? Firm level evidence. *Journal of Development Economics*, *83*(1), 63–75. doi:10.1016/j.jdeveco.2005.09.009

Fisman, R., & Wei, S. J. (2009). The smuggling of art, and the art of smuggling: Uncovering the illicit trade in cultural property and antiques. *American Economic Journal. Applied Economics*, *1*(3), 82–96. doi:10.1257/app.1.3.82

Forbes India. (2016). *Nirav Modi - Forbes India Magazine*. Retrieved from https://www.forbesindia.com/richprofile2016/nirav-modi/1557/141

Forbes. (2016). *Chanda Kochhar-Profile*. Retrieved from https://www.forbes.com/profile/chanda-kochhar/?sh=59e7fb25674c

Forbes. (2017, November 1). No. 5: Chanda Kochhar -Power women: Most powerful women in finance. Retrieved from https://www.forbes.com/pictures/ 59f4ea1ca7ea436b47b47be6/ no-5-chanda-kochhar/?sh=5217f8a22b8f Forbes. (2018). *Rana Kapoor*. https://www.forbes.com/profile/rana-kapoor/?sh=7275f1213efd

Freeman, M., & Ruehsen, M. (2013, August). Terrorism financing methods. *Perspectives on Terrorism*, *7*(4), 5–26. https://www.universiteitleiden.nl/binaries/content /assets/customsites/perspectives-on-terrorism/2013/issue-4/terrorism-financing-methods-an-overview--michael-freeman-and-moyara-ruehsen.pdf

Frunza, M. (2013). Aftermath of the VAT fraud on carbon emissions markets. *Journal of Financial Crime*, *20*(2), 222–236. doi:10.1108/13590791311322382

Frunza, M. C. (2018). *Value Added Tax Fraud*. Routledge., doi:10.4324/9781315098722

Gandolfo, G., & Trionfetti, F. (2014). *International Trade Theory and Policy*. Springer. doi:10.1007/978-3-642-37314-5

Gangwani, M. (2021). Suitability of forensic accounting in uncovering bank frauds in India: An opinion survey. *Journal of Financial Crime*, *28*(1), 284–299. doi:10.1108/JFC-07-2020-0126

Gao, X., Ritter, J. R., & Zhu, Z. (2013). Where have all the IPOs gone? *Journal of Financial and Quantitative Analysis*, *48*(6), 1663–1692. doi:10.1017/S0022109014000015

Gärber, A. (1992). *slam, finanzielle Infrastruktur und wirtschaftliche Entwicklung*. Frankfurt: Peter lANG.

Gayle, G. L., Li, C., & Miller, R. A. (2022). Was Sarbanes Oxley costly? Evidence from optimal contracting on CEO compensation. *Journal of Accounting Research*, *60*(4), 1189–1234. doi:10.1111/1475-679X.12436

Geiger, H., & Wuensch, O. (2007). The fight against money laundering: An economic analysis of a cost-benefit paradox on. *Journal of Money Laundering Control*, *10*(1), 91–105. doi:10.1108/13685200710721881

Geisst, C. R. (2004). *Wall Street: a history: from its beginnings to the fall of Enron*. Oxford University Press.

Ghoneim, A. F., & Ezzat, A. M. (2016). Growth and corruption in Arab countries: What type of relationship connects them? *Journal of Economics and International Finance*, *8*(5), 44–55. doi:10.5897/JEIF2015.0675

Ghosh, S., & Bagheri, M. (2006). The Ketan Parekh fraud and supervisory lapses of the Reserve Bank of India (RBI): A case study. *Journal of Financial Crime*, *13*(1), 107–124. doi:10.1108/13590790610641279

Gilmour, P. M. (2020). Lifting the veil on beneficial ownership: Challenges of implementing the UK's registers of beneficial owners. *Journal of Money Laundering Control*, *23*(4), 717–734. doi:10.1108/JMLC-02-2020-0014

Giordano, C., & Lopez-Garcia, P. (2018). Is corruption efficiency-enhancing? A case study of the central and eastern European region. *European Journal of Comparative Economics*, *15*(1), 119–164.

Glaum, M. S., Street, D., & Vogel, S. (2013). Compliance with IFRS 3 and IAS 36-required disclosures across 17 European countries: Company- and country-level determinants. *Accounting and Business Research*, *43*(3), 163–204. doi:10.1080/00014788.2012.711131

Goedhuys, M., Mohnen, P., & Taha, T. (2016). Corruption, innovation and firm growth: Firm-level evidence from Egypt and Tunisia. *Eurasian Business Review*, *6*(3), 299–322. doi:10.100740821-016-0062-4

Goldberg, J. (2002). In the party of God. *The New Yorker*. Retrieved from https://www.newyorker.com/magazine/2002/10/28/in-the-party-of-god-2

Goodwin v. Agassiz 186 N.E. 659 (Mass. 1933).

Goyal, K. A., & Joshi, V. (2012). Indian banking industry: Challenges and opportunities. [IJBRM]. *International Journal of Business Research and Management*, *3*(1), 18–28.

Greene, W. H. (2011). *Econometric analysis*. Pearson Education.

Gros, D. (2017, July 27). Is Germany's current account surplus bad for the world economy? *CEPS Commentary*. Retrieved from http://gesd.free.fr/gros2012.pdf

Gründler, K., & Potrafke, N. (2019). Corruption and economic growth: New empirical evidence. *European Journal of Political Economy*, *60*, 101810. doi:10.1016/j.ejpoleco.2019.08.001

Gujarati, D. (2003). Basic Econometrics. Fourth Edition. Singapura: McGraw-Hill.

Guo, K., & Stepanyan, V. (2011). *Determinants of bank credit in emerging market economies* (Working Paper No. 11–51). Washington D.C.: International Monetary Fund.

Gupta, A. (2021). The Devil's laugh at corporate governance: The case of Punjab and Maharashtra Co-operative Bank (PMC Bank) India. *Indian Journal of Corporate Governance*, *14*(2), 248–267. doi:10.1177/09746862211047315

Gupta, P. K., & Gupta, S. (2015). Corporate frauds in India - Perceptions and emerging issues. *Journal of Financial Crime*, *22*(1), 79–103. doi:10.1108/JFC-07-2013-0045

Gupta, S., Davoodi, H., & Alonso-Terme, R. (2002). Does corruption affect income inequality and poverty? *Economics of Governance*, *3*(1), 23–45. doi:10.1007101010100039

Habib, M., & Zurawicki, L. (2002). Corruption and foreign direct investment. *Journal of International Business Studies*, *33*(2), 291–307. doi:10.1057/palgrave.jibs.8491017

Hafez, Z. (2009). The culture of rent, factionalism, and corruption: A political economy of rent in the Arab World. *Contemporary Arab Affairs*, *2*(3), 458–480. doi:10.1080/17550910903034989

Hanousek, J., & Kochanova, A. (2016). Bribery environments and firm performance: Evidence from CEE countries. *European Journal of Political Economy*, *43*, 14–28. doi:10.1016/j.ejpoleco.2016.02.002

Hansen, L. (2021). Regulatory Ambiguity: The Underbelly of Insider Trading. In A. Rafay (Ed.), *Handbook of Research on Theory and Practice of Financial Crimes* (pp. 132–148). IGI Global., doi:10.4018/978-1-7998-5567-5.ch008

Hawkins, D. F., & Cohen, J. (2003). *Arthur Andersen LLP. Case 9-102-061*. Harvard Business School.

Haydaroğlu, C. (2016). Corruption, Institutions and Economic Growth in Sub-Saharan Africa. *International Journal of Economic Research*, *7*, 14–26.

Healy, P., & Palepu, K. (2001). Information asymmetry, corporate disclosure, and the capital markets: A review of the empirical disclosure literature. *Journal of Accounting and Economics*, *31*(1-3), 405–440. doi:10.1016/S0165-4101(01)00018-0

He, L. (2020). Discount rate behaviour in fair value reporting. *Journal of Behavioral and Experimental Finance*, *28*, 100386. doi:10.1016/j.jbef.2020.100386

He, L., Wright, S., & Evans, E. (2021). The impact of managerial discretion on fair value information in the Australian agricultural sector. *Accounting and Finance*, *61*(S1), 1897–1930. doi:10.1111/acfi.12647

Helbling, T., & Terrones, M. E. (2009). From deficit to surplus: Recent shifts in global current accounts. *World Economic Outlook*, •••, 35–39.

Hendriyetty, N., & Grewal, S. B. (2017). Macroeconomics of money laundering: Effects and measurements. *Journal of Financial Crime*, *24*(1), 65–81. doi:10.1108/JFC-01-2016-0004

Hermanson, D. R., Justice, S. E., Ramamoorti, S., & Riley, R. A. Jr. (2017). Unique characteristics of predator frauds. *Journal of Financial Accounting Research*, *2*(1), A31–A48. doi:10.2308/jfar-51747

Heywood, P. (Ed.). (2015). *Routledge handbook of political corruption*. Routledge.

Heywood, P. M.Paul M. Heywood. (2017). Rethinking corruption: Hocus-pocus, locus and focus. *Slavonic and East European Review*, *95*(1), 21–48. doi:10.5699laveasteurorev2.95.1.0021

Hillier, D., McColgan, P., & Tsekeris, A. (2022). How did the Sarbanes Oxley Act affect managerial incentives? Evidence from corporate acquisitions. *Review of Quantitative Finance and Accounting*, *58*(4), 1395–1450. doi:10.100711156-021-01028-6

Hofmann, B. (2004). The determinants of bank credit in industrialized countries: Do property prices matter? *International Finance*, *7*(2), 203–234. doi:10.1111/j.1367-0271.2004.00136.x

Hoye, J. M. (2022). Famine, remittances, and global justice. *World Development Perspectives*, *27*, 100446. doi:10.1016/j.wdp.2022.100446

Hsiao, C. (2007). Panel data analysis-advantages and challenges. *Test*, *16*(1), 1–22. doi:10.100711749-007-0046-x

Huntington, S. P. (1968). *Political order in changing societies*. Yale University Press.

Husmann, S., & Schmidt, M. (2008). The discount rate: A note on IAS 36. *Accounting in Europe*, *5*(1), 49–62. doi:10.1080/17449480802088762

IASB. (2018). *Conceptual framework for financial reporting*. London: IFRS Foundation. Retrieved from https://www.ifrs.org/content/dam/ifrs/publications/pdf-standards/english/2021/issued/part-a/conceptual-framework-for-financial-reporting.pdf

IASB. (2019). Discount rates in IFRS standards. London: IFRS Foundation. Retrieved from https://cdn.ifrs.org/content/dam/ifrs/project/discount-rates/project-summary.pdf

Ibrahim, M., & Alagidede, I. P. (2020). Asymmetric effects of financial development on economic growth in Ghana. *Journal of Sustainable Finance & Investment*, *10*(4), 371–387. doi:10.1080/20430795.2019.1706142

ICICI. (n.d.). *ICICI Bank: About us | History*. Retrieved from https://www.icicibank.com/about-us/history

IDBI. (2019). *Information on the constitution of IDBI*. Retrieved from https://www.idbibank.in/pdf/BriefHistoryofIDBI.pdf

ILO. (2022). *Informal economy in Sri Lanka and the Maldives*. Geneva: International Labour Organisation. Retrieved from https://www.ilo.org/colombo/areasofwork/informal-economy/lang--en/index.htm

Im, K. S., Pesaran, M. H., & Shin, Y. (2003). Testing for unit roots in heterogeneous panels. *Journal of Econometrics*, *115*(1), 53–74. doi:10.1016/S0304-4076(03)00092-7

Imran, K., & Nishat, M. (2013). Determinants of bank credit in Pakistan: A supply side approach. *Economic Modelling*, *35*, 384–390. doi:10.1016/j.econmod.2013.07.022

India News. (2020). *Hawala dealer Naresh Jain generated black money worth ₹ 565 crore: Probe agency*. Press Trust Of India. Retrieved from https://www.ndtv.com/india-news/hawala-dealer-naresh-jain-generated-black-money-worth-rs-565-crore-enforcement-directorate-2320129

Issah, M., Antwi, S., Antwi, S. K., & Amarh, P. (2022). Anti-Money Laundering Regulations and Banking Sector Stability in Africa. *Cogent Economics & Finance*, *10*(1), 2069207. doi:10.1080/23322039.2022.2069207

Ivanovic, M. (2016). Determinants of credit growth: The case of Montenegro. *Journal of Central Banking Theory and Practice*, *2*(2), 101–118. doi:10.1515/jcbtp-2016-0013

Iwasaki, I., & Suzuki, T. (2012). The determinants of corruption in transition economies. *Economics Letters*, *114*(1), 54–60. doi:10.1016/j.econlet.2011.08.016

Jagannath, J. (2023, April 22). ICICI Bank Q4 results: Net profit rises 30% to Rs 9,122 cr; lender declares Rs 8 dividend. *Business Today*. Retrieved from https://www.businesstoday.in/industry/banks/story/icici-bank-q4-results-net-profit-rises-30-to-rs-9122-cr-378445-2023-04-22

Jalil, A., Qureshi, A., & Feridun, M. (2016). Is corruption good or bad for FDI? Empirical evidence from Asia, Africa and Latin America. *Panoeconomicus*, *63*(3), 259–271. doi:10.2298/PAN1603259J

James, H. L., & Lirely, R. (2022). The propensity to save: The effect of Sarbanes Oxley Act. *Review of Financial Economics*, *40*(1), 77–96. doi:10.1002/rfe.1140

Jayasekara, S. D. (2022). Trade-based money laundering and informal remittance services: implications on the sustainability of the balance of payments of a small open economy. *Journal of Money Laundering Control, ahead-of-print*. doi:10.1108/JMLC-03-2022-0042

Jegede, C. (2014). Effects of monetary policy on the commercial banks' lending in Nigeria. *Review of Public Administration and Management, 3*(5), 134–146.

Jin, J. Y., Kanagaretnam, K., & Lobo, G. J. (2011). Ability of accounting and audit quality variables to predict bank failure during the financial crisis. *Journal of Banking & Finance, 35*(11), 2811–2819. doi:10.1016/j.jbankfin.2011.03.005

Johnson, J., & Madura, J. (2009). The pricing of IPOs post-Sarbanes-Oxley. *Financial Review, 44*(2), 291–310. doi:10.1111/j.1540-6288.2009.00219.x

Kandil, M., & Greene, J. E. (2002). The impact of cyclical factors on the US balance of payments (IMF Working Paper No. 02/45). International Monetary Fund.

Kapuria-Foreman, V. (2007). Economic freedom and foreign direct investment in developing countries. *Journal of Developing Areas*, •••, 143–154.

Karnik, M. (2017, January 23). Once an intern at Citibank, Yes Bank's Rana Kapoor is now India's newest banking billionaire. *Quartz*. Retrieved from https://qz.com/india/891891/once-an-intern-at-citibank-yes-banks-rana-kapoor-is-now-indias-newest-banking-billionaire

Kassem, R., & Higson, A. (2012). The new Fraud Triangle model. *Journal of Emerging Trends in Economics and Management Science, 3*(3), 191–195.

Kasyan, A., Santos, P. G. D., Pinho, C., & Pinto, V. (2017). Disclosure of fair value measurement techniques of financial instruments: Study applied to the Portuguese banking sector according to IFRS 7. *International Review of Management and Business Research, 6*(4), 1453–1468.

Katerji, O. (2021, October 25). *Hezbollah has no choice but escalation*. FP. Retrieved from https://foreignpolicy.com/2021/10/25/hezbollah-escalation-lebanon-beirut-port-blast-amal-movement/

Kaufmann, D., & Wei, S. J. (1999). *Does "grease money" speed up the wheels of commerce?* (NBER Working Paper No. 7093). The National Bureau of Economic Research.

Kaufmann, D., Kraay, A., & Mastruzzi, M. (2011). The worldwide governance indicators: Methodology and analytical issues. *Hague Journal on the Rule of Law, 3*(2), 220–246. doi:10.1017/S1876404511200046

Kedia, S., Koh, K., & Rajgopal, S. (2010). *Evidence on contagion in corporate misconduct* (AFA 2011 Denver Meetings Paper). SSRN Electronic Journal. Retrieved from https://papers.ssrn.com/sol3/papers.cfm?abstract_id=1571538

Keen, M., & Smith, S. (2006). VAT fraud and evasion: What do we know and what can be done? *National Tax Journal, 59*(4), 861–887. doi:10.17310/ntj.2006.4.07

Kelejian, H. H., & Mukerji, P. (2022). Causal factors of terrorist attacks on countries, and corresponding spill-overs between them. *European Journal of Political Economy, 72*, 102092. doi:10.1016/j.ejpoleco.2021.102092

Kens, P. (2009). The Crédit Mobilier Scandal and the Supreme Court: Corporate power, corporate person, and government control in the mid-nineteenth century. *Journal of Supreme Court History, 34*(2), 170–182.

Khalife, D., Yammine, J., & El Bazi, T. (2022). How to put the collapsed Lebanese banking sector on the right track? *The Arab Economics and Business Journal, 14*(1), 31–46. doi:10.38039/2214-4625.1007

Khan, M. M., & Amoozegar, A. (2022). Effect of corporate and shariah governance on prevention of frauds in banking sector of Pakistan: Mediating role of compliance audit. [Ziran Kexue yu Gongcheng Jishu Ban]. *Tianjin Daxue Xuebao, 55*(2), 160–176. doi:10.17605/OSF.IO/MXU8K

Khwaja, A. I., & Mian, A. (2005). Do lenders favor politically connected firms? rent provision in an emerging financial market. *The Quarterly Journal of Economics, 120*(4), 1371–1411. doi:10.1162/003355305775097524

Kim, M. S., Dandu, J., & Iren, P. (2019). The effect of SOX on audit quality. *Journal of Financial Crime, 26*(3), 897–909. doi:10.1108/JFC-08-2018-0088

Kim, R., & Luo, W. (2022). Customer concentration and earnings management: Evidence from the Sarbanes Oxley Act. *European Accounting Review, 31*(4), 905–936. doi:10.1080/09638180.2020.1858915

Klapper, L., Laeven, L., & Rajan, R. (2004). *Barriers to entrepreneurship* (NBER Working Paper, Paper No: 10380), National Bureau of Economic Resaerch.

Klapper, L., & Love, I. (2011). The impact of the financial crisis on new firm registration. *Economics Letters, 113*(1), 1–4. doi:10.1016/j.econlet.2011.05.048

Koh, K., Matsumoto, D. A., & Rajgopal, S. (2008). Meeting or beating analyst expectations in the post-scandals world: Changes in stock market rewards and managerial actions. *Contemporary Accounting Research, 25*(4), 1067–1098. doi:10.1506/car.25.4.5

Ko, K., & Samajdar, A. (2010). Evaluation of international corruption indexes: Should we believe them or not? *The Social Science Journal, 47*(3), 508–540. doi:10.1016/j.soscij.2010.03.001

Kosinski v. United States, 976 F.3d 135 (2d Cir. 2021).

KPMG. (2017). Fair value measurement - Questions and answers US GAAP and IFRS. Retrieved from https://assets.kpmg/content/dam/kpmg/xx/pdf/2017/12/fair-value-qa-2017.pdf

Kraidy, M. M. (2019). The Lebanese rise up against a failed system. *Current History (New York, N.Y.), 118*(812), 361–363. doi:10.1525/curh.2019.118.812.361

Kranacher, M. J., & Riley, R. A. (2019). *Forensic accounting and fraud examination.* John Wiley & Sons.

Krishnamurthy, S., Zhou, J., & Zhou, N. (2006). Auditor reputation, auditor independence, and the stock-market impact of Andersen's indictment on its client firms. *Contemporary Accounting Research, 23*(2), 465–490. doi:10.1506/14P1-5QRR-1NAF-3CE1

Krishnan, G. V. (2005). Did Houston clients of Arthur Andersen recognize publicly available bad news in a timely fashion? *Contemporary Accounting Research, 22*(1), 165–193. doi:10.1506/EGQD-BTG1-4RHD-7MU6

Krishnan, G. V. (2007). Did earnings conservatism increase for former Andersen clients? *Journal of Accounting, Auditing & Finance, 22*(2), 141–163. doi:10.1177/0148558X0702200205

Krishnan, J., Raghunandan, K., & Yang, J. S. (2007). Were former Andersen clients treated more leniently than other clients? Evidence from going-concern modified audit opinions. *Accounting Horizons, 21*(4), 423–435. doi:10.2308/acch.2007.21.4.423

Krugman, P. (2010). The theory of interstellar trade. *Economic Inquiry, 48*(4), 1119–1123. doi:10.1111/j.1465-7295.2009.00225.x

Krugman, P. R., Obstfeld, M., & Melitz, M. (2018). *International Economics: Theory and Policy.* Pearson Education Limited.

Kunieda, T., Okada, K., & Shibata, A. (2014). Corruption, capital account liberalization and economic growth: Theory and evidence. *Inter Economics*, *139*, 80–108. doi:10.1016/j.inteco.2014.03.001

Kunz, B. (2015). The scope of disclosures of fair value measurement methods of financial instruments in financial statements of banks listed on the Warsaw stock exchange. *Research Papers of the Wroclaw University of Economics / Prace Naukowe Uniwersytetu Ekonomicznego we Wroclawiu*(381),158–176. https://doi:10.15611/pn.2015.381.12

Kuratko, D. F., Hornsby, J. S., Naffziger, D. W., & Hodgetts, R. M. (2000). Crime and small business: An exploratory study of cost and prevention issues in US firms. *Journal of Small Business Management*, *38*(3), 1–13.

Kvaal, E. (2010). The discount rate of IAS 36 – A comment. *Accounting in Europe*, *7*(1), 87–95. doi:10.1080/17449480.2010.485378

La Porta, R., Lopez-de-Silanes, F., Shleifer, A., & Vishny, R. W. (1998). Law and finance. *Journal of Political Economy*, *106*(6), 1113–1155. doi:10.1086/250042

Laidlaw v. Organ, 15 US 178 (1817).

Laila, B., Azhari, T., Gebeily, M., & Perry, T. (2022, May 17). *Lebanon's Hezbollah, allies likely to lose parliamentary majority*. Reuters. Retrieved from https://www.reuters.com/world/middle-east/anti-hezbollah-lebanese-forces-party-says-it-has-won-least-20-seats-2022-05-16/

Lambsdorff, J. G. (2003). How corruption affects persistent capital flows. *Economics of Governance*, *4*(3), 229–243. doi:10.100710101-002-0060-0

Lambsdorff, J. G. (2007). *The institutional economics of corruption and reform: Theory, evidence and policy*. Cambridge university press. doi:10.1017/CBO9780511492617

Lamensch, E. M. (2018). *VAT fraud: Economic impact, challenges and policy issues*. EPRS: European Parliamentary Research Service. Retrieved from https://policycommons.net/artifacts/1335646/vat-fraud/1942306/

Lara-Rodríguez, J. S. (2021). How institutions foster the informal side of the economy: Gold and platinum mining in Choco, Colombia. *Resources Policy*, *74*, 101582. doi:10.1016/j.resourpol.2020.101582

Law, S. H., Azman-saini, W. N. W., & Ibrahim, M. H. (2013). Institutional quality thresholds and the finance – growth nexus. *Journal of Banking & Finance*, *37*(12), 5373–5381. doi:10.1016/j.jbankfin.2013.03.011

Lee, C. C., Wang, C. W., & Ho, S. J. (2020). Country governance, corruption, and the likelihood of firms' innovation. *Economic Modelling*, *92*, 326–338. doi:10.1016/j.econmod.2020.01.013

Leenders, R. (2012). *Spoils of truce: Corruption and state-building in postwar Lebanon*. Cornell University Press.

Leff, N. H. (1964). Economic development through bureaucratic corruption. *The American Behavioral Scientist*, *8*(3), 8–14. doi:10.1177/000276426400800303

Legas, H. (2015). Challenges to entrepreneurial success in Sub-Saharan Africa: A comparative perspective. *European Journal of Business and Management*, *7*(11), 23–35.

Leuz, C. (2007). Was the Sarbanes Oxley Act of 2002 really this costly? A discussion of evidence from event returns and going-private decisions. *Journal of Accounting and Economics*, *44*(1-2), 146–165. doi:10.1016/j.jacceco.2007.06.001

Leuz, C., Triantis, A., & Wang, T. (2008). Why do firms go dark? Causes and economic consequences of voluntary SEC deregistrations. *Journal of Accounting and Economics*, *45*(2-3), 181–208. doi:10.1016/j.jacceco.2008.01.001

Levi, M. (2006). Why we need a new theory of government. *Perspectives on Politics*, *4*(1), 5–19. doi:10.1017/S1537592706060038

Levine, R. (2005). Finance and growth: Theory and evidence. In Handbook Of Economic Growth, 1, 865–934.

Levine, R. (1997). Financial development and economic growth: Views and agenda. *Journal of Economic Literature*, *35*(2), 688–726.

Levine, R. (1998). The legal environment, banks, and long-run economic growth. *Journal of Money, Credit and Banking*, *30*(3), 596–613. doi:10.2307/2601259

Levitt, M. A. (2002). The Political economy of Middle East terrorism. *Middle East Review of International Affairs*, *6*(4), 49–65.

Leys, C. (1965). What is the problem about corruption? *The Journal of Modern African Studies*, *3*(2), 215–230. doi:10.1017/S0022278X00023636

Lien, D. H. D. (1986). A note on competitive bribery games. *Economics Letters*, *22*(4), 337–341. doi:10.1016/0165-1765(86)90093-5

Litigation Releases. (2021, September 9). Retrieved from https://www.sec.gov/litigation/litreleases.htm

Livemint. (2022, December 26). ICICI Bank loan fraud case: Why has the CBI arrested Videocon's Venugopal Dhoot? *Mint*. Retrieved from https://www.livemint.com/news/india/icici-bank-loan-fraud-case-the-arrest-of-videocon-founder-venugopal-dhoot-and-cbi-custody-of-chanda-kochhar-11672036632789.html

Livemint. (2023, March 17). IDBI Bank privatisation on track, says DIPAM Secretary. *Mint*. Retrieved from https://www.livemint.com/news/india/idbi-bank-privatisation-on-track-says-dipam-secretary-11679039514740.html

Loayza, N., Villa, E., & Misas, M. (2019). Illicit activity and money laundering from an economic growth perspective: A model and an application to Colombia. *Journal of Economic Behavior & Organization*, *159*, 442–487. doi:10.1016/j.jebo.2017.10.002

Lobo, G. J., & Zhou, J. (2006). Did conservatism in financial reporting increase after the Sarbanes Oxley Act? Initial evidence. *Accounting Horizons*, *20*(1), 57–73. doi:10.2308/acch.2006.20.1.57

Looney, R. (2003). Hawala: The terrorist's informal financial mechanism. *Middle East Policy*, *10*(1), 164–167. doi:10.1111/1475-4967.00099

Loss, L. (1988). *Fundamentals of securities regulation* (2nd ed.). Aspen Publishers.

Lucas, R. E. (1990). Why doesn't capital flow from rich to poor countries? *The American Economic Review*, *80*(2), 92–96.

Lui, F. T. (1985). An equilibrium queuing model of bribery. *Journal of Political Economy*, *93*(4), 760–781. doi:10.1086/261329

MacDonald, S. B. (2017). *Separating fools from their money: A history of American financial scandals*. Routledge.

Maia, D., & Martins, P. (2014). Internacional Financial Reporting Standards - IFRS: Percepção dos profissionais de contabilidade sobre a nova contabilidade e o impacto dessa na controladoria. *Revista de Contabilidade do Mestrado em Ciências Contábeis da UERJ*, *19*(1), 42–57. doi:10.12979/8191

Majed, R., & Salman, L. (2019). Lebanon's thawra. *Middle East Report (New York, N.Y.)*, *292*(3), 6–9.

Markham, J. W. (2002). *A Financial History of the United States: From Christopher Columbus to the Robber Barons (1492-1900)* (Vol. 1). ME Sharpe.

Marks, J. (2012). The Mind behind the fraudsters crime: Key behavioral and environmental elements discussion leader. *Crowe Horwath LLP*. Retrieved from https://www.fraudconference.com/uploadedFiles/Fraud_Conference/Content/Course-Materials/presentations/23rd/ppt/10C-Jonathan-Marks.pdf

Markusen, J. R., & Maskus, K. E. (2002). Discriminating among alternative theories of the multinational enterprise. *Review of International Economics, 10*(4), 694–707. doi:10.1111/1467-9396.00359

Marques, C. (2015). Provisões e Contingências - Análise das divulgações das entidades do PSI20. Master thesis in Accounting and Finance, Universidade de Coimbra - Faculdade de Economia.

Martins, L., Cerdeira, J., & Teixeira, A. A. C. (2020). Does corruption boost or harm firm's' performance in developing and emerging economies? A firm-level study. *World Economy, 43*(8), 2119–2152. doi:10.1111/twec.12966

Matiş, D., Damian, M. I., & Bonaci, C. G. (2013). Fair value measurement disclosures: Particularities in the context of listed companies and European funding. *Annales Universitatis Apulensis Series Oeconomica, 15*(1), 40–53. doi:10.29302/oeconomica.2013.15.1.3

Matti, J., & Ross, M. (2016). Does crime affect entrepreneurship? A discussion of the current literature. *Journal of Entrepreneurship and Public Policy, 5*(3), 254–272. doi:10.1108/JEPP-05-2016-0018

Mauro, P. (1995). Corruption and growth. *The Quarterly Journal of Economics, 110*(3), 681–712. doi:10.2307/2946696

Mauro, P. (1998). Corruption and the composition of government expenditure. *Journal of Public Economics, 69*(2), 263–279. doi:10.1016/S0047-2727(98)00025-5

Mbaku, J. M. (2010). *Corruption in Africa: Causes, consequences, and cleanups*. Lexington Books.

McDowell, J., & Novis, G. (2001). The consequences of money laundering. *Economic Focus, 6*(2), 6–8.

McGinley, I. (2022). 'US v. Trovias': Lessons from the first dark web insider trading case. *New York Law Journal, 267*(48).

Meek, G., Roberts, C., & Gray, S. (1995). Factors influencing voluntary annual report disclosures by U.S., U.K and continental European multinational corporations. *Journal of International Business Studies, 26*(3), 555–572. https://www.jstor.org/stable/155561. doi:10.1057/palgrave.jibs.8490186

Mehta, M. N., Reeb, D. M., & Zhao, W. (2021). Shadow trading. *The Accounting Review, 96*(4), 367–404. doi:10.2308/TAR-2017-0068

Mekpor, E. S., Aboagye, A., & Welbeck, J. (2018). The determinants of anti-money laundering compliance among the Financial Action Task Force (FATF) member states. *Journal of Financial Regulation and Compliance, 26*(3), 442–459. doi:10.1108/JFRC-11-2017-0103

Memdani, L., Kademi, T. T., & Rafay, A. (2021). Effect of Terrorism Financing on selected Global Indices: The Case of 2015 Paris Attacks. In A. Rafay (Ed.), *Money Laundering and Terrorism Financing in Global Financial Systems* (pp. 183–205). IGI Global., doi:10.4018/978-1-7998-8758-4.ch008

Méndez, F., & Facundo, S. (2006). Corruption, growth and political regimes: Cross-country evidence. *European Journal of Political Economy, 22*(1), 82–98. doi:10.1016/j.ejpoleco.2005.04.005

Mendoza, R., Lim, R., & Lopez, A. O. (2015). Grease or sand in the wheels of commerce? Firm level evidence on corruption and SMES. *Journal of International Development, 27*(4), 415–439. doi:10.1002/jid.3077

Méon, P. G., & Sekkat, K. (2005). Does corruption grease or sand the wheels of growth? *Public Choice, 122*(1), 69–97. doi:10.100711127-005-3988-0

Méon, P. G., & Weill, L. (2010). Is corruption an efficient grease? *World Development*, *38*(3), 244–259. doi:10.1016/j.worlddev.2009.06.004

Michaels, D. (2021, December 14). SEC takes rare court loss in insider-trading case. *Wall Street Journal.* Retrieved from https://www.wsj.com/articles/sec-takes-rare-court-loss-in-insider-trading-case-11639515867

Mishkin, F. (1996). The channels of monetary transmission: lessons for monetary policy. In *Banque de France-Universite Conference*. National Bureau of Economic Research. 10.3386/w5464

Mishra, C. S., & Zachary, R. K. (2014). *The Theory of Entrepreneurship*. Palgrave Macmillan. doi:10.1057/9781137371461

Mo, P. H. (2001). Corruption and economic growth. *Journal of Comparative Economics*, *29*(1), 66–79. doi:10.1006/jcec.2000.1703

Morakabati, Y. (2013). Tourism in the Middle East: Conflicts, crises and economic diversification, some critical issues. *International Journal of Tourism Research*, *15*(4), 375–387. doi:10.1002/jtr.1882

Morck, R., Yavuz, M. D., & Yeung, B. (2011). Banking system control, capital allocation, and economy performance. *Journal of Financial Economics*, *100*(2), 264–283. doi:10.1016/j.jfineco.2010.12.004

Munemo, J. (2018). Entrepreneurial success in Africa: How relevant are foreign direct investment and financial development? *African Development Review*, *30*(4), 372–385. doi:10.1111/1467-8268.12345

Munemo, J. (2021). The effect of regulation-driven trade barriers and governance quality on export entrepreneurship. *Regulation & Governance*, *16*(4), 1119–1140. doi:10.1111/rego.12384

Mungiu-Pippidi, A. (2017). *The Quest for Good Governance: How Societies Develop Control of Corruption*. Cambridge University Press.

Murthy, N., & Gopalkrishnan, S. (2022). Creating a nexus between dark triad personalities, Non-Performing Assets, Corporate Governance and frauds in the Indian banking sector. *Journal of Financial Crime*, *30*(4), 859–876. doi:10.1108/JFC-05-2022-0097

Myers, S. C. (1977). Determinants of corporate borrowing. *Journal of Financial Economics*, *5*(2), 147–175. doi:10.1016/0304-405X(77)90015-0

Myers, S. C., & Majluf, N. S. (1984). Corporate financing and investment decisions when firms have information that investors do not have. *Journal of Financial Economics*, *13*(2), 187–221. doi:10.1016/0304-405X(84)90023-0

Nakhoul, S. (2020, August 5). *Initial investigations point to negligence as cause of Beirut blast*. Retrieved from https://www.reuters.com/article/us-lebanon-security-blast-warehouse-idUSKCN2511G7

Nakhoul, S., Francis, E., & Georgy, M. (2020). *In Beirut port, all of Lebanon's ills are laid bare*. Retrieved from https://www.reuters.com/article/uk-lebanon-crisis-port-insight-idAFKBN27D1JF

Nakitende, M. G., Rafay, A., & Waseem, M. (2021). Frauds in Business Organizations: A Comprehensive Overview. In A. Rafay (Ed.), *Handbook of Research on Theory and Practice of Financial Crimes* (pp. 21–38). IGI Global., doi:10.4018/978-1-7998-5567-5.ch002

Nassar, C. K., & Nastacă, C. (2021). The Beirut port explosion: Social, urban and economic impact. *Theoretical and Empirical Researches in Urban Management*, *16*(3), 42–52.

Ndanshau, M. O., & Semu, A. M. (2023). Determinants of bank credit supply to the private sector in Tanzania. *African Journal of Economic Review*, *11*(2), 92–115.

Newar, B. (2022, July 05). Indian crypto trading volumes slump following hefty taxes. *Cointelgraph*. Retrived from https://cointelegraph.com/news/indian-crypto-trading-volumes-slump-following-hefty-taxes

Nitzan, J., & Bichler, S. (2009). *Capital as power - A study of order and creorder*. Routledge. doi:10.4324/9780203876329

Niyetullayev, N. N., & Almond, P. (2014). Money laundering and the shadow economy in Kazakhstan. *Journal of Money Laundering Control*, *17*(2), 128–140. doi:10.1108/JMLC-05-2013-0015

Nizameddin, T. (2006). The political economy of Lebanon under Rafiq Hariri: An interpretation. *The Middle East Journal*, *60*(1), 95–114. doi:10.3751/60.1.15

Nonnenberg, M. J. B., & Mendonça, M. J. C. D. (2005). Determinantes dos investimentos diretos externos em países em desenvolvimento. *Estudos Econômicos*, *35*(4), 631–655. doi:10.1590/S0101-41612005000400002

Norawati, S., Zulher, Z., Kasmawati, K., & Ratnasih, C. (2022). The effectiveness of the determinants of banking credit growth. *Accounting*, *8*(3), 287–292. doi:10.5267/j.ac.2021.12.001

North, D. (1990). *Institutions, Institutional Change and Economic Performance*. Cambridge University Press. doi:10.1017/CBO9780511808678

Ofoeda, I., Agbloyor, E. K., & Abor, J. Y. (2022b). How do anti-money laundering systems affect FDI flows across the globe? *Cogent Economics & Finance*, *10*(1), 2058735. doi:10.1080/23322039.2022.2058735

Ofoeda, I., Agbloyor, E. K., Abor, J. Y., & Osei, K. A. (2020). Anti-money laundering regulations and financial sector development. *International Journal of Finance & Economics*, *24*(2), 1–20.

Ofoeda, I., Agbloyor, E. K., Abor, J. Y., & Osei, K. A. (2022a). Foreign direct investment, anti- money laundering regulations and economic growth. *Journal of International Development*, *34*(3), 670–692. doi:10.1002/jid.3582

Okunlola, O. C. (2014). Money Laundering: A Threat to Sustainable Democracy in Nigeria. *Journal of Economics and Sustainable Development*, *5*(2), 85–98.

Olaniyi, C. O., & Oladeji, S. I. (2021). Moderating the effect of institutional quality on the finance–growth nexus: Insights from West African countries. *Economic Change and Restructuring*, *54*(1), 43–74. doi:10.100710644-020-09275-8

Oliveira, L., Rodrigues, L., & Craig, R. (2006). Firm-specific determinants of intangibles reporting: Evidence from the Portuguese stock market. *Journal of Human Resource Costing & Accounting*, *10*(1), 11–33. doi:10.1108/14013380610672657

Olson, J. S., & Mendoza, A. O. (2015). *American Economic History: A dictionary and chronology*. ABC-CLIO.

Olunuga, A. (2022). Determinants of bank lending and credit accessibility of micro, small and medium enterprises. *Journal of Business Science*, *10*(3), 299–313. doi:10.22139/jobs.1093265

Olusanya, S., Oyebo, A., & Ohadebere, E. (2012). Determinants of lending behaviour of commercial bank: Evidence from Nigeria. A co-integration analysis (1975-2010). *Journal of the Humanities and Social Sciences*, *5*(5), 71–80.

Omri, A. (2020). Formal versus informal entrepreneurship in emerging economies: The roles of governance and the financial sector. *Journal of Business Research*, *108*, 277–290. doi:10.1016/j.jbusres.2019.11.027

Online, E. T. (2022, December 26). Loan fraud case: CBI arrests Videocon CEO Venugopal Dhoot. *The Economic Times*. Retrieved from https://economictimes.indiatimes.com/news/india/loan-fraud-case-cbi-arrests-videocon-ceo-venugopal-dhoot/articleshow/96510207.cms?from=mdr

Online, F. E. (2022, April 19). Nirmala Sitharaman's latest statement on cryptocurrency tax: Here's why Govt imposed 30% crypto tax, 1% TDS. *Financial Express*. Retrieved from https://www.financialexpress.com/business/blockchain-nirmala-sitharamans-latest-statement-on-cryptocurrency-tax-heres-why-govt-imposed-30-crypto-tax-1-tds-2496309/

Ouédraogo, I. M. (2017). Governance, Corruption, and the Informal Economy. *Modern Economy*, *8*(2), 256–271. doi:10.4236/me.2017.82018

Owusu-Ansah, S. (1998). The impact of corporate attributes on the extent of mandatory disclosure and reporting by listed companies in Zimbabwe. *The International Journal of Accounting*, *33*(5), 605–631. doi:10.1016/S0020-7063(98)90015-2

Oyebowale, A. Y. (2020). Determinants of bank lending in Nigeria. *Global Journal of Emerging Market Economies*, *12*(3), 376–398. doi:10.1177/0974910120961573

Özbaran, H. (2003). Yolsuzluk ve bu alanda mücadele eden uluslararası örgütler ve birimler. *Sayıştay Dergisi*, *50*(51), 17–34.

Palmiter, A. (2011). *Securities regulation* (5th ed.). Wolters Kluwer.

Pande, S., & Prakash, M. V. (2019). Case study on scam in Indian banking industry (Nirav Modi). *Pramana Research Journal, 9*(6), 626–630. https://www.pramanaresearch.org/gallery/prj-p1051.pdf

Pandey, M. (2018, April 26). Rs 600 crore loan fraud: How top bankers helped in looting IDBI bank. *India Today*. Retrieved from https://www.indiatoday.in/india/story/rs-600-crore-loan-fraud-how-top-bankers-helped-in-looting-idbi-bank-1221074-2018-04-26

Parameswar, N., Dhir, S., & Dhir, S. (2017). Banking on innovation, innovation in Banking at ICICI Bank. *Global Business and Organizational Excellence*, *36*(2), 6–16. doi:10.1002/joe.21765

Park, B., & Khanoi, O. (2017). How does the globalization of firms affect corruption in developing economies? *Journal of Korea Trade*, *21*(3), 256–270. doi:10.1108/JKT-02-2017-0022

Parker, S. C. (2009). *The Economics of Entrepreneurship*. Cambridge University Press. doi:10.1017/CBO9780511817441

Patel, V., & Putnins, T. J. How much insider trading happens in stock markets? (January 11, 2020). *American Finance Association (AFA) Annual Meeting*. Retrieved from http://dx.doi.org/10.2139srn.3764192

Patrick, H. T. (1966). Financial development and economic growth in underdeveloped countries. *Economic Development and Cultural Change*, *14*(2), 174–189. doi:10.1086/450153

Paugam, L., Ramond, O., Husson, B., Philippe, H., & Casta, J. F. (2013). Risque d'estimation, coût du capital et communication des tests de dépréciation. *Finance Contrôle Stratégie*, *16*(1). Advance online publication. doi:10.4000/fcs.1260

Peasnell, K. (1977). The present value concept in financial reporting. *Journal of Business Finance & Accounting*, *4*(2), 153–168. doi:10.1111/j.1468-5957.1977.tb00702.x

Pellegrini, L., & Gerlagh, R. (2006). Corruption, democracy, and environmental policy: An empirical contribution to the debate. *Journal of Environment & Development*, *15*(3), 332–354. doi:10.1177/1070496506290960

Perino, M. A. (2019). The lost history of insider trading. *University of Illinois Law Review*, *2019*(3), 951–1004.

Pigou, A. (1932). *The Economics of Welfare* (4th ed.). Macmillan.

Pincus, M. (2020). Did accrual earnings management decline and real earnings management increase Post-SOX? A re-examination and replication. *Journal of Financial Reporting*, *7*(2), 179–205. doi:10.2308/JFR-2019-0009

Piotroski, J. D., & Srinivasan, S. (2008). Regulation and bonding: The Sarbanes-Oxley Act and the flow of international listings. *Journal of Accounting Research*, *46*(2), 383–425. doi:10.1111/j.1475-679X.2008.00279.x

Pluskota, A. (2020). The Impact of corruption on economic growth and innovation in an economy in developed European countries. *Annales Universitatis Mariae Curie-Skło-Dowska, Sectio H – Oeconomia*, *54*(2), 77–87. doi:10.17951/h.2020.54.2.77-87

PNB. (2023a). Origin. *Punjab National Bank*. Retrieved from https://www.pnbindia.in/origin-of-PNB.html

PNB. (2023b). Profile. *Punjab National Bank*. Retrieved from https://www.pnbindia.in/profile.html

Podlipnik, J. (2012). Missing trader intra-community and carousel VAT frauds-ECJ and ECtHR case law. *Croatian Yearbook of European Law & Policy*, *8*(1), 457–472. doi:10.3935/cyelp.08.2012.135

Pozner, J. E., Mohliver, A., & Moore, C. (2022). Shine a light: How firm responses to announcing earnings restatements changed after Sarbanes Oxley. In K. Martin, K. Shilton, & J. Smith (Eds.), *Business and the Ethical Implications of Technology* (pp. 121–137). Springer. doi:10.1007/978-3-031-18794-0_8

Pratama, D. P. I., & Putri, P. I. (2022). Determinants of Bank Credit in Indonesia. *Indonesian Journal of Development Economics*, *5*(3), 254–266.

Press Trust of India. (2014, December 16). Yes Bank chief Rana Kapoor awarded 'Business Innovator Award'. *The Economic Times*. Retrieved from https://economictimes.indiatimes.com/news/company/corporate-trends/yes-bank-chief-rana-kapoor-awarded-business-innovator-award/articleshow/45534475.cms?from=mdr

Press Trust of India. (2021a, September 2). PMC Bank: PMC bank fraud: Enforcement Directorate attaches HDIL group's shares worth Rs 233 crore. *The Economic Times*. Retrieved from https://economictimes.indiatimes.com/industry/banking/finance/banking /pmc-bank-fraud-enforcement-directorate-attaches-hdil-groups-shares-worth-rs-233-crore/articleshow/85868445.cms?from=mdr

Press Trust of India. (2021b, December 7). Sivasankaran, serving and retired top officials of IDBI Bank booked by CBI in ₹600-cr loan fraud. *The Hindu Business Line*. Retrieved from https://www.thehindubusinessline.com/info-tech/sivasankaran-serving-and-retired-top-officials-of-idbi-bank-booked-by-cbi-in-600-cr-loan-fraud/article23687454.ece

Press Trust of India. (2022a, April 23). Rs 5,000-Crore fraud by Yes Bank's Rana Kapoor, Wadhawans: probe agency. *NDTV*. Retrieved from https://www.ndtv.com/india-news/yes-bank-fraud-rs-5-000-crore-fraud-by-yes-banks-rana-kapoor-wadhawans-probe-agency-2913012

Press Trust of India. (2022b, November 9). Explainer: How Nirav Modi cheated PNB of Rs 14,000 crore through fraudulent LoUs. *The Economic Times*. Retrieved from https://economictimes.indiatimes.com/news/india/explainer-how-nirav-modi-cheated-pnb-of-rs-14000-crore-through-fraudulent-lous/articleshow/95410291.cms?from=mdr

Press Trust of India. (2023, June 11). FY24 to be golden year for Punjab National Bank: MD. *The Economic Times*. Retrieved from https://economictimes.indiatimes.com/industry/banking/finance/banking/fy24-to-be-golden-year-for-punjab-national-bank-md/articleshow/100917556.cms?from=mdr

Profit, N. D. T. V. (2023). *Yes Bank Ltd.: Reports, company history, director's report, chairman's speech, auditor's report of Yes Bank*. Retrieved from https://www.ndtv.com/business/stock/yes-bank-ltd_yesbank/reports

PwC. (2015). *A look at current financial reporting issues - IFRS 13 disclosure requirements - questions and answers*. Retrieved from https://www.PwC.co.za/en/assets/pdf/indepth-ifrs-13-questions-and-answers-march-2015.pdf

PwC. (2018). *Applying discount rates under the future European Public Sector Accounting Standards (EPSAS)*. Retrieved from https://circabc.europa.eu/sd/a/12a99051-5c46-4dc4-add5-d6464877ed3f/Issue%20paper%20on%20applying%20discount%20rates.pdf

Qian, J., Strahan, P. E., & Zhu, J. L. (2009). *The economic benefits of the Sarbanes Oxley Act?: Evidence from a natural experiment*. Financial Institutions Center, Wharton School, University of Pennsylvania.

Quagliariello, M. (2009). Macroeconomic uncertainty and banks' lending decisions: The case of Italy. *Applied Economics*, *41*(3), 323–336. doi:10.1080/00036840601007286

Qureshi, F., Qureshi, S., Vo, X. V., & Junejo, I. (2021). Revisiting the nexus among foreign direct investment, corruption and growth in developing and developed markets. *Borsa Istanbul Review*, *21*(1), 80–91. doi:10.1016/j.bir.2020.08.001

Rabab'ah, M. (2015). Factors affecting the bank credit: An empirical study on the Jordanian commercial banks. *International Journal of Economics and Finance*, *7*(5), 166–178. doi:10.5539/ijef.v7n5p166

Rafay, A. (2022). Related party disclosures in financial reporting for Islamic banks. *Journal of Islamic Accounting and Business Research*, *13*(7), 997–1017. doi:10.1108/JIABR-03-2020-0066

Rafay, A. (Ed.). (2021). *HandBook of Research on Theory and Practice of Financial Crimes. Pennsylvania*. IGI Global., doi:10.4018/978-1-7998-5567-5

Rafay, A. (Ed.). (2021a). *Money Laundering and Terrorism Financing in Global Financial Systems*. IGI Global., doi:10.4018/978-1-7998-8758-4

Rafay, A. (Ed.). (2023). *Concepts, Cases, and Regulations in Financial Fraud and Corruption. Pennsylvania*. IGI Global., doi:10.4018/978-1-6684-5007-9

Rafay, A., & Farid, S. (2018). Shariah Supervisory Board Report (SSBR) in Islamic Banks: An experimental study of Investors' perception and behaviour. *International Journal of Islamic and Middle Eastern Finance and Management*, *11*(2), 274–296. doi:10.1108/IMEFM-07-2017-0180

Rafay, A., & Gilani, U. J. (2016). Banking Competition and Stability: Evidence from Inter-continental Markets. *DLSU Business and Economics Review*, *25*(2), 24–40.

Rafay, A., Mohsan, T., & Sadiq, R. (2017). Structural Mix of Credit Portfolios in Islamic Banking System: Evidence from a South Asian Economy. In D. Mutum, M. M. Butt, & M. Rashid (Eds.), *Advances in Islamic Finance, Marketing, and Management: An Asian Perspective* (pp. 185–210). Emerald Group Publishing Limited., doi:10.1108/978-1-78635-899-820161010

Rafay, A., Sadiq, R., & Ajmal, M. M. (2016). The effect of IAS-24 disclosures on governance mechanisms and ownership structures in Pakistan. *Lahore Journal of Business*, *5*(1), 15–36. doi:10.35536/ljb.2016.v5.i1.a2

Rafay, A., Yasser, F., & Khalid, Z. (2019). Revaluation of Non-Current assets under IAS-16: Possibility of any managerial inducement - Evidence from a South Asian economy. *DLSU Business and Economics Review*, *29*(1), 93–105.

Rai, N. (2018). Yes Bank: 3 reasons cited by RBI for sacking Rana Kapoor as CEO and now his board seat in jeopardy. *The Economic Times*. Retrieved from https://economictimes.indiatimes.com/industry/banking/finance/banking/3-reasons-cited-by-rbi-for-sacking-rana-kapoor-as-ceo-and-now-his-board-seat-in-jeopardy/articleshow/65904385.cms?from=mdr

Ramamoorti, S., Morrison, D., & Koletar, J. W. (2009). Bringing freud to fraud: Understanding the state-of-mind of the C-level suite/white collar offender through "ABC" analysis. Institute for Fraud Prevention (IFP), West Virginia University.

Ramamoorti, S. (2008). The psychology and sociology of fraud: Integrating the behavioral sciences component in to fraud and Forensic Accounting curricula. *Issues in Accounting Education*, *23*(4), 521–533. doi:10.2308/iace.2008.23.4.521

Ramamoorti, S., Morrison, D. E., Koletar, J. W., & Pope, K. R. (2013). *ABC's of behavioral forensics: Applying psychology to financial fraud prevention and detection*. Wiley. doi:10.1002/9781118740422

Ramchandani, K., & Jethwani, K. (2021). Yes bank: An untold story. *Emerald Emerging Markets Case Studies*, *11*(1), 1–37. doi:10.1108/EEMCS-04-2020-0123

Raweh, B. A., Erbao, C., & Shihadeh, F. (2017). Review the literature and theories on anti-money. *Asian Development Policy Review*, *5*(3), 140–147. doi:10.18488/journal.107.2017.53.140.147

RBI. (2023). Annual Report 2022-23. *Reserve Bank of India*. Retrieved from https://rbidocs.rbi.org.in/rdocs/AnnualReport/PDFs/0ANNUALREPORT20222322A548270D6140D998AA20E8207075E4.PDF

Regulation FD, 17 C.F.R. § 243.100.

Reuter, P., & Truman, E. M. (2004). *Chasing Dirty Money: The Fight against Money Laundering*. Institute for International Economics.

Rezaee, Z., & Riley, R. (2010). *Financial statement fraud prevention and detection*. John Wiley&Sons, Inc.

Ricour-Brasseur, J. (2021, December 24). Lebanon: From Switzerland of the Middle East to modern-day dystopia. *Middle East Eye*. Retrieved from https://www.middleeasteye.net/opinion/lebanon-switzerland-middle-east-modern-day-dystopia

Riggs, T. (Ed.), *Gale encyclopedia of US economic history* (2nd ed., Vol. 1, pp. 312–314). Gale Group.

Rodrigues Brás, G., & Soukiazis, E. (2018). The determinants of entrepreneurship at the country level: A panel data approach. *Entrepreneurship Research Journal*, *9*(4), 20160060. doi:10.1515/erj-2016-0060

Rodríguez-Pose, A., & Di Cataldo, M. (2015). Quality of government and innovative performance in the regions of Europe. *Journal of Economic Geography*, *15*(4), 673–706. doi:10.1093/jeg/lbu023

Rosa, S. (2013). *A importância da informação financeira nas PME: mensuração do ativo fixo tangível*. Tese de Doutoramento. Especialidade de Economia da Empresa, Universidade Autónoma de Lisboa.

Rose, A. M., Rose, J. M., Suh, I., Thibodeau, J., Linke, K., & Norman, C. S. (2021). Why financial executives do bad things: The effects of the slippery slope and tone at the top on misreporting behavior. *Journal of Business Ethics*, *174*(2), 291–309. doi:10.100710551-020-04609-y

Rose-Ackerman, S. (2009). Governance and Corruption. In L. Bjorn (Ed.), *Global Crises, Global Solutions*. Cambridge University Press.

Rose-Ackerman, S., & Palifka, B. J. (2016). *Corruption and government: Causes, consequences, and reform*. Cambridge university press. doi:10.1017/CBO9781139962933

Rosenthal, S., & Ross, A. (2010). Violent crime, entrepreneurship and cities. *Journal of Urban Economics*, *67*(1), 135–149. doi:10.1016/j.jue.2009.09.001

Rotberg, R. I. (2019). The Corruption of Latin America. In *Corruption in Latin America* (pp. 1–25). Springer.

Roy, D. (2022, December 24). Chanda Kochhar biography, career, husband, fraud, education, net worth, age, height and more. *Indias Magazine*. https://indiasmagazine.in/chanda-kochhar-biography/

Rudner, M. (2010). Hizbullah terrorism finance: Fund-raising and money-laundering. *Studies in Conflict and Terrorism*, *33*(8), 700–715. doi:10.1080/1057610X.2010.494169

Rule 10b-5, 17 C.F.R. § 240.10b5-1.

Rule 10b5-2, 17 C.F.R. § 240.10b5-2.

Safieddine, H. (2019). *Banking on the state: The financial foundations of Lebanon*. Stanford University Press.

Saha, A., & Bose, S. (2021). Do IFRS disclosure requirements reduce the cost of capital? Evidence from Australia. *Accounting and Finance*, *61*(3), 4669–4701. doi:10.1111/acfi.12744

Saha, S., & Sen, K. (2021). The corruption–growth relationship: Does the political regime matter? *Journal of Institutional Economics*, *17*(2), 243–266. doi:10.1017/S1744137420000375

Sahgai, R. (2018). PNB Fraud: Former MD of PNB was aware of Nirav Modi fraud, says CBI. *Economic Times*. Retrieved from https://economictimes.indiatimes.com/industry/banking/finance/banking/former-md-of-pnb-was-aware-of-nirav-modi-fraud-says-cbi/articleshow/64260412.cms?from=mdr

Salamey, I. (2009). Failing consociationalism in Lebanon and integrative options. *International Journal of Peace Studies*, *14*(2), 83–105.

Salinger, L. M. (Ed.) (2005). Insider trading. In Encyclopedia of White-Collar and Corporate Crime (Vol. 2, pp. 428-432). SAGE.

Salman v. United States, 580 US _, 137 S. Ct. 420 (2016).

Salti, N., & Chaaban, J. (2010). The Role of Sectarianism, in the Allocation of Public Expenditure in Postwar Lebanon. *International Journal of Middle East Studies*, *42*(4), 637–655. doi:10.1017/S0020743810000851

Saluja, S., Aggarwal, A., & Mittal, A. (2021). Understanding the fraud theories and advancing with integrity model. *Journal of Financial Crime*, *29*(4), 1318–1328. doi:10.1108/JFC-07-2021-0163

Samaha, K., & Stapleton, P. (2008). Compliance with International Accounting Standards in a national context: Some empirical evidence from the Cairo and Alexandria Stock Exchanges. *Afro-Asian Journal of Finance and Accounting*, *1*(1), 40–66. doi:10.1504/AAJFA.2008.016890

Sánchez-Martín, M. E., De Arce, R., & Escribano, G. (2014). Do changes in the rules of the game affect FDI flows in Latin America? A look at the macroeconomic, institutional and regional integration determinants of FDI. *European Journal of Political Economy*, *34*, 279–299. doi:10.1016/j.ejpoleco.2014.02.001

Santos, E. S., Ponte, V. M., & Mapurunga, P. V. (2014). Adoção obrigatória do IFRS no Brasil (2010): Índice de conformidade das empresas com a divulgação requerida e alguns fatores explicativos. *Revista Contabilidade & Finanças*, *25*(65), 161–176. doi:10.1590/S1519-70772014000200006

Sarquis, R., Santos, A., Lourenço, I., & Braunbeck, G. (2021). Joint venture investments: An analysis of the level of compliance with the disclosure requirements of IFRS 12. *Journal of International Financial Management & Accounting*, *32*(2), 207–232. doi:10.1111/jifm.12130

Saunders, K. M. (2001). *Practical internet law for business*. Artech House.

Schramm, M., & Taube, M. (2003). Evolution and institutional foundation of the hawala financial system. *International Review of Financial Analysis*, *12*(4), 405–420. doi:10.1016/S1057-5219(03)00032-2

Schumpeter, J. A. (1934). *Theorie Der Wirtschaftlichen Enwicklung* [the Theory of Economic Development]. (R. Opie, Trans.). Duncker and Humblot.

Scully, W. G. (2002). Economic freedom, government policy, and the trade-off between equity and economic growth. *Public Choice*, *113*(1-2), 77–96. doi:10.1023/A:1020308831424

SEC v. Clark, 2021 WL 6932689 (E.D. Va. 2021).

SEC v. Panuwat, 2022 WL 633306 (N.D. Cal. 2022).

SEC v. Switzer, 590 F. Supp. 756 (W.D. Okla. 1984).

SEC v. Texas Gulf Sulphur Corp., (401 F.2d 833 (2d Cir. 1968).

SEC v. Trovias, Complaint, No. 1:21-cv-05925 (S.D.N.Y. Jul. 9, 2021), ECF No. Retrieved from https://www.sec.gov/litigation/complaints/2021/comp-pr2021-122.pdf

Serhan, C., Mikhael, S., & Warrak, S. E. (2016). Anti-Money laundering rules and the future of banking secrecy laws: Evidence from Lebanon. *International Finance and Banking*, *3*(2), 148–161. doi:10.5296/ifb.v3i2.10165

Shafiu Ibrahim Abdullahi, S. I., Shuaibu, M., Yusufu, M., Shehu, K. K., & Rafay, A. (2023). Economic Growth, Financial Development and Bank Failure: The Case of Corruption in Nigeria. In A. Rafay (Ed.), *Concepts, Cases, and Regulations in Financial Fraud and Corruption* (pp. 144–163). IGI Global., doi:10.4018/978-1-6684-5007-9.ch006

Shahbaz, M., & Rahman, M. (2012). The Dynamic of Financial Development, Imports, Foreign Direct Investment and Economic Growth: Cointegration and Causality Analysis in Pakistan. *Global Business Review*, *13*(2), 201–219. doi:10.1177/097215091201300202

Sharma, M. (2018, April 27). IDBI Bank fraud: CBI books former Aircel promoter Sivasankaran, top bankers for Rs 600-crore loan scam. *Business Today*. Retrieved from https://www.businesstoday.in/industry/banks/story/idbi-bank-fraud-aircel-promoter-sivasankaran-arrested-cbi-600-crore-loan-104148-2018-04-27

Sharma, C., & Mitra, A. (2015). Corruption, governance and firm performance: Evidence from Indian enterprises. *Journal of Policy Modeling*, *37*(5), 835–851. doi:10.1016/j.jpolmod.2015.05.001

Sharman, J. (2012). Chasing kleptocrats' loot: Narrowing the effectiveness gap. *U4 Issue*. Retrieved from https://www.cmi.no/publications/4514-chasing-kleptocrats-loot

Sharma, N. J., & Aggarwal, D. (2022). Yes Bank fraud: Examining the softer underbelly of the fraud from a behavioral model. *Journal of Financial Accounting Research*, *7*(1), 133–150. doi:10.2308/JFAR-2021-022

Shijaku, G., & Kalluci, I. (2013). *Determinants of bank credit to the private sector: the case of Albania* (Working Paper No. 09/48). Albania: Bank of Albania.

Shi, Y., Nie, D., & Chen, L. (2022). Management earnings forecasts, earnings management, and the Sarbanes Oxley Act. *Journal of Forensic & Investigative Accounting*, *14*(1), 106–132.

Shleifer, A., & Vishny, W. (1993). Corruption. *The Quarterly Journal of Economics*, *108*(3), 599–617. doi:10.2307/2118402

Shumba, C. (2022, March 28). India identifies 11 crypto exchanges accused of tax evasion. *CoinDesk*. Retrieved from https://www.coindesk.com/policy/2022/03/28/india-identifies-11-crypto-exchanges-accused-of-tax-evasion/

Shumetie, A., & Watabaji, M. D. (2019). Effect of corruption and political instability on enterprises' innovativeness in Ethiopia: Pooled data based. *Journal of Innovation and Entrepreneurship*, *8*(11), 1–19. doi:10.118613731-019-0107-x

Sikka, P. (2009). Financial crisis and the silence of the auditors. *Accounting, Organizations and Society*, *34*(6-7), 868–873. doi:10.1016/j.aos.2009.01.004

Singh, C., Pattanayak, D., Dixit, D. S., Antony, K., Agarwala, M., Kant, R., Mukunda, S., Nayak, S., Makked, S., Singh, T., & Mathur, V. (2016). *Frauds in the Indian banking industry* (Working Paper No. 505). IIMB. Retrieved from https://www.iimb.ac.in/sites/default/files/2018-07/WP_No._505.pdf

Singh, H. (2019). PMC Bank fraud case: Full detail of the bank fraud. *Jagran Josh*. Retrieved from https://www.jagranjosh.com/general-knowledge/pmc-bank-fraud-case-1570456027-1

Sobel, R. S. (2008). Testing Baumol: Institutional quality and the productivity of entrepreneurship. *Journal of Business Venturing*, *23*(6), 641–655. doi:10.1016/j.jbusvent.2008.01.004

Sokanović, L. (2020). *Fraud in criminal law: A normative and criminological analysis of fraudulent crime in croatia and the regional context*. Duncker & Humblot.

Spaic, A., Nolasco, C. A., Tsai, L. C. F., & Vaughn, M. S. (2019). Does insider trading pay? An analysis of trading and tipping activities in insider trading litigation. *Journal of Financial Crime*, *26*(2), 647–664. doi:10.1108/JFC-07-2018-0068

Speed v. Transamerica Corp., 71 F. Supp. 457 (D. Del. 1947).

Springborg, R. (2020). *Political Economies of the Middle East and North Africa*. Polity Press.

Srinivas, A. (2009, February 5). How to be a 'Yes' man. *Business Today*. Retrieved from https://www.businesstoday.in/magazine/new-business/story/how-to-be-a-yes-man-244278-2009-01-21

Stigler, G. (1971). The theory of economic regulation. *The Bell Journal of Economics and Management Science*, *2*(1), 3–21. doi:10.2307/3003160

Street, D., & Gray, S. (2002). Factors influencing the extent of corporate compliance with International Accounting Standards: Summary of a research monograph. *Journal of International Accounting, Auditing & Taxation*, *11*(1), 51–76. doi:10.1016/S1061-9518(02)00054-X

Strong v. Repide, 213 US 419 (1909).

Sutherland, E. H. (1940). White-Collar Criminality. *American Sociological Review*, *5*(1), 1–12. doi:10.2307/2083937

Sutherland, E. H. (1945). Is 'White Collar Crime' Crime? *American Sociological Review*, *10*(2), 132–139. doi:10.2307/2085628

Swaleheen, M. (2011). Economic Growth with Endogenous Corruption: An Empirical Study. *Public Choice*, *146*(1), 23–41. doi:10.100711127-009-9581-1

Swaleheen, M., & Stansel, D. (2007). Economic Freedom, Corruption, and Growth. *The Cato Journal*, *27*, 343–358.

Taha, R. (2020, December 05). *Beirut Blast: Mystery over murder of two customs colonels killed three years apart*. Alarabiya News. Retrieved from https://english.alarabiya.net/News/middle-east/2020/12/05/Beirut-Blast-Mystery-over-murder-of-two-customs-colonels-killed-three-years-apart

Talisse, R., & Aikin, S. F. (2006). Two forms of the straw m an. *Argumentation*, *20*(3), 345–352. doi:10.100710503-006-9017-8

Talley, E. (2009). Going-Private decisions and the Sarbanes Oxley Act of 2002: A cross-country analysis. *Journal of Law Economics and Organization*, *25*(1), 107–133.

Tanzi, V., & Davoodi, H. (1997). *Corruption, public investment, and growth* (Working Paper WP/97/139). International Monetary Fund.

Teweles, R. J., Bradley, E. S., Farwell, L. C., & Leffler, G. L. (1982). *The stock market* (4th ed.). Wiley.

Thakur, P. (2022). Over Rs. 4000 Cr laundered via cryptos unearthed By ED in 1 year. *Times of India*. Retrieved from https://timesofindia.indiatimes.com/india/over-rs-4000cr-laundered-via-cryptos-unearthed-in-1-year/articleshow/87939180.cms

Thauvron, A., Astolfi, P., & Desban, M. (2022). Valuation and discount rates under IFRS: Does a size premium exist on the French market? *Accounting Auditing Control*, *28*(4), 101–141.

The Indian Express. (2022, January 26). India ranks 85 in Transparency International's corruption index. Retrieved from https://indianexpress.com/article/india/india-ranks-85-in-transparency-internationals-corruption-index-7741760/

The New Indian Express. (2019, June 12). Former chairman of Indian Bank gets 3-yr jail in fraud case. *The New Indian Express*. Retrieved from https://www.newindianexpress.com/cities/chennai/2019/jun/12/former-chairman-of-indian-bank-gets-3-yr-jail-in-fraud-case-1989137.html

The WB. (2020, August 31). *Decisive action and change needed to reform and rebuild a better Lebanon*. The World Bank. Retrieved from https://www.worldbank.org/en/news/press-release/2020/08/30/beirut-explosion-decisive-action-and-change-needed-to-reform-and-rebuild-a-better-lebanon

The WB. (2022, November 23). *Lebanon Economic Monitor: Time for an Equitable Banking Resolution*. The World Bank. Retrieved from https://www.worldbank.org/en/country/lebanon/publication/lebanon-economic-monitor-fall-2022-time-for-an-equitable-banking-resolution

TI. (2020). *The Beirut blast recovery and reconstruction monitor*. Transparency International. Retrieved from https://www.transparency.org/en/press/the-beirut-blast-recovery-and-reconstruction-monitor

TI. (2022). *Corruption perceptions index*. Transparency International. Retrieved from https://images.transparencycdn.org/images/Report_CPI2022_English.pdf

Timko, M. (2019). The gig economy: An annotated bibliography. *Northern Illinois University Law Review*, *39*, 361–378.

Transparency International. (2021). *Corruption Perceptions Index 2020*. https://www.transparency.org/en/cpi/2020/index/nzl

Transparency International. (2023). *Corruption Perceptions Index 2022*. https://www.transparency.org/en/cpi/2022

Tsalavoutas, I. (2011). Transition to IFRS and compliance with mandatory disclosure requirements: What is the signal? *Advances in Accounting*, *27*(2), 390–405. doi:10.1016/j.adiac.2011.08.006

Tsang, D. (2019). *Crypto-Friendly countries: Crypto regulation around the world*. Retrieved from https://blog.lumiwallet.com/crypto-regulation-around-the-world/

Tuwiner, J. (2023, January 1). *63+ Cryptocurrency statistics, facts & trend*. Retrieved from https://buybitcoinworldwide.com/cryptocurrency-statistics/#:~:text=Key%20Cryptocurrency%20Statistics%3A&text=300%2B%20million%20people%20around%20the,cryptocurrency%20users%20are%20bitcoin%20owners

U.N. (2019). About the Sustainable Development Goals. United Nations. https://www.un.org/sustainabledevelopment/sustainable-development-goals/. Accessed 26 April 2022.

Ugur, M. (2014). Corruption's direct effects on per-capita income growth: A meta-analysis. *Journal of Economic Surveys*, *28*(3), 472–490. doi:10.1111/joes.12035

UNCTAD. (2020). Tackling illicit financial flows for sustainable development in Africa. Geneva: *United Nations Conference on Trade and Development*.

UNESCO. (2022). *Global flow of tertiary-level students*. Quebec: UNESCO Institute of Statistics. Retrieved from http://uis.unesco.org/en/uis-student-flow

United States v. O'Hagan, 521 US 642 (1997).

Ünlü, H., & Ulusoy, M. K. (2021). Innovation and Corruption in Turkey: "Grease the Wheels" or "Sand the Wheels". In A. Rafay (Ed.), *Handbook of Research on Theory and Practice of Financial Crimes* (pp. 80–103). IGI Global., doi:10.4018/978-1-7998-5567-5.ch006

UNODC. (2018). *Afghan opiate trafficking along the northern route.* Vienna: United Nations Office on Drugs and Crime. Retrieved from https://www.unodc.org/rpanc/en/Sub-programme-4/afghan-opiate-trafficking-along-the-northern-route.html

UNODC. (2020). *Money-Laundering and globalization.* Vienna: United Nations Office on Drugs and Crime. Retrieved from https://www.undp.org/unodc/in/money-laundering/globalization.html

Unvan, Y. A. (2020). Determinants of bank credit in Turkey: An autoregressive distributed lag (ARDL) approach. *Turkish Studies – Economics, Finance. Politics, 15*(1), 675–686.

Urquiza, F., Navarro, M., & Trombetta, M. (2009). Disclosure indices design: Does it make a difference? *Revista de Contabilidad, 12*(2), 253–277. doi:10.1016/S1138-4891(09)70008-1

Vaithilingam, S., & Nair, M. (2007). Factors affecting money laundering: Lesson for developing countries. *Journal of Money Laundering Control, 10*(3), 352–363. doi:10.1108/13685200710763506

Van Erven, G. C., Carvalho, R. N., de Holanda, M. T., & Ralha, C. (2017, June). Graph database: A case study for detecting fraud in acquisition of brazilian government. In *2017 12th Iberian Conference on Information Systems and Technologies (CISTI)* (pp. 1-6). IEEE. 10.23919/CISTI.2017.7975974

Vézina, P. L. (2015). Illegal trade in natural resources: Evidence from missing exports. *Inter Economics, 142*, 152–160. doi:10.1016/j.inteco.2014.09.001

Vinšalek Stipić, V. (2020). Korporativno upravljanje i ekonomija trećeg puta. *Obrazovanje za poduzetništvo – E4E: Znanstveno stručni časopis o obrazovanju za poduzetništvo, 10*(1), 132–146.

Vinšalek Stipić, V. (2022). The concept and importance of social audit for sustainable community development. *BH Ekonomski forum, 16(1)*, 151–165. Retrieved from https://ef.unze.ba/OJS/index.php/BHF/article/view/255

Vinšalek Stipić, V., & Blažević, L. (2011). Upravljanje primjenom pristupa temeljenog na procjeni rizika poslovanja i rizika od pranja novca. *Praktični Menadžment - stručni časopis za teoriju i praksu menadžmenta, II*(3), 73–79. Retrieved from https://www.bib.irb.hr/996346

Vousinas, G. L. (2019). Advancing theory of fraud: The S.C.O.R.E. model. *Journal of Financial Crime, 26*(1), 372–381. doi:10.1108/JFC-12-2017-0128

Vucetic, S. (2011). *The Anglosphere: A genealogy of a racialized identity in international relations.* Stanford University Press. doi:10.1515/9780804777698

Warf, B. (2002). Tailored for Panama: Offshore banking at the crossroads of the Americas. *Geografiska Annaler. Series B, Human Geography, 84*(1), 33–47. doi:10.1111/j.0435-3684.2002.00112.x

Wartzman, R. (2002, July 3). A 1920s insider trade was ruled by court to be merely a perk. *Wall Street Journal*. Retrieved from https://www.wsj.com/articles/SB1025637858937126040

WDI. (2022). *World Development Indicators*. Retrieved from https://databank.worldbank.org/source/world-development-indicators

Wei, S. J. (2000). How taxing is corruption on international investors? *The Review of Economics and Statistics*, *82*(1), 1–11. doi:10.1162/003465300558533

Wei, S. J., & Shleifer, A. (2000). Local corruption and global capital flows. *Brookings Papers on Economic Activity*, *2000*(2), 303–354. doi:10.1353/eca.2000.0021

Wells, J. T. (2001). Why employees commit fraud. *Journal of Accountancy*, *191*(2), 89.

Wennekers, S., Van Stel, A., Carree, M., & Thurik, R. (2010). The relationship between entrepreneurship and economic development: Is it U-shaped? *Foundations and Trends in Entrepreneurship*, *6*(3), 167–237. doi:10.1561/0300000023

WGI. (2022). *Worldwide Governance Indicators*. Retrieved from http://info.worldbank.org/governance/wgi/

Williams, K. (2019). Do political institutions improve the diminishing effect of financial deepening on growth? Evidence from developing countries. *Journal of Economics and Business*, *103*, 13–24. doi:10.1016/j.jeconbus.2018.11.003

Williamson, O. (2000). New Institutional Economics. *Journal of Economic Literature*, *38*(3), 595–613. doi:10.1257/jel.38.3.595

Wolfe, D. T., & Hermanson, D. R. (2004). The Fraud Diamond: Considering the four elements of fraud. *The CPA Journal*, *12*(74), 38–42.

Wooldridge, J. (2012). In Introductory econometrics: A modern approach (5th ed.). South-Western: Cengage Learning.

Wooldridge, J. M. (2010). *Econometric Analysis of Cross Section and Panel Data*. The MIT Press. Retrieved from https://mitpress.mit.edu/books/econometric-analysis-cross-section-and-panel-data-second-edition

World Bank. (2011). World trade report 2011. Retrieved from https://www.wto.org/english/res_e/booksp_e/anrep_e/world_trade_report11_e.pdf

World Bank. (2018). *The State of Social Safety Nets 2018*. Washington, DC: World Bank. Retrieved from https://www.worldbank.org/en/topic/socialprotectionandjobs/publication/ the-state-of-social-safety-nets-2018

World Bank. (2020). *Informality, job quality, and welfare in Sri Lanka*. Washington: The World Bank. Retrieved from https://documents.worldbank.org/en/publication/documents-reports/documentdetail/341681597688560604/informality-job-quality-and-welfare-in-sri-lanka

World Bank. (2021). *Informal economy database*. Washington: The World Bank. Retrieved from https://www.worldbank.org/en/research/brief/informal-economy-database

Wright, R. E. (2005). *The first Wall Street: Chestnut Street, Philadelphia, and the birth of American finance*. University of Chicago Press. doi:10.7208/chicago/9780226910291.001.0001

Yakubu, I. N. (2019). Does corruption grease or sand the wheels of bank profitability in Ghana? *Cogent Economics & Finance*, *7*(1), 1–12. doi:10.1080/23322039.2019.1701909

Yakubu, I. N., & Musah, A. (2022). The nexus between financial inclusion and bank profitability: A dynamic panel approach. *Journal of Sustainable Finance & Investment*, •••, 1–14. doi:10.1080/20430795.2022.2105792

Yakubu, I. N., Sulemana, A. M., & Abdallah, I. (2020). Small and medium-sized enterprises financing. *Gading Journal for Social Sciences*, *23*(2), 1–8.

Yazbeck, N., Mansour, R., Salame, H., Chahine, N. B., & Hoteit, M. (2022). The Ukraine–Russia war is deepening food insecurity, unhealthy dietary patterns and the lack of dietary diversity in Lebanon: Prevalence, correlates and findings from a national cross-sectional study. *Nutrients*, *14*(17), 3504. doi:10.3390/nu14173504 PMID:36079761

Yeh, Y. H., Chung, H., & Liu, C. L. (2011). Committee independence and financial institution performance during the 2007-08 credit crunch: Evidence from a multi-country study. *Corporate Governance*, *19*(5), 437–458. doi:10.1111/j.1467-8683.2011.00884.x

Yes Bank. (2016, February 26). Yes bank has ranked top 500 global banking brands list by the banker. Retrieved from:// www.yesbank.in/about-us/media/press-releases-details/3000000212277-copy-of-press-release-list-item-feb-15-16-02

Yildirim, Y., & Rafay, A. (2021). Anti-Money Laundering in Insurance Sector: The Turkish Case. In A. Rafay (Ed.), *Money Laundering and Terrorism Financing in Global Financial Systems* (pp. 108–127). IGI Global., doi:10.4018/978-1-7998-8758-4.ch005

Yurdakul, F., & Ucar, B. (2015). The relationship between current deficit and economic growth: An empirical study on Turkey. *Procedia Economics and Finance*, *26*, 101–108. doi:10.1016/S2212-5671(15)00885-0

Zeff, S. A. (2014). A Evolução do IASC para o IASB e os Desafios Enfrentados. *Revista Contabilidade & Finanças*, *25*(spe), 300–320. doi:10.1590/1808-057x201400040

Zheng, C., & Musteen, M. (2018). The impact of remittances on opportunity-based and necessity-based entrepreneurial activities. *Academy of Entrepreneurship Journal*, *24*(3), 1–13.

About the Contributors

Abdul Rafay is a practitioner cum academician. For more than 25 years, Mr. Rafay has been working as a freelance advisor, consultant & trainer to a wide variety of public & private sector national and multinational companies in the areas of Corporate Finance, Financial Policy & Implementation, Auditing & Assurance, Accountancy, Corporate Tax Management, Financial Technology, and System Consultancy. He has been providing consultancy to various industries including Textile, Auto Assembling, Footwear, Industrial/Agro Chemicals, Ice Cream/Dairies, Glass/Ceramics, Healthcare, Mining/Natural Resources, Packaging/Paper Sacking, Steel/Pipe Casting, Rice Processing, Brokerage/Co-operative Financing, Software Development, Real Estate, Printing/Publishing, and Construction/Civil Engineering, etc. Mr. Rafay is a Fellow member of the Institute of Chartered Accountants of Pakistan. He is also a member of various national and international professional bodies including the Institute of Internal Auditors (IIA), USA; Association of Certified Fraud Examiners (ACFE), USA. Since 2001, he has been a lifetime member of the Lahore Tax Bar Association. He has served as Co-regional Director (Founding) of Lahore-Islamabad Chapter of Professional Risk Managers International Association (PRMIA), Washington, USA (2011-2013). In 2012, he was nominated as Member: Education & Training Committee (ETCOM) of The Institute of Chartered Accountants of Pakistan (ICAP). He is also a member of ICAP's "Islamic Finance working group" which is closely in liaison with the State Bank of Pakistan and other stakeholders for Islamic Finance Accounting and Auditing Standards. He is an Alumnus of Rausing Executive Development Center (REDC), Lahore University of Management Sciences (LUMS), Pakistan. In 2014, International Finance Corporation (World Bank Group) selected him for Training of Trainers (ToT) for Corporate Governance Action Planning for SMEs. He is also an approved trainer for the Institute of Financial Markets of Pakistan (IFMP) established by the Securities and Exchange Commission of Pakistan (SECP), the corporate regulator. In 2013, his name got included in the list of "Certified Directors" as per Clause (xi) of The Code of Corporate Governance 2012 issued by SECP. Currently, he is on the board of a Listed Company as an Independent Director. For the last 27 years, Mr. Rafay has also been associated with teaching in some of the top business schools of Pakistan. His specialized subjects of interest include Strategic Corporate Finance, Financial Crimes, Financial Derivatives, Investments/Portfolio Analysis, International Financial Reporting Standards, Corporate Restructuring (Mergers & Acquisitions), Financial Statement Analysis & Corporate Taxation. He also served as an instructor in Civil Services Academy, Pakistan to train the CSS Officers selected by the Federal Public Service Commission of Pakistan (FPSC). Currently, he is a Professor of Finance & Accounting at the University of Management & Technology, Pakistan. He has published more than two dozen research papers in SSCI, ESCI and Scopus indexed journals published by reputed global publishers including Emerald, Sage, Taylor & Francis, Routledge and IGI Global. He contributed multiple chapters in

Books edited by International Editors. He also edited international books on FinTech, Islamic Finance, Financial Crimes, Money Laundering, Terrorism Financing, Energy Finance, Environmental Finance and Technological/Financial Frauds published by IGI Global, USA. For the last 27 years, Mr. Rafay has also been associated with teaching in some of the top business schools of Pakistan. He has published more than two dozen research papers/books/book chapters/cases in SSCI/ESCI/Scopus indexed journals/books published by Emerald, Sage, Taylor & Francis, and IGI Global. Mr. Rafay is a Fellow member of the Institute of Chartered Accountants of Pakistan.

***

Folorunsho Ajide holds a PhD in Economics from the Obafemi Awolowo University, Ile-Ife, Nigeria. He is currently a faculty member of the University of Ilorin, Ilorin, Nigeria. He is a Chartered Accountant(ACA), Tax consultant (ACTI) and Full member of Nigerian Economic Society (FNES). His area of research interests include: Crime Economics, Financial/ Business Economics, Development and Economics of Entrepreneurship.

Fábio Albuquerque holds a PhD in Economic and Business Sciences from the University of Extremadura, UNEX, Spain. Currently, he is an Assistant Professor at Lisbon Accounting and Business School, Portugal. His professional experience includes technical work in different entities in the areas of accounting, reporting and statistics, as well as the provision of consulting and business training services on international and national accounting and financial reporting standards and risk management in Auditing.

Faris Nasif Alshubiri holds a PhD from Amman Arab University, Jordan. Currently, he is a professor at Dhofar University, Oman. Prof. Faris is the Director of the Department of Postgraduate Studies at Dhofar University. Prof. Faris has published more than 60 professional papers, most of them included in Scopus and Web of Science. Faris Alshubiri is also the Regional Editor International Journal of emergency services, He received an international award for outstanding scientist finance and accounting for the year (2016) from VENUS International Research Awards. Furthermore, He received an international award for a best researcher for this year (2020) from CEEMAN (The international Association for management development in dynamic societies.

Miguel Assunção is a master's student at the Instituto Politécnico de Lisboa, Portugal. He has been working in an auditing firm for more than 10 years.

Alhassan Bunyaminu holds a PhD in Finance from the University of Central Nicaragua. Currently, he is a Lecturer at the University of Professional Studies, Accra-Ghana. His research interests include Energy Finance, Financial Modelling, Financial Market and institutions, corporate finance & Corporate Governance. He possesses 15 years of experience as an advisor/consultant to Government, multinational companies and he is a local governance expert and offers consultancy and research services to Metropolitan, Municipal and District Assemblies (MMDAs) across Ghana. Dr. Bunyaminu is also a capacity building and training provider for public and private organizations in management and finance. He has over 25 publications including research articles and book chapters.

Felippe Clemente holds a PhD in Applied Economics from the Federal University of Viçosa, Brazil, with a thesis on Tax Evasion: Essays on Tax Evasion. Currently, he is a faculty member at the University of Lisbon, Portugal. Previously he worked with Goethe Frankfurt University, Germany, His research interests focus on corruption and economic crisis, tax evasion and the economics of crime in Europe and abroad.

Thiago C. Ferreira holds a Masters Degree in Applied Economics from University of Viçosa, Brazil. Currently he is a PhD. Student at the Laboratório Nacional de Computação Científica. His research interests include Environmental Economics, International Economics and Applied Mathematics.

Perihan Iren holds a Doctorate in Business Administration from Cleveland State University, USA. Previously she obtained M.Sc. in Accounting and Finance and B.Sc. in Management Sciences degrees from Hacettepe University, Türkiye. Currently, she is an Associate Professor of Finance at Zayed University, UAE. She has published research on a wide range of financial issues including banking sector stability, corporate governance issues, and international finance. She is particularly interested in crisis literature. She also conducts interdisciplinary research, particularly in the innovation area. Her work has been published in well reputable international journals and presented at leading international academic conferences.

S G Sisira Dharmasri Jayasekara has been with the Central Bank of Sri Lanka (CBSL) for more than 15 years and currently holds office as Deputy Director, of the Financial Intelligence Unit of CBSL. He is an experienced examiner in conducting supervision of financial institutions. He has published several articles on risk-based supervision in international and local journals. Mr. Jayasekara is a Fellow of the Institute of Chartered Accountants of Sri Lanka, a Fellow of the Association of Chartered Certified Accountants (UK), and an Associate Member of the Institute of Certified Management Accountants of Sri Lanka. Mr. Jayasekara also holds an MBA from the University of Peradeniya, Sri Lanka, MSc from the University of Birmingham, UK. He has also been involved as an assessor in conducting a mutual evaluation under the FATF 2012 methodology.

Moo Sung Kim holds PhD in Finance from Temple University, USA. Previously he obtained his MBA degree in finance from St Joseph's University, USA. Currently, he is an Associate Professor of Finance in the College of Business at Zayed University, UAE. Prior to his doctorate, he had several years of professional experience first in the Korean military, and then with a major advertising company in Korea. His research focus is on corporate structure, governance, and strategic decisions. He has had his papers presented at leading international academic conferences in finance.

Fatih Kırşanlı holds a PhD in economics from Colorado State University, USA. Previously he holds a master's degree in economics from Texas A&M University. Currently, he is an Assistant Professor of Economics at Yozgat Bozok University, Turkey. His scholarship relies on macroeconomics, institutional economics, and political economy. More particularly, Fatih concentrates on corruption, governance, and bureaucracy and their impacts on macroeconomic variables.

Viviani Silva Lirio holds a PhD in Applied Economics from University of Viçosa, Brazil. Currently she is a Professor at the same university. Her research interests include Economics of Crime, Agricultural Economics and Development Microeconomics.

Beemamol M is a PhD candidate at Pondicherry University, India. Her research interest includes forensic accounting, financial fraud detection, anti-fraud disclosure, behavioral forensics, business ethics and banking. She is an awardee of the CMA (IMA) Doctoral Scholarship in 2023, the SJSGC fellowship from the University Grant Commission (UGC (2022-23)), and the JNMF scholarship for doctoral studies in 2021-2022. Before entering her PhD track, Beema holds a Bachelor of Commerce degree from the University of Kerala and a Master of Business Administration in Finance and Marketing from the National Institute of Technology, India.

Alhassan Musah holds a PhD in Endogenous Development from the University for Development Studies, Ghana. He is an interdisciplinary professional and a senior lecturer in the Department of Sustainable Development Studies of the University for Development Studies. Alhassan is a Fellow of the Association of Chartered Certified Accountants (ACCA, UK) and a member of the Institute of Chartered Accountants, Ghana. His current research interests include inclusive finance, sustainable development, corporate sustainability and greening of business. Dr. Musah has over 20 publications.

Tayo Oke holds a PhD and is a principal partner at the financial and economic law firm; ASIKO Chambers. Currently, he is also a senior academician at Afe Babalola University, Ado-Ekiti, Nigeria

Luis Perez received his Bachelor of Science in Business Administration from California State University, Northridge, where he is currently a student in the Masters of Business Administration program. He also serves as Graduate Assistant to the faculty of the Department of Business Law.

Kurt M. Saunders holds J.D. from the University of Pittsburgh, USA and an LL.M. in Intellectual Property Law from George Washington University, USA. Currently, he is a Professor of Business Law at California State University, Northridge. He is the author of the books, Intellectual Property Law: Legal Aspects of Innovation and Competition (2016) and Practical Internet Law for Business (Artech 2001), as well as numerous law review articles on intellectual property law, business and commercial law, internet law, and legal education. Professor Saunders currently serves as the Chair of the Department of Business Law and teaches courses in intellectual property law, business law, estates and trusts law, and international business law. Prior to joining the faculty at California State University, he practiced law in Pennsylvania. As an attorney, his main areas of practice were business planning and estate law. He also served as Jury Commissioner in Pennsylvania during 1995-1997. Professor Saunders has also served as an instructor at the George Washington University Law School and the University of Pittsburgh School of Law and as a Clinical Professor of Law at the Duquesne University Law School.

Sachin Shah is a CAMS certified Financial Crime Compliance professional associated with one of the Big 4 in India. He has worked with 4 of the top 15 global banks in a career spanning 20 years. He is also a regular writer on the Fincrime matters and has various global publications in his name. Recently his academic paper got featured in the Central Bank of Future Conference, co-hosted by Reserve Bank of San Francisco in USA.

Valentina Vinsalek Stipic holds a PhD from the Faculty of Economic Studies at the University of Modern Sciences in Mostar, Bosnia, and Herzegovina. Currently, she is a Professor at the Polytechnic "Nikola Tesla" in Gospic, Croatia. Her research interests include Corporate Social Responsibility and Financial management, Organizational Management, and SME. She possesses sixteen years of experience as a CFO in multinational companies. She has published more than eighty papers, ten teaching materials, and two books.

Ibrahim Nandom holds a PhD in Banking and Finance. He received his MSc. in International Business from the University of Liverpool, UK and BSc. in Banking and Finance (First Class Honours) from the University of Professional Studies, Accra. He also holds an Investment Foundations Certificate from the CFA Institute (USA). His research focuses on banking, corporate finance, corporate governance, international business, and energy finance. Ibrahim has over 40 publications including articles and book chapters. His research works have appeared in various internationally ranked journals and he has presented his research findings in international and national conferences. Dr. Ibrahim serves as an ad hoc reviewer for a number of journals published by Emerald, Taylor & Francis, SAGE and Springer.

Index

L

M

N

O

P

R

S

T

U

V

W

www.ingramcontent.com/pod-product-compliance
Lightning Source LLC
LaVergne TN
LVHW080527300926
849162LV00007B/1552